THE NEW ENCYCLOPEDIA OF
AMERICAN
TREES

THE NEW ENCYCLOPEDIA OF
AMERICAN TREES

TONY RUSSELL
CATHERINE CUTLER
MARTIN WALTERS

HERMES HOUSE

This edition is published by Hermes House, an imprint of Anness Publishing Ltd
Hermes House, 88–89 Blackfriars Road, London SE1 8HA
tel. 020 7401 2077; fax 020 7633 9499; info@anness.com

www.hermeshouse.com; www.annesspublishing.com

Anness Publishing has a new picture agency outlet for images for publishing, promotions or advertising. Please visit our website www.practicalpictures.com for more information.

Publisher: Joanna Lorenz
Editor Director: Helen Sudell
Editor: Simona Hill
Designer: Nigel Partridge
Production Controller: Pedro Nelson
Editorial Reader: Jay Thundercliffe
Consultant: Clive King
Photographers: Peter Anderson, Sidney Teo
Illustrators: Peter Barrett, Penny Brown, Stuart Carter, Anthony Duke,
    Stuart Lafford, David More, Sebastian Quigley

ETHICAL TRADING POLICY
Because of our ongoing ecological investment programme, you, as our customer, can have the pleasure and reassurance of knowing that a tree is being cultivated on your behalf to naturally replace the materials used to make the book you are holding. For further information about this scheme, go to www.annesspublishing.com/trees

Parts of this title have been previously published as part of another volume, *Trees: An Illustrated Identifier and Encyclopedia*

PUBLISHER'S NOTE
Although the advice and information in this book are believed to be accurate and true at the time of going to press, neither the authors nor the publisher can accept any legal responsibility or liability for any errors or omissions that may be made.

P1 Red horse chestnut, *Aesculus* x *carnea*.
P2 Fall foliage.
P3 American mountain ash, *Sorbus americana*.
P4 Left: Japanese chestnut, *Castanea crenata*.
Center: Bristlecone fir, *Abies bracteata*. Right: Oriental plane, *Platanus orientalis*.
P5 Top: Douglas fir, *Pseudotsuga menziesii*. Below top: Pagoda tree,
Sophora japonica. Center: West Indian Jasmine, *Plumeria alba*. Below: Black locust,
Robinia pseudoacacia. Bottom: Showy mountain ash, *Sorbus decora*.

CONTENTS

INTRODUCTION

Trees are the most complex and successful plants on earth. They have been around for 370 million years and quite likely will be around for many millions of years to come. Today, they cover almost a third of the earth's dry land and comprise more than 80,000 different species ranging from small Arctic willows that are just a few inches high to the lofty giant redwoods, which stand at an amazing 368ft (113m).

Trees are the oldest living organisms on earth. In California, there are Bristlecone pines which are known to be over 4,500 years old and in the United Kingdom there are yew trees of a similar age. Ever since the first primates appeared in the Palaeocene epoch, 65 million years ago, trees have played an integral part in human development, providing food, shelter, safety, medicines, timber and fuel among other things.

Trees are indeed essential to all life. They reduce pollution by absorbing vast amounts of carbon dioxide from the atmosphere while at the same time replacing it with "clean" oxygen. Each day 1 acre

Above: Giant redwoods, Sequoiadendron giganteum, *can reach heights in excess of 325ft (100m).*

(0.4 ha) of trees will produce enough oxygen to keep 18 people alive. Forests of trees help to regulate water flow and can reduce the effects of flooding and soil erosion. They even influence weather patterns by increasing humidity and generating rainfall.

With their myriad shades of green, trees make our cities and towns more colorful. They increase wildlife diversity, and create a more pleasant living and working environment. They provide shade in summer and shelter in winter. It is also a fact that post-operative hospital stays are shortened when patients are in rooms with views of trees.

For centuries, poets, writers and artists have been inspired by the beauty of trees. Works such as Wordsworth's *Borrowdale Yews* and John Constable's

Left: Robinia pseudoacacia *trees have been used to create avenues for at least 400 years. Pollarding keeps the shape neat and even.*

Above: Ancient trees are important points of reference in our towns and the countryside, and help determine the character of an area.

majestic elms in *The Hay Wain* will live on long after the original trees depicted have died. Trees help to bring beauty to our gardens and parks. Chosen well, they will provide stunning flowers, foliage, fruit and bark every day of the year. Nothing brings structure and maturity to a garden as successfully as a tree.

With so many obvious values it should be safe to assume that trees are venerated the world over. Unfortunately that is not the case. More than ten percent of the world's tree species are endangered. More than 8,750 species are threatened with extinction—some are down to their last one or two specimens. Across the world we are losing at least 100 acres (40 ha) of trees every minute.

This book is a celebration of trees in all their forms, from hardy evergreens and deciduous broadleaves, to desert survivors and tropical palms. It reveals what incredible organisms trees are, and describes the diversity that exists throughout the world and how they each contribute to the planet. The first section describes the origins of trees, how they have evolved, how they live, grow, reproduce and why they die. It looks in detail at their leaves, bark, fruit, flowers, buds, cones and seeds, and

details the fascinating role each plays in the life of the tree. Trees inhabit many natural landscapes, from the highest mountain ridges all the way down to sea level, and have adapted to different circumstances. The heat of the tropics, the biting cold of northern lands, the salt and wind of the sea and the pollution of the city have all contributed to the evolution of the tree.

The second section of this book features a comprehensive encyclopedia of the most well-known, unusual, or economically and ecologically important species that thrive in the Americas. Each entry provides a detailed description of the tree, its height, habit, color and leaf shape, and whether it produces flowers, fruit or cones. Its habitat and most interesting features are described to aid identification, and a map helps to locate wild populations for each entry.

This book aims to bring a greater understanding and appreciation of trees to a wider audience. It should encourage you to look more closely at the diversity of trees in your own locality and, if you have the opportunity to visit far-flung regions, to appreciate the diversity that exists in the world.

Below: The monkey puzzle tree, Araucaria araucana, *has a distinctive and instantly recognizable silhouette.*

HOW TREES LIVE

Trees have three obvious features that together distinguish them from all other living plants. First, they produce a woody stem, roots and branches which do not die back each winter, but continue to grow year upon year. This means that from the time a tree begins to germinate until the time it dies it is always visible. Be it the smallest Arctic willow or the largest Californian redwood, this basic principle of growth remains the same.

Second, trees live longer than any other living organism on the planet. It is not exceptional to find living trees that are more than 1,000 years old and many are considerably older. Third, trees are the largest living organisms on the planet. Around the world there are trees in excess of 328ft (100m) tall or 1,360 tons in weight.

Trees have been growing on earth for 370 million years, and today can be found growing almost everywhere from the Arctic and Antarctic circles to the Equator. For much of the world, trees are the climax species of all plants. In simple terms this means if land is left untended long enough, it will eventually become colonized by trees.

So why are trees so successful? Well, as with all plants, trees need light to survive. Without light, photosynthesis cannot take place and food for growth cannot be made. Trees are superb competitors for light; their woody stem enables them to hold their leaves way above the leaves of any other plant. This means they can absorb vast quantities of light while shading out other plants in the process.

Such is the extensive nature of a tree's root system that it can access moisture from deep in the subsoil—something few other plants can do. As such, trees are well equipped to survive periods of drought, particularly as their structure and size allows them to store food and water for times of deficiency. All in all trees are an incredibly competitive and successful group of plants—which is why they have been around so long. They are also a fascinating group of plants, as the following pages will clearly show.

Left: Cedars of Lebanon, Cedrus libani, *in the remnants of a forest in the Bcharre Valley, in Lebanon. This species is known to live for over 2,000 years.*

THE EVOLUTION OF TREES

The first trees evolved more than 300 million years ago. By 200 million years ago they were the most successful land plants on earth, growing in all but the most inhospitable places, such as the Polar regions. Their ability to produce vast amounts of oxygen has enabled other life forms, including humans, to evolve.

The first living organisms appeared on earth 3,800 million years ago. These primitive, single-celled life forms were followed 500 million years later by the earliest cyanobacteria or blue-green algae. Also single-celled, these were the first organisms able to harness the sun's energy to produce food. This process, known as photosynthesis, had an important by-product—oxygen, which gradually began to accumulate in the earth's atmosphere.

Archaeopteris: the first tree

The first known land plant, which was called *Cooksonia*, evolved around 430 million years ago. *Cooksonia* was erect and green-stemmed with a simple underground root system. It was followed about 60 million years later by *Archaeopteris*, the first real tree.

Below: The timeline below shows the evolution of life forms from the first ammonites of the Devonian period, 417–360 million years ago, through to the development of flowering trees such as magnolias during the Cretaceous period, 144–65 million years ago.

With a woody trunk up to 16in (40cm) across, *Archaeopteris* had branches and a large root system. It also had the ability to produce buds and continue growing year after year. Fossils of *Archaeopteris* found recently suggest that it may have been able to live for as long as 50 years. As forests of *Archaeopteris* spread across the earth, the amount of oxygen in the atmosphere rapidly increased, paving the way for an explosion in the evolution of new land animals.

The Carboniferous period

During the Carboniferous period, the earth's climate was warm and humid. Great forests and swamps of trees, ferns and mosses covered the land. One of the most common trees was *Lepidodendron*. Known as the scale tree, it reached heights of 98ft (30m) and had a trunk more than 10ft (3m) across. It looked like a palm tree, but instead of fans of long, thin leaves it had fern-like fronds, each ending with cone-shaped structures containing spores for reproduction.

At the close of this period, the first primitive conifers, or gymnosperms, began to appear. These plants protected their seeds in cones and had a much more efficient reproductive system than their predecessors. None of these early conifers survives today. Their nearest relatives are species of *Araucaria* (monkey puzzle), *Taxus* (yew) and *Podocarpus*.

Pangaea

A vast supercontinent that existed 280–193 million years ago was known as Pangaea. The northern part, called Laurasia, comprised the landmasses of North America, Europe and Asia all joined together. The southern part, Gondwanaland, was made up of South America, Africa, Arabia, India, Australia and Antarctica.

Since they were part of Pangaea the continents have moved. Fossil evidence taken from samples of ice deep in the Antarctic ice cap show that relatives of *Nothofagus moorei*, the Antarctic beech, grew in that region more than 200 million years ago.

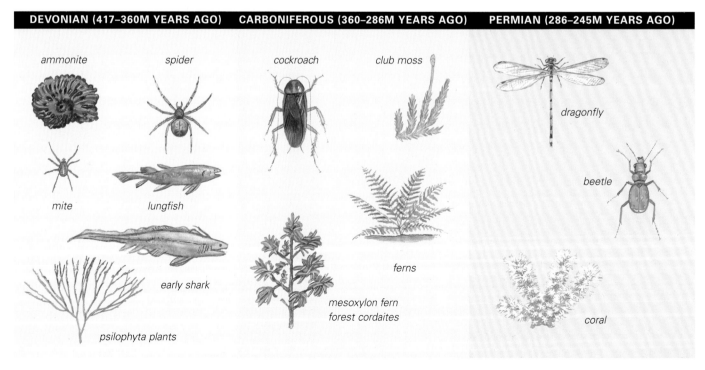

| DEVONIAN (417–360M YEARS AGO) | CARBONIFEROUS (360–286M YEARS AGO) | PERMIAN (286–245M YEARS AGO) |

ammonite

spider

cockroach

club moss

dragonfly

mite

lungfish

beetle

early shark

ferns

psilophyta plants

mesoxylon fern
forest cordaites

coral

Above: One very early tree that is still around today is the deciduous Ginkgo biloba, *or maidenhair tree. It is the last surviving member of a family of trees called the ginkgos; along with conifers, they dominated the land for 250 million years.*

The Mesozoic era

This era lasted from 245–65 million years ago. It was the age of dinosaurs and saw dramatic fluctuations in world climate. Conifers adapted to these changes so successfully that different species evolved for almost every environment. Today, they survive in some of the coldest and hottest parts of the planet.

Ginkgos were also successful: fossils show that they grew throughout the Northern Hemisphere, from the Arctic Circle to the Mediterranean and from North America to China. Fossils of the Jurassic period (208–144 million years ago) also show the dawn redwood, *Metasequoia glyptostroboides*. Previously thought to have been extinct since that time, the dawn redwood was discovered growing in China in 1941. During the Cretaceous period (144–65 million years ago) flowering plants (angiosperms) evolved and began to exert their dominance over conifers. Among the earliest were magnolias, which are common today, many providing superb flowers.

The Tertiary era

Many of the trees that grew during the Tertiary era (65–2 million years ago) still grow today. The main difference between the Tertiary and the present was the scale of the forests. During the early Tertiary era the planet was warmer than it is today. Europe and North America had a similar climate to that of present-day Southeast Asia, and vast swathes of forest covered virtually every available piece of land. Oak, beech, magnolia, hemlock, cedar, maple, chestnut, lime and elm occurred alongside tropical trees such as the nypa palm. As the era progressed however, the climate began to cool.

The ice ages

By 1.5 million years ago, the climate had cooled so much that the first of four ice ages began. Trees that we now regard as tropical began to die at the far north and south of their ranges. As the temperature dropped further so more temperate species succumbed. Only those trees close enough to the Equator were able to survive. Each glaciation was interspersed with warmer interglacial periods lasting anything up to 60,000 years. During these warmer periods, many trees recolonized their previous ranges. Every continent suffered; however, some fared better than others because of differences in topography. In North America, for example, the mountain ranges all run from north to south. Heat-loving trees were able to spread south as the ice sheets advanced, using the valleys between mountain ranges to reach refuges nearer the equator. The trees recolonized their old ranges using these routes. In Europe, however, recolonization was impossible. The Pyrenees and the Alps, which stretched from east to west, prevented many trees from moving south ahead of the ice. Once trapped they perished, leaving Europe with a far less diverse tree flora than that of North America or Asia.

The modern era

Since the last ice age began to wane 14,000 years ago, the temperature of the earth has gradually increased and trees have begun to recolonize temperate areas of the world. Today there are over 80,000 different species of trees on earth.

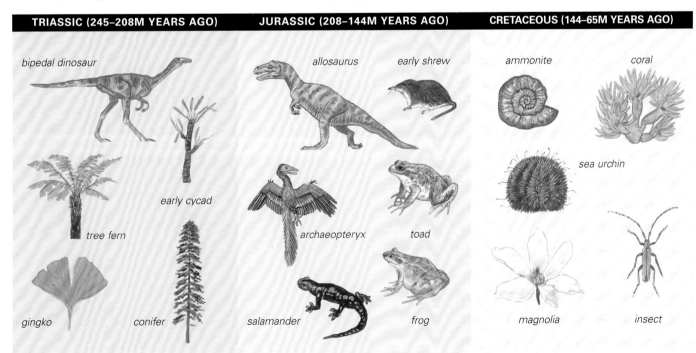

TRIASSIC (245–208M YEARS AGO)　　**JURASSIC (208–144M YEARS AGO)**　　**CRETACEOUS (144–65M YEARS AGO)**

bipedal dinosaur

early cycad

tree fern

gingko　　*conifer*

allosaurus　　*early shrew*

archaeopteryx　　*toad*

salamander　　*frog*

ammonite　　*coral*

sea urchin

magnolia　　*insect*

CLASSIFICATION OF TREES

Classification is the process by which plants or animals are grouped and named according to their specific similarities. The theory and practice of classification is called taxonomy, and those that work in this field are known as taxonomists.

There are over 300,000 different species of flowering plants and gymnosperms or conifers in the world. Botanists have classified them in order to try and make sense of the way that they are related to each other. Rudimentary grouping of trees has occurred for centuries, not always with great accuracy. For example the Northern red oak, *Quercus rubra*, and the holm (evergreen) oak, *Q. ilex*, have always been regarded as being closely related because of the fruit they produce. However, the sweet chestnut, *Castanea sativa*, and the horse chestnut, *Aesculus hippocastanum*, which were also once classified on the basis of their fruit, are now thought to belong to two quite different families.

The science of classification starts to become ever more complex as botanists study trees more closely. Where trees were once classified on the basis of just one or perhaps two characteristics, now many more of their features are compared before any decision is made.

Below: The horse chestnut (left) and sweet chestnut (right) were once thought to be related.

Carl Von Linné (1707–1778)

Ever since the time of the Greek philosopher Aristotle (384–322 B.C.) it had been recognized that, both in the plant and animal world, there was a natural order where everything had its place and was linked to other species by a common thread. However, it was not until the eighteenth century that the Swedish botanist Carl Von Linné (also known as Linnaeus—the Latin name that he gave himself) made the first attempt to link all plants by one specific feature. He classified them by the way they reproduced themselves and the make-up of their reproductive systems—in the case of flowering plants, their flowers. As he admitted, his choice of feature for classification was artificial. Linnaeus had not found the common thread, the natural order of all living things. Nevertheless, he did create a system of classification that is still in use today.

Linnaeus invented the principle of using two Latin words to name a species. He chose Latin because it was the language of scholarship, and was understood across the world but no longer used as a spoken language, so

Above: Trees often have common names that refer to their place of origin, coloring, or use.

the meaning of its words would not change over time. The first of the two words is known as the generic (genus) name and the second the specific (species) name. The generic name gives a clue to the species' relationship with others. Closely related species are given the same generic name but different specific names. For example, the Northern red oak is called *Quercus rubra* and the closely related turkey oak is called *Quercus cerris*. All species with the same generic name are said to belong to the same genus.

Similar genera (the plural of genus) are combined into larger groups known as families. For example the oak genus, *Quercus*, belongs to the same family as the beech genus, *Fagus*. This family is called Fagaceae, and is commonly known as the beech family. Similar families are gathered together in turn into larger groups called orders. The beech family, Fagaceae, combines with the birch family, Betulaceae, to make the beech tree

order Fagales. Similar orders are then combined into subclasses. The beech order is part of the hazel subclass, which is called Hamamelidae. In turn, Hamamelidae is combined with all of the other plant subclasses that are characterized by embryos that contain two seed leaves, to form a group that is known as the dicotyledons. This group is then joined together with all plants that have an embryo that contains only one seed leaf (monocotyledons) into one group that contains all flowering plants—the Magnoliophytina. Finally, this is gathered together with all of the other groups of seed-producing plants, and then combined with the non seed-producing plants, such as ferns, into the Plant Kingdom.

Charles Darwin (1809–1882)

The "common thread" or natural order of all living things was left for Charles Darwin to discover. Darwin recognized that plants, or animals for that matter, were usually alike because of their common ancestry.

Trees alive today can be classified in terms of their relatedness because they have all evolved "over time" from a single common ancestor that existed millions of years ago. The science of the ancestry of all living things is called phylogeny, and it goes hand in glove with taxonomy.

Once the interrelatedness of all plants was understood, scientists began to trace back the evolution of trees. In

many ways this process is similar to tracing back one's own family tree. The major difference is that fossil records are used. The different characteristics of trees living today, compared to fossils of those from the past, reflect the evolutionary changes that have occurred to the common ancestral line over millions of years. Each evolutionary change has been in response to a different environmental condition and has resulted in a different tree.

For most of us, classification only becomes pertinent when we are trying to identify a species.

Below: The cork oak (left) and common beech (right) look different, but in fact they are both members of the beech family, Fagaceae.

Above: It is possible to recognize trees that belong to the same family by certain obvious characteristics. For example hazel (above left), alder (above center), birch (above right), and hornbeam (not shown) all belong to the birch family, Betulaceae, and all produce catkins.

For botanists and taxonomists however, classification is an everyday procedure and a frequent cause of disagreement. It is now more than 200 years since Linnaeus developed his system of classification, and 150 years since Darwin announced his theory of evolution. Nevertheless, taxonomists still move species from one genus to another, and some botanists cast doubt on whether plant classification should be based upon the evolutionary process at all.

ROOTS

Tree roots provide anchorage, ensuring that the tree does not fall over. They obtain water, the lifeblood of any tree, by sucking it from the soil, and provide the tree with minerals which are essential for growth. They also store food, such as starch, which is produced by the leaves, for later use.

Roots have the ability to influence the size of a tree. Around 60 percent of the total mass of any tree is made up by its trunk. The remaining 40 percent is split evenly between the branches and the root system, each having a direct relationship with the other. If there are not enough roots, the canopy and leaves will not be able to obtain enough water and branches will start to die back. In turn, if branches are damaged or removed and there are fewer leaves to produce food, a tree's roots will begin to die back.

A shallow existence
Contrary to popular belief, tree roots do not penetrate deep into the soil. In most cases the roots of even the tallest tree seldom reach down more than 10ft (3m). In reality the overall shape of a tree will look like a wine glass, with the roots forming the shallow but spreading base.

More than three-quarters of most trees' roots can be found within 24in (60cm) of the surface. They seldom

Below: Few trees can survive indefinitely in waterlogged conditions, but mangroves can.

need to go deeper: the top layers of the soil are usually rich in organic material, minerals and moisture, which are just the ingredients that roots require.

However, roots do spread extensively outwards within the upper layers of the soil. The bulk of a root system will be found within 10–13ft (3–4m) of a tree's trunk. However, very fine roots may spread anything up to twice the radius of the canopy, which in a large tree can mean anything up to 98ft (30m) away from the trunk.

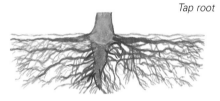

Tap root

Tap roots
The first root that every tree grows from its seed is called a tap root. Tap roots grow straight down and, from day one, have the ability to extract moisture and minerals from the soil. Within days of the tap root emerging from a seed, side roots (known as laterals) grow off the tap root and begin to move horizontally through the top layers of the soil. With some trees,

such as the oak, the tap root will persist for several years. In most species, however, the tap root withers and the lateral roots take over.

Lateral roots

Lateral roots
Most lateral roots stay close to the surface for the whole of a tree's life. Sometimes they may develop from the tap root or grow directly from the base of the trunk, and in the latter case can be more than 12in (30cm) across. Within 3ft (1m) of the trunk they taper to around 4in (10cm) across, and at 13ft (4m) away they are usually under 2in (5cm) in diameter and far more soft and pliable.

Symbiotic associations
Within the soil, tree roots come into contact with the living threads, or *hyphae*, of numerous fungi. Quite often this association is beneficial to both the tree and the fungus. Usually the tree acquires hard-to-obtain nutrients such as phosphorus from the fungus, and the fungus gets carbohydrates from the tree. These structures formed between tree roots and fungi in these mutually beneficial, or symbiotic, associations are known as mycorrhiza. Sometimes, however, contact with fungus can be damaging for a tree.

Roots and water
Tree roots require water to survive, but they also need to obtain a supply of oxygen. It is important that they have water readily available, but roots will not do well if they are continually submerged. In constantly waterlogged conditions roots will not be able to obtain enough oxygen from the soil, and a tree will effectively drown.

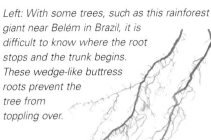

Left: With some trees, such as this rainforest giant near Belém in Brazil, it is difficult to know where the root stops and the trunk begins. These wedge-like buttress roots prevent the tree from toppling over.

Roots and oxygen

As its name suggests, the swamp cypress from the southeastern United States grows in wet conditions. To counter the lack of soil oxygen, its roots have strange knobbly growths, called knees. These grow out of the water or wet ground to gain access to the air, and therefore to a supply of oxygen. Swamp cypress knees can reach a height of 13ft (4m). They not only absorb oxygen, but also provide support to the tree, making it less likely to blow over in a strong wind.

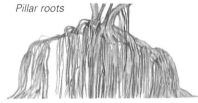

Pillar roots

Pillar roots

Both the weeping fig, *Ficus benjamina*, and the banyan, *F. benghalensis*, have roots that grow and hang down from the branches. These roots grow remarkably quickly—up to ½in (1cm) a day—and once anchored in the soil they form prop-like pillars, capable of bearing the weight of the spreading branches, which they grew

Below: The breathing roots of this mangrove protrude through the sand on Mafia Island, off the coast of Tanzania.

Left: The farther they are from the trunk, the finer roots become. Growing from these fine roots are millions of tiny hairs, each one made up of a single cell. It is these root hairs that collect the necessary ingredients, such as nitrogen and potassium, for a tree to grow. Each is in contact with the soil particles around it, and is able to absorb both the moisture and the diluted minerals that surround each particle. Root hairs have a lifespan of no more than a few weeks but, as they die, new ones are formed.

from. This system enables the tree to continue to grow outwards almost indefinitely. A single banyan tree planted in the Royal Botanic Garden of Calcutta in 1782, for example, now covers an area of 3 acres (1.2ha) and has 1,775 pillar roots.

Below: Honey fungus, Armillariella mellea, is one of the biggest killers of trees in the temperate world. Once it has made contact with a tree's roots, it rapidly spreads through the entire vascular system of the tree, killing tissue as it goes.

Stilt roots

Stilt roots

Mangroves grow throughout the tropics on coastal mudflats. Many species of mangrove have stilt-like roots that arch from the main stem down into the mud. Once these have taken root, they help to anchor the tree so that it remains stable in the constantly moving mudflat silt. The stilt roots graft together, creating a three-dimensional framework that holds and supports the mangrove tree clear of the mud.

TRUNK AND BARK

What makes a tree different from all other plants is the tough, woody framework it raises above the ground: the framework, made up of a trunk and branches, lasts for the entire life of the tree. As each year passes, this framework gets bigger as the trunk and branches expand upwards and outwards.

The main purpose of the trunk is to position the leaves as far as possible from the ground. The higher they are, the less competition there is from other plants for light, and without light, trees die. The trunk supports the branches, and the branches support the leaves.

The trunk and branches have two other functions. They transport water, which has been collected by the roots, up through the tree to the leaves. Second, they move food, which is produced in the leaves, to every other part of the tree, including the roots.

Considering the importance of the functions that the trunk and branches perform, it is extraordinary that more than 80 percent of their mass are made up of dead cells. The only living cells in a tree's trunk and branches are those in the area immediately beneath the bark. It is here that all of the activity takes place.

The inner tree

A tree's bark is like a skin. It is a corky waterproof layer that protects the all-important inner cells from disease, animal attack and, in the case of redwoods and eucalyptus, forest fires.

Some barks, such as that of the rubber tree, exude latex to "gum up" the mouths of feeding predators. Pine trees have a similar defense mechanism, exuding a sticky resin, which can literally engulf a whole insect. Some trees, such as the South American quinine tree, *Cinchona corymbosa*, produce chemicals in their bark which are poisonous to attackers.

Bark is perforated with millions of tiny breathing pores called lenticels, which pass oxygen from the outside atmosphere through to the living cells beneath. In cities and along busy roads these lenticels get clogged up with dirt and carbon. Some trees, such as the London plane, *Platanus* x *hispanica*, have adapted by regularly shedding their old bark. All trees are constantly growing and their girth expanding. This is reflected in the cracks and crevices that appear in the bark of many trees. As bark splits, new corky cells are produced to plug the gap.

Beneath the outer bark is the inner bark, or phloem. This is a soft spongy layer of living tissue that transports sap—sugary liquid food—from the leaves to the rest of the tree.

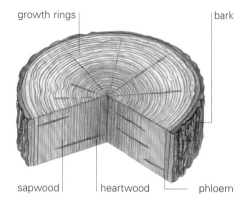

Above: A section through the trunk of a larch tree showing the darker heartwood and the lighter sapwood.

Beneath the phloem is a thin tissue known as the cambium. Although it is only one cell thick, the cambium is extremely important. It is here that all tree growth takes place. Cambium cells are constantly dividing, producing phloem cells on the outside and on the inside wood cells, or xylem.

Xylem has two parts: the sapwood, made up of living cells, and the heartwood, composed of dead cells. The sapwood transports water and minerals from the roots to the leaves. Most of these are carried in sapwood made by the cambium during that year. The heartwood forms the dense central core of the trunk, supporting the tree and giving the trunk rigidity. The two main constituents of xylem are cellulose and lignin. Cellulose, a glucose-based carbohydrate, makes up three-quarters of the xylem and is used in the construction of cell walls. Lignin comprises most of the remaining quarter and is a complex organic polymer. It is lignin that gives wood its structural strength. If water and air reach the heartwood as a result of damage to the outer layers of the trunk, decay will occur and in time the tree may become hollow.

Left: Most trees that are more than 500 years old are hollow. Eight people sitting around a table can fit inside the trunk of this tree.

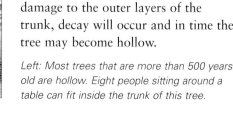

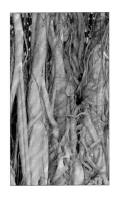
Banyan tree

Cola nut

Kapok

Papaya

Flame of the forest

Tembusu

Bark invaders

While bark exists to provide a protective barrier over the living tissue of a tree's trunk and branches, there are plenty of creatures capable of penetrating that barrier. Bark beetles and wood-boring insects eat cellulose and excavate breeding chambers and galleries for egg-laying purposes. Often the damage inflicted by insects is much greater than just the physical effects of their mining. Insects may carry fungal diseases. Beetles that bore into infected trees become coated with fungal spores, which they carry to other, healthy trees. Once underneath the bark, the fungus quickly blocks the cells transporting food and water, leading to the tree's demise.

How we use bark

Bark not only forms protection for trees, it can also be very useful to us.

Below: Trees grow from terminal and lateral buds positioned toward the tip of the branches.

Much of the wine that we drink is sealed in bottles with bark from the cork oak tree, *Quercus suber*. In Mediterranean regions, cork oaks are grown in orchards. Every ten years or so, the outer corky bark is carefully removed, leaving the cambium layer intact. The cambium then produces more cork cells to replace the bark that has been harvested.

Bark also provides us with food and medicine. The spice cinnamon is made from the dried and ground bark of the Sri Lankan cinnamon tree, *Cinnamomum zeylanicum*, while the bark of the Pacific yew, *Taxus brevifolia*, contains a substance called taxol, which has been highly effective in the treatment of some forms of cancer.

Some trees have very attractive bark, making them ideal ornamental plants for parks and gardens. The Tibetan cherry, *Prunus tibetica*, has highly polished mahogany-red bark, for example, and the Himalayan birch,

Himalayan cherry

Indian horse chestnut

Floss silk tree

Eucalyptus

Paperbark maple

Birch 'Snow Queen'

BUDS

Buds act as protective sheaths for the growing tips of trees during the coldest months of the year. In winter, even though deciduous trees will have shed their leaves, they can still be readily identified by their buds.

For trees to grow they need water, minerals, nutrients and the right growing conditions, namely sunlight and warmth. In parts of the world where there is little seasonal variation, such as the tropics, favorable climatic conditions may allow growth to continue all year round. However, even in tropical rainforests very few trees grow non-stop. The normal pattern for most trees, particularly those in temperate regions, is for a period of growth followed by a period of rest. The period of rest coincides with the time of year when the climate is least favorable to growth. Across North America, Britain and Europe this is during the cold and dark of winter.

Throughout the winter resting period, the growing tips of a tree, known as the meristem, are vulnerable to cold winds and frost. Prolonged low temperatures can very easily damage or even kill the meristem. Trees have therefore evolved ways to protect this all-important tissue.

Protective sheath

During early autumn, as the growing season approaches its end, the last few leaves to be produced by the tree are turned into much thicker but smaller bud leaves, known as scales. These

Above: A lime tree breaking bud.

Above: A maple breaking bud.

toughened leaves stay on the tree after all the other leaves have fallen off, and form a protective sheath around the meristem. This sheath is known as a leaf-bud. Its thick scales are waterproof and overlap each other, creating a defense system able to withstand the onslaught of winter. Often a coating of wax, resin or gum is used to strengthen these defenses.

Inside the bud

Winter buds contain all that the tree will need to resume growing once the days lengthen and the temperature increases in spring. Inside is a miniature shoot, miniature leaves all carefully folded over one another and, in some species, such as the horse chestnut, *Aesculus hippocastanum*, miniature flowers.

Trees without buds

Not all trees produce buds, even in temperate regions. Some, such as the wayfaring tree, *Viburnum lantana*, have "naked buds" with no bud scales. At the end of the growing season its last leaves to be formed stop growing before they are fully

developed. A dense layer of hair then forms on them to provide protection from the cold, and they proceed to wrap themselves around the meristem. When spring arrives the protective leaves simply start growing again from where they left off.

Eucalyptus trees also have "naked buds" but, as back-up, they produce tiny concealed buds beneath the leaf base. These are only activated if the growing tip gets damaged.

Below: An Indian horse chestnut bud opening to reveal long, thin, down-covered leaves.

Below: Some buds contain all of the cells needed for the whole of the following year's growth. Others contain just enough to start growing in spring, and then produce more growth cells once the leaves have emerged from the bud.

Some conifers, such as western red cedar, *Thuja plicata*, and lawson cypress, *Chamaecyparis lawsoniana*, have no distinct buds at all; instead they produce little packets of meristematic cells, which are hidden beneath the surface of each frond of needles.

The growing season

As spring arrives, buds open and the leaves begin to emerge. For all trees the trigger for this to happen is increasing warmth and light. Individual species each have their own trigger point, which is determined by their geographical origins. Species that originated in colder regions, such as birch or willow, burst bud earlier than those such as horse chestnut or sweet chestnut, which evolved in warmer parts of the world. Birch instinctively knows that northern European summers are relatively short affairs, and that it needs to get going as quickly as possible to make the most of the growing season. Sweet chestnut, on the other hand, instinctively expects a long, Mediterranean summer, and so is in less of a rush to get started.

Growth cycle of a horse chestnut bud

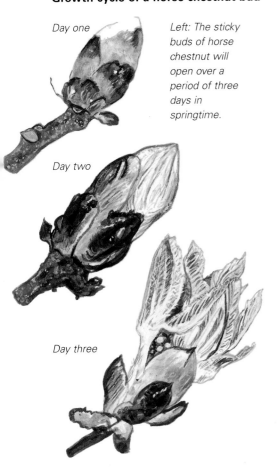

Day one

Day two

Day three

Left: The sticky buds of horse chestnut will open over a period of three days in springtime.

BUD ARRANGEMENTS

Even in winter, when deciduous trees display bare branches, trees can still be identified by the shape, size, color and arrangement of the buds on the twigs.

Opposite buds

The buds of trees such as maple and ash are said to be opposite—that is, in pairs on each side of the twig, exactly opposite each other. Ash buds are easily recognizable by their distinctive black coloring.

Alternate buds

The buds of trees such as beech and willow are arranged alternately on different sides of the twig. Willow buds are generally longer and more slender than those of beech.

Hairy buds

Magnolia buds are very distinctive and easily recognized by their covering of thick gray fur. Magnolia buds are some of the largest found on any tree.

Clustered buds

Oak buds appear almost randomly on the twig, but always with a cluster of buds at the tip. Cherries also adopt this clustered approach.

Whiskered buds

As well as being clustered, some oaks, such as the turkey oak, also have thin whiskers surrounding the buds.

Naked buds

The wayfaring tree does not have a true bud. Instead it has immature hairy leaves which surround the growing tip to protect it from the cold.

Trees that have everything for the coming year's growth pre-packaged inside the bud, tend to have a single growth spurt immediately after their leaves emerge. This can mean that they achieve virtually all their growth for the whole year within the first four weeks of spring. Those trees that over-winter with just enough growth cells in the bud to aid emergence in spring grow more slowly, but grow for a longer period of time. In some instances these species may continue growing for more than 100 days. However, by the end of the season the overall growth of each will be similar.

Below: Sweet cherry buds.

Below: Magnolia bud.

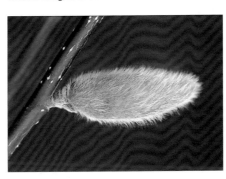

Below: Wingnut bud.

Below: Horse chestnut bud.

LEAVES

Each leaf on a tree is a mini power station generating food, which the tree uses to provide the necessary energy for living and growing. The process by which leaves produce food is called photosynthesis. During this process the leaves absorb carbon dioxide and emit oxygen.

Leaves contain a green pigment called chlorophyll, which absorbs light energy from the sun. This energy is used to combine carbon dioxide, which the leaf absorbs from the atmosphere, with water taken from the soil. The resulting products are glucose and oxygen. Glucose provides the energy to fuel the tree and can be turned into starch for storage, or cellulose, which forms the tree's cell walls. Oxygen is then released by the leaf back into the atmosphere. A mature tree can produce the same amount of oxygen every year as that used by ten people.

Leaf structure

Each leaf is covered by a skin of tightly packed cells known as the epidermis. This skin is coated by a waxy covering called the cuticle. The cuticle acts as waterproofing, preventing the leaf from losing any more water than is necessary. The transfer of oxygen and carbon dioxide to and from the atmosphere takes place through tiny holes in the cuticle known as stomata. Stomata are concentrated on the underside of the leaf away from the direct heat of the sun to minimize water loss. The cells around the stomata have the ability to enlarge and decrease the size of the hole. Despite this, water is lost from the leaf through the stomata. This loss of water is known as transpiration. Even though stomata normally

Left: Tiny breathing holes in the leaf are known as stomata.

cover less than one percent of a leaf's total area, the amount of water lost in this way can be astonishing. A large deciduous tree can lose up to 66 gallons (300 liters) per day in summer. The lost water is usually replaced by water drawn from its roots. In times of drought the amount of water lost may exceed that available to the roots. When this happens the leaves wilt and die, stopping the tree from producing food.

Inside the leaf cells, the chlorophyll is contained in millions of tiny cell-like vessels called chloroplasts. Most of these are found in the upper part of the leaf, which receives the most light. Beneath the chloroplasts are the vascular tissues that make up the xylem, and which transport the raw ingredients for photosynthesis, such as water and minerals, all the way from

Below: Cross section of a leaf.

upper layer of leaf — xylem — stomata — cells containing chlorophyll

phloem

Above: In the fall, when chlorophyll production ceases and any residue decays, other pigments are revealed in the leaves.

Life cycle of leaves

Above: In spring new leaves form.

Left: Summer.

Below: The changing tones of fall.

Above: Winter profile.

the roots to the leaf. Alongside the xylem is the phloem, which transports the sugary products of photosynthesis from the leaf to all other parts of the tree. Both vascular systems rely on a process called osmosis to move liquid. Osmosis is a process whereby liquid moves from one cell to another. The catalyst for this to happen is the fullness, or turgidness, of each cell. As one cell becomes full, so the liquid within it permeates through the cell wall into a neighboring cell that is less turgid. Once this cell is full, liquid starts to permeate from it into the next empty cell and so on.

Leaf size and shape

One of the most interesting things about leaves is the incredible range of shapes and sizes. The smallest so-called broad leaf is produced by the Arctic willow, *Salix nivalis*. This tundra species has leaves less than ¼in (5mm) long. Some conifers have needles that are even smaller.

All broad-leaved tree leaves have one thing in common: a network of visible veins, which spread out across the leaf from its base. It is within these veins that the xylem and phloem are found. The veins join together at the leaf base to form the stalk, or petiole.

Simple leaves

These come in a wide variety of shapes. At their most basic they may be entirely round or heart-shaped, or have no

indentation around the leaf edge. Many leaves, such as those of cherry trees, are oval in shape and have small serrations around the edge. On others the serrations may be more pronounced, as with the sweet chestnut, *Castanea sativa*. Some trees, such as the oak, produce leaves with distinctive lobing. These lobes may be rounded, or more angular.

Compound leaves

At first glance the leaflets of compound leaves look like separate leaves growing off the same stalk. However, closer inspection of a new compound leaf reveals that the whole stalk and its leaflets all emerge from the same leaf bud. It is in essence all one leaf. Many of the trees in our cities have compound leaves. One of the most easily recognized is the horse chestnut, which has seven or nine large leaflets all attached to the same point of the main leaf stalk. The golden-leaved robinia, *Robinia pseudoacacia* 'Frisia', has paired leaflets that appear opposite each other (pinnate leaflets) on the leaf stalk, as with the American ash, *Fraxinus americana*. Occasionally the leaf stalk to which the leaflets are attached may sub-divide, producing side stalks and a bipinnate leaf. One of the best examples of a tree with bipinnate leaves is the Japanese angelica tree, *Aralia elata*, which has leaves in excess of 20in (50cm) long.

Evergreen leaves

A deciduous tree keeps its leaves for only part of the year; they grow in the spring and drop in the fall. By contrast, evergreen trees, which include most conifers and trees such as holly, box and laurel, have leaves all year around. This does not mean the same leaves stay on the tree for the whole of its life. Evergreen leaves fall from trees and are replaced throughout the year. The real difference between evergreen and deciduous trees is that the leaves of deciduous trees all fall at around the same time, while those of evergreens do not. On average, evergreens keep their leaves for between three and five years, although on some firs and spruces the needles may be retained for up to ten years.

Needles

Pines, firs, larches, spruces and cedars all have needles, as do yews and redwoods. Although visually quite unlike other leaves, needles are in fact just compact versions of simple leaves, and do the same job of producing food for the tree. Needles lose far less water than the leaves of broadleaf trees. They are therefore better equipped to survive in areas where water is in short supply, such as northern temperate regions where the ground is frozen for months at a time.

Below: The soft, feathery needles of the western red cedar.

Below: The 3ft- (1m)-long leaves of the tropical breadfruit tree.

Below: The fine pencil-like leaves of Eucalyptus champmaniana.

FLOWERS

Flowers contain the tree's reproductive organs. Some trees, such as cherry, have both male and female reproductive organs within the same flower. Others, such as hazel, have separate male and female flowers on the same tree. Some trees only produce flowers of one sex.

Flowers are the sex organs of a tree. What happens in them determines the ability of the tree to reproduce itself. Trees are passive organisms; they cannot actively go out and search for a mate, so they have to engage in sex by proxy. Each tree needs a go-between to get its pollen either to another tree or from the male to the female part of its own flowers. Depending on the species of tree, this go-between may be wind, water or an animal, such as a bird or insect. Over countless generations each species has developed its own flower to suit a specific go-between. The African baobab tree, *Adansonia digitata*, for example, has developed large flowers that produce vast quantities of nectar at night. These flowers attract bats, which feed on the nectar and, in the process, get covered in pollen. The bats transfer that pollen from flower to flower and tree to tree.

Inside the flower

There are almost as many different forms of tree flower as there are trees. Indeed the whole classification system for trees (and other flowering plants) is built around the design of the flowers. Although tree flowers may not resemble other flowers, their basic components are the same. Most flowers have four main parts: the stamen, which is the male reproductive organ and produces the pollen; the stigma, which receives the pollen; the

Below: Magnolia flowers are pollinated by insects.

style, which links the stigma to the ovary; and the ovary, which contains ovules that, after fertilization, develop into seeds. A few tree flowers have only male or female parts.

If both male and female components are present in the same flower, then the flower is said to be "perfect." The tree is then capable of self-pollination and it is known as an hermaphrodite. Self-pollination is far from ideal, and can lead to genetic weaknesses in the same way as inbreeding does in animals. Cross-pollination with another tree is better because it enables different genes to mix. Trees that are hermaphrodites include cherry, laburnum and lime.

To avoid self-pollination, some trees have developed separate male and female flowers. Such trees are known as monoecious and are particularly common where the main vector for pollination is the wind. Monoecious trees include beech, birch and hazel.

Some species only produce male or female flowers on any one tree. These species are "dioecious." This division of trees into sexes overcomes the problem of self-pollination but raises a new problem. Trees of opposite sexes must be relatively close together to have any chance of breeding at all. Trees that are dioecious include yew, holly and the New Zealand kauri pine. Holly berries are found only on female trees, and then only when there is a male tree not too far away.

Below: The flowers of the Italian alder are pollinated by the wind.

Life cycle of a flower from bud

Left: In winter the flowers are protected within buds.

Left: The flowers emerge as the temperature rises in spring.

Right: Once fully open the flowers are pollinated by insects.

Left: Fertilized flowers produce berries in summer.

Right: Birds eat the berries and the seed they contain are dispersed within the birds' droppings.

Welcoming guests

Tree flowers come in all manner of sizes, shapes and colors. Much of this diversity is linked to the pollinator. In general, flowers that are pollinated by animals tend to be larger and showier then those that are pollinated by wind. The wind is indiscriminate but animals need to be attracted. Some animal pollinators are attracted to flowers of certain colors, and a few trees actually

alter their flowers' colors once they have been pollinated to discourage further visitors. For example the color of the markings inside the flowers of the horse chestnut, *Aesculus hippocastanum*, changes from yellow to red after pollination. To a bee, red looks black and very unattractive, so it visits a flower that has yet to be pollinated instead.

Sometimes tree flowers themselves may be quite inconspicuous but are surrounded by showy sterile flowers or leaf bracts to attract pollinators to them. The handkerchief tree, *Davidia involucrata*, from China, for example, has large white bracts that guide pollinating moths to its flowers.

Gone with the wind

Most wind-pollinated trees evolved in places where there was a shortage of insects. Wind pollination is common in the colder northern temperate regions of the world. All conifers are wind pollinated and most produce such large amounts of tiny-grained pollen that on breezy days, clouds of it may fill the air around them. Conifer stamens are positioned at the tips of the branches to aid dispersal. Those of pine trees are bright yellow and stand upright like candles.

Alder, birch and hazel are also wind pollinated. Rather than having erect

Below: The Burmese fish tail palm is pollinated by insect and by wind.

stamens like those of pines they have drooping catkins, each containing millions of pollen grains. In many places, these catkins are one of the first signs of spring. They are made all the more conspicuous by the fact that they appear before the tree comes into leaf. Oak also has pollen-bearing catkins, but these are hardly ever seen because they open in late spring after the tree's leaves have emerged.

Insect pollinators

Pollination by insects is by far the most common method of reproduction among trees. More than 60 per cent of tree species in equatorial regions are pollinated by some kind of insect. Trees that use insects as pollinators tend to produce flowers with copious amounts of sugar-rich nectar. Their pollen grains are larger than those of wind-pollinated species and also quite sticky so that they adhere to insects' bodies.

Below: Male and female persimmon flowers are borne on separate trees.

Above: Magnolia grandiflora has some of the largest flowers borne by any tree.

Birds and mammals

In the tropics, birds are important pollinators of tree flowers. Flowers that are pollinated by birds tend to be tubular in shape (to keep the nectar out of reach of other animals), brightly colored and unscented, since most birds have a poor sense of smell. Hummingbirds use their long beaks to reach inside the flowers of trees such as the angel's trumpet, *Brugmansia*, from Brazil. In Australia and South Africa, bottle-brush trees, *Banksia*, have masses of protruding pollen-covered stamens, which brush against birds' feathers as they collect nectar. Few temperate trees are pollinated by birds. The giraffe is the most unique pollinator of all. It transfers pollen between the flowers of the knobthorn acacia, *Acacia nigrescens*, which grow high up in the tree's branches.

Below: The Prunus x yedoensis *is grown for its stunning display of spring flowers.*

SEEDS

Seeds are the next generation of trees. They contain all that is necessary for the creation of mature trees virtually identical to their parents. Seeds come in a variety of forms; they may be contained within nuts, fruit or berries, or have "wings" to aid dispersal by the wind.

Every tree seed has the potential to develop and become part of the next generation. "From little acorns mighty oak trees grow" is a well-known and accurate saying, although only a tiny proportion of acorns will ever have the opportunity to become mighty oaks. A mature oak tree can produce up to 90,000 acorns in a good year, but fewer than 0.01 percent will grow to become anything like as mighty as their parent. Most acorns will be eaten by mammals or birds (a wood pigeon can eat up to 120 acorns a day), or simply land in a spot where germination and growth are impossible. It is because of this low success rate that the oak needs to produce so many acorns. In terms of seed production, 90,000 is quite modest; alder trees will produce around 250,000 seeds a year.

Different seed types

Seeds are produced from the female part of the flower once it has been pollinated and one or more of its ovules has been fertilized. Just as tree flowers have evolved over millions of years in their quest to find the most effective method of pollen dispersal, so tree seeds also take on many different forms. The main problem facing pollen is exactly the same as that for seeds; trees cannot move, so they have to find other ways of distributing what they produce.

Some trees wrap their seeds inside brightly colored, sweet-tasting fruits or berries. The fruit or berry has two roles; firstly to protect the seed, and

Left: Apple seeds are contained within an edible, fleshy, protective fruit.

Left: The first year's growth from an acorn.

secondly to tempt animals to take it away from the tree. After a fruit or berry is eaten, the seed passes through the animal's digestive system and is excreted, often far from the parent tree, in its own ready-made package of fertilizer. Other trees enclose their seeds within tough outer casings or nuts. Once again, these casings help to protect the seed, but in this case it is the actual seed inside that is the attraction. Squirrels will collect and hoard the nuts, eating some in the process, but many of the nuts are never eaten and, wherever the squirrel has stored them, they will proceed to germinate and grow.

Conifer seed is known as "naked seed" because each individual seed is produced without a protective coat or cover. Conifer seeds are encased together in a cone, but the scales of each cone can be bent back to reveal the unprotected seed inside. Each seed is often equipped with light, papery wings, which enable it to "fly" away from the parent tree on the wind. Other seeds, such as those of alder,

Below: The seeds of the crab apple are contained within a berry loved by birds.

are contained in cones, but rely on water for their distribution.

Whatever the method of seed dispersal there is always one aim: to get the seed as far away from the parent plant as possible. There is no point competing for living space with one's own progeny. Dispersal also reduces the risk of cross-pollination between parent and offspring in years to come.

Matters of time

Most ovules are fertilized within days of pollen landing on the stigma. How long seed takes to ripen varies from tree to tree. Elm seed can be ready for dispersal less than ten weeks after fertilization.

Most temperate broad-leaved trees disperse their seed in the autumn of the year in which their flowers were fertilized. In many conifers, on the other hand, seed takes two years to develop. This is because fertilization is delayed for a year after pollination. Some conifers will hold seed in a sealed cone for many years after it has ripened, waiting for a special event to trigger its release. For the giant redwood this trigger is a forest fire, which kills off all competing vegetation and provides a thick bed of nutrient-rich ash for its seeds.

Below: The seeds of the Douglas fir are paper-thin and borne on bracts within a woody cone.

Above: Tamarind pods grow to 7in (18cm) long and contain a soft pulp.

Above: The nuts or seeds of the cream nut tree are edible, but difficult to find because they are also irresistible to monkeys.

Above: Some seed heads are incredibly attractive, such as these remarkable magnolia seed capsules.

Right: The seeds of sweet chestnut are contained within a spiny casing to protect them from predation.

Berries and fruit

Most fruit and berries are brightly colored to attract birds. Bright red rowan berries are loved by starlings, while red holly berries attract waxwings and fieldfares. The berries of hawthorn provide a vital source of food for many different birds in winter.

Normally, the flesh of berries is digested but the seed is not, and it gets passed out in the bird's droppings.

Fruit ranges in size from large tropical varieties, such as mango and papaya, to the small, glossy, black berry of the European elder tree. Many kinds of fruit are eaten by humans, and some trees, such as apple and olive, are farmed specifically for this produce. Some fruit only becomes good for human consumption as it begin to rot, such as the fruit of the medlar tree, *Mespilus germanica*.

Nuts and other seeds

Essentially, nuts are edible seeds. Some, such as hazelnuts, are encased in a

Above: Seeds such as this from a maple are attached to wings to aid dispersal.

Right: Walnut seeds are protected within a hard wooden casing.

woody shell. Others, like chestnuts, are surrounded by an inedible but more fleshy outer coating. They are distributed by birds and mammals. Squirrels and jays both bury those nuts that they are unable to eat straight away. Some of the store is never returned to, and these nuts may germinate. Some seed casings are impenetrable to all but the most determined of foragers. The Brazil nut has one of the toughest cases of all but it is staple food for the agouti, a cat-sized rodent. Agoutis collect Brazil nuts and bury them, just like squirrels do in temperate forests.

Many dry seeds rely on the wind for their dispersal. Eucalyptus seed is like fine dust and can be borne considerable distances on the wind. Some heavier seeds also ride on the wind. Those of maple and ash trees have extended wings known as keys, which help to keep the seed airborne. Sycamore seeds have paired keys.

Alder trees grow beside rivers and watercourses. Each of their seeds is attached to a droplet of oil, which acts like a tiny buoyancy aid. After falling from the tree into the water, the seed floats downstream until it is washed ashore. Wherever it lands it will then attempt to grow.

The world's largest seed comes from the coco de mer palm, *Lodoicea maldivica*, which is found in the Seychelles. It looks like an enormous double coconut and takes ten years to ripen. The heaviest of these seeds can weigh up to 45lb (20kg).

Germination

Inside every ripe tree seed are the beginnings of a root, a shoot and two specialized leaves, which are known as cotyledons. If a seed arrives in a suitable location it will germinate straight away, or wait until conditions become right for it to do so. In temperate areas this is in spring, when air and soil temperatures begin to rise.

Germination to seedling

Below: The first growth to emerge from the seed is the root. No matter which way the seed is lying, the root will instinctively grow downward into the soil. Once the root has become established and is providing additional food and moisture, the two cotyledons emerge and begin the process of photosynthesis. Shortly afterwards, true leaves appear from a bud between the cotyledons and the tree begins to grow.

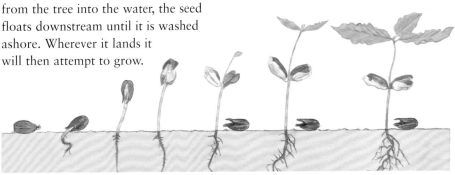

LIFE CYCLE OF TREES

The life cycle of a tree is a fascinating, and in many cases very long, process of change and development.
It begins with the initial struggle, coupled with rapid growth, when a sapling establishes itself, through a
middle period of relative inactivity, ending in its slow decline into old age and death.

There is a saying that "An oak tree spends 300 years growing, 300 years resting and 300 years dying." Although these time spans may be optimistic for some oaks and very optimistic for most other tree species, there are, in fact, several important truths within this statement.

There is no doubt that trees have the potential to live for a very long time. They include by far the oldest living organisms on earth. The oldest tree in the world is a bristlecone pine, *Pinus longaeva*, growing 10,000ft (3,050m) up in the White Mountains of California, which has been verified as 4,700 years old. Close on its heels is Scotland's Fortingall yew, which is estimated to be somewhere between 3,000 and 5,000 years old.

Trees go through various stages of growth in much the same way as humans. In our early years we develop and grow at a relatively fast rate. By

Below: This sweet chestnut is in the final stages of its life cycle. It is still alive even though its trunk is hollow.

the end of our teens, growth slows down and stops and our bodies stay pretty much the same for the next 40 years or so. Then, as our three score years and ten approaches, we begin our decline into old age and eventual demise. This is similar to a tree's life cycle, the only real difference being the amount of time that it takes.

So how do trees grow?

As with any living organism, it all begins with a birth. In the case of trees it is the germination of a seed. However, it can also occur naturally when a piece of an older tree breaks away, develops its own root system and grows as a completely new tree. This frequently happens with willows growing along riverbanks. When the river floods, a lower branch may be broken off by the force of the water and swept downstream. Eventually this branch will come to rest and from it roots will develop, grow down into the mud and a new willow tree will grow. A tree grown in this way is known as a

Above: Some trees in old age need a helping hand to prevent their branches from crashing to the ground.

cutting. Cuttings have the same DNA as the tree they were once part of.

Seeds do not have the same DNA as the tree that produces them. A seedling tree will develop its own genetic identity, taking on characteristics from both its male and female parent or, in the case of a self-fertilized tree, the characteristics contained in the genes of the male and female sex cell that initially produced it.

Once a seed or cutting has put down roots and sprouted its first leaves, the process of growth begins. The first few years, known as the establishment years, are critical in the life of any tree and the odds are stacked against survival. A young tree is vulnerable to being eaten or trampled by animals, its root system may not be able to withstand drought and it is far more vulnerable to forest fire than a larger tree. Other major threats include long periods of frost or waterlogging, which a fully grown tree would survive more easily.

The growing years

Once a tree is established, it can get down to some serious growing. Trees grow upwards, downwards and outwards. The rate of growth will be determined by many factors, including the availability of water, light and climatic conditions.

Upward growth

There is a popular misconception that trees grow from the bottom up and are continually moving skywards. In other words, if you were to go to any tree and paint a ring around it 6½ft (2m) above the ground, and then return to it five years later when the tree was 6½ft (2m) taller, then the ring would be 13ft (4m) above the ground. Well, this is not the case; the tree may well be 6½ft (2m) taller but the painted ring will still be 6½ft (2m) above the ground. Growth occurs year on year only from the tips of the previous year's growth.

At the tip of each branch are growing cells. As these divide, they make the branch grow longer, so the tree becomes taller and wider. How fast these cells divide will depend on the species and many other external factors, such as the availability of water and light. Some plants, such as bamboo, can grow more than 20in (50cm) a day, but there are no trees that grow anywhere near this rate. The fastest-growing trees come from tropical parts of the world, simply because there are no seasonal changes and so growing conditions remain good throughout the year. One species of tropical eucalyptus from New

Below: Tree growth is determined by the amount of sunlight the leaves can absorb, and the uptake of water through the roots.

Guinea, *Eucalyptus deglupta*, can grow 33ft (10m) in just over a year, as can *Albizia falcata*, another tropical tree, from Malaysia. Willow is one of the fastest-growing temperate trees. When it is coppiced (the stem is cut back down to the stump) it can grow more than 10ft (3m) in a year.

Growth in any tree is affected by age; as trees get older their growth rate decreases until they eventually stop growing altogether.

Downward growth

There is a direct relationship between the growth put on above ground by the branches and that achieved below ground by the roots. This relationship is known as the root:shoot ratio. The leaves on the branches provide food for the roots and, in turn, the roots provide water and minerals for the leaves. As a tree grows, it produces more leaves. These require more water and minerals, so the root system needs to grow in order to provide these minerals. To do that it needs more food from the leaves. All parts of the tree must work in harmony in order to continue the growth of the tree. The tree roots must develop to provide sufficient anchorage for the tree. The balance is a fine one; if leaves or roots fail, the tree will suffer and may die.

Outward growth

As the branches grow longer, so the trunk, branches and roots become thicker. In temperate regions, a mature tree trunk increases in diameter by about 1in (2.5cm) every year. This growth is a result of the need for the tree to be able to transport increasing amounts of water and food to and from its branches. This process occurs immediately below the bark surface in the vascular system, which contains the phloem and xylem. Throughout a tree's life, the cambium constantly produces new phloem and xylem cells, which cover the inner wood. As these cells are added, so the tree's girth expands. In tropical regions this growth continues throughout the year. In temperate areas, growth only occurs in the spring and summer.

Above: Without competition for light from other trees, saplings will establish much more quickly than those trying to grow in another tree's shade.

Growth rings

The cycle of growth in a temperate tree can be clearly seen when the tree is cut down. Each year the new cells that are produced under the bark create a new ring of tissue, visible in a cross section of the trunk. Each ring has light and dark sections. The light tissue is less dense and is made up of cells produced in the spring when the tree is growing fastest. The dark part of the ring is composed of cells laid down in the summer when the rate of growth has slowed. These rings are known as growth rings. By counting them it is possible to work out the age of a tree.

Old age

As a tree gets older, so its rate of growth slows down and eventually it stops. In theory, provided that the root:shoot ratio remains stable the tree should live for many years. However, as a tree ages and its growth slows, so it also loses the ability to defend itself from attack. Opportunistic fungi will exploit this, and eventually disease and decay upset the root:shoot ratio, and the tree starts to decline.

Rejuvenation

Some trees can respond to hard pruning or coppicing. The re-growth is effectively young wood, and it displays all the characteristics of a tree still in the early years of its life. Coppicing carried out on a regular basis can extend a tree's life almost indefinitely. In England, there is a coppiced small-leafed lime, at least 2,000 years old, which is still growing as a juvenile.

TREES AND WEATHER

Climate is the main influence controlling where and how trees grow. Throughout time, climate changes have dictated the pattern of tree distribution and evolution across the world. In times of intense cold, such as the ice ages, billions of trees perished.

The relatively settled climate of the last 12,000 years has resulted in fairly static patterns of tree distribution over that time. However, even minor changes in the earth's climate now, perhaps due to the greenhouse effect, could have a dramatic effect on future patterns of tree distribution and growth. An increase in the mean temperatures of just 35°F (2°C) would result in a significant northward migration of temperate trees in the Northern Hemisphere. Thousands of acres of sugar maple plantations in New England would disappear as the climate became too warm for them. Spruce would have difficulty surviving in the United States, Great Britain and central Europe for the same reason. Deserts would expand into the Mediterranean-type regions of the world, threatening the natural diversity of trees in California, Spain and France. In the Southern Hemisphere more than half of the rainforest of

Below: In areas of severe exposure, trees will grow away from the direction of the prevailing wind.

northern Australia would disappear, along with vast areas of rainforest in central Africa and South America.

Influencing weather patterns

Whereas the climate controls tree distribution on a global scale, trees actually influence weather patterns on a regional or local level. The process of photosynthesis raises humidity in the air. Where trees are found in large numbers, as in equatorial rainforests, this humidity has an effect on daily rainfall. In the morning the sun warms up the forest and warm, moist air rises from the trees. As the air rises, it cools and condenses into water droplets, causing clouds to form, and it begins to rain. This process is repeated daily throughout the year in the world's equatorial regions.

Reducing the effects of weather

Ever since humans evolved, trees have been used to reduce the effects of cold and wind exposure. Forests and woodlands provided natural shelter, and many original human settlements

Above: Palm trees are well equipped to cope with the heat and drought of the tropics.

were created in clearings cut from the forest. Trees were also used to shelter stock. The practice of "wood pasture" —grazing cattle or sheep within a forest—has occurred in Britain since the second century. Timber from trees has been used to build shelters and dwellings for thousands of years, and early man discovered that wood from trees could be burnt to provide heat.

Today, our use of trees to control the extreme effects of the weather has become far more sophisticated. We now know which are the best species to include within wind shelter belts, for example. We know how tall, how wide and how dense the belt should be. We also know how far away it should be from the area we wish to shelter. On average, a shelter belt 66ft (20m) wide and 66ft (20m) tall will provide wind protection on the leeward side for a distance of 1,312ft (400m). Such protection can increase cereal crop production by as much as 20 percent.

Trees also help reduce the effects of frost. If tree shelter belts are planted across a hillside, cool air descending the slope will become "trapped" by

the trees. Frost "ponds up" above the trees rather than traveling farther down the hillside or into the valley bottom. The same principle applies to snow. Strategic planting of trees on lower mountain slopes dramatically reduces the chance of avalanches occurring and their effects, if and when they do occur.

Another important function trees have is the stabilization of soil and prevention of erosion. Tree roots help bind soil to the ground and soak up rainfall, while leaves and branches reduce the effects of wind on the ground. The latter is particularly important in areas of low rainfall where soil is often dry and loose. One of the biggest causes of soil erosion is deforestation. Once trees have been felled, fragile topsoil becomes exposed to both wind and rain, and is soon washed or blown away. Once the soil

Above: Cooler temperatures in the fall will trigger an explosion of color as the leaves begin to die.

Below: Many conifers have adapted to regular heavy snowfall by developing weeping branches, which are able to shed their load.

has gone, so has the opportunity to grow food crops. Trees are now being re-planted in the Sahel region of Africa to try to reduce the effects of soil erosion, and also the expansion of the Sahara Desert.

Trees also help protect against the effects of heavy rainfall and flooding. Those planted in water catchment areas soak up excessive amounts of rain, enabling the soil to release smaller volumes of water into the watercourses gradually, thus reducing the possibility of flash-flooding farther downstream. Trees such as willow, planted beside river banks, reduce the effects of river bank erosion when water levels are high.

Above: Welwitschia mirabilis *has adapted successfully to the Namibia Desert, where less than 1¼in (3cm) of rain falls each year.*

Indicators of climate change

In many parts of the world where there are seasonal differences in rainfall and temperature, trees form clear annual growth rings in their trunks. The width of these rings varies depending on the growing conditions in any one year. In cold, dry years, tree growth is slow, producing a narrow ring. In warm, wet years, tree growth is faster and the ring is wider. As tree rings build up, they provide a year-by-year record of changes in climate. These records may cover hundreds or thousands of years.

TREES AND POLLUTION

Trees are the air filters of the world. They absorb carbon dioxide from the air and replace it with oxygen. They also trap airborne particle pollutants, which are one of the main causes of asthma and other respiratory problems.

The process by which trees produce food and thereby harness energy for growth is called photosynthesis. As part of the process, trees absorb vast amounts of carbon dioxide from the atmosphere and break it down. The carbon is effectively locked up within the trees' woody structures of roots, trunk and branches. A healthy tree can store about 13lb (6kg) of carbon a year. On average, 1 acre (0.4ha) of trees will store 2.5 tons of carbon per year. Trees are the most effective way of removing carbon dioxide from the atmosphere, and thereby reducing the effects of global warming.

When trees die naturally, the carbon they contain is gradually released into the atmosphere as carbon dioxide. This happens so slowly that the gas can be reabsorbed by the next generation of trees growing alongside. However, when trees, or coal (fossilized wood), are burnt, the carbon they contain is released much more quickly. Living trees and other plants are only able to reabsorb some of it—the remainder stays in the atmosphere. Continual burning means a continual build-up of carbon dioxide.

The practice of "slash and burn" agriculture, carried out in tropical rainforests to create agricultural land,

Below: Across the world 100 acres (40ha) of forest are felled every minute.

Above: One of the biggest threats to South American tropical rainforests is the continuing expansion of agriculture.

releases hundreds of thousands of tons of carbon dioxide back into the atmosphere. Even more serious is the large-scale burning of fossil fuels, such as coal and oil, in the West. The carbon dioxide produced traps more of the sun's energy than normal inside the atmosphere, and so contributes to global warming.

During the photosynthesis process trees not only remove carbon dioxide from the atmosphere, they also replace it with oxygen, effectively producing clean air. Every day 1 acre (0.4ha) of trees produces enough oxygen to keep 18 people alive.

Biological filters

As well as removing carbon dioxide from the atmosphere, trees absorb sulphur dioxide produced by the burning of coal; hydrogen fluoride and tetrafluoride released in steel and phosphate fertilizer production; and chlorofluorocarbons, which are produced by air-conditioning units and refrigerators. Trees also trap other particle pollutants, many of which are by-products of the internal combustion engines in cars. These particles are one

of the main reasons for the increasing incidence of asthma and other respiratory illness in people across the world. Research has shown that trees act as excellent biological filters, removing up to 212 tons of particle pollutants every year in cities the size of Chicago.

Trees cause pollution

Some trees emit large amounts of certain volatile organic compounds (VOC), which react with nitrogen oxides and sunlight to form ozone—a significant ground-level air pollutant. Volatile organic compounds exist in fossil fuels, such as gasoline. Most nozzles are fitted with filters to stop the VOC from escaping into the atmosphere. It is, of course, impossible to stop trees from emitting high rates of VOC, but some tree species produce more than others. Scientists suggest that these trees should not be grown in large quantities where high levels of nitrogen oxides already exist, such as in and around towns and cities.

Trees that produce high levels of VOC include eucalyptus, oaks and poplars. The blue haze often seen over the Blue Mountains near Sydney, Australia, is in part caused by the release of VOC by eucalyptus trees. Ten thousand eucalyptus trees will emit about 22lb (10kg) of VOC an hour, which is equivalent to that released by the spilling of 12 gallons (54 liters) of gasoline an hour.

There is evidence to suggest that certain tree species, particularly conifers such as spruce and fir, increase acidification of streams, rivers and lakes. This increased acidification can cause the decline of freshwater flora and deplete stocks of freshwater fish. The evidence for this effect is not clear-cut however. Acid deposition from the atmosphere (acid rain) can increase acidification in freshwater, and therefore the decline of freshwater flora and fauna may be attributable to that. There is much debate over whether conifer plantations in water-catchment areas actually do increase the level of acidification. Long-term studies are currently underway in

North America, Great Britain and Scandinavia to establish the truth. In the meantime, forest policy in North America has been revised so that coniferous tree species are no longer being planted directly adjacent to lakes and rivers.

Trees are subject to pollution

Although trees can act as natural "air filters," ideally they need clean air to live and grow. Photosynthesis becomes more difficult for trees in areas of high air pollution. In highly polluted cities such as Mexico City, it is estimated that less than ten percent of the tree population is healthy. Some trees, such as the London plane, *Platanus* x *hispanica*, are able to cope with relatively high levels of air pollution, but it is estimated that more than half of the trees in large cities are in decline due to air pollution. In New York City the average lifespan of trees is less than 40 years.

In many parts of the world the air is now highly polluted. Pollutants, such as sulphur dioxide, reach high into the atmosphere where they vaporize and

mix with other chemicals and moisture to form acid rain. The damage caused by acid rain affects both coniferous and broad-leaved trees. The effects are more obvious on evergreen trees than deciduous ones because their needles or leaves are replaced less often. Discoloration of foliage is the first sign of acid rain damage. This is followed in extreme cases by defoliation and death. Nutrients are stripped from the leaves as acid rain falls through the canopy, and the roots are slowly killed as the acid soaks into the soil.

There are a range of other sources of pollution that affect trees. Too much ozone disrupts the process of photosynthesis and can sterilize pollen, so reducing seed production. Particles of soot are also harmful because they coat leaves and thus prevent vital sunlight getting through. Even salt that is spread to de-ice roads can affect the chemistry of the soil around the roots of roadside trees.

Below: Views of greenery make traveling by road less stressful for motorists, but the pollution emitted by vehicles is ultimately damaging to the trees.

ANCIENT TREES

The oldest living things in the world are trees. The life span of most is measured in centuries rather than years, and there are some that have existed for millennia. Temperate trees generally live longer than tropical trees; although there are baobabs in South Africa said to be more than 3,000 years old.

Until recently we knew more about the ages of trees in temperate than tropical regions (because there are no annual growth rings to count in tropical trees), but now evidence suggests that tropical trees can live just as long as their temperate counterparts. For many years it was thought that the rapid growth and decay that occurs in tropical rainforests meant that tropical trees rarely lived for more than 200–300 years. However, recent advances in carbon-dating have clearly shown that many tropical trees are capable of living for more than 1,000 years.

Ancient tropical trees

There is speculation that some tropical trees may be more than 1,500 years old. The oldest tropical tree recorded with any certainty is a *castanha de macaco* (monkey nut), *Cariniana micrantha*, which is related to the Brazil nut. One specimen of this

Below: Africa's oldest known tree is a baobab growing in Sagole, South Africa. It could be over 5,000 years old.

Amazonian rainforest tree is known to be 1,400 years old. The cumaru tree, *Dipteryx odorata*, from Brazil, is also known to live for more than 1,000 years. One of the best known and largest of all tropical rainforest trees, the Brazil nut, *Bertholletia excelsa*, regularly attains heights in excess of 164ft (50m), but none of those carbon-dated so far has been found to be more than 500 years old.

Africa's oldest known tree is a baobab, *Adansonia digitata*, growing in Sagole, in South Africa's Northern Province. Near its base it is 45ft (13.7m) in diameter, and it is thought to be more than 5,000 years old.

The oldest tree in the world with a known and authenticated planting date is a fig tree, *Ficus religiosa*. It grows in the temple gardens in Anuradhapura, Sri Lanka, and was planted as a cutting taken from another fig tree given to King Tissa in 288 B.C. King Tissa planted it and prophesied that it would live forever: over 2,000 years later it is still going strong.

Above: English oaks, Quercus robur, *have been known to live for more than 1,000 years.*

The world's oldest?

People have a fascination for the oldest and biggest. Over the years ancient trees have grabbed their fair share of the headlines. An 11,700-year-old creosote bush, *Larrea tridentata*, was said to grow in California's Mojave Desert. A 10,000-year-old huon pine, *Dacrydium franklinii*, was "discovered" in Tasmania. The most incredible is a king's holly, *Lomatia tasmanica*, also from Tasmania, which was reported to be up to 40,000 years old. These are all great stories, but are they true?

Close scrutiny reveals that these are all clones that have grown from plants that were on the same site before. In terms of the age of the growth that can be seen above ground today, none is any older than 2,000 years. Whether or not they qualify for the title of oldest living trees is debatable. They have the same genetic material as the seedlings that first grew on the same spot all those millennia ago, but then all living things that reproduce asexually have the same genetic make-

up as their ancestors. We would not consider a female aphid produced asexually to be the same animal as its mother. No doubt the veracity of these claims will continue to be debated for some time to come.

Ancient temperate trees

The oldest living tree in the temperate world is the bristlecone pine, *Pinus longaeva*. Bristlecone pines originate from the White Mountains of eastern

Below: Olive trees will live for centuries; the oldest in the world is believed to be 2,000 years old.

California. The oldest are found in an area known as Schulman Grove, named after Dr Edward Schulman, who spent more than 20 years studying the trees there. In 1957 he discovered that many of them were over 4,000 years old and one of them, which he christened Methuselah, was considerably older. All these trees have solid centers, so Schulman was able to bore right into the center of each one and take out pencil-thick radial cores, from which he was able to count the growth rings. Carbon-dating since then has confirmed Dr Schulman's original age for these trees, and Methuselah is verified as being 4,700 years old.

For many years the giant redwoods, *Sequoiadendron giganteum*, were assumed to be the oldest trees because they were the biggest. We now know that isn't the case. The oldest redwood is a giant known as General Sherman, which stands in the Sequoia National Park, California, and is approximately 2,700 years old.

The oldest tree in Europe is believed to be the Fortingall Yew, which stands

Above: Methuselah, the world's oldest pine, grows in the White Mountains of eastern California.

in a churchyard in Perthshire, Scotland. Although much of its trunk has rotted away, its girth suggests that it is at least 4,000 years old. There are many contenders for the oldest oak tree, *Quercus robur*, and in truth we will probably never know for certain which is the oldest. Oaks have a habit of looking more ancient than they actually are. England and Wales have possibly the best collection of ancient oaks in western Europe. There are several oaks in Britain and across Europe that are believed to be up to 1,000 years old, but their exact age is anyone's guess. Three oaks are locally proclaimed as being 1,500 years old: one in Brittany, France, another one in Raesfeld, Germany, and a third in Nordskoven, Denmark. The oldest olive tree, *Olea europaea*, grows in the Garden of Gethsemane, at the foot of the Mount of Olives in Jerusalem. It is said to have been planted at the time of Christ.

GIANT TREES

Trees are by far the largest living organisms on earth. Some of the tallest specimens would dwarf the Leaning Tower of Pisa in Italy, or a tall cathedral. A single banyan tree in India covers an area that is larger than several tennis courts.

Not only are trees the oldest living things on earth, they are also the largest. The world's biggest trees include the most famous individual trees of all. Some of these arboreal giants are local celebrities, others are nationally famous and a few are well-known throughout the world.

Almost every country has its dendrologists (tree buffs) and tree measurers, who can always be readily identified by their measuring tapes and skyward gaze. Countries such as the United States and Britain even have their own tree registers, which detail the largest specimen of just about every tree species that grows in that country. Books are written about the biggest trees and photographs taken. Champion trees are big news and interest in them is growing.

What is a champion tree?

A champion tree is the tallest or fattest living example of a species. In order to be proclaimed champion it must have been accurately measured, with those measurements being recorded in an agreed way. The height is taken to be the distance from the ground to the top of the tallest living part of the tree. Girth is considered to be the distance around the trunk, and is read at 4ft 3in (1.3m) from the ground.

Right: Compare the height of trees to the Leaning Tower of Pisa, which stands 190ft (58m) tall. From the left: Montezuma cypress, 115ft (35m); New Zealand kauri, 167ft (51m); giant redwood, 272ft (83m).

Tropical giants

The tallest tropical tree, which is called *Araucaria hunsteinii*, is a relative of the monkey puzzle and grows in New Guinea. When last measured the largest specimen was 293ft (89m) tall. In Africa, Dr David Livingstone (1813–1873) camped under a baobab tree, *Adansonia digitata*, which had a girth of 85ft (26m). This tree appears not to exist now and the largest baobab alive today is 45ft (13.7m) in circumference.

One of the largest trees in the world is found in the Calcutta Botanic Garden in India. It is a banyan tree, *Ficus benghalensis*, that was planted in 1782. In not much over 200 years it has grown into an arboreal titan with vital statistics that are simply astounding. The tree covers an area of about 3 acres (1.2ha) and can provide shade for more than 20,000 people. It has 1,775 "trunks" (pillar roots) and an average diameter of more than 430ft (131m).

Temperate giants

For sheer volume, the largest single living thing on earth is a giant redwood, *Sequoiadendron giganteum*, called

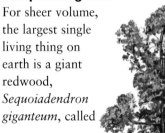

Above: One of the largest trees in South America is this Fitzroya cupressoides, which has a girth of 14¾ft (4.5m).

General Sherman. The tree, which stands in the Sequoia National Park, California, has a diameter of 58ft (17.6m), is 311ft (95m) tall and weighs 1,088 tons.

General Sherman is not the tallest tree in the world, however. This accolade belongs to a specimen of its cousin, a coastal redwood, *Sequoia sempervirens*, which goes by the simple but appropriate name of "Tall Tree." It grows on the Californian coast and when last measured, in October 1996, was 368ft (112.2m) tall. If it could be stood beside one of the Apollo space rockets, it could just be seen over the top.

General Sherman is not the fattest tree in the world either. That title is held by a Montezuma cypress, *Taxodium mucronatum*, growing in the grounds of a church at Santa Maria del Tule, near Oaxaca in southern Mexico. This enormous tree is made even more impressive by its very close proximity to the church and other buildings, which take on toy-town proportions in its shade. The Santa Maria del Tule Montezuma cypress has a girth of 119ft (36.3m), outstripping even the mighty African baobabs.

Two trees from New Zealand also deserve a mention. They are the kauri, *Agathis australis*, which grows in the north of the North Island, and the totara, *Podocarpus totara*, which grows on both the North and South Islands. Both trees are antipodean giants, reaching ages approaching 2,000 years, with girths of 43ft (13m) and heights approaching 197ft (60m). They hold great religious significance for the Maori people, who believe that important spirits live within the trees. Both species have suffered at the

hands of the loggers over the last 200 years, and many of the biggest specimens have gone. Those that remain are protected within special sanctuaries, such as Waipoua State Forest, north of Auckland.

The tallest tree ever recorded was an Australian eucalyptus called the mountain ash, *Eucalyptus regnans*, measured in 1872 in Victoria. Unfortunately it never qualified as a champion tree because when it was measured it was already on the ground. It was 435ft (132.6m) tall at the time, and thought to have been over 500ft (150m) tall when it was at its peak. At one time giant mountain ash trees clothed the valleys that run from Melbourne to Tasmania. Today, only remnants of this mighty forest remain. There are still some big eucalyptuses in Australia, but nothing approaching these dimensions. There are now no trees over 328ft (100m) tall.

There are no world-record-breaking trees in Britain, but there is plenty of time for that situation to change. Britain has a good climate for tree growth. It is moist with few extremes of temperature as a result of its proximity to the Gulf Stream. A large number of exotic trees from America have been introduced into Britain in the last 200 years, and many of them are world-beaters in their native habitats. The British examples are still babies, but their growth rates so far suggest that some have the potential to develop into record-breaking giants. The title of tallest tree in Britain is currently shared between two Douglas firs, *Pseudotsuga menziesii*, both growing in Scotland. Each measures 203ft (62m) tall—taller than the Leaning Tower of Pisa, which stands at 190ft (58m).

Below: In southern California, the giant redwoods regularly attain heights in excess of 328ft (100m).

THE PLANT HUNTERS

For centuries people have sought out new tree species, firstly for food, medicine and timber, and latterly for ornamental purposes. Over the last 200 years plant hunters have scoured the world in search of previously unknown species to introduce to gardens and arboreta.

Ever since they first appeared on earth, trees have spread to new places by natural means. Sometimes their movements have been the result of large-scale geological events, such as the break up of the supercontinent Pangaea, which began to occur around 193 million years ago. Sometimes they have been in response to changes in global climate. For example, successive ice ages saw a migration of plants away from the poles and towards the Equator. Interglacial warm periods saw a movement back towards the poles but also away from low-lying land, which became flooded as the polar caps melted and sea levels rose. These movements occurred over many plant generations, and sometimes took tens of thousands of years.

Later, the development of human civilization brought an accompanying quickening in the rate at which trees migrated and species settled in entirely new areas. Humans quickly realized that trees were useful. They could be used to make basic tools, produce food and provide shelter and fuel. As humans moved around the earth, they

Below: The Arnold Arboretum, Boston, Massachusetts has one of the finest ornamental tree collections in North America.

started using the trees that surrounded them and took parts of other trees with them, sometimes in the form of their fruits and berries. Inadvertently to begin with, but then consciously, humans became the vehicle for seed distribution and then, ultimately, tree movements. Trees took on new importance, becoming symbols in pagan worship. As time passed, their medicinal properties became better understood too.

The early plant hunters

The first record of plant hunting and tree collecting dates from 1495 B.C. Queen Hatshepsut of ancient Egypt sent out expeditions to Somalia to collect the incense tree, *Commiphora myrrha*, which produced a resin that was burned in Egyptian temples.

The Romans sped up the process of distribution, taking many trees with them as their empire expanded. Later, during medieval times, monks were also responsible for moving trees right across Europe, as they developed a network of monasteries from Russia to Portugal.

As civilization developed, so did the aesthetic appreciation of trees. Trees were considered an integral part of

Above: The Oriental plane is indigenous to Albania and Greece. It was introduced to much of Europe by the Romans.

garden creation and, from the 16th century onwards, European plant hunters started to look outside their own continent for new introductions. One of the first trees to be brought in was the horse chestnut, *Aesculus hippocastanum*, which was introduced into Vienna and then into France and England from Constantinople by the Austrian botanist Clusius in 1576. It was followed shortly afterwards by the Oriental plane, *Platanus orientalis*, introduced into Britain from Greece in the late 1590s.

It was in the early 1600s, as the exploration of North America began, that plant hunting really started to take off. Stories of amazing new trees swept through Europe, and everyone with influence and money wanted their own collection. The Englishman John Tradescant (1570–1638) and his son, also called John (1608–1662), were the first organized plant hunters. After starting out as gardeners for the rich and famous (including King Charles I), they introduced a phenomenal range of plants including dogwoods, *Cornus* species; lilac, *Syringa* species; red maple, *Acer rubrum*; the tulip tree,

Liriodendron tulipifera; and the false acacia, *Robinia pseudoacacia*, from North America into Britain.

The past 200 years

As travel became easier, European plant hunters ventured farther and farther away in search of ever more exotic and wonderful trees. North and South America, the Himalayas, China, Japan, Australia and New Zealand all contained huge, largely unexplored tracts of land, ripe for discovery. Expeditions were funded by wealthy landowners or botanical institutions such as London's Kew Gardens, keen to build up their collections of botanical rarities. Arboreta sprang up all over Europe. Among the first was Westonbirt Arboretum in England, created by Robert Holford in 1829.

Charles Sargent (1841–1927)

Born in Boston, U.S.A., Sargent created the Arnold Arboretum. A botanist and plant hunter, he collected mainly in North America and Japan. Sargent had several plants named after him. Perhaps the best-known are the Chinese rowan, *Sorbus sargentiana* and the Chinese cherry, *Prunus sargentii*.

David Douglas (1799–1834)

Born in Perthshire, Scotland, David Douglas was probably one of the greatest tree collectors of all time.

Below: The tulip tree, Liriodendron tulipifera, *was introduced into Europe from America by John Tradescant in 1650.*

From an early age he displayed a great interest in all things horticultural. By the time he was ten he was apprentice gardener to the Earl of Mansfield at Scone Palace. In his early twenties he was commissioned by the Horticultural Society in London (later to become the Royal Horticultural Society) to collect for them in North America. Over the next ten years Douglas walked almost 10,000 miles, exploring the Pacific coast of North America. Along the way he collected over 200 species never seen in Europe before, which included the Monterey pine, *Pinus radiata*, from Southern California; the noble fir, *Abies procera*; the grand fir, *Abies grandis*; and perhaps the finest tree of them all, the Douglas fir, *Pseudotsuga menziesii*.

William Lobb (1809–1864)

A Cornishman, William Lobb was the first plant hunter employed by Veitch and Sons, nurserymen of London and Exeter. His first journey in 1840 took him to the South American Andes, where, among other things, he collected more than 3,000 seeds from the monkey puzzle tree, *Araucaria araucana*. The seed was dispatched to Veitch and Sons, and by 1843 the first seedlings were on sale. In 1849 Lobb was sent on his second trip, this time to North America, with the aim of picking up from where Douglas had left off 20 years before. It was on this trip that he discovered the western red cedar, *Thuja plicata*, and collected seed from the coastal redwood, *Sequoia sempervirens*. Lobb's third trip in 1852, again to North America, was the one for which he is best remembered. It was on this trip that he discovered the largest tree in the world, the giant redwood, *Sequoiadendron giganteum*. Lobb arrived back at Veitch and Sons with seed from this remarkable tree just before Christmas in 1853. The tree was immediately named "Wellingtonia" in honor of the Duke of Wellington, who had recently died. The Victorians fell in love with Wellingtonia and, virtually overnight, it became the most sought-after tree for estates across the British Isles.

Above: General Sherman, the world's tallest giant redwood, grows in North America. This species was introduced to Europe by William Lobb. The species grows taller in its native habitat.

Ernest Wilson (1876–1930)

Another employee of Veitch and Sons, Ernest Wilson was sent to China in 1899 to find what had been described as "the most beautiful tree in the world". The description was for the handkerchief tree, *Davidia involucrata*. When he arrived in China, he was presented with a scruffy piece of paper with a map on it. The map covered an area of roughly 20,000 miles^2 (51,200km^2). On it was marked the rough position of a single handkerchief tree. Amazingly Wilson found the tree's location, but all that was left was a stump. The tree had been cut down and its timber used to build a house. Undaunted, Wilson continued to search the area and eventually found another handkerchief tree, from which he collected seed to send back to England. In 1906 Wilson left the employment of Veitch and Sons to become a plant hunter for the Arnold Arboretum in Boston, North America. From there he carried out further trips to China and to Japan. During his plant-hunting career Wilson introduced more than 1,000 new plant species to the western world.

TREE CULTIVATION

People grow trees for several reasons. Foresters plant on a large scale to produce trees for timber, while farmers and landowners cultivate trees for their fruit. Many trees are grown for pure ornament, to brighten up public spaces or add structure to gardens.

Ever since people first appeared on earth they have lived in a world dominated by trees. When modern humans finally arrived 35,000 years ago, trees covered more than two-thirds of all dry land on the planet. The other third was covered by ice or occupied by grassland or desert.

Modern humans have grown up alongside trees and forests. People have used them for shelter, as a source of food and fuel, and for all the necessary implements for life. In the beginning,

Above: Fruit trees have been cultivated in orchards for more than 2,000 years.

Below: The first roadside tree planting was carried out by the Romans, to provide shade for their marching legions.

they would have used whatever tree happened to be near. Gradually, however, awareness grew that certain tree species were better used for specific purposes. Harvesting trees from the wild had one serious disadvantage however—the more that were taken, the farther people had to travel from home to find the right tree for the job.

Semi-natural forests

Eventually people learnt that trees could be "managed." Seed could be collected, seedlings grown and trees planted in more convenient locations closer to human settlement. These were the first artificial plantations. At the same time, people realized that some trees did not die once they had been cut down, but re-grew from the stump. They learned that regular cutting (coppicing) provided a ready supply of thin, straight sticks, which could be used for a variety of purposes. The trees were all native to the area, and had been part of the original natural forest, but now that people were managing them in these ways, the forest had become semi-natural.

Above: The para rubber tree is indigenous to the Amazon rainforest, but is grown in plantations throughout Southeast Asia, where it is widely cultivated for its harvest.

Early plantations

The idea of growing specific trees together in one place for a clearly defined purpose dates back almost to prehistory. Ancient Egyptians grew plantations of sandalwood so that they could have a ready supply of incense, for example. Both the ancient Greeks and Romans planted groves of olives, as well as orchards of cork oak. Fruit, such as apples and pears, has been grown in orchards in much of western Europe since early medieval times. In Britain from the sixteenth century, forests of oak were planted to supply timber to build wooden ships for the navy. One large warship could consume as many as 3,000 trees.

With the advent of the Industrial Revolution came the need for vast quantities of raw materials, many of which came from trees. One tree that typifies this change is the para rubber tree, *Hevea brasiliensis*, which originates from the Amazon rainforest. As early as the fifteenth century,

rubber was being extracted from this tree to make shoes, clothes and balls. In 1823, Charles Macintosh, a Scots inventor, coated cloth with rubber and invented the raincoat we now know as the mackintosh. Just 16 years later, an American, Charles Goodyear, discovered that heating rubber with sulphur caused the rubber to stabilize. This led to many new uses for rubber, including the manufacture of tyres. In 1872, Joseph Hooker, director of the Royal Botanic Gardens at Kew in England, sent plant hunter James Wickham to Brazil to collect seed from the para rubber tree. There, Wickham collected more than 70,000 seeds. Out of these seeds, 9,000 grew into young saplings, which were then shipped to Sri Lanka and Singapore. These saplings began rubber growing on an entirely new continent, and formed the basis for plantations that now cover more than 2,500,000 acres (a million ha) across Southeast Asia.

Plantation forestry

The form of tree cultivation that we are most familiar with is the growing of trees in manmade forests for timber. Around 3 billion acres (1.2 billion ha) of the temperate world are now covered with commercial timber plantations. More than 80 percent of

Below: In many areas, timber-producing, fast-growing conifers have replaced traditional broad-leaved woodlands.

these are plantations of softwood trees —fast-growing conifers, such as the Monterey pine, *Pinus radiata*, which is widely planted in New Zealand, Australia and South Africa, and Sitka spruce, *Picea sitchensis*, from the west coast of North America, which is grown right across the Northern Hemisphere. Both of these species have the potential to grow more than 3ft (1m) in height per year. They are both harvested at 20–60 years of age, depending on growth rates, for use in construction or to create pulp for papermaking. Once harvested the forest is re-planted and the whole process begins again.

This "sustainable" forestry has far less impact on the environment than the wholesale destruction of natural forests, such as that which occurs in many parts of the tropics. Even so, it does have its disadvantages. Conifer plantations are normally made up of just one species, often not native to the country it is being grown in. The trees are planted close together in rows, thus creating poor habitats for wildlife. Some organizations have begun to acknowledge that this is unacceptable, and have taken steps to remedy the problem. In Britain, the Forestry Commission, for example, now ensures that at least 20 percent of the ground is left unplanted and that other, native tree species are also grown within the conifer plantation.

Above: There are more than 20 different varieties of fir which are now cultivated for Christmas trees.

Plantation forestry is not restricted to temperate countries, though. Large areas of Java are now planted with teak, for instance, to provide wood for furniture-making. Like the softwoods from conifer plantations, this timber is sustainably produced—the trees are replaced with new saplings immediately after they are cut down. Sustainable forestry is now being developed all over the world and is actively encouraged by organizations such as the Forestry Stewardship Council (FSC), based in Oaxaca, Mexico. Consumers are also better informed about where wood comes from—most products made from timber grown in certified sustainable forests now carry an FSC label.

Christmas trees

Growing Christmas trees is now big business, with thousands of acres being devoted to their cultivation. These are "short rotation crops" being harvested normally in less than ten years from planting. Traditional Christmas trees, such as pine, now have competition from many other species, such as the Nordman fir, *Abies nordmanniana*, which has citrus-scented needles that remain on the tree for longer.

TREES FOR LUMBER

Wood is humanity's oldest natural resource. It has provided us with food, fuel, weapons, shelter and tools for thousands of years. Wood can be easily shaped, it has great strength and is durable, hard-wearing and naturally beautiful.

If you look around any room, you will see several things that are made of wood. Furniture, paneling, doors and window frames are the most obvious, but even the paint on the doors, the paper this book is printed on and the photographic film the photographs were taken with, all have a proportion of wood in them.

Wood is unique because it is the one basic natural resource that mankind can renew. When all of the world's oil, gas and coal has been exhausted, there will still be trees and we will still have wood—that is, as long as we manage our forests and woodlands properly.

What is wood?
Wood is a type of tissue produced within trees by a specialized cell layer known as the cambium. Cambium encircles a tree, producing on its outside phloem cells, which transport food manufactured in the leaves to other parts of the tree, and on its inside xylem cells, or living sapwood, which transport water and minerals from the roots to the leaves. This

Below: Acer saccharum, the sugar maple, is indigenous to the USA. Its timber is used for dance floors.

sapwood is constantly being renewed, overlaying the existing sapwood and so enlarging the core of the tree. As each growing season passes, so the core of the tree gets larger. Only the xylem cells in the current year's sapwood are able to transport water and minerals; the cells beneath gradually die. As they die the old cells undergo a chemical change, turning drier, harder and normally darker. It is this change that creates the visually distinctive banding in a sawn log, demarcating the boundary between the young, soft sapwood and the older, harder inner wood, or heartwood.

Is there a difference between wood and timber?
No, both refer to the woody cells that make up the structure of a tree. The difference between the two words is a matter of timing. When a tree is standing and growing, its bulk is referred to as wood. Once the tree has been cut down and sawn up, that bulk becomes timber. We buy planks from a lumberyard, but once the planks have been turned into something, the object that they have been turned into is generally referred to as being made of wood, rather than lumber.

A global business
Lumber is produced by almost every country in the world. In general, softwood lumber, such as spruce, larch and pine, is more likely to have been grown in temperate regions, whereas hardwood lumber, such as teak, mahogany and ebony, is more likely to have come from the tropics. Some countries, such as Canada and Brazil, are virtually self-sufficient in lumber supplies. Others, such as Great Britain and Japan, must import up to 90 percent of their requirements. Over the last 100 years or so, the global trade in lumber has increased dramatically. For

many developing countries, it is financially by far their single most important export. Unfortunately, this has resulted in the destruction of millions of acres of natural forest. It is estimated that 200–500 million acres (80–200 million ha) of natural forest were destroyed in the last ten years of the twentieth century.

Lumbers of the world
The world's most famous types of lumber are household names. But, perhaps surprisingly, not every type is sourced from trees of just one species. Ebony, for instance, may come from any one of five different trees.

Mahogany
Ever since the sixteenth century, when it was first brought to Europe by the Spanish, mahogany has been the most prized wood for cabinet- and furniture-making in the world. Mahogany is the collective name for the lumber of several species of tree in the genus *Swietenia*, which originate from Central and South America. The most

Below: The red-brown coloring of mahogany lumber has long been valued for cabinet and furniture production.

Above: Pine lumber is used for general construction work and was traditionally used for economy furniture.

favored species is *S. mahoganii*, but because this tree is now very rare most commercial supplies of mahogany come from *S. macrophylla*. Mahogany has distinctive, rich red-brown coloring, complemented by dark figuring. As well as being beautiful, it is also very durable and is quite impervious to rot and woodworm.

Teak

Indigenous to India, Burma and Indonesia, teak, *Tectona grandis,* has been introduced to Central America, where it is widely planted. Its lumber has beautiful golden brown heartwood and is extremely strong and durable. Teak lumber is used to make all manner of things, including furniture, boats, staircases and sea defenses.

Ebony

Certain species of *Diospyros* provide the lumber known as ebony. There are two main types: African ebony, produced by trees that originated from West Africa and Madagascar, and East Indian ebony, produced by trees from Sri Lanka and southern India. Both types have a distinctive almost jet-black coloring. Ebony has always been used for furniture and sculpture, but it is best known as the lumber used to make the black keys of pianos.

Oak

There are more than 450 species of oak, most of which occur in temperate regions. The most important group for lumber production is known as the "white oaks" and includes the English oaks, *Quercus robur* and *Q. petraea*; the American oak, *Q. alba*; and the Japanese oak, *Q. mongolica*. Lumber from white oak has a creamy fawn sapwood and yellow-brown heartwood with silver-gray veining. It is one of the world's most popular lumbers. Oak beams were used in the construction of many of the most important old buildings in western Europe, including the majority of old barns, churches and cathedrals.

Spruce

This is a group of 20 evergreen conifers found growing naturally in most of the cool temperate regions of the Northern Hemisphere. Of those, only two are commercially important: Norway spruce or "whitewood", *Picea abies*; and sitka spruce, *Picea sitchensis*. Norway spruce occurs in the wild throughout much of northern Europe, while sitka spruce originates from the Pacific coast of North America. Both lumbers are widely used for interior building work, general joinery and the manufacture of pallets. Sitka spruce produces a significant amount of the world's virgin pulp supply for newspapers.

Pine

European redwood, red deal and Scots pine are just three of the names given to the lumber of *Pinus sylvestris*, a tree that occurs right across Eurasia from Spain to Siberia. Pine is one of the heaviest softwoods, and has attractive pale red-brown heartwood. It is often used in the manufacture of economy furniture, as well as for general building work. In Britain, pine has been used for many years for making railroad sleepers and telegraph poles.

Elm

The elm occurs naturally throughout northern temperate regions of North America, Europe and Asia. Although different species grow in different regions, the characteristics of the lumber are broadly similar. The heartwood is dull brown with a reddish tinge and has prominent, irregular growth rings, which give an attractive figuring. Elm is very water-resistant—in Roman times it was used as a conduit for water, the heartwood being bored out to create a basic drainpipe. The Rialto bridge in Venice stands on elm piles. Sadly, because of Dutch elm disease, elm lumber is in short supply across much of North America and Europe and elm trees are much rarer than they once were.

Below: Oak was traditionally grown for building ships and for roofing beams. It has a straight grain and is very durable.

GENERAL USES OF TREES

It is easy to take wood for granted because it features in almost every area of life. Humans have had a long association with trees, and consequently there is an impressively wide range of useful products that can be obtained from them.

Over the centuries and to the present day, tree products have found their way into the pantry, medicine cabinet, wine cellar, paint store, garage, garden shed, bathroom, library and jewelry box.

Medicinal uses

Although the bark and wood of trees is seldom edible, extracts from them have given rise to some of the world's most important medicines. Malaria is said to have killed more people than all of the wars and plagues in history combined. Oliver Cromwell and Alexander the Great are two of the most famous people to have died at its hands. For centuries the only known treatment was quinine, an alkaloid found in the bark of the evergreen cinchona tree, which grows in the tropical forests of Peru and Bolivia. Quinine was first used to treat malaria by the Quechua Indians, and in the sixteenth century the Spanish Conquistadors realized its potential. Called the "miracle cure" when it finally arrived in Europe, it was used to treat King Charles II, King Louis XIV and the Queen of Spain, among countless others. Quinine has been chemically reproduced since the 1940s; however, in recent years some forms of malaria have developed resistance to synthetic quinine and the

Below: Aspirin was derived from the bark of the white willow, from the willow family.

Above: Extracts of the leaves of Ginkgo biloba *have been used to improve memory loss and to treat Parkinson's disease.*

cinchona tree has once again become the center of attention.

If you have ever had a headache then the chances are that you will have reached for a bottle of aspirin, the world's most widely used drug. Before aspirin came in bottles, aches and pains could be cured by walking to the nearest river and finding a piece of willow bark to chew on. Aspirin is a derivative of salicylic acid, which comes from the bark of the white willow, *Salix alba*. Nowadays aspirin is produced synthetically.

The last remaining member of a family that existed when dinosaurs roamed the earth, the maidenhair tree, *Ginkgo biloba*, has long been used for medicinal purposes. The leaves have traditionally been a staple of Chinese herbal medicine, being used to treat everything from asthma to hemorrhoids. Now maidenhair tree leaves have found their way into western medicine and are used to treat memory loss and coronary conditions. Fluid extracted from the leaves helps

to improve blood circulation. It relaxes blood vessels, enhancing blood flow throughout the body but in particular that going to the brain.

More than 2,000 different trees are currently used for medicinal purposes. Many, such as the Pacific yew, *Taxus brevifolia*, are helping in the fight against cancer. *Castanospermum australe*, the Australian Moreton Bay chestnut, contains an unusual alkaloid called castanospermine, which is able to help neutralize the Aids virus HIV. Witch hazel, *Hamamelis virginiana*, is a North American tree with strong antiseptic qualities. Native American tribes such as the Cherokee made a "tea" of the leaves, which they used to wash sores and wounds. Another important medicinal tree species is *Eucalyptus globulus*. Its leaves contain the oil cineol, which is very effective in the treatment of coughs, sore throats, bronchitis and asthma.

Trees in the home

One of the world's favorite drinks—coffee—is made from the seeds (beans) of three small evergreen trees, *Coffea arabica*, *C. canephora* and *C. liberica*. Now cultivated extensively throughout the tropical world, they originate from the montane forests of Ethiopia, where they grow to approximately 20ft (6m) tall.

Products made from the Amazonian tree *Hevea brasiliensis* have found their way into just about every home in the world. Better known as the para rubber tree, its cultivation accounts for about 90 percent of the world's raw rubber supply. *Hevea brasiliensis* produces a gummy, milky white sap beneath its bark as a natural defense against attack from wood-boring insects. This sap, known as latex, is tapped and collected once the tree reaches seven years old. An experienced tapper can harvest about

Above: A mature cork oak may produce up to 4,000 bottle stoppers per harvest. Plastic corks damage the industry.

450 trees a day. *Hevea brasiliensis* is cultivated on more than 17 million acres (7 million ha) of land across the tropics. These plantations yield about 5.9 million tons of natural rubber every year.

Cork comes from the outer bark of the cork oak tree, *Quercus suber*. An evergreen tree, the cork oak is grown in Mediterranean countries, such as Portugal, Spain and Italy, and in California. Cork is a great insulator, and it protects the tree's inner bark from forest fires and hot dry summer winds. It is also resistant to moisture and liquid penetration. The Romans used cork to insulate their houses and beehives, as soles for their shoes, stoppers for bottles, pitchers and vases, floats for fishing nets and buoys for navigation purposes. Today its main use is in the wine industry. The cork oak is not stripped of its bark until it reaches 25 years old. After that, the cork is harvested every nine to twelve years, giving the tree time to grow a new "skin." Cork oaks are long-lived, regularly exceeding 200 years old. A mature tree provides enough cork to make 4,000 bottle stoppers per harvest.

Much of the food that stocks our superstore shelves comes from trees. Citrus fruits, such as oranges and lemons, are produced by evergreen trees of the *Citrus* genus, originally from Southeast Asia. The species that yields Seville oranges, *Citrus aurantium*, was introduced to Spain in the twelfth century and its fruit became a valuable provision on long sea voyages, helping to prevent scurvy among the sailors. Today the orange is the most widely grown fruit in the world—every year more than 63 million tons are harvested.

Olive trees, *Olea* species, have been grown for their fruit for more than 5,000 years. Originally from Europe's Mediterranean region, they are now cultivated across the world, from Australia to California. The fruit is either eaten whole or pressed for its

Above: Olive trees provide an important crop of fruit for Californian regions. The fruit is distilled to make olive oil.

oil, which has significant health benefits. A ripe olive is about 20 percent oil.

Even when we brush our teeth we are using products from trees. Toothpaste contains carboxymethal cellulose, which is basically pulped up wood. In Africa, small sticks made from the wood of a tropical tree called *Diospyros usambarensis* are chewed to clean teeth. The wood contains antifungal bacteria, which help combat gum disease and tooth decay.

Below: Lightweight lumber has been used for boat building and aircraft.

NATURAL DISTRIBUTION OF TREES

The natural distribution of trees around the world is influenced by the weather. Over millions of years each tree species has adapted to a particular set of climatic conditions and so their distribution is limited to where those conditions exist.

Trees in different parts of the world function in much the same way. They all require the same things to survive, namely water, minerals, air and light. They all have leaves, roots and a persistent woody stem containing a vascular transport system, which takes water and minerals from the roots to the leaves, and food from the leaves to the rest of the tree. That, however, is where the similarity ends.

Throughout the world, trees have adapted to the climate that surrounds them. The amount of rainfall, the temperatures they have to endure, the number of daylight hours and the angle of the sun all influence both the behavioral patterns of trees and their natural distribution across the planet.

Trees growing in the tropics look very different to those found in temperate parts of the world. In a large number of cases they represent very different groups of plants. In general, conifers dominate the colder and drier areas of the world, and broad-leaved trees are more common in warmer and wetter regions.

Below: The world is broken up into zones that experience different climatic conditions. Individual tree species seldom occur within more than one zone.

Equatorial rainforest

Five degrees latitude north and south of the Equator is the area where Equatorial rainforest exists. The conditions in these rainforest areas are perfect for tree growth: the morning sun heats up the vegetation, causing water to evaporate from the leaves. Warm, wet air rises from the trees, forms clouds and produces rain in the afternoon. This happens on every day of the year, and there are no major seasonal changes. Numerous trees thrive here, among them rosewood, *Dalbergia nigra*, and the gaboon, *Aucoumea klaineana*.

Monsoon forest

Moving away from the Equator, the climate becomes drier. Within 5 and 25 degrees north and south of the Equator there is a marked dry season during the winter months when the air is colder and clouds do not form. Trees can only grow during the summer months when warm air allows clouds to form and causes rain to fall. This seasonal change is monsoon period and the forest that grows in these regions is monsoon forest. Monsoon forest covers a vast proportion of the Indian subcontinent, parts of Central

America, East Africa, Madagascar and southeastern China. Trees of the monsoon forest include Indian rosewood, *Dalbergia latifolia*, and East Indian ebonys, among them *Diospyrus melanoxylon*.

Savanna and desert

Between 25 and 35 degrees of latitude, clouds seldom form, rain rarely falls and the climate becomes progressively drier. Savanna grassland, which borders the monsoon areas, eventually gives way to desert. Few trees can survive in this harsh environment. Those that do include the giant saguaro cactus, *Carnegiea gigantea*, from North America, and the dragon's blood tree, *Dracaena cinnabari*, from Yemen.

Mediterranean forest

Beyond latitudes of 35 degrees, the conditions for tree growth gradually improve. At 40 degrees from the Equator, the Mediterranean forest region begins. This region contains most European Mediterranean countries, California, Chile and parts of Australia. Typically, the climate is characterized by hot, dry summers, and winters with moderate rainfall. Mediterranean trees include the holm oak, *Quercus ilex*, and the olive tree, *Olea europaea*.

Temperate forest

Between 40 and 50 degrees of latitude the climate becomes damp and windy, with cold temperatures in winter months restricting tree growth. This temperate region covers central and western Europe (including the British Isles), central North America, New Zealand, Japan and parts of China. The natural tree cover of this area is primarily broad-leaved. Trees that thrive here include oak, beech, ash, birch and maple.

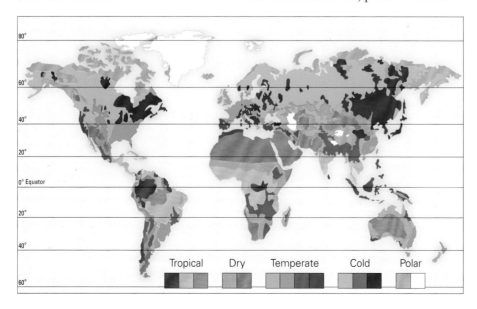

| Tropical | Dry | Temperate | Cold | Polar |

Above: Conifers are particularly well adapted to cold conditions. Their needle-like leaves help to protect them from severe weather.

Boreal forest

From 50 to 70 degrees of latitude, the length of the tree growing season diminishes and winter lengthens. Known as the boreal region, this area covers by far the greatest landmass of all the forest regions. It includes most of central Canada, northern Europe and Russia, right across to the Pacific coast. The natural tree cover of this region is primarily conifer and includes Scots pine, *Pinus sylvestris*, and sitka spruce, *Picea sitchensis*. The tree density of this region is greater than in temperate or Mediterranean regions, but less than both Monsoon and the Equatorial regions.

Tundra

Above 70 degrees, winter lasts almost all year and very few trees are able to survive. Known as tundra, this area includes northern Canada, Iceland, Greenland and the far north of Europe and Russia. One tree that does survive is the dwarf willow, *Salix reticulata*.

Micro climates

There is a blurring of these divisions at the edges of every climatic forest region. Land close to the sea will generally be warmer than that which is landlocked. Consequently a greater diversity of tree species will grow here than would be expected at this latitude. The west coasts of Britain and Ireland benefit from the Gulf Stream, which brings warm, moist air from the Caribbean. This allows trees that grow naturally in the Mediterranean forest region to survive and sometimes to flourish. One Mediterranean forest tree that tends to grow well in gardens in Cornwall, the Isles of Scilly and the west coast of Scotland is the Chilean azara, *Azara lanceolata*.

Montane forest

In mountainous areas, trees typical of regions farther from the Equator thrive. Because of their latitudes, both the Alps of central Europe and the Rocky Mountains of North America are technically within the temperate region. But because of their high altitude, which decreases average temperatures and effectively shortens the summers, the tree cover is more typical of boreal forest. In the Alps, Norway spruce, *Picea abies*, is the dominant species.

Tree zoning

Whether or not a tree will survive in any region, given its basic requirements of water, minerals, air and light, depends on the lowest temperatures it will have to endure. Over the years, through trial and error, botanists and horticulturalists have identified the average annual minimum temperatures that individual tree species can withstand. Maps of the world have been produced that put countries or regions into zones, according to the average annual minimum temperatures that occur in them. North America includes six of the nine zones, with 3, 4 and 5 in the far north, 6 making a wide curve from New York City to the Midwest and up to parts of British Columbia, and 7 and 8 to the south. Most of Britain is in zone 8 where trees can withstand a minimum of about 41°F (5°C).

Below: Savanna grassland is the harsh intermediate zone between Mediterranean forest and desert. The closer conditions are to a desert, the fewer trees exist.

TEMPERATE TREES

Temperate trees are found in the bands 40 to 50 degrees north and south of the Equator. These areas include most of North America, Britain and Europe, southern Russia, northern China, Japan, New Zealand, Tasmania, southern Argentina and Chile.

In temperate regions the climate is suitable for tree growth for six months of the year, when temperatures average more than 50°F (10°C). There are well-defined seasons but few extremes in either temperature or rainfall.

Although the temperate regions are suitable for both deciduous and evergreen trees, it is deciduous broad-leaved trees, such as oak, which predominate. Many trees that live in the windy conditions of the world's temperate regions are wind pollinated.

Temperate diversity
There is far less tree diversity within temperate regions than in the tropics. This is partly because the climate is less favorable, and partly due to historical climatic changes.

Temperate trees have been forced to migrate towards the Equator and back again several times during the last two million years because of successive ice ages. Inevitably these mass movements had casualties. Some tree species perished as they were unable to successfully disperse their seeds with enough speed to escape the freezing conditions expanding outwards from the polar regions. Other species became extinct because their escape routes were blocked by high mountain ranges, such as the Alps and Pyrenees.

Temperate pioneers
The density of temperate woodlands is such that light is rarely in short supply and there are few other plants, such as climbers, that have the ability to stifle tree growth. Temperate pioneer trees have large canopies and their branches and

leaves are free to grow right down the trunk. Their wood is light in color. Birch is one of the most successful temperate pioneer tree species. It will colonize land far more readily than any other species, and is quite often found growing on disused industrial sites, spoil heaps, landfills and railway embankments. Willow, poplar and pine are also quick to colonize inhospitable land.

Other temperate species
The temperate tree species that has been around longer than any other is the maidenhair tree, *Ginkgo biloba*. Today it grows wild in a small area of Chekiang province, China, although it has been widely planted elsewhere.

There are more than 450 species of oak tree across the temperate world. In Europe the two main species are the English oak, *Quercus robur*, and the

1 Oak
2 Beech

Above: Oak is the predominant tree species in temperate regions of the world.

Below: Species such as oak and beech (below) are slow to establish on new sites, and move in only after pioneer species, such as birch, willow, pine and poplar, have improved soil conditions with their fallen leaves. Oak, beech and maple are the predominant deciduous woodland species of North America.

sessile oak, *Q. petraea*. The holm or evergreen oak, *Q. ilex*, originates from the Mediterranean but also grows well in southern temperate regions of Europe and America.

Close to 80 species of oak are native to North America, including the red oak, *Q. rubra*, which has large, sharply pointed leaves that turn red in the fall.

One of the most recognizable temperate trees is the monkey puzzle or Chile pine, *Araucaria araucana*. This hardy evergreen grows up to the snow line in its native Andes Mountains. It has rigid, spiny, prickly leaves.

One temperate tree that looks like it belongs in the tropics is the tree fern, *Dicksonia antarctica*. Native to Tasmania, it grows well in warm, moist temperate regions, such as southern Ireland, where frosts are not too severe. *D. antarctica* is a very exotic-looking tree with a fibrous trunk and large fern-like fronds, which can reach over 10ft (3m) long. In Tasmania there are tree fern forests with specimens growing to more than 33ft (10m) tall.

Perhaps the most beautiful of all temperate trees is the tulip tree, *Liriodendron tulipifera*. It is native to North America, where it grows from Nova Scotia to Florida. The tulip tree is a large species, growing in excess of 131ft (40m) tall. It has flowers that resemble greenish-orange tulips. Quite often a mature tree will be covered with a stunning display of flowers.

TROPICAL TREES

Tropical trees are found in three main parts of the world: central Africa, Amazonia in South America, and Southeast Asia. The total area they cover amounts to about 3½ million square miles (9 million square kilometres) and represents 7 percent of the earth's land surface.

In the rainforest, levels of rainfall, warmth and sunlight are constant, creating ideal conditions for tree growth throughout the year. Most tropical trees have evergreen leaves with pointed tips. These "drip tips" help the trees to keep their leaves dry, shedding excess water during tropical rainstorms. Tropical trees include the fastest growing trees in the world; 16½ft (5m) of vertical growth per year is commonplace. Fast growth means a fast metabolism; consequently everything happens at a fast rate, including the advent of senility. Very few of the tropical trees live beyond 500 years of age, whereas many temperate trees are much older.

Tropical diversity

The range of tropical species is amazing —there are over 2,000 tree species, in Madagascar alone.

The reason for so many different species is not fully understood. However, the fact that today's tropical rainforests have existed for millions of years means that there has been plenty of time for new species to evolve. Evolution takes place primarily as a response to outside influence. It is possible there are so many tropical tree species because there are so many potential killers of trees in tropical forests. The climate is ideal for tree growth and for insects, fungi and viruses. New tree species may have evolved specifically to repel attackers.

Despite their great diversity of species, most tropical rainforest trees look very similar to one another; they have tall, thin trunks supported by roots with prominent buttresses. The crowns of these trees are comparatively small and bear large, thick, evergreen leaves not dissimilar to those of laurel. Most tropical trees have thin bark because there is no need to provide protection against frost or water loss. Often,

however, the wood of tropical trees is stained dark with chemicals for protection against fungal attack.

Tropical pioneers

Such is the competition for space and light in a tropical rainforest that only those trees that can react quickly to changes in the density of the canopy survive. If a gap opens up in the canopy when a mature tree dies, light reaches the forest floor and there is a scramble by other plants to fill that gap. The first species to colonize gaps are herbaceous plants and climbers. These plants do their best to smother the ground to prevent another tree from filling the gap because they need the light to survive. Eventually a branchless, umbrella-like tree shoot with a thick, slippery trunk will emerge

Below: Rainforests are characterized by layers of planting. At the top are the tallest trees, usually with large leaves to absorb any moisture and light, and buttress roots to anchor them into the ground. Below these are smaller trees with glorious flowers and luscious fruit to attract pollinators.

1 Kapok
2 Palm tree
3 Brazil nut

from the ground. At the top of this trunk a huge canopy of leaves unfolds, desperate to capture as much light as possible. The thick, slippery trunk provides nothing for climbing plants to grip on to, and the tree's leaves are held well out of reach of grasping tendrils. These pioneer trees can grow up to 33ft (10m) tall in their first year, quickly filling the space left by the fallen trees.

Tropical species

Outside the tropics most tropical trees are known for their products. Brazil nut, *Bertholletia excelsa*, is probably one of the best-known tropical trees because of the nuts it produces. It grows wild in Brazil and throughout Peru, Columbia, Venezuela and Ecuador. The Brazil nut is among the largest tropical trees, reaching heights in excess of 131ft (40m). It has thick, leathery, oval-shaped leaves up to 8in (20cm) long. Brazil nuts flower in November, producing fruit pods at the end of thick branches the following June. Up to 25 individual nuts can be found in each large, spherical, woody fruit pod. Each tree can produce up to 300 fruit pods a year, and thousands of

tons of Brazil nuts are exported from South America each year. In economic terms, the Brazil nut is second only to rubber in importance to Brazil as an export cash crop.

The weeping fig, *Ficus benjamina*, originates from the tropical forests of Southeast Asia and today is grown from India through to northern Australia. It is an attractive tree with narrow, leathery leaves, which can be

Above: Such is the diversity of the Amazon rainforest that over 500 different species have been found within 2½ acres (1 hectare).

up to 4¾in (12cm) long. Mature weeping figs can have dramatic twisting branches. In temperate areas this species is grown as a conservatory or house plant. In the warmer tropical regions it produces small red figs in pairs along its twisting branches.

Palm trees have different leaf shapes to the Brazil nuts and weeping figs. Long, narrow and strap-like, the leaves branch out from the tree top. There are around 3,000 species of palm in the world, and the vast majority of them grow in the tropics.

DESERT TREES

There are few places on earth, other than the polar regions, where plants will not grow. Even in the harsh environment of the desert, plants—including trees—somehow manage to cling to life. That's a remarkable fact because deserts are extremely inhospitable for trees.

Trees that survive in the desert have developed unique ways of coping with the day-to-day difficulties of survival. The main problems facing desert trees relate to water—or the lack of it. Hot sun, drying winds and low, erratic rainfall make it difficult for tree roots to supply enough water to make up for that lost by transpiration from the leaves. Desert trees have adapted to the extremes of heat and aridity by using physical and behavioral mechanisms.

Plants that have adapted by altering their physical structure are called either xerophytes or phreatophytes. Xerophytes, such as cacti, usually have special means of storing and conserving water. They often have few or no leaves, which helps them to reduce transpiration. Phreatophytes are plants, such as the African acacias, that have adapted to parched conditions by growing extremely long roots, allowing them to acquire moisture from the water table.

Other plants have altered their behavior to cope. They have to make the most of the times of greatest moisture and coolest temperatures, remaining dormant in dry periods and springing to life when water is available. Many germinate after heavy seasonal rain, and then complete their reproductive cycle very quickly. These plants produce heat- and drought-resistant seeds that remain dormant in the soil until rain eventually arrives.

The Joshua tree

The *Yucca brevifolia*, or Joshua tree, grows in the Mojave Desert of California, Nevada, Utah and Arizona. It has spiky, leathery, evergreen leaves at the tips of the branches, thus reducing the effects of transpiration. The leaves have a hard, waxy coating that also helps to reduce water loss. Originally considered a member of the agave family, the Joshua tree is now known to be the largest yucca in the world. It can grow up to 40ft (12m) tall with a trunk diameter of 3ft (1m).

Welwitschia

A dwarf species from Africa, *Welwitschia mirabilis* is one of the strangest trees on earth. It grows on the dry gravel plains of the Namib Desert in southern Angola, and is a throwback to the prehistoric flora that existed on the supercontinent of Gondwanaland millions of years ago. Its shape and growing characteristics are so unusual that there is no comparable living plant. It is a unique species occupying its own genus.

The bulk of *Welwitschia's* "trunk" grows under the sand like a giant carrot. Its girth can be up to 5ft (1.5m)

1 Baobab
2 Date palm
3 *Welwitschia mirabilis*

Above: Mormon pioneers are said to have named this species the Joshua tree because it reminded them of the Old Testament prophet Joshua, with arms outstretched, waving them on toward the promised land.

Below: Tropical areas of the world include deserts and savanna. Trees that live in these habitats are exceptionally good at storing water. The Welwitschia mirabilis *has a long tap root that can reach down to the water table. Succulents have few leaves and are best adapted to the desert. The baobab can store vast amounts of water in its trunk.*

and its height (or in this case length) up to 13ft (4m), less than a third of which appears above ground. Its subterranean trunk is a water storage organ made of hard wood and covered with a cork-like bark. Broad, leathery leaves emerge from the part of the trunk that appears above ground. The leaves, which can reach 6½ft (2m) long, sprawl across the desert floor. They have specially adapted pores to trap any moisture that condenses on the leaves during the night when the temperature falls. As rain falls about once in four years in the Namib Desert this method of moisture collection is vital. Recent carbon-dating has established that some of these trees are more than 2,000 years old.

Other desert trees

The acacias and tamarisks, which grow in African deserts, are phreatophytes – they have developed incredibly long root systems to cope with the absence of surface water. These roots take water from the permanent water table, which may be anything up to 164ft (50m) below the desert surface. Once mature, they have little trouble combating harsh desert conditions—the difficulty is in establishing themselves, as the roots first have to grow through great depths of bone-dry soil before they reach the water. Phreatophytes grow in places where the soil is occasionally wet, such as dried-up riverbeds, as these are the only spots where they can get started.

Perhaps the most successful desert plants are cacti. The giant saguaro cactus, *Carnegiea gigantea*, is the ultimate desert tree. It has no leaves at all, but does have a thick green trunk, which is capable of photosynthesis and storing water. The giant saguaro can grow to heights in excess of 33ft (10m). It grows in the Sororan desert, U.S.A. and is the state flower of Arizona.

The prickly pear cactus (*Opuntia* genus) are well represented in North American deserts. They have large flat pads for leaves, which are covered with large spines. They grow to 6–7ft (1.5–1.7m) tall, and the pad dimensions can vary in length, width and shape.

MOUNTAIN TREES

Mountains tend to be covered with conifers and most are members of the Pinaceae family, which includes pines, spruces, hemlocks and firs. The higher the altitude, the slower the trees grow. The point beyond which no trees will survive is known as the timberline.

In many ways mountains have the same climate as subarctic regions, having short summers, cold winters and a mean temperature that rarely rises above 50°F (10°C). Wind speeds tend to be greater at high altitudes. These drying winds and shallow soils, often frozen for long periods of time, mean that only those trees that are protected against water loss and frost damage will survive.

Conifers and evergreens

A characteristic that conifers and broad-leaved evergreens share is leaves that are resistant to water loss and cold. Broad-leaved evergreens often have thick, leathery leaves with a waxy coating. Conifers further reduce water loss by having fine, rolled, needle-like leaves that expose just a small surface area to the elements.

Conifers and other evergreens are efficient at functioning in low light and temperature conditions. Once deciduous trees have lost their leaves in the fall they cannot produce food or grow until the next year's leaves grow—anything up to six months. Yet, during this time there are periods when the temperature and light is sufficient for photosynthesis to occur. Evergreens and conifers take advantage of this. Deciduous trees are also vulnerable when their young leaves are bursting from the bud in spring. These new leaves are sensitive to frost and can easily be damaged. Evergreens have tough leathery leaves that are not so vulnerable.

Mountain characteristics

Trees become progressively shorter as they approach the timberline. The reason for their shortness is not the cold but increasing wind—constant stem movement stunts a tree's growth. High winds can also damage trees, and to avoid this, some species have evolved a low-growing, almost sprawling habit.

Many mountain trees have adopted characteristics to cope with this harsh environment. They are conical or spire-shaped with branches and twigs that point downwards. This prevents snow from building up on the branches and breaking them. Instead it simply slides off the tree to the ground.

Mountain trees will also grow away from the direction of the prevailing wind, giving them a windswept appearance. The reason for this is that the waxy coating on the leaves or needles on the windward side gets worn away by the sandpaper effect of harsh winds carrying ice particles. Once the coating has gone the leaves and shoots are open to dehydration,

1 Sitka spruce
2 Brewer spruce

Above: As trees approach the altitude beyond which they will not grow (known as the timberline), they become stunted and eventually prostrate.

Below: Most of the conifers found in mountainous regions are members of the Pinaceae family. Such trees have adapted to cope with the harsh and extreme conditions of the weather, from freezing snow to fierce winds, driving rain, and the blistering heat of the summer sun.

clump moves slowly downwind. Research has shown that the average movement of these clumps is 6½–23ft (2–7m) per century.

Often the branches at the bottom of mountain trees grow much better than those at the top, giving a skirted effect around the tree's base. This is because in the depths of winter these lower branches are protected from the ravages of the wind by snowdrifts.

Mountain species

Brewer's spruce, *Picea breweriana*, is a tree that originates from the Siskiyou Mountains of California and Oregon, where it grows at altitudes of up to 7,000ft (2,100m). In Scotland the rowan or mountain ash, *Sorbus aucuparia*, grows at altitudes in excess of 2,300ft (700m).

Sorbus americana, the American mountain ash is a small shrub-like tree, growing to 10–20ft (3–6m) tall. It grows naturally along the Appalachian Mountain ridge, and produces small white flowers in spring and bright red berries in autumn.

and slowly die. The tree compensates for the lack of leaves and shoots on the windward side of the crown by producing more on the leeward side.

In exposed mountain regions, young trees can only grow in the shelter of other trees. This leads to clumps of trees scattered across the mountainsides. As trees die on the windward side and new ones grow on the leeward side, the whole

COASTAL TREES

The coast is one of the most difficult environments of all for trees to grow in. Those that survive have adapted to the strong winds and salt-laden water by growing additional roots on their windward sides to improve anchorage, and their habit becomes low and squat, thus offering less resistance to the wind.

Only the toughest tree species can survive a combination of strong winds and salt spray. Exposure to ocean storms, with winds in excess of 100mph (160km/h), is only part of the problem. Strong wind alone is something that many trees are able to withstand. However, if those winds are laden with huge quantities of sea salt, most trees will simply die.

The Everglades in southeast U.S.A. are home to many terrestrial plants that have adapted to life in almost continual wet conditions. One of the best tree examples is the swamp cypress, *Taxodium distichum*, which produces "knee roots" that appear above the water, and pipe air to the roots beneath the surface.

Salt damage

Trees can be damaged by salt in two ways: through direct contact with the foliage, and by absorption from the soil through the roots. Direct and prolonged contact with salt will cause leaf-burn, branch die-back and defoliation. This in turn will reduce the ability of the tree to photosynthesize and produce its own food, so eventually it dies. Salt can also dramatically reduce the amount of seed and fruit produced.

The most common cause of tree death by salt is through its uptake from the soil. When salt-laden winds that have traveled across the ocean reach land they condense, producing rain or dense sea mists. The salt precipitation from these mists and rain

soaks into the soil. The highest salt concentrations are deposited closest to the coast.

Salt causes the soil structure to deteriorate, leading to a decrease in soil fertility. Natural calcium in the soil is replaced by sodium chloride. This increases soil alkalinity, making it dramatically harder for trees to survive. Salt also makes the soil less permeable and reduces the moisture content, causing root systems to dehydrate and die back. The moisture that is absorbed by the roots can literally poison the tree. It takes only half a percent of a tree's living tissue to contain salt before the tree starts to die. This process is also what damages trees planted on roadsides, where the road is regularly covered with salt to clear it of ice.

Below: Mangroves have developed root systems that not only cope with waterlogging but also with the high salinity of sea water. The black, red and white mangroves are found in coastal regions of southeastern U.S.A.

1 Black mangrove
2 Red mangrove
3 White mangrove
4 Gumbo-limbo

Mangroves

One genus of trees has adapted so well to life alongside the coast that its members can actually grow with their roots in salt water. Mangroves are found throughout the tropics, particularly in shallow, muddy estuarine and coastal situations. They have to cope not only with waterlogging but also with the high salinity of seawater.

The most notable feature of mangroves is their roots. Many species are anchored in the soft mud by prop roots, which grow from the trunk, or drop roots, which grow from the branches. Oxygen is piped from the roots above ground to those below the waterline. This aeration is particularly important to mangroves because they need oxygen to carry out the process of ultra-filtration, which they use to exclude salt from the tree. Each root cell works like a mini-desalination plant, screening out the salt and allowing only freshwater to flow into the root system and on through the rest of the tree.

Mangroves display several other adaptations to their situation. They have leathery, evergreen leaves, which are able to conserve the freshwater

Above: Mangroves have developed their curious root system to cope with continual immersion in water.

within, but keep out salt-laden water that lands on them. They also have wind-pollinated flowers, which are able to take full advantage of sea breezes, and spear-shaped seed pods, which can stab into the mud or float away from the mother tree, coming to rest elsewhere.

Monterey cypress

At the Monterey Peninsula in San Francisco, clinging to the cliff edge and life, are two groves of Monterey Cypress, *Cupressus macrocarpa*.

The trees grow on the shore cliffs and, being undermined by the waves, occasionally fall into the sea. There are fewer than 300 trees left, ancestors of a species that covered great swathes of the temperate world at the start of the glacial cool-down a million years ago. The Monterey cypress, with other American giants, such as the Douglas fir and the giant redwood, retreated to the Pacific coast to escape the worst of the cold. When the climate warmed up 12,000 years ago and the glaciers withdrew, the trees moved back to the land they had occupied before the ice ages—all, that is, except the Monterey cypress, which remained on the Californian coast, where it has been growing in decreasing numbers since.

The trees that are left are stunted and gnarled, seldom reaching more than 50ft (15m) tall. Collect seed from any of them and sow it anywhere else in the temperate world, however, and it grows into a magnificent giant. Wherever there is the need for shelter from the wind and salt spray off the sea, this is the tree to plant.

ISLAND TREES

Islands often contain a diversity of plant life that is very different to that of the nearest mainland. This is because evolution on islands occurs in isolation. Some islands, such as New Caledonia in the Pacific Ocean, still have a range of trees which evolved during the Jurassic period.

The reason for the often unique plant life on individual islands lies in the earth's history, and how each island was formed. Islands are normally formed as a result of continental drift or volcanic activity on the seabed.

About 200 million years ago, most of the world's land was clumped together in a single supercontinent, known as Pangaea. Pangaea began to

Below: Islands have unique ecosystems. Their weather conditions, landmass and the vegetation thriving there can differ dramatically to that on the nearest mainland.

break up about 190 million years ago. First it split in two. The northern part, Laurasia, contained what are now North America, Europe and Asia, while the southern part, Gondwanaland, consisted of present-day South America, Africa, India, Antarctica and Australasia. Gradually Laurasia and Gondwanaland also broke up to form the continents we recognize today.

This fragmentation process created the major continents, and thousands of islands. When these islands broke away from the continents, they carried with them a collection of the flora and fauna that existed on the larger land-masses at that time. Over the following millions of years, plants and animals on these isolated fragments of land adapted to their new environments, and often evolved in different ways to those on the mainland.

In some cases, evolution has continued on the continents, while little has changed on some of the islands. The island of New Caledonia, off the east coast of Australia, is home to an amazing collection of ancient trees no longer found anywhere else on earth. So primeval is its landscape that it has been used as a backdrop for films on dinosaurs. In other cases the reverse has been true, with island life forms changing quite dramatically.

Not all of the world's islands were created by the breakup of the continents. Many were formed more recently by undersea volcanic activity and have never been attached to the continents at all. At first these islands had no plants of their own.

The Hawaiian Islands

Archipelagos such as the Hawaiian Islands began as barren outcrops of rock. Hawaii's native trees are all descendants of the few plants whose seeds washed up on its shores, or were carried there by birds.

Tarweed is a daisy-like plant from California. Fragments of this plant floated across the ocean to Hawaii millions of years ago. Tarweed gradually colonized the island and then began to evolve into new plants, filling the empty niches. Today Hawaii has 28 species whose ancestry can

❷

1 Coco-de-mer
2 Palm tree

Above: Coconut palms have large seeds that can float for hundreds of miles across the ocean.

be traced back to tarweed. One, *Dubautia reticulata*, is a tree that can grow to more than 33ft (10m) tall.

The Galapagos Islands

Like the Hawaiian Islands, the Galapagos Islands formed in volcanic activity after the breakup of the continents. Mangroves were among the first and most successful tree colonizers of the Galapagos Islands. Four species exist there today: the black mangrove, *Avicennia germinans*; the red mangrove, *Rhizophora mangle*; the button mangrove, *Conocarpus erecta*; and the white mangrove, *Laguncularia racemosa*. Mangroves are able to live in shallow seawater and grow on the shores of almost all the islands. They are a vital part of the coastal ecosystem, as fallen leaves and branches provide nutrients and shelter for a wide variety of sea creatures, and their tangled roots protect the coastline from erosion and storm damage. The Galapagos Islands' mangroves are thought to have established themselves from plants and seeds that floated from the Far East across the Pacific Ocean.

The Virgin Islands

The warm, moist climate on the northern coasts of the Virgin Islands, in the West Indies, supports an amazing array of tree species. Growing wild here are West Indian locust, bay rum, sandbox, kapok and hog plum. To the south and east the climate becomes much drier, creating ideal growing conditions for the turpentine tree, acacia, white cedar and the poisonous manchineel tree.

The Seychelles

More than 80 species of tree grow on the Seychelles, in the Indian Ocean, that grow nowhere else on earth. Among them is the record-breaking coco de mer palm with its 45lb (20kg) nut. This is the largest seed of any plant in the world, and it has been found washed ashore in places as far away as Africa, India and Indonesia. Before the islands were discovered the coco-de-mer seed was thought to have grown on the seabed, hence its name.

New Caledonia

Situated off Australia's east coast, this island has been described as having "one of the richest and most beautiful flora in the world." The island is home to trees that are remnants of families that became extinct elsewhere millions of years ago, some as far back as the Jurassic period. *Araucaria columnaris* is a rocket-shaped relative of the monkey puzzle tree which grows wild in Chile and Argentina. Of the 19 living species of *Araucaria*, 13 are found in New Caledonia and nowhere else. The island also has unique members of the podocarp family, to which most of New Zealand conifers belong, and proteas, which only occur elsewhere in South Africa.

New Caledonia is also home to some of the tallest tree ferns in the world, many of them over 98ft (30m) tall. The island's rarest tree is a small evergreen called *Xeronema moorei*; this unique tree grows in isolated pockets high in the mountains and is found nowhere else on earth.

URBAN TREES

Trees have become a vital part of urban areas around the world. From the leafy avenues of downtown Manhattan to the cherry-covered walkways of Tokyo, they bring beauty and environmental benefits right to the heart of our cities.

Trees have been planted in large numbers in our towns and cities ever since the eighteenth century. Before that time, urban trees were the privilege of royal palaces, cathedrals, churches, monasteries and universities. Some of the earliest town plantings were in specially landscaped town gardens, squares and crescents, such as Berkeley Square in London, which was planted with London plane trees in 1789. These trees still exist today, tall spreading giants bringing shade and cool in summer.

Quite often these early plantings only took place in the more affluent areas of towns, and were for the private enjoyment of those who lived there. The poorer residential and industrial areas were left largely devoid

Below: The London plane tree, Platanus x hispanica, *is popular in urban settings throughout the temperate world. It grows quickly, is hardy and tolerates the pollution of modern cities.*

of trees. It wasn't until the Victorian era that municipal parks were laid out for the benefit of all town dwellers. At this time, the idea of parks as the "green lungs" of towns and cities developed, improving citizens' health as well as giving them opportunities to walk, meet and relax. Public parks began to appear in North America and all over the British Empire, and trees were an integral part of them. Today some of the finest tree collections in the world are found in city parks.

Urban street planting also became prevalent during this time, although the planting of trees lining roads linking towns had been going on for centuries. Plane and poplar trees were planted by the Roman troops to provide shade and shelter for their legions as they marched back and forth across southern Europe. This tradition was repeated by Napoleon for his armies, and many Napoleonic roadside trees can still be seen today in France, Germany and Spain.

The environmental benefits of trees in towns and cities were recognized towards the end of the Victorian era by Ebenezer Howard. His book, *Garden Cities of Tomorrow,* inspired the early landscaping of suburbs and new towns that were being built outside the cities to house rapidly increasing populations. These new towns were built on "green field" sites and the inclusion of street trees, park trees and areas of woodland between housing were drawn into landscape plans long before the houses were even built. Howard's ideas quickly spread, and were used by town planners across Europe and the Americas.

Urban trees today

Trees have become an integral part of cities around the world. In terms of planning, they have almost become as important a feature of the urban landscape as the buildings themselves. Trees have a higher priority in our towns and cities now than at any time previously.

1 London plane tree

Above: Urban trees provide shade in summer and shelter in winter.

The architectural value of trees and the health benefits they offer are now well-recognized, and some cities have instigated massive tree-planting campaigns.

Benefits of urban trees

Trees reduce air pollution. They help to trap particle pollutants such as dust, ash and smoke, which can damage human lungs, and they absorb carbon dioxide and other dangerous gases, releasing vital oxygen in their place. In a year, 1 acre (0.4ha) of trees in a city park absorbs the same amount of carbon dioxide as is produced by 26,000 miles (41,850km) of car driving.

Urban trees also conserve water and reduce flooding. They lessen surface runoff from storms as their roots increase soil permeability. Reduced overloading of drainage systems, the main cause of localized flooding, occurs in towns with a high tree population.

Trees modify local climates as they help to cool the "heat island" effect in inner cities caused by the storage of thermal energy in concrete, steel and tarmac. They also provide a more pleasant living and working environment. They reduce wind speed around high-rise buildings, increase humidity in dry climates and offer cooling shade on hot, sunny days.

Without trees, towns and cities are sterile landscapes. Trees add natural character; they provide color, flowers, fragrance, and beautiful shapes and textures. They screen unsightly buildings and soften the outline of masonry, mortar and glass.

Trees for urban environments

One of the finest large trees for planting in towns and cities is the London plane, *Platanus* x *hispanica*. Most trees suffer in urban areas as their bark's "breathing pores," known as lenticels, get clogged with soot and grime. The London plane frequently sheds its old bark, revealing fresh, clean bark beneath.

The maidenhair tree, *Ginkgo biloba*, native to China, is also tolerant of air pollution. Its slow growth can easily be kept in check and it narrow habit make it an ideal tree for street planting. Other trees suitable for planting in the urban environment include laburnum, *Laburnum* x *watereri* 'Vossii'; black locust, *Robinia pseudoacacia*; hawthorn, *Crataegus laevigata* 'Paul's Scarlet'; Indian bean tree, *Catalpa bignonioides*; and cherry, *Prunus* species.

ENDANGERED TREES

Trees are one of the most successful groups of plants on earth, but despite their proliferation, some are increasingly under threat. Ten percent of the world's tree species are currently threatened with extinction. Across the world more than 100 acres (40 ha) of forest are felled every minute.

One third of the land on earth is covered by trees. But that figure is set to decrease. As the human population continues to expand at a rapid rate, so ever larger areas of the natural world are changed to meet people's growing needs. One of the first things to go is forest.

Ten percent threatened with extinction

There are more than 80,000 different species of tree in the world. At the moment around 8,750 of them are threatened with extinction. Almost 1,000 of those are critically endangered, and some species are literally down to just one or two trees.

The threats to tree species are many and varied. They include felling of woodlands and forests for lumber and fuel, agricultural development, expansion of human settlements, uncontrolled forest fires and the introduction of invasive alien tree species. Across the world we are losing at least 100 acres (40ha) of forest every minute. At the same time we are planting only 10 acres (4 ha).

Can we live in a world without trees?

The simple answer is no. Trees are essential to all life and incredibly important to the planet as a whole. They provide services of incalculable value to humans, including climate control, production of oxygen, pollution control and flood prevention. They also prevent soil erosion and provide food, medicine, shelter and lumber. Forests are also extremely important from an ecological point of view—tropical forests contain almost 90 percent of the world's land-based plant species, for example.

The threat of extinction

The monkey puzzle tree, *Araucaria araucana*, has become one of the most familiar trees in the temperate world. As an ornamental species, it is grown in virtually every botanical garden in Europe and North America. Yet, in its native homeland, high in the Andes Mountains of Chile and southern Argentina, the monkey puzzle is threatened with extinction. Thanks to its tall, straight trunk, its timber is highly sought after, and the land it once stood on is now claimed for new uses. Monkey puzzle forests have been felled on a massive scale, and it is thought there are now more monkey puzzle trees growing in Britain than there are in South America.

Another native of Chile and Argentina, the alerce tree, *Fitzroya cupressoides*, is a magnificent slow-growing conifer. Its Latin name was given in honor of Captain Robert Fitzroy, who captained HMS *Beagle* on Charles Darwin's epic voyage around the world in the 1830s. Even back then alerce was being felled for lumber.

Below: Destruction of woodland and unsustainable forestry have contributed to the rarity of some of the world's trees.

Today it is one of the world's rarest conifers, with only 15 percent of the original trees remaining. Although international trade in alerce timber is banned, illegal felling still continues.

Wilmott's whitebeam, *Sorbus wilmottiana*, grows in only one place in the entire world and that is the Avon Gorge, west of Bristol, England. This beautiful little tree, which produces clusters of attractive creamy white flowers in June and bunches of red berries in September, is critically endangered. There are only 20 trees now remaining at this site in the wild.

The Australian wollemi pine, *Wollemia nobilis*, was thought to be extinct until 40 survivors were found in a remote canyon in the Blue Mountains of New South Wales in 1994. A distant relative of the monkey puzzle tree, the wollemi pine has existed unchanged for almost 200 million years.

The Pacific yew, *Taxus brevifolia*, hit the headlines in the 1990s when it was found to contain a toxin called

Below: Fitzroya cupressoides *is one of the world's rarest conifers.*

Above: The American Lawson cypress has become an endangered species since felling for lumber and disease have taken their toll on the world's population.

taxol, which, when administered to humans, helped in the treatment of breast, ovarian and lung cancer. The greatest concentrations of taxol were found to exist in the tree's bark and, for a while, wholesale bark stripping took place, threatening the survival of what was already a rare species of tree. Bark from ten trees is needed to produce enough taxol to treat a single patient, but steps have now been taken to protect the tree in the wild. Pacific yew plantations have been established and this, with the recent chemical synthesis of taxol, has taken the pressure off the species in the wild.

Madagascar has some of the world's most extraordinary flora, including six different species of baobab, three of which are found nowhere else in the world. *Adansonia grandidieri*, named after Grandidier, is the grandest of them all. It is also the rarest. Although recognized by botanists the world over as a tree that must be conserved, numbers continue to dwindle. The problem here is not logging but human overpopulation. As Madagascar's people continue to increase in number, more and more of the island's wilderness is turned into agricultural land.

Hope for the future

The problem with man's exploitation of trees is that it is very often done in an unsustainable way. Areas of forest are felled and cleared, often with little regard to replanting. Once the tree cover is removed, the animals, insects and birds that populated the area move away or die and soil erosion occurs, making it very difficult for trees to recolonize the felled area.

In some parts of the world, notably western Europe, sustainable silviculture is now practiced with excellent results. Large areas of forest or woodland are never felled; trees are selectively thinned and removed one at a time, or in small clearings. These trees are then replaced by young seedlings that thrive naturally in the gaps once the light is allowed in. If this sustainable method of management could be adopted in other parts of the world then the future for some of the world's endangered trees might not be so bleak.

Below: Due to over-exploitation for timber, the monkey puzzle tree is now threatened with extinction in the wild.

TREES OF THE AMERICAS

Identifying trees can be an absorbing, rewarding and fascinating pastime to involve the whole family. Recognizing trees in their natural habitat helps create a stronger sense of familiarity with the area in which you live. In each locality, certain trees will thrive. This is because the soil conditions, weather and geography of the area are beneficial to the survival of the tree.

Each tree has specific characteristics making exact identification possible. It may be the overall profile, the flowers, fruit, shape of the cones, size of the leaves or even the bark that helps identify each tree with the family to which it belongs.

This section of the book will help you to identify the most popular and best-known trees in different locations, throughout the Americas. The associated descriptions will clarify how each tree can be identified at all times of the year, even in winter when deciduous trees have only bare branches, bark and twigs to show. The fact boxes provide general information of interest about each tree. Not every tree species is included, but those that feature on the following pages are a good representative sample of some of the most beautiful, culturally significant and ecologically important trees in the Americas today. Many included species originated in the Americas, while others have naturalized in the continent, after being cultivated by plant hunters of the past.

Left: Swamp cypress, Taxodium distichum, *displaying their distinctive "knee-like roots," which allow them to grow in waterlogged conditions.*

HOW TO IDENTIFY A TREE

Looking at and identifying trees can be an immensely enjoyable and fascinating pastime, but, unless you know what to look for, it can be confusing. The following information should help to reduce the confusion and provide a clear route to tree identification.

Whether growing in a woodland or forest, lining the hedgerows of our fields, bringing green to our city streets or standing in defiant isolation on some windswept hillside, trees form an integral part of the landscape. They are the most diverse group of plants on the planet, providing variation in shape, size, color and texture, and in the detail of their leaves, flowers, fruit and bark.

What to look for

There are many clues to a tree's identity, primarily built around seven main features. These features will generally not all be visible at the same time, flowers and berries normally only being present during certain seasons, for example, but some features are constant. The color and texture of bark changes little throughout the lives of most trees.

Shape and size—Is the tree tall and spire-like or low and wide-spreading?
Evergreen or deciduous—Are there leaves on the tree all year round or does the tree lose its leaves in the fall?
Leaves—Are they long and needle-like or broad and flat?

Below: It is quite often possible to identify a tree from a distance by its overall shape.

Flowers—Are flowers (or flower buds) present? If so, what color and shape are they?
Fruit—Does the tree have any fruit, berries, seeds, nuts or cones on it, and if so what are they like?
Bark—Does the bark have distinctive coloring or patterning?
Buds—In winter, buds can be a tremendous help in identifying temperate trees. What color and shape are they, and how are they positioned on the twig?

By working through these features step by step, it should be possible to identify any tree.

There are other points to consider that relate to the tree's location and the environment surrounding the tree, which may yield some clues. The acidity of the soil will dictate what species will grow successfully, for example. Some trees, such as the Northern red oak, *Quercus rubra*, will only grow well on acidic soil (low pH), while others, such as whitebeam, *Sorbus aria*, prefer chalky, alkaline soil (high pH). The position of wild trees should also be taken into account. Some trees grow well alongside, or even in, water, for instance. Willow or alder enjoy damp conditions and grow

Above: In winter the buds and bark are important clues to identification.

naturally next to rivers; hawthorn on the other hand does not. Some trees, such as beech, will grow well in dense shade; others, such as the Judas tree, will only thrive in full sun.

It is generally easier to identify trees in the wild than in a park or arboretum. This is simply because the pool of species is likely to be greater in a park or arboretum than in a natural setting. Most hedgerows will contain fewer than ten tree species, for example, and the majority of those will be common native species. At the other extreme, an arboretum may contain up to 4,000 species, brought together from various habitats in different countries all over the world.

Shape and size

Some trees have such a distinctive shape that it becomes almost unnecessary to continue down the identification trail, other than to confirm the initial assumption. The Lombardy poplar, *Populus nigra*

'Italica', is particularly distinctive with its remarkable narrow shape and upright habit. This shape is known as "fastigiate." Another very distinctive tree is the monkey puzzle, *Araucaria araucana*. No other tree has such sharply toothed evergreen foliage and stiff branching. Once a tree has been identified, stand well back from it and try to commit its overall shape to memory. Then look for other trees with similar shape and confirm their identity. After a while you will find that certain species become instantly recognizable.

Evergreen or deciduous

In winter, in temperate regions, this is a fairly obvious feature to substantiate; at other times of year, or in the tropics, it may require a little more detective work. Most evergreen leaves fall into two categories. They will either be long, thin and needle-like, which will suggest that they belong to a conifer, or they will be thick and leathery, quite often with a shiny surface. In most temperate countries the latter are few and far between, making identification relatively easy. A non-conifer evergreen in America is quite likely to be either holly, *Ilex aquifolium*, or holm oak, *Quercus ilex*, for example. In the tropics, you may well need to look at the leaves more closely and take other features of the tree into account before its identity becomes clear.

Below: Palm trees are clearly identifiable by their frond-like leaves and single trunk.

Spherical *Coniferous spreading* *Deciduous spreading*

Ovoid *Conical* *Weeping* *Columnar*

Leaves

For most trees, the leaves are probably the most important aid to identification. There are many different leaf shapes but almost all of them fall into the following six categories. Leaves may be "entire," which means that they are undivided and have no serrations around the edge, such as those of magnolia. They may be "serrated" with sharp serrations around the edge, as with the leaves of sweet chestnut, or be "lobed," curving

Below: Deciduous trees are easier to identify when in full leaf in summer.

Above: Tree shape or form is the first step in identifying trees.

in toward the center of the leaf and then back out again, as in oak. They may be "palmate," which means hand or palm-like—maple leaves are palmate. On some leaves the indentations may go right down to the petiole (leaf-stalk) as with horse chestnut, then the leaf is called a "compound palmate" leaf. Sometimes the leaf is subdivided into smaller leaflets, the leaf is then called "pinnate."

Below: Evergreen trees can be identified by their cones or flowers.

  (entire / serrated / lobed)

entire   *serrated*   *lobed*

palmate   *compound palmate*   *pinnate*

leaf scale   *needles in clusters*   *needles in bunches*

Temperate trees with pinnate leaves include ash and rowan. Many tropical trees have pinnate leaves.

Flowers

Most trees produce flowers in spring, although some, such as the Indian bean tree, *Catalpa bignonioides*, which is native to the U.S.A., wait for summer. Relatively few temperate trees flower in fall or winter although some tropical trees flower all year round. Tree identification can be much easier when flowers are evident. Knowing whether a tree produces flowers in early or late spring, for example, can also help to identify it. Cherries are instantly recognizable by their flowers, as are magnolias. The difficulty arises when individual species or varieties of cherry or magnolia are required. Here again the flower can help. Ask yourself the following questions. What color is it? Does it have double or single petals? How long are the flower stalks? Close examination of flowers will always enable trees to be separated. The way that flowers are

Below: Indian bean tree flower clusters help identify the tree in summer.

held on the tree is also important. Where do they appear, on the ends of twigs or in the leaf axils? Are they individual or do they appear in clusters? If they are held in clusters, what are those clusters like?

Fruit

Late summer to fall is the best time to identify trees by their fruit. Some fruit or seeds are instantly recognizable—acorns will immediately identify an oak tree and conkers a horse chestnut tree. Fallen fruit are particularly useful indicators for tropical trees, which may be too tall for flowers or leaves to be visible. Some fruit are particularly

Below: Fruit and seeds appear in a variety of forms to attract a wide range of pollinators.

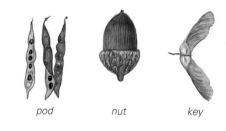

pod   *nut*   *key*

Below: Simpoh air has distinctive yellow flowers that form in racemes.

Above: There are hundreds of different leaf shapes, colors and arrangements to help identify trees. Needles too are quite distinct, and like leaves, are arranged differently on different trees.

distinctive, such as those of spindle trees, *Euonymus* species. The casing is normally bright pink and opens very much like a parasol to reveal orange seeds, which hang on tiny threads.

Bark

Some trees are probably better known by their bark than any other feature. Silver birch, for example, has striking silvery white bark, while the Tibetan cherry, *Prunus serrula*, has bark that is polished, peeling and mahogany red. Other trees may not have such striking bark color but bark may still be a useful feature to aid identification. For instance, beech has smooth light gray bark, cherry has distinctive horizontal banding and plane trees have buff-colored bark which is constantly "flaking" to reveal fresh, light fawn bark beneath. Bark can vary between young and mature trees.

Below: Buds and flowers can help identify a willow tree that is not in leaf.

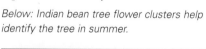

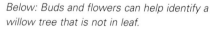

Above: Breadfruit are instantly recognizable in their native West Indies.

Above: The cones of the Likiang spruce age to become almost purple in color.

Above: The sweet chestnut tree can be identified by its distinctive fruit in the fall.

Buds

Winter is the time when tree identification can be most difficult. However, close inspection of the buds can be of considerable help. Ash has very distinctive black buds, for example, while those of magnolias tend to be large and covered with a dense coating of light-gray hairs. Horse chestnut buds are large and sticky, sycamore buds lime-green in color. The positioning of buds can also help identify a tree. They may be in pairs on opposite sides of the twig, or they may be alternately positioned with one on the left followed by one on the right. Some buds hug the twig, such as those of willow, while others, such as oak buds, appear in clusters.

Equipment

When identifying trees, a good field guide is essential. It is worth getting one that fits inside your pocket and preferably has a waterproof cover. A pair of binoculars can be useful to look at leaves, flowers or buds, which may be at the top of the tree. A notepad and pencil will allow you to sketch relevant features and make notes on locations. Finally, sealable plastic bags

Right: In winter the overall shape of a tree and its bark, twigs and buds will all help towards identification. Quite often, in managed woodlands, the task of identification will be made simpler by the fact that many trees of the same species will be planted together.

are useful. They enable you to collect specimen leaves, fruit or seeds and take them home for closer examination.

How to use the encyclopedia

The trees in the following pages are arranged according to two major groups of trees: trees of temperate America and trees of tropical America; both groups include conifers and broad leaves. Within each chapter the trees are subdivided using Arthur Cronquist's system for classification of flowering plants.

Each main group of trees is divided into families, then genus and finally species. Under the common name of

each tree species, is any other common name the tree is known by. It is followed by the Latin name, which is always given in italics. Each species is presented with general information of interest and then with more specific information to help in identification. The fact boxes contain brief details of the most salient features, and the map shows where in the world the tree originates from. This may differ to its current distribution around the world. Where trees have been introduced by plant collectors as specimen trees, for use in gardens and arboreta, a hardiness zone range has been given (see the map in the index).

TREES OF TEMPERATE AMERICA

Temperate America roughly equates to an area from Alaska to Mexico and from southern Argentina to Patagonia. Within these regions there are vast differences in temperature and landscapes, ranging from cold northern tundra, and high mountain ranges, to arid deserts, and exposed coastlines. This has resulted in the evolution of a large, diverse and fascinating population of native tree species. Within the following pages you will find representatives of great diversity, including northern tundra dwarf willows, West Coast giant conifers, swamp species of the Everglades and the amazing drought-tolerant Joshua tree of the Mojave Desert. In addition to native tree species, the Americas contain vast numbers of cultivated ornamental species that have their origins in other parts of the world, and many of which are included here.

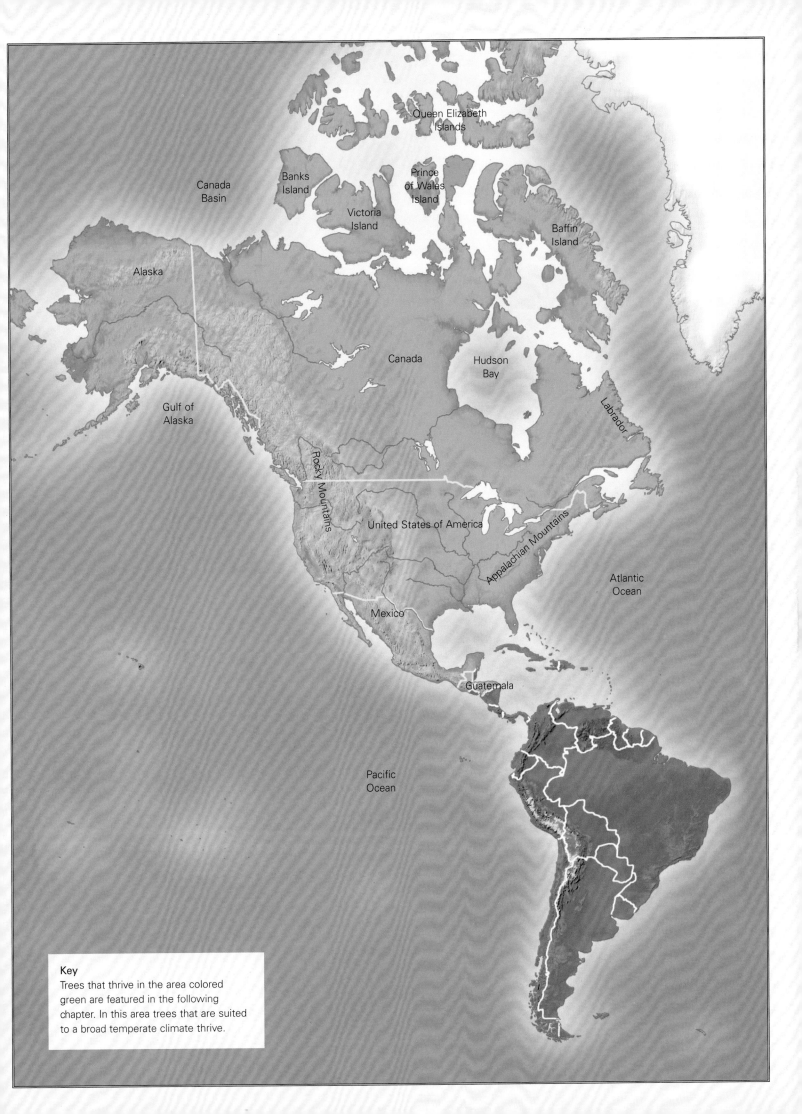

Queen Elizabeth
Islands

Canada
Basin

Banks
Island

Prince
of Wales
Island

Victoria
Island

Baffin
Island

Alaska

Gulf of
Alaska

Canada

Hudson
Bay

Labrador

Rocky Mountains

United States of America

Appalachian Mountains

Atlantic
Ocean

Mexico

Guatemala

Pacific
Ocean

Key

Trees that thrive in the area colored
green are featured in the following
chapter. In this area trees that are suited
to a broad temperate climate thrive.

PODOCARPS

The podocarps are predominantly forest trees from the Southern Hemisphere. They are all coniferous evergreens with linear or scale-like leaves. The most extensive genus is Podocarpus, *with over 70 species that range from southern temperate regions through all the tropics to the West Indies and Japan. Many can be grown in a temperate environment and are a major component of temperate rainforests.*

Japanese Podocarp

Podocarpus nagi

This tender, slow-growing tree was described by Charles Sprague Sargent, one-time director of the Arnold Arboretum, Boston, as "one of the most strikingly beautiful of all evergreen trees." It has wider leaves than most other podocarps, and was originally mistaken by the Dutch botanist Kaempfer for a species of laurel. It is popular as a street tree in the Bay Area and around San Diego.

Identification: The bark is at first smooth and purple-brown, flaking into large scales in maturity. The leaves are opposite, dark glossy green and leathery with pronounced veins running down their length; they are pointed at the tip and tapered at the base and 2in (5cm) long. Male flowers are catkin-like spikes clustered along the shoot and are up to 1in (2.5cm) long. Female flowers are solitary or in pairs and develop into a globular fruit about ½in (1cm) wide which is covered in a plum-like bloom.

Distribution: Southern Japan, Taiwan and China, and widely planted in southwest U.S.A. from California to Arizona.
Height: 80ft (25m)
Shape: Broadly conical
Evergreen
Pollinated: Wind
Leaf shape: Ovate

Left: The male flowers are catkin-like spikes, up to 1in (2.5cm) long, and are clustered along the shoot.

Bigleaf Podocarp

Podocarpus macrophyllus

An attractive, formal-shaped tree, which is extremely hardy, and able to withstand severe and prolonged frost. It is a prominent feature in many Japanese temple gardens. There is a magnificent specimen at the entrance to the Kyoto Botanic Gardens, Japan. In the U.S.A. it is found from Sacramento to California, and is commonly grown against walls, and occasionally clipped and shaped into hedging and screening. It grows particularly well on moist acid soils.

Left: The pointed linear leaves are leathery, dark green and glossy.

Far left: The fruit is globular, purple-green and contained in a fleshy bowl.

Identification: The bark is red-brown, smooth on juvenile trees becoming heavily fissured in maturity and shredding vertically. The leaves are dark green and glossy above, and a lighter pea-green beneath. They are arranged spirally around the shoots in clusters. The fruit appears in late summer and is purple-green, about ½in (1cm) long, and held in a fleshy bowl not dissimilar to an acorn cup.

Distribution: Japan and China. It is widely planted in Los Angeles, in Phoenix, Arizona and in southern California.
Height: 70ft (20m)
Shape: Broadly conical
Evergreen
Pollinated: Wind
Leaf shape: Linear

Right: The leathery leaves are pointed, up to ½in (1cm) wide and up to 6in (15cm) long.

Totara

Podocarpus totara

The totara is a slow-growing evergreen tree that is noted for its longevity (it usually lives between 800 and 1,000 years). It grows in milder regions of the U.S.A. Growing up to 100ft (30m) it has a straight, deeply grooved trunk that often reaches nearly two-thirds of its overall height. The bark peels off in long strips to reveal a beautiful golden brown hue. Its timber is valued for general construction. Montane totara, *P. cunninghamii*, is a similar species, which has thinner, papery bark.

Above right: The cherry-like fruit contains two round seeds.

Identification: The crown develops from conical to a more broadly ovoid shape as it matures. It is noted for its massive trunk, which can be up to 6½ft (2m) in diameter, and for the huge strips of bark that peel away in a curtain-like fashion until finally falling from the tree's trunk.

Distribution: Throughout the North Island of New Zealand and into the northeastern regions of the South Island. Hardy to zone 9.
Height: 100ft (30m)
Shape: Broadly conical
Evergreen
Pollinated: Wind
Leaf shape: Linear

Left: The dull green needles are stiff and leathery with a sharp point at the tip.

Plum-fruited Yew *Podocarpus andina* (*Prumnopitys andina*)
This tree has foliage similar to the common yew. It produces fruit ¾in (2cm) long, which is yellow in color and similar to a plum with an edible fleshy covering. The seed is noted for not having a resinous odor. The tree is cultivated throughout the warmer temperate regions as an ornamental specimen. Canelo, a yellow hardwood obtained from this podocarp, is used in the production of furniture.

Below: The foliage is similar to common yew.

Manio *Podocarpus salignus*
Native to Chile, this tree is commonly referred to as the willowleaf podocarp as its leaves are linear and sickle-shaped, resembling those of a willow. It can grow to 66ft (20m) tall, forming an attractive tree with gently pendulous branching and graceful foliage.

Prince Albert's Yew

Saxegothaea conspicua

The genus *Saxegothaea* is monotypic, meaning there is only one tree in the genus. *S. conspicua* is an evergreen tree forming part of the temperate rainforests of southern Chile and adjacent Argentina. It is found growing in association with other forest species, such as *Nothofagus dombeyi*, *Drimys winteri* and *Podocarpus nubigena*, all prized for lumber. It is cultivated throughout warmer regions of the Northern Hemisphere as an ornamental tree. The generic and common names are in commemoration of the husband of Queen Victoria of the United Kingdom.

Above: Needles of Prince Albert's yew are slightly curved with a sharp tip and are up to 1¼in (3cm) long.

Distribution: Along lowland areas at the base of the west Andean slopes, from Chile (Biobio to the Chiloé province), and into southwest Argentina.
Height: 50ft (15m)
Shape: Broadly conical
Evergreen
Pollinated: Wind
Leaf shape: Linear

Identification: Grows to a height of 50ft (15m) or more, developing a slender, conical crown in its native environment and a more bushy habit in cultivation. The foliage is similar in appearance to the genus *Taxus*. The fruit is thick, round and composed of fleshy scales.

Right: The leaf on the right shows the topside view, and that on the left shows the underside coloring.

PLUM YEWS AND CHILE PINES

The plum yews or Cephalotaxus are very similar to the podocarps in that they produce cones or fruit that are drupe-like. This is a characteristic also shared by the false nutmegs, or Torreya species. Of much greater difference is the Chile pine, belonging to the unique Southern-Hemisphere family Araucariaceae. It shares the characteristics of this family, being an evergreen, long-lived coniferous tree.

Plum Yew

Cephalotaxus harringtonia

The plum yew is the most widely cultivated of the four species of *Cephalotaxus*. It is a useful landscape plant in southern U.S.A. It forms a small evergreen tree up to 33ft (10m) tall with foliage similar to that of yew, but with much broader and drupe-like fruit that resembles a plum. When crushed, the foliage is pungent. In cultivation it is useful for tolerating shade, where it can develop an impressive, mound-like appearance.

Identification: Leaves are broader and longer than yew. The upper surface is pale green and glossy, and the underside is slightly gray in color with two distinctive green bands. The leaf apex is acute and often spine-tipped.

Above: Needles are up to 2in (5cm) long, glossy dark green above with two light bands of stomata beneath.

Distribution: Japan and Korea. In the U.S.A. it survives in hardiness zones 6–9.
Height: 33ft (10m)
Shape: Spreading
Evergreen
Pollinated: Wind
Leaf shape: Linear

Left: The fruit has distinctive pale banding and browns as it matures.

Chile Pine

Monkey puzzle *Araucaria araucana*

This is a uniquely bizarre tree for its triangular, very sharp, pointed leaves and distinctive whorls of long branches. It was introduced into cultivation in the late eighteenth century. It is widely admired for its architectural habit, but often looks misplaced. Even in its native Andean forest it is an impressive oddity.

Female trees of the Chile pine produce cones 6in (15cm) in length, which take over two years to ripen. The seed is edible.

Identification: As a young tree it has a slightly rounded conical outline, with foliage to ground level. As it matures, the crown broadens and the lower branches fall away. This reveals an impressive trunk with horizontal folds of gray bark, similar in appearance to elephant hide.

Above: The distinctive bark of the Chile pine.

Right: Male cones are borne in clusters at the tips of each shoot.

Distribution: Forms groves in the Andean forests of Chile and southwestern Argentina.
Height: 164ft (50m)
Shape: Broadly conical, becoming domed in maturity
Evergreen
Pollinated: Wind
Leaf shape: Linear to triangular

Left: The female ovoid brown cone is 6in (15cm) long.

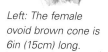

Right: The leaves.

Stinking Cedar

Torreya taxifolia

This tree is very similar in foliage to the yew, *Taxus*, but differs in having incredibly sharp, spine-like tips to the needles. When crushed, the needles release a pungent, disagreeable odor, hence the common name. In outline this tree forms a broad-based pyramid, rarely growing taller than 50ft (15m) in height. As is the case with other *Torreya* species, it is commonly found in moist woodland areas. Its lumber has been used for fencing, but it is not an abundant tree in its native Florida and is now considered to be under threat in the wild. It has been widely planted in ornamental collections worldwide.

Right: The fruit is a purple-green berry containing one seed.

Far right: Needles are sharply pointed, glossy dark green above and light green beneath.

Identification: This evergreen tree differs from the Californian nutmeg in having much shorter, convex needles which can be up to 1¼ in (3cm) long and sharply pointed. The needles are simple and linear in shape, and arranged alternately. The bark is gray-brown in color and furrows as the tree ages. The fleshy seed is poisonous if eaten. It is cultivated as an ornamental tree.

Distribution: Restricted to the Apalichicola River in northwest Florida, and then moves northwards into Georgia.
Height: 50ft (15m)
Shape: Broadly conical
Evergreen
Pollinated: Wind
Leaf shape: Linear

OTHER SPECIES OF NOTE
Kaya Nut *Torreya nucifera*
This *Torreya* originates from the lowland valley areas of Honshu, Shikoku and Kyushu in Japan. A similar species to the Californian nutmeg, it develops a rather more open crown and has much shorter leaves. It survives in U.S.A. hardiness zones 7–9.

Below: Kaya nut needles.

Fortune Plum Yew
Cephalotaxus fortunei
Native of east and central China, where it forms a tree up to 50ft (15m) tall. It develops an open habit, largely as a result of its long needles, which can be 6in (15cm) long. It can survive in U.S.A. hardiness zone 7.

Californian Nutmeg

Torreya californica

The Californian nutmeg is very similar to some of the podocarps and plum yews in having drupe-like fruit and linear foliage. It is distinctive in producing very sharp spines at the tips of its leaves. Beneath the resinous, fleshy fruit the seed is grooved and resembles commercial nutmeg, but has no similarity in use. It is largely grown as an ornamental tree in gardens and arboreta, as the crown forms a very attractive conical outline, and the branching develops in open whorls.

Identification: An evergreen to 66ft (20m) tall. The leaves are thin and short (up to 2in (5cm)). They are deep yellowish-green and have a shiny upper surface. Their underside has two distinctive ranks of white stomatal bands. The bark is reddish-brown and flaky.

Above: There is no botanical connection between the fruit of the Californian nutmeg (above) and the spice nutmeg, Myristica fragrans.

Distribution: Restricted to forested areas of California.
Height: 100ft (30m)
Shape: Broadly conical
Evergreen
Pollinated: Wind
Leaf shape: Linear

Below: Needles are reminiscent of some of the silver fir species, Abies. They are up to 2in (5cm) long and sharply pointed.

GINKGO, YEWS AND INCENSE CEDAR

The maidenhair tree is the only surviving representative of the Ginkgoaceae family, the other members being known solely from fossil records. The genus Taxus is present in three continents across the Northern Hemisphere and has related characteristics to the Torreya species. Incense cedar is one of only three species belonging to the genus Calocedrus.

Maidenhair Tree

Ginkgo biloba

Distribution: Originating from China, thought to be from the provinces of Anhwei and Kiangsu. It is widely cultivated throughout the Northern Hemisphere including Japan and U.S.A.
Height: 130ft (40m)
Shape: Broadly conical
Deciduous
Pollinated: Wind
Leaf shape: Fan

Fossil records show that *Ginkgo biloba* existed over 200 million years ago. It was introduced to general cultivation in 1754. It produces male and female flowers on separate trees. When ripe, the fruit has a rancid odor; the seed beneath this pungent flesh is edible if roasted. *Ginkgo* has an attractive outline.

Identification: A deciduous tree, unique in producing fan-shaped leaves which resemble those of the maidenhair fern, *Adiantum*, hence its common name. The foliage is produced on characteristic short shoots, most apparent in winter. The bark is a pale gray.

Above left: The foliage turns golden yellow in fall.

Left: The foliage is tolerant of the urban landscape.

Above right: The fruit is orange-brown when ripe and has a single edible kernel.

Common Yew

Taxus baccata

The common yew develops a very dense, evergreen canopy. It has become associated, over recent centuries, with churchyards. In the U.S.A. it is a popular hedging tree. Yew wood is extremely durable, and is valued in the production of furniture and decorative veneers used in cabinetmaking. It was commonly used for making bow staves. A number of cultivars have been created. One of the most striking is 'Standishii', which has an upright habit and golden-yellow foliage.

Identification: Common yew develops a broad and loosely conical outline. The leaves are glossy above with a central groove. The bark is rich brown with a purple hue. In spring the male cones shed pollen with cloud-like abundance. The fruit is a red fleshy aril, turning red at maturity, around an olive-green seed.

Below: Yew leaves are needle-like in appearance. The canopy-like foliage creates a somber feel.

Distribution: Europe, including Britain, eastwards to northern Iran and the Atlas mountains of North Africa. It survives in U.S.A. zones 5–7.
Height: 66ft (20m).
Shape: Broadly conical
Evergreen
Pollinated: Wind
Leaf shape: Linear

Right: Poisonous yew berries are not digested by birds.

Incense Cedar

Calocedrus decurrens

Incense cedar is native to western North America. The natural habit of this tree is unusual in that it develops a columnar, almost fastigiate form. Shiny, mid-green leaves develop in flattened sprays produced on branches that are almost horizontal to the main stem. It has a very attractive, exfoliating gray to reddish-brown bark. There are only two other species of tree in this genus, *C. macrolepis* from China and *C. formosana* from Taiwan.

Identification: The foliage of the incense cedar is dense, dark green and usually present to the base of the tree with only a short, exposed bole. The male and female flowers are produced on the same tree. Often, abundant quantities of oblong cones are produced, and become pendulous with their own weight.

Above: The red-brown bark of the incense cedar is similar to that of the giant redwood.

Far left: The yellow-brown cones have six overlapping scales.

Distribution: Western North America from mid-Oregon southwards to Baja California in northern Mexico.
Height: 130ft (40m)
Shape: Narrowly columnar
Evergreen
Pollinated: Wind
Leaf shape: Linear scale-like

OTHER SPECIES OF NOTE

Above: Japanese yew is a wide-spreading, open growing tree.

Japanese Yew *Taxus cuspidata*
Occurring naturally throughout Japan and most of northeast Asia. It can survive in U.S.A hardiness zones 8–10. Reaching a height of 66ft (20m) in the wild, but more shrub-like in cultivation, it has spine-tipped leaf apices. This is one of the parents, together with the common yew, of a hybrid *Taxus* x *media*, the most common form of which is the fastigiate 'Hicksii'.

Canadian Yew *Taxus canadensis*
This small tree or large shrub is native to eastern North America from Newfoundland to Virginia. It is the hardiest of all yews and the only yew which has male and female flowers on the same tree. The leaves are more pointed than on the English yew and the foliage is not so poisonous.

Pacific Yew

Taxus brevifolia

The Pacific yew is endemic to the rainforests of western North America. It is a small tree, which grows in the shade of larger trees, often beside streams and gullies. Ever since its bark was found to contain an alkaloid called taxol, which inhibits the growth of some forms of cancer, it has become increasingly rare in the wild. It takes about ten Pacific yew trees to yield enough bark for the 2g of taxol needed to treat a single patient. Consequently thousands of yews have been felled and stripped of their bark in the quest for taxol.

Identification: This small to medium-size tree has thin reddish-brown bark not dissimilar to that of the English yew. The branches are slender and slightly pendulous, and the winter buds are covered with golden scales. The leaves are needle-like, dark green above and sage green beneath. The needles are arranged on the shoot in two opposite horizontally spreading rows.

Above: The seed is contained in a red fleshy fruit known as an aril.

Right: The needles are approximately 1in (2.5cm) long.

Distribution: Western North America from British Columbia to California.
Height: To 70ft (20m)
Shape: Broadly conical
Evergreen
Pollinated: Wind
Leaf shape: Linear

FALSE CYPRESSES

Trees belonging to the genus Chamaecyparis, *or false cypress, have a number of obvious characteristics in common. All are evergreen, and their leaves are arranged in flattened sprays and have a pungent aroma when crushed. The habitats from which they originate are generally wet and they all produce very durable lumber. The genus is present in western North America, Taiwan and Japan.*

Leyland Cypress

x *Cupressocyparis leylandii*

This fast-growing conifer is a hybrid between two American species; Monterey cypress, *Cupressus macrocarpa*, and Alaska cedar, *Chamaecyparis nootkatensis*. The hybrid cross has never naturally occurred in the U.S.A. because the natural ranges of the two parents do not overlap. It originated in 1888 at Leighton Hall, Powys, Wales, where the two parents were growing close to each other in a garden. Since then, Leyland cypress has become one of the most popular trees for hedging and screening. It is extremely fast growing, quite often exceeding 6ft (2m) growth in one year.

Right: The fruit is a small brown cone.
Far right: The leaves are scale-like.

Identification: The bark is red-brown developing shallow fissures as it matures. The leaves are small, with pointed tips. They are dark green above, lighter green beneath and borne in flattened sprays. Male and female flowers are found on the same tree. The male flowers are yellow, the female's green; both appear in early spring at the tips of the shoots. The fruit is a globular woody brown cone approximately ¾in (2cm) diameter.

Distribution: Of garden origin. Originated as a hybrid in the United Kingdom. Widely planted throughout the U.S.A.
Height: 100ft (30m)
Shape: Narrowly columnar
Evergreen
Pollinated: Wind
Leaf shape: Scale-like

Alaska Cedar

Nootka cypress, *Chamaecyparis nootkatensis*

The nootka cypress is common throughout the coastal forests of western North America, where there are living examples many thousands of years old. It is distinctively conical in outline; the branches are flexible and develop a weeping appearance that distinguishes it from other *Chamaecyparis* species. There is an elegant naturally occurring form called 'Pendula', which produces elongated sprays of foliage that hang from pendulous branches. Referred to as yellow cedar, the wood is noted for being fine textured, straight grained and yellow.

Identification: Up to 100ft (30m) tall. The bark resembles the western red cedar in that it produces thin strips when peeled. It is brown in color with a pinkish hue. Both male and female flowers are produced on the same tree. The cones, which take two years to develop, are about ½in (1cm) across and a deep plum color.

Below: The foliage has pale green margins.

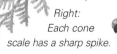

Right: Each cone scale has a sharp spike.

Below: The branches have a graceful upward sweep towards the tip.

Distribution: From Alaska, south towards northern California. At varying altitudes, from sea level to above the timberline, where competition is reduced. Found in the Olympic Mountains, the Cascades of Washington and Oregon, and east to the Blue Mountains.
Height: 100ft (30m)
Shape: Narrowly conical
Evergreen
Pollinated: Wind
Leaf shape: Linear scale-like

Henry's Cypress

Chamaecyparis henryae

Henry's cypress is named after the North American traveler and plant collector Mrs J. Norman Henry who first collected it in the 1960s. It is closely related to the American white cypress, *Chamaecyparis thyoides*, with which it shares many characteristics. However, in maturity it more closely resembles *C. nootkatensis*. Despite originating from southeastern U.S.A., it is perfectly hardy and grows well in Virginia and in the United Kingdom.

Identification: This medium-size tree has red-brown smooth bark which becomes finely fissured with age. On young trees the foliage is a bright yellow-green color, but as the tree matures it gradually turns dull green. The scale-like leaves are borne on flattened fan-shaped sprays, and give off a citrus, fruity aroma when crushed. The cones are small, ½in (1cm) across, ovoid, green ripening to brown. When they first appear in summer they are covered with a soft glaucous bloom.

Below: Each cone is at first almost spherical, but then ripens to an irregular, angular woody structure.

Distribution: Coastal plains of Florida, Alabama and Mississippi.
Height: 70ft (20m)
Shape: Narrowly conical
Evergreen
Pollinated: Wind
Leaf shape: Scale-like

Left: Scale-like leaves are borne on flattened fan-shaped sprays.

Port Orford Cedar

Lawson cypress, Oregon cedar

Chamaecyparis lawsoniana

It originates from North America and develops into a tall, columnar tree, to 130ft (40m), with reddish-brown fibrous bark. The scented foliage has distinctive stomatal markings on the underside of the leaves. In Pacific northwestern America it is a very important source of lumber with many uses, from boatbuilding to cabinetmaking. An incredible diversity of cultivars has been produced, which vary in form, foliage and color.

Identification: Young trees have smooth, brown-green and shiny bark, with a pendulous dominant shoot that is distinct from the mature trees. It produces globular cones on the foliage tips, which begin fleshy with a bluish-purple bloom and become woody and wrinkled.

Below: The cones are globular, ⅓in (7mm) in diameter, purple-brown and remain on the tree long after the seed has been shed.

Distribution: Northwestern U.S.A. from southwest Oregon to northwest California. Present in the Klamath and Siskiyou Mountains to an altitude that approaches 6,561ft (2,000m).
Height: 130ft (40m)
Shape: Narrowly conical
Evergreen
Pollinated: Wind
Leaf shape: Linear scale-like

Below: The top side of the foliage is dark green to blue, and when crushed smells of parsley.

TRUE CYPRESSES

These trees are closely related to the genus Chamaecyparis, *since their leaves are scale-like and produced in sprays. Unlike the false cypresses the foliage is not flattened. Their cones are composed of fewer scales, between six and eight, and are twice the diameter, but contain less seed. True cypresses are distributed throughout regions of North America, Europe and Asia.*

Santa Cruz Cypress

Cupressus abramsiana

Distribution: Santa Cruz Mountains in California.
Height: 70ft (20m)
Shape: Columnar
Evergreen
Pollinated: Wind
Leaf shape: Scale-like

This fast-growing, dense-foliaged, symmetrical tree only grows in a few locations in the Santa Cruz Mountains of California. It was not named until 1948 and is very closely related to Californian cypress, *Cupressus goveniana*. At one stage it was considered to be just a variation of that species. However, the cones are larger and the foliage a brighter green than the Californian cypress. On young trees the branches are strongly ascending.

Right: Seeds of the Santa Cruz cypress are contained within globular cones which may be up to 1in (2.5cm) across.

Identification: The bark is red-brown with a silver sheen when young, becoming fissured in maturity. The stem has a tendency to fork low down. Each strongly ascending branch is covered with finely divided sprays of bright, rich green scale-like foliage. Cones are large and appear from a very early age, sometimes when the tree is less than 3ft (1m) tall. They are irregularly globular, 1in (2.5cm) across with a slight beak to each scale. The seeds within are glaucous dull brown.

Arizona Cypress

Cupressus arizonica

The Arizona cypress belongs to a group of cypresses that are found in south-western U.S.A. along the northern border with Mexico. They are distinguished from each other largely by their geographical distribution through this region. All have blue-gray glaucous foliage composed of scale-like leaves, and tolerate the dry, sun-drenched conditions. Other cypresses in this group include the smooth cypress, *C. glabra*; San Pedro cypress, *C. montana*; Piute cypress, *C. nevadensis*; and the Cayamaca cypress, *C. stephensonii*.

Identification: Develops a conical habit to a height of 66ft (20m). Has a textured, finely fissured bark. The foliage is dull gray-green, often lacking the white, resin-secreting glands common to other cypresses in this group.

Above and right: The rounded cones are 1in (2.5cm) across with six large scales and a short stalk.

Distribution: From the central region of Arizona south towards the northern border of Mexico.
Height: 66ft (20m)
Shape: Narrowly conical
Evergreen
Pollinated: Wind
Leaf shape: Linear scale-like

Right: The scale-like needles closely overlap, and are pale to gray-green with a sharp point.

Right: The scales are arranged irregularly along the shoot.

Monterey Cypress

Cupressus macrocarpa

With an incredible ability to withstand exposure to salt-laden winds, this tree has become as common a sight along the exposed coastal habitats of Europe as in its native California. It can attain a height of 130ft (40m), but individual trees are often stunted by the extreme conditions. In cultivation it is best known for being the female parent of the leyland cypress, × *Cupressocyparis leylandii*. Since cypress lumber is strong and durable it is often used for structural work.

Right: Juvenile trees are pyramidal to columnar.

Left: Mature trees become flat-topped with widespread horizontal branches.

Identification: Mature trees display a great variability in habit, from a dense crown of ascending branches to a more horizontal cedar-like form. Leaves are arranged in loose, circular sprays around the shoots. When crushed its foliage releases an aromatic odor.

Distribution: Known from two sites along the coastline near Monterey, California: at Cypress Point and Point Lobos.
Height: 130ft (40m)
Shape: Broadly conical
Evergreen
Pollinated: Wind
Leaf shape: Linear scale-like

Above: Cones are up to 1½ in (4cm) across.

OTHER SPECIES OF NOTE

Guadelupe Cypress *Cupressus guadelupensis*
Grows to a height of 66ft (20m) in the wild. This cypress is restricted in natural distribution to Guadelupe off the coast of Baja California. The island is part of a series of ridges once connected to the mainland. The tree is seldom seen in cultivation.

Mexican Cypress *Cupressus lusitanica*
Height 66ft (20m). The Mexican cypress was first named in Portugal, having been brought over from Mexico and cultivated there. It was also believed to have been of Asiatic origin, hence its other common name, cedar of Goa.

Sargent's Cypress *Cupressus sargentii*
This bushy small tree occurs on dry mountain slopes up to elevations of 2,200ft (670m) throughout the coastal range of California. This species is closely related to *C. goveniana*, but is distinguishable by its short trunk, spreading branches and handsome open crown. The branches are covered with attractive smooth bark which is at first orange, becoming bright red-brown, and on maturity, purple-brown.

Modoc Cypress *Cupressus bakeri*
The Modoc cypress is native to the dry hills and low slopes in the Siskiyou Mountains of California and Oregon, particularly in Shasta County and southeast Siskiyou County. It is a tree which grows to 50ft (15m) tall with smooth red-brown bark which matures to gray but with minimum fissuring. The scale-like, dark gray-green leaves are arranged all around the shoot.

Californian Cypress

Cupressus goveniana

Otherwise known as Gowen's cypress, after James Gowen, the renowned British rhododendron nurseryman, this multi-stemmed tree has small natural populations on Point Pinos Ridge, two miles west of Monterey, and along a narrow coastal strip in Mendocino county. In the wild it is more often a small tree, or large shrub, but in cultivation elsewhere it attains heights around 70ft (20m). It appears to be a short-lived tree, regularly dying back after 50 years or so.

Identification: The Californian cypress has bright red-brown thin bark with shallow, linear fissures, which separate the surface into long thread-like scales. The leaves are acutely pointed, dark green and scale-like. The cones are smaller than *C. abramsiana*, about ¾ in (1.5cm) across, more oval than spherical with six to ten scales. The seed they contain is almost black.

Distribution: Monterey peninsula, Southern California.
Height: 70ft (20m)
Shape: Broadly columnar
Evergreen
Pollinated: Wind
Leaf shape: Scale-like

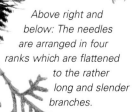

Above right and below: The needles are arranged in four ranks which are flattened to the rather long and slender branches.

PATAGONIAN CYPRESS AND ARBORVITAE

A common characteristic of Fitzroya *is the three-whorled arrangements of the leaves, which distinguish it from the closely related* Cupressus. *The arborvitae, or* Thuja *species, are similar to Lawson cypress, but have much larger and broader leaves, and* Thujopsis, *or hiba, differs from* Thuja *in having thick white markings on the underside of its leaves.*

Patagonian Cypress

Fitzroya cupressoides

This unique genus of tree has a restricted distribution and is one of the world's oldest trees, recorded at over 3,500 years. It is often referred to as the redwood of South America. Its reddish, lightweight and straight-grained timber, commonly used for shingles, furniture and masts, has been highly prized for centuries.

Identification: It has reddish brown, deeply ridged bark that peels off in strips. The foliage is produced in pendulous sprays and is blue-green with distinctive white markings on both surfaces. In cultivation it is slow-growing and forms a multibranched, shrub-like habit.

Above: The cones develop at the end of each spiky shoot.

Left: Needles are bright blue-green with two white stomatal bands.

Left: The angular cones have nine woody scales.

Distribution: South America: From southern Chile to Argentina. It is now restricted to higher altitude rainforests along the coastal ranges from south of Valdira, including Chiloe Island, to the Andean slopes.
Height: 165ft (50m)
Shape: Broadly columnar
Evergreen
Pollinated: Wind
Leaf shape: Linear scale-like

White Cedar

Thuja occidentalis

This slow-growing evergreen tree's origins are in eastern Canada and southeastern U.S.A., where it is predominantly a tree of upper forest levels, surviving in rocky outcrops as well as sites with high moisture content. Similar to its more westerly cousin, it is valued commercially as a timber that has good resistance to decay and tolerates contact with moisture. Many cultivars have been developed, mostly from dwarf forms. 'Rheingold' has attractive golden yellow foliage.

Identification: Twisted sprays of foliage give this tree a distinctive outline. During fall and winter the foliage has attractive hints of orange and brown. The bark is brown with a golden orange hue and shreds with age. Yellow cones develop from as early as six years.

Right: Needle scales are dark green above, yellow-green below. Below: When crushed, the foliage smells of fresh apples.

Left: The upright cones are ⅓in (1cm) across. Yellow-green at first, they ripen to brown.

Distribution: Southeastern Canada and U.S.A. From Nova Scotia and New Brunswick, west to Quebec and northern Ontario; through Michigan, Illinois and Indiana to the states of New England.
Height: 66ft (20m)
Shape: Narrowly conical
Evergreen
Pollinated: Wind
Leaf shape: Linear scale-like

Western Red Cedar

Thuja plicata

Also known as giant arborvitae, this evergreen tree originates from the northwestern Pacific coastline of America, where it is a major component of the moist, lowland coniferous forests. Some trees have been recorded at over 1,000 years old. The timber has been utilized for centuries. Native American Indians used to burn out the trunks to make canoes. It has become an economically important timber, being straight-grained, soft and easily worked. It has been widely used to make roofing shingles. Many cultivars have been produced, including a distinctive variegated form called 'Zebrina'.

Identification: A very tall, narrow, conical evergreen tree up to 165ft (50m). Individual specimen trees with low branching can layer to form a secondary ring of vigorous, upright trunks. The foliage is dark green and glossy above, with a sweetly aromatic scent when crushed. The bark is reddish brown, forming plates with maturity. It is fibrous and ridged.

Left: The shoots are coppery brown with sprays of deep glossy green, scale-like needles that are flattened in one plane.

Distribution: Originating from the Pacific coastline of North America, it grows from southern Alaska, through British Columbia, south to Washington and Oregon to the giant coastal redwood forests of California.
Height: 165ft (50m)
Shape: Narrowly conical
Evergreen
Pollinated: Wind
Leaf shape: Linear scale-like

Oriental Arborvitae

Thuja orientalis

Distribution: China and Korea.
Height: 50ft (15m)
Shape: Columnar
Evergreen
Pollinated: Wind
Leaf shape: Scale-like

Below: When crushed, the needles emit a strong "pine" aroma.

Otherwise known as Chinese thuja, this medium-size tree is frequently planted from Texas to California and north to Nevada. It is common in parks and cemeteries, and is quite often seen planted on each side of the front door of houses. It is different to all other thujas in having distinctive erect or upward-curving branches which bear the foliage in vertical sprays. It has given rise to several popular cultivars including 'Aurea Nana', 'Conspicua' and 'Elegantissima'.

Identification: The oriental arborvitae is frequently multi-stemmed, forming a dense crown of foliage virtually to ground level, which obscures the copper-red bark of the trunk. The dark green coloring of the leaves is virtually identical on both the upper and lower surfaces. The cones are an irregular shape, about ¾in (1.5cm) long with approximately six scales each with a protuberance shaped like a Rhino's horn. The seeds inside are dark red-purple and without wings.

OTHER SPECIES OF NOTE

Japanese Thuja *Thuja standishii*
Native of Japan, from Honshu and Shikoku. An evergreen tree, to 66ft (20m), with very deep, rich red-brown bark that peels off in square plates. It is similar in form to hiba, in having branches that curve sharply upwards, and foliage that is hard and irregular in outline. The young, growing leaf tips are blue-gray. When crushed, the foliage has a lemon-like scent.

Hiba *Thujopsis dolabrata*
A monotypic genus and single species, this broadly conical, evergreen tree originates from Japan. It is distinguished from thuja by its broader scale-like leaves, which have strong bands of white stomata on their underside. Hiba is a slow-growing tree, eventually reaching 70ft (20m) in height. It has bark that is red-brown to gray, peeling with maturity into fine strips.

Korean Thuja *Thuja koraiensis*
Native to Korea and the Jilin province of China, this is a small tree, to 33ft (10m). A similar species to the Japanese thuja, it has blue-green foliage, that is unique in having silvery undersides to the leaves.

Right: In spring, the new growth is vivid lime-green. As it matures, so its appearance becomes progressively darker.

JUNIPERS

The junipers are similar to the true cypresses, Cupressus, *in that they have two types of leaves on the same plant, both juvenile and scale-like. Unlike cypresses, the fruit consists of a cone in which the scales have fused together to give a berry-like appearance. The common juniper is probably found in more regions of the world than any other tree.*

Western Juniper

Sierra juniper *Juniperus occidentalis*

This tough, medium-size tree is a common species in western U.S.A. where it inhabits rocky slopes and dry hillsides, quite often in conjunction with the Western yellow pine, *Pinus ponderosa*. In the Sierra Nevada 2,000 year-old specimens with huge trunks can be seen growing out of what appears to be solid rock. It was first identified and introduced into cultivation by plant collector David Douglas in 1829.

Identification: The bark is red-brown and smooth, becoming fissured and flaky in maturity. The leaves are scale-like, small, silver-gray-green and held closely to the shoot. Individual, stiff, spiny leaves are quite often found towards the ends of growing tips. Male flowers are yellow and the female's green. They are normally produced on separate trees in spring. The fruit is an egg-shaped, blue-black cone, ½ in (1cm) long, and covered with a glaucous bloom.

Right: The leaves are scale-like and silver-gray-green.

Distribution: West Coast U.S.A. from Washington to California.
Height: 70ft (20m)
Shape: Broadly conical
Evergreen
Pollinated: Wind
Leaf shape: Scale-like

Eastern Red Cedar

Juniperus virginiana

The most widely distributed conifer through central and eastern North America, the eastern red cedar is tolerant of dry, exposed, and elevated sites—a characteristic that has made it a useful tree for screening and wind protection. The heartwood is a beautiful reddish brown and has a typical cedar scent, which is retained through drying. The wood has moth-repellent properties and is commonly used to make blanket boxes and chests. The oil is extracted from the fruit and leaves for use in soaps and fragrances.

Identification: An evergreen tree to 100ft (30m). Eastern red cedar develops a dense pyramidal to columnar habit, with two types of foliage. It has red-brown bark, which exfoliates in long strips. The fruit is berry-like, light green in spring and dark blue when mature.

Above: The dense scale-like foliage is ¼ in (6mm) long, sage-green above and gray-green beneath.

Left: The small cones have a blue-gray bloom when ripe.

Distribution: Eastern and central U.S.A. Great Plains eastwards. Southwest Maine to southern Minnesota into the Dakotas and southwards to Nebraska and central Texas. East to Florida and Georgia.
Height: 100ft (30m)
Shape: Narrowly conical
Evergreen
Pollinated: Wind
Leaf shape: Linear scale-like

Common Juniper

Juniperus communis

The common juniper is believed to be the most widespread tree in the world, growing naturally from Alaska, Greenland, Iceland and Siberia, south through most of Europe, temperate Asia, and North America. It is a hardy tree, tolerating intense cold, exposed coastal locations, and high mountain ranges. In North America it seldom attains heights in excess of 16ft (5m) tall.

Below: The whorls of three needles can be clearly seen below.

Identification: Depending on its location, the overall shape of common juniper may be thin and tree-like or wide-spreading and shrub-like. It has thin, dark red-brown bark that peels in vertical papery strips. The leaves are needle-like, sharply pointed and up to ½in (1cm) long. They are gray-green and carried in whorls of three along the shoot. The yellow male, and green female, flowers are borne on separate trees in clusters within the leaf axils. The fruit is a green, berry-like cone that takes between two and three years to ripen. When ripe it turns a glaucous, purple-black. The fruit is used to give gin its characteristic flavor.

Distribution: Europe, Asia and North America.
Height: 20ft (6m)
Shape: Narrowly conical
Evergreen
Pollinated: Wind
Leaf shape: Needle-like

Utah Juniper

Juniperus osteosperma

This small, candelabra-shape tree makes a distinctive feature in deserts from Wyoming and Utah to California and Arizona around the Grand Canyon, where some arid slopes are clothed in dense, almost pure forests of Utah juniper. It is a hardy tree withstanding long periods of drought and dramatic changes of temperature. It has been recorded at altitudes in excess of 8,000ft (2,500m).

Identification: The Utah juniper has ash-gray to silvery-white, fibrous bark that peels into long thin scales in maturity. It has bright yellow-green, blunt, scale-like leaves, which are held either opposite or in threes on the shoot. Male flowers are yellow and the female's green, and they are borne on separate trees in spring. The fruits are rounded, ½in (1cm) across, reddish-brown, with a thick, firm skin covered with a glaucous bloom. Each fruit contains up to two seeds. The fruit used to be ground into flour and made into cakes by Native Americans.

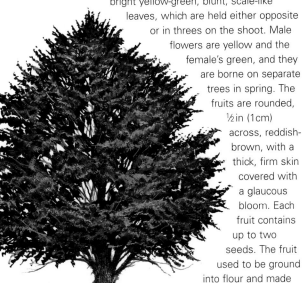

Distribution: From Wyoming to California in U.S.A.
Heigh: 20ft (6m)
Shape: Conical
Evergreen
Pollinated: Wind
Leaf shape: Scale-like

Above: True to its name, the Utah juniper is the most abundant species of juniper in Utah state.

REDWOODS AND BALD CYPRESS

This group of conifers are all members of the Taxodiaceae family and are found in the Northern Hemisphere. The group includes some of the biggest, tallest and oldest trees in the world. The coast and giant redwoods are evergreens originating from California, U.S.A. The dawn redwood and swamp cypress are deciduous conifers. All have distinctive, fibrous, reddish-brown bark.

Coast Redwood

Sequoia sempervirens

The *Sequoia* takes its name from a native American Cherokee called Sequoiah. This majestic tree attains heights in excess of 328ft (100m). The current champion, known as the "Stratosphere Giant," is 374ft (114m). The trunk is quite often branchless for two-thirds of the height.

Left: The cones are ¾–1¼ in (2–3cm) long.

Identification: Young trees have a cone-like form with widely spaced, level, slender branches, upcurved at the tips. Old trees become columnar with flat tops and branches that sweep down. Leading shoots have small pinkish-green needles arranged spirally. Needles on main and side shoots are arranged in two flat rows, ½–¾ in (1–2cm) long, dark green above, and speckled with two bands of white stomata on the underside. Male flowers are yellowish-brown; female flowers are green, in separate clusters on the same tree.

Distribution: Found in a narrow coastal band running for approximately 500 miles (800km) from Monterey, California, to the Oregon border.
Height: 328ft (100m)
Shape: Narrowly conical
Evergreen
Pollinated: Wind
Leaf shape: Linear

Left: The fissured, reddish-brown thick, spongy bark acts as a fire-resistant blanket.

Giant Redwood

Sequoiadendron giganteum

Distribution: Restricted to 72 groves on the western slopes of the Sierra Nevada, California.
Height: 262ft (80m)
Shape: Narrowly conical
Evergreen
Pollinated: Wind
Leaf shape: Linear

Right: The trunk of a redwood may grow to more than 10ft (3m) in diameter.

The largest living thing in the world is a giant redwood called "General Sherman," which is estimated to weigh 5,440 tons. Some giant redwoods live up to 3,500 years. They thrive in any soil, site or exposure with a moderate supply of moisture, but do not grow well in heavy shade. The bark is red-brown, soft, thick and fibrous.

Left: Needles and cones.

Identification: The crown of the tree is conical, becoming broad in old age. The leaves grow to ⅛ in (8mm), and are sharp-pointed with spreading tips. They are matt gray-green at first, covered with stomata, and turn a dark, shiny green after three years. When crushed, the foliage emits a fragrance of aniseed. The male flowers are yellowish-white ovoid, held at the end of minor shoots, and shed pollen in early spring. The female flowers are green, and develop into bunches of green ovoid cones, which ripen to brown in their second year.

Swamp Cypress

Bald cypress *Taxodium distichum*

Also known as the bald cypress because of its deciduous habit, this tree grows naturally in wet conditions and can tolerate having its roots submerged for several months. In these conditions it will produce aerial roots known as "knees" or "pneumatophores," which provide oxygen to the roots. An excellent tree for color; the leaves turn from old gold to brick red in early to mid-fall.

Right: Autumn needles.

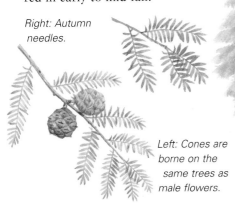

Left: Cones are borne on the same trees as male flowers.

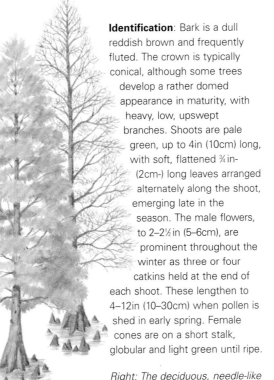

Identification: Bark is a dull reddish brown and frequently fluted. The crown is typically conical, although some trees develop a rather domed appearance in maturity, with heavy, low, upswept branches. Shoots are pale green, up to 4in (10cm) long, with soft, flattened ¾in- (2cm-) long leaves arranged alternately along the shoot, emerging late in the season. The male flowers, to 2–2½in (5–6cm), are prominent throughout the winter as three or four catkins held at the end of each shoot. These lengthen to 4–12in (10–30cm) when pollen is shed in early spring. Female cones are on a short stalk, globular and light green until ripe.

Right: The deciduous, needle-like foliage turns red in autumn.

Distribution: Southeastern U.S.A.: from Delaware to Texas and Missouri.
Height: 130ft (40m)
Shape: Broadly conical
Deciduous
Pollinated: Wind
Leaf shape: Linear

OTHER SPECIES OF NOTE

Pond Cypress
Taxodium ascendens
This broadly conical tree from the southeastern U.S.A. reaches 130ft (40m) tall. It has linear leaves ½in (1cm) long, which are closely pressed around upright, deciduous shoots. The bark is red-brown, thick and heavily fluted. Male flowers are yellow-green, and held in catkins up to 8in (20cm) long. Female flowers are green and appear in clusters at the base of the male catkins. The fruit is a green globular cone, which will not exceed 1¼in (3cm) across.

Chinese Swamp Cypress
Glyptostrobus pensilis
This small tree seldom reaches more than 33ft (10m). It originates from southeast China and grows wild in swamps and along riverbanks. It is rare in the wild. It has linear, scale-like leaves, ⅔in (1.5cm) long, arranged spirally on deciduous side shoots. The bark is gray-brown and the flowers insignificant. The fruit is an egg-shape green cone, to 1in (2.5cm) long. This fairly tender tree does not thrive in northern Europe, where the temperatures will dive too low.

Dawn Redwood

Metasequoia glyptostroboides

Until this beautiful tree was discovered growing in east Szechwan by Chinese botanist T. Kan in 1941, it had only been seen as a fossil and was deemed extinct. It was introduced to the West in 1948. Since then it has become a popular species for ornamental planting. It has bright orange-brown stringy bark, and the trunk is quite often fluted.

Identification: The crown is conical in most trees. When grown in the open, the crown is dense, but in shade it becomes sparse. The leaves are down-curved at the tips, ¾in (2cm) long, bright green above with a pale band each side of the midrib below. Male flowers are ovoid, and set on panicles, which are up to 10in (25cm) long. The female cone is green ripening to brown, and ¾in (2cm) across with stalks ¾in (2cm) long.

Distribution China: The Shui-sha valley, in the northwest part of Hueph Province and into Szechwan Province. U.S.A. zone 4.
Height: 130ft (40m)
Shape: Narrowly conical
Deciduous
Pollinated: Wind
Leaf shape: Linear

Below: The leaves are positioned opposite each other on the shoot.

TRUE CEDARS AND HEMLOCKS

Although there are only four true cedars, they are without doubt the real stars of the coniferous world. Nothing can touch them for sheer majesty and dignity. Three are clustered around the Mediterranean and the fourth makes it a little further east into the Himalayas. The hemlocks, on the other hand, are all to be found in either North America or Asia.

Eastern Hemlock

Tsuga canadensis

Otherwise known as the Canada hemlock, this beautiful, tall, fast-growing tree is common in parks and gardens throughout North America. On the northern plains it makes a broad and strongly branched tree, but in the mountain valleys to the south it is far more slender and conical. There is an ancient wood of eastern hemlocks on one of the hills in the Arnold Arboretum near Boston, Massachusetts. Some of the trees in the wood have girths over 10ft (3m).

Identification: The bark is purple-gray, smooth when juvenile becoming fissured with scaly ridges in maturity. The male flowers are yellow, and the female flowers small green cones which are borne at the shoot tip. Both are found on the same tree. The fruit is a small, pale fawn, oval hanging cone, up to 1in (2.5cm) long.

Distribution: Eastern U.S.A. from Nova Scotia south to Alabama and Georgia.
Height: 100ft (30m)
Shape: Broadly conical
Evergreen
Pollinated: Wind
Leaf shape: Linear

Left: The fruit is a cone, to 1in (2.5cm) long, and may contain up to 50 tiny winged seeds.

Right: The linear leaves are ½in (1.2cm) long, dark glossy green above, with two white stomatal bands on the underside.

Cedar of Lebanon

Cedrus libani

This large, stately tree is probably the best known of all the cedars. It has been revered for thousands of years. In biblical times it stood as a symbol for fertility. King Solomon is believed to have built his temple out of its lumber. On Mount Lebanon it grows at altitudes up to 7,021ft (2,140m). Although in the wild, numbers are decreasing, it has been widely planted as an ornamental tree in parks, gardens and arboreta in Britain and North America.

Identification: The bark is dull brown with even, shallow fissures. For the first 40 years of its life, cedar of Lebanon is a narrow, conical tree; thereafter it broadens rapidly with long level branches which seem, in some cases, to defy gravity: such is their length. The needles are gray-blue to dark green (depending on the provenance of the individual tree), 1¼in (3cm) long and grow in dense whorls on side shoots and singly on fast-growing main shoots. The cone is barrel-shaped, erect, gray-green and matures to purplish brown.

Distribution: Mount Lebanon, Syria and the Taurus Mountains in southeast Turkey. U.S.A. zones 6–8.
Height: 130ft (40m)
Shape: Broadly columnar
Evergreen
Pollinated: Wind
Leaf shape: Linear

Right: Cones are 4¾in (12cm) long.

Atlantic Cedar
Cedrus atlantica
Also known as the Atlas cedar after the mountain range where it originates. It is the fastest growing of all the cedars reaching 10ft (3m) in less than seven years. It is also the straightest, maintaining its leading stem into old age. The form 'Glauca' is far more widely planted, in arboreta, than the true species because of its strikingly beautiful silvery blue foliage.

Cyprus Cedar *Cedrus brevifolia*
The tree is confined to forests surrounding Mount Paphos in Cyprus. At one time considered a form of Lebanon cedar, it is now treated as a separate species. It does not look much like Lebanon cedar as it maintains a single stem, has shorter needles, a more open habit and, from a distance, has a yellow-green crown. In the U.S.A it grows in arboreta and parks.

Deodar *Cedrus deodara*
This beautiful large tree is commonly planted as an ornamental along the Gulf Coast into Texas and along the Mississippi Valley. It is also grown in the west around Vancouver and in California. It has blue-gray foliage which turns dark green with age. The overall shape is at first narrowly conical becoming broad in maturity. It is easily distinguished from other cedars by the way that the ends of the branches droop down.

Western Hemlock

Tsuga heterophylla

This tall, elegant tree has weeping branches and soft pendulous foliage. However, this softness is deceptive; western hemlock is as hardy as any conifer. It thrives in the Rockies up to 6,000ft (1,830m) above sea level and is extremely shade-tolerant, out-growing its competitors in the thickest forest.

Distribution: West coast U.S.A. from Alaska to California.
Height: 200ft (60m)
Shape: Narrowly conical
Evergreen
Pollinated: Wind
Leaf shape: Linear

Identification: Bark is reddish-purple in young trees, becoming dark purple-brown with age. The tree has a narrow conical shape, with ascending branches that arch gently downwards towards the tip. The leading shoot is always lax. Needles are ¾in (2cm) long, deep dark green above with two broad blue-white stomatal bands beneath. New growth is bright lime green in spring, contrasting dramatically against the rather sombre mature foliage. Male and female flowers are red. Much pollen is shed in late spring. Cones are pendulous, egg-shaped, 1in (2.5cm) long, with few scales, and are pale green ripening to deep brown.

Left and below: Small egg-shaped cones appear in late summer at the tips of branches.

Mountain Hemlock

Tsuga mertensiana

Native to the west coast of America from Alaska to California, this handsome tree has a columnar crown of gray pendulous foliage. The mountain hemlock is sometimes mistaken for *Cedrus atlantica* 'Glauca', as it has thick blue-gray needles, which radiate all around the shoot.

Identification: The bark is dark orange-brown, becoming vertically fissured into rectangular flakes in maturity. The branches are slightly drooping with weeping branchlets hanging from them. The shoot is a shiny pale brown color. The needles are similar to a cedar's, ¾in (1.5cm) long, dark gray-green to blue-gray, and are borne radially all over the shoot. The cone is spruce-like, 2¾ in- (7cm-) long, cylindrical and buff pink maturing to brown. Male flowers are violet-purple and borne on slender drooping stems. The female flowers are erect and have dark purple and yellow-green bracts.

Below: Cones before and after opening.

Distribution: Alaska to California, U.S.A.
Height: 100ft (30m)
Shape: Columnar
Evergreen
Pollinated: Wind
Leaf shape: Linear

Left: The needles have a definite bluish tinge to them and radiate out from the twigs. From their ends, shoots appear star-like.

TRUE FIRS

The term "fir" has become a general description for anything vaguely coniferous-looking. In reality this is erroneous; the true, or silver, firs are a select band of conifers botanically linked within the genus Abies. They include some of the finest conifers and nine of the best are found in North America. They range across the continent, from the balsam firs of Canada to the Santa Lucia firs of California.

Noble Fir

Abies procera

This is a superb species which truly deserves its name. It has a stately, noble appearance with a long, straight stem and large cones that stand proudly above the surrounding foliage. It is particularly hardy, growing at up to 4,921ft (1,500m) in the Cascade Mountains, U.S.A. Noble fir has been planted widely outside its natural range for its timber, which is light brown, close-grained and very strong.

Identification: The bark is silvery-gray, smooth and has occasional resin blisters. Young trees are conical, with widely spaced whorls of branches. Older trees become flat-topped, with characteristic twisted, dead branches. Needles are gray-green above with two distinct white stomata bands on the underside. They are strongly parted on the shoot, curving upwards and then down. Needles on top of the shoot are ½in (1cm) long; beneath the shoot, they are 1½in (3.5cm) long. When crushed, they emit a pungent smell, like cat's urine. Cones are broad cylinders up to 10in (25cm) long, and are held erect from the branch.

Above: Cones are normally confined to the topmost branches.

Below: Male flowers are clustered beneath the shoot in spring.

Right: Female flowers are upright on the shoot.

Distribution: Cascade Mountains of Oregon, Washington State and northern California, U.S.A.
Height: 262ft (80m)
Shape: Narrowly conical
Evergreen
Pollinated: Wind
Leaf shape: Linear

Santa Lucia Fir

Bristlecone fir *Abies bracteata*

Sometimes known as the bristlecone fir because of the long bristle attached to each cone scale, this west coast species is the rarest native North American fir. It is only found growing naturally in the bottom of a few rocky canyons. It is rare in the wild and in cultivation. Although relatively hardy, it has not been widely planted. In 1852 it was introduced to Europe by William Lobb.

Above: New needles often have a purple tinge to them.

Identification: Bark on young trees is dark gray with wrinkles and black lines around branch knots. Older trees develop black or purple-black bark with deep cracks. The shape is broad at the base, narrowing rapidly to a long, conical crown. Branches tend to fan out and droop towards their tips. Needles are strongly parted each side of the shoot. They are forward pointing, up to 2in (5cm) long with a sharp tip, dull green above and have two bright white bands beneath. Cones are found on the topmost branches, like candles. Each cone scale has a long bristle, giving it a very distinctive appearance. Cones normally disintegrate on the tree.

Distribution: Santa Lucia Mountains, southern California, U.S.A.
Height: 115ft (35m)
Shape: Narrowly conical
Evergreen
Pollinated: Wind
Leaf shape: Linear

Left: The cone has hair-like protrusions, giving it a very scruffy appearance.

OTHER SPECIES OF NOTE

Alpine Fir *Abies lasiocarpa*
Native to mountain terrain from Alaska to northern Arizona, the Alpine fir is rare in the wild. It is a tall, slender tree, which looks at home on the snow-covered mountain slopes. The alpine fir is characterized by a dense covering of needles, all pointing forwards on the shoot. They are 1in (2.5cm) long, shiny gray-green above, with two narrow white stomatal bands beneath.

Pacific Fir *Abies amabilis*
Found along the Pacific coast from California to Alaska, this is a luxuriant-looking, tall, spire-like tree with dense foliage. Needles sweep flat on each side of the shoot and are dusty gray-blue when young, maturing to glossy rich green. When crushed they emit a strong fragrance of tangerines. The upright cone is cylindrical and up to 6in (15cm) long.

Low's Fir *Abies concolor* var. *lowiana*
This hardy, fast-growing tree is an intermediate between grand fir, *A. grandis*, and Colorado white fir, *A. concolor*. It grows wild from mid-Oregon to the south of the Sierra Nevada. It has, however, been planted commercially as far north and east as Boston. The needle-like leaves are blue-gray, up to 1½in (4cm) long, parted on the shoot and rising at 45 degrees, creating a V-shaped gap along the top of the shoot. It has gray, corky and fissured bark in maturity. In cultivation it may be confused with *A. concolor* but can be distinguished by its shorter needles.

Grand Fir

Giant fir *Abies grandis*

This silver fir is one of the true giants of North American coniferous forests. Before deforestation took its toll, many grand firs exceeded 300ft (90m) in height. It is an extremely fast-growing tree, attaining 160ft (50m) within 100 years. It was first discovered by the plant collector Douglas on the Columbia River in 1825.

Identification: When young the bark is olive-brown, smooth but pockmarked with resin blisters. In maturity the bark fades to silver-gray and the base of the trunk become fissured. The needle-like leaves are 2in (5cm) long, glossy deep green above and silver gray beneath. They are parted uniformly at each side of the shoot, and when crushed have a scent of oranges. The male flowers are reddish-yellow, and the female, greenish-yellow, borne in clusters on the same tree in spring.

Distribution: North of Vancouver Island, through British Columbia and south to Navarro River, California, U.S.A.
Height: 200ft (60m)
Shape: Narrowly conical
Evergreen
Pollinated: Wind
Leaf Shape: Linear

Right: Female flowers.

Below: The light brown cone, which is 4in (10cm) and cylindrical, stands upright towards the top of the tree.

Red Fir

Abies magnifica

This is a tree of the high mountains, where snow lies for months on end before being followed by long periods of summer drought. It is named after the red color of its bark, but the botanical name *magnifica* is more appropriate, because this truly is a magnificent species. Its short, regularly spaced, horizontal branches create perfect symmetry.

Identification: Bark, even on relatively young trees, is thick, corky and has deep fissures. Overall, red fir has a very regular shape, keeping its neat, conical appearance into old age. The needles are almost round in cross-section, 1⅓in (3.5cm) long, wide-spreading, and curving back in towards the shoot at the tips. They are dark gray-green in color with two lighter bands of stomata on both the upper and lower surfaces. The upright cones are seldom seen, growing right at the top of the tree and disintegrating *in situ*. They grow up to 8in (20cm) long, are barrel-shaped, smooth and golden green.

Above: Upright cones are borne at the top of the tree.

Distribution: Cascade Mountains of Oregon, Mount Shasta and Sierra Nevada, California, U.S.A.
Height: 130ft (40m)
Shape: Narrowly conical
Evergreen
Pollinated: Wind
Leaf shape: Linear

Left: Male cones are purple-red and appear in spring.

Balsam Fir

Abies balsamea

A common tree in North America and one of the most important in northern U.S.A and Canada. It is probably the most resinous of all the silver firs and a popular choice for Christmas trees. It has an average lifespan of 200 years. Large blisters of resin occur under the bark, and the foliage needs only to be touched to release its fragrant balsam scent, which is valued by aromatherapists. This tree is the main source of Canada balsam, which is used for mounting microscopic specimens. It is a hardy tree, growing well inside the Arctic Circle, and at altitudes in excess of 4,000ft (1,220m).

Below: Upright purple-brown cones are normally covered with sticky white resin.

Identification: The bark is dark gray, smooth at first except for resin blisters, but becoming heavily and vertically fissured in maturity. The narrow needle-like leaves are 1in (2.5cm) long, dark green above, with a triangular, white patch of stomata near the tip, and two silver-gray bands beneath. They are parted on the shoot. The upright, purple-brown, pointed cones are up to 4in (10cm) long. They are normally coated in silver sticky resin, and borne on the topmost branches from where they disintegrate upon ripening.

Distribution: Eastern Canada and U.S.A. from Newfoundland to Virginia.
Height: 65ft (20m)
Shape: Narrowly conical
Evergreen
Pollinated: Wind
Leaf shape: Linear

Right: The branches of balsam fir are dense, and the needles are dark green. At ground level in open spaces live branches may thrive. In forests low branches dieback.

Fraser's Fir

Abies fraseri

Distribution: Virginia, North Carolina and East Tennessee, U.S.A.
Height: 65ft (20m)
Shape: Narrowly conical
Evergreen
Pollinated: Wind
Leaf Shape: Linear

Right: Narrow, needle-like leaves are dark green above and banded silver-gray beneath. The needles spread out each side of the shoot in two distinct ranks.

This hardy, handsome, symmetrical tree is common in the Great Smoky Mountains, where it grows at altitudes in excess of 6,500ft (2,000m), but has a limited natural range elsewhere. It is planted widely as an ornamental in parks and arboreta, and in recent years has found favor in the UK as a Christmas tree. It was identified by John Fraser in 1811 and named in his honor in 1817.

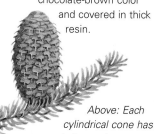

Identification: The bark is a rich brown color when young, becoming pink-gray in maturity and covered in resin-blisters. The needle-like leaves are dark green above and silvery white beneath, spreading out in two distinct ranks at each side of the shoot. They are ¾in (1.5cm) long and broadest near the blunt notched tip. The upright cylindrical cones are 2¼in (5.5cm) long, dark purple, with pale brown bracts between each scale. The winter buds are distinctive, being a deep chocolate-brown color and covered in thick resin.

Above: Each cylindrical cone has pale brown bracts between each scale.

Vejar Fir

Abies vejari

In the wild this is a rare mountain species, found mainly in the Mexican state of Tamaulipas, where it grows up to elevations around 10,000ft (3,000m), in mixed forests, with *Pinus hartwegii* and *P. rudis*. It is closely related to sacred fir, *Abies religiosa*, but differs in having irregularly arranged leaves, and shorter, squatter cones. Vejar fir was identified and named by Martinez in 1942. It is infrequently found in cultivation in arboreta and botanic gardens.

Distribution: Northeast Mexico, U.S.A.
Height: 100ft (30m)
Shape: Broadly conical
Evergreen
Pollinated: Wind
Leaf shape: Linear

Identification: The needle-like leaves are forward-pointing, and borne all around the pale orange shoots. They are 1in (2.5cm) long, slightly grooved down the center and tapering to a fine yellow point. They are dark blue-green above, with two lines of blue-white stomata beneath. As they twist forward some of the leaf underside points upwards. The barrel-shape cones are purple-black and covered in specks of hard white resin. On individual trees cone size may vary from 2–6in (5–15cm) in length.

Below: Each needle-like leaf is forward-pointing and borne on pale orange shoots.

Left: The barrel-shape cone stands upright.

OTHER SPECIES OF NOTE

European Silver Fir *Abies alba*
This is the native silver fir of central Europe, particularly France, Switzerland and Germany where it can attain heights in excess of 130ft (40m). It is a handsome tree, with glossy dark green needles, which have two distinctive white bands of stomata beneath. It is widely planted in parks and gardens right across temperate regions of the world, including North America. The silver fir is commonly used as a Christmas tree in many parts of Europe.

Abies oaxacana
This rare Mexican species is found in only a few locations in the western Sierra Madre Mountains of central Mexico, where it grows up to elevations of 6,500ft (2,000m). It is fairly tender, and consequently is only found as an ornamental species in botanical collections in California, Texas, and other southern states through to Florida. It is a medium-size tree, with conspicuous orange shoots, which contrast well with its dark green, needle-like leaves.

Corkbark Fir *Abies lasiocarpa* var. *arizonica*
This beautiful, narrow, spire-shape tree is a variety of the alpine fir, *A. lasiocarpa*. It grows wild in the Colorado Rocky Mountains, south into Arizona. It grows at high altitudes above the snowline, and has adapted to these conditions by producing a spire-like crown that does not allow snow to lie heavily upon the branches and break them—it simply slides off the sides to the ground. It appropriately takes its name from the fawn-colored, thick corky bark.

Sacred Fir

Mexican fir *Abies religiosa*

Otherwise known as the Mexican fir, this tender species is common in the mountains of central Mexico, up to altitudes around 10,000ft (3,000m). In Mexico, its branches are used during religious festivals as decoration around mission halls. Outside Central America the sacred fir is relatively uncommon in cultivation. It has foliage and buds that look similar to the Douglas fir, *Pseudotsuga menziesii*, and the lower branches have a tendency to sweep down to the ground.

Distribution: Central and southern Mexico and northern Guatemala, U.S.A.
Height: 100ft (30m)
Shape: Broadly conical
Evergreen
Pollinated: Wind
Leaf shape: Linear

Identification: The bark is smooth and gray when young, becoming rough and scaly in maturity. The 1in (2.5cm) needles have two silver bands of stomata beneath. Leaves on the lower side of the shoot spread horizontally; those on the upper side point up and forward. The cones are 4–6in (10–15cm) long, barrel-shaped, purple-black, with distinctive reflexed tips to each cone scale, from which blue-black bracts protrude.

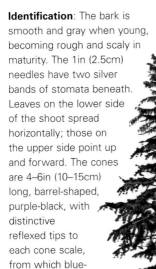

Right: The needle-like leaves are dark glossy green above.

Below: As the cone ripens it turns chestnut-brown.

FALSE FIRS AND CEDARS

A group of ancient conifers belonging to the Pinaceae and Taxodiaceae families. The origins of all lay in the Jurassic period, 208–144 million years ago. Today, the Douglas fir and the Japanese red cedar are planted in their millions around the world for timber production. The others are scarcely seen outside botanical collections.

Japanese Red Cedar

Cryptomeria japonica

Distribution: Found in Japan in Honshu, Shikuka and Kyushu. It also grows in Chekiang and Fukien provinces in China. U.S.A. zones 5–9.
Height: 100ft (30m)
Shape: Broadly conical
Evergreen
Pollinated: Wind
Leaf shape: Linear

This stately conifer produces a large, straight trunk which tapers quickly from a broad base above the roots. It has reddish-brown bark which is soft, fibrous and peels off, hanging in long strips from the trunk. This tree has been extensively planted throughout Japan and China for its timber, which is strong, light and pink-brown. In the U.S.A. it grows at heights of 3,600–8,200ft (1,100–2,500m).

Identification: The crown is narrow when young, broadening with age. Often the heavy branches sweep downwards before ascending at the tips. The foliage consists of bright green branchlets covered with hard, forward-facing needles ⅔in (1.5cm) long. Male flowers are yellowish-brown, ovoid, and clustered along the final ½in (1cm) of each branchlet. They are bright yellow when ripe. Female flowers are green rosettes and are on the same tree as male flowers. Cones are globular, ¾in (2cm) across, and held on upright, stiff stalks.

Above: Branches occasionally touch the ground, causing layering.

Right: At the base of each needle is a protruding keel that runs down the branchlet.

Rocky Mountain Fir

Pseudotsuga menziesii var. *glauca*

This medium-size tree is the form of Douglas fir that grows away from the coast in the Rocky Mountains up to altitudes around 10,000ft (3,000m). It is hardier than the species, and more tolerant on soils with a high lime content. It is easily distinguished from the species by its glaucous-blue foliage, and the fact that when the foliage is crushed it emits the odor of paint thinner. The Rocky Mountain fir is widely grown as an ornamental in parks and gardens across the U.S.A.

Above: Rocky Mountain fir has rigid blue needles which are held at right-angles to the shoot.

Distribution: Eastern crests of the Rocky Mountains from Montana to New Mexico.
Height: 80ft (25m)
Shape: Narrowly conical
Evergreen
Pollinated: Wind
Leaf shape: Linear

Identification: The bark is black-brown and extremely rough, even when young. The blue needle-like leaves are shorter and stouter than the species, up to 1in (2.5cm) long, and stand proud from the shoot. The female flowers are bright red, while those of the Douglas fir are greenish-pink. The copper-colored cones are smaller than the species, less than 3in (7.5cm) long, with trident-shape, protruding bracts, which curve outwards from the cone.

Right: The cones are distinctive by their trident-shaped bracts which protrude from beneath each cone scale.

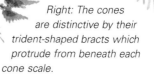

Bigcone Douglas Fir

Pseudotsuga macrocarpa

This is the only Douglas fir with sharp, rigid, spine-tipped leaves. It grows wild on steep, rocky mountain slopes, up to altitudes around 6,500ft (2,000m), from the Santa Inez Mountains to the San Bernardino Mountains, and south to the Mexican border. It has a broad crown with sparse, long horizontal branches from which the foliage weeps. There are many forest fires in this part of the world and this tree has adapted to this by producing thick corky bark that is reasonably fire-resistant.

Left: The winged seed is contained beneath each large rounded cone scale and released when the cone matures in late winter.

Identification: The bark is heavily fissured, with the old bark showing gray, and that more recently exposed, pinky-brown. The needle-like leaves are dark blue-gray, up to 3in (7.5cm) long, and arranged in two neat ranks on each side of the reddish-brown shoot. Male flowers are orange-red, female's green-red, and both appear in spring on the same tree. The trident-shaped bract is present, as with all Douglas fir's, but not nearly so obvious on this species.

Right: As the name suggests the cone is large—the largest in the genus—up to 18cm (7in) long.

Distribution: Southern California, U.S.A.
Height: 80ft (25m)
Shape: Broadly conical
Evergreen
Pollinated: Wind
Leaf shape: Linear

Douglas Fir

Pseudotsuga menziesii

Distribution: Northwest Pacific Seaboard, from Mexico through U.S.A. to Canada including Vancouver Island.
Height: 250ft (75m)
Shape: Narrowly conical
Evergreen
Pollinated: Wind
Leaf shape: Linear

Below: Cones have bracts that project from each scale.

Douglas fir is commercially one of the most important timber-producing trees in the world. It has been planted throughout North America, Europe, Australia and New Zealand. It is a huge tree, attaining heights in excess of 250ft (75m). Quite often there is no branching for the first 110ft (33m). The bark is corky and deeply fissured in maturity; young trees have smooth, shiny gray-brown bark that is pockmarked with resin blisters.

Identification: When young this majestic tree is slender, regularly conical, with whorls of light, ascending branches. In old age it becomes flat-topped with heavy branches high up in the crown. Needles are linear to 1¼in (3cm) long, rounded at the tip. They are rich green with distinctive white banding beneath, and arranged spirally on the shoot. When crushed the foliage emits a sweet citrus aroma. Male flowers are yellow, and grow on the underside of the shoot. Female flowers are green, flushed pink to purple at the tip, and grow in separate clusters on the same tree. The fruit is a hanging cone up to 4in (10cm) long, green, ripening to orange-brown, with distinctive three-pronged bracts.

TWO- AND THREE-NEEDLED PINES

There are over 100 different pine species in the world, and almost half are native to North America and Mexico. They naturally divide into west-coast pines, central and east-coast pines, and southern pines. North American pines include the oldest and some of the biggest trees in the world. Many are important timber-producing trees, and some have provided food for Native Americans for centuries.

Monterey Pine

Pinus radiata

Distribution: Californian coast around the Monterey Peninsula, U.S.A.
Height: 100ft (30m)
Shape: Broadly conical
Evergreen
Pollinated: Wind
Leaf shape: Linear

Right: Needles are held in threes, are shining dark green and are 4–6in (10–15cm) long.

The Monterey pine is a Californian coastal species with a very limited range. It is seldom found growing wild more than 6 miles (10km) from the coast. Discovered by the plant collector David Douglas in 1833, it has become one of the most widely planted trees for timber production in the world. In New Zealand it makes up more than 60 percent of all conifers growing there, and covers more than 1 million acres (400,000ha).

Above: Cones may persist on the tree for up to 30 years.

Identification: The bark is dark gray and deeply fissured in old age. Young trees are conical, with sharply ascending branches. Older trees develop a large domed crown, which looks black from a distance. The male flowers are bright yellow and shed copious amounts of pollen in early spring. The cone is reddish brown with dark gray scale centers. It is roughly ovoid in shape, up to 4in (10cm) across and held on a curved stalk ½in (1cm) long. Large, irregular scales tend to distort its overall shape.

Western Yellow Pine

Pinus ponderosa

The natural range of this pine is vast, stretching from the Pacific coast to elevations of 9,000ft (2,750m) in the Rocky Mountains in Colorado. It is planted as an ornamental species in large parks and gardens because of its attractive bark, fast growth and yellow leading shoots.

Identification: The bark is pale purple-gray, flaking to reveal attractive yellow, red and cinnamon-colored bark beneath. As a young tree, it is narrow with strongly ascending branches. Older trees develop an irregular crown with several large, horizontal branches and dense foliage. The shoot is stout, bright yellow-brown and has clusters of needles, held in threes, along its length. The needles are up to 10in (25cm) long, dark gray-green and all face forward. Male flowers are dark purple and female flowers red. Both occur on the same tree. The cone is egg-shaped, up to 4in (10cm) long, glossy reddish-brown and has a hard spiny tip to each scale.

Above: Older trees often have an irregular clumped crown.

Distribution: North America, from British Columbia to Mexico.
Height: 165ft (50m)
Shape: Broadly conical
Evergreen
Pollinated: Wind
Leaf shape: Linear

Left: The needles are extremely long, each measuring up to 10in (25cm) from base to tip.

Lodgepole pine

Shore pine, Beach pine *Pinus contorta* var. *latifolia*

The lodgepole pine is so called because it was used by native Americans to support their lodges. This prolific pine is not only common in the wild but has also been extensively planted in forests as a lumber-producing tree. There are four different varieties of lodgepole pine. *Latifolia* is the true lodgepole pine, and is the pine of the Yellowstone Park geyser-basins and gorge. The natural range of the coastal form, *P. contorta* var. *contorta*, is along the Pacific coast in a belt about 100 miles (160km) broad, from the Alaska Panhandle to Point Arena in California.

Left: Each cone scale bears a blunt spine up to ¼in (5mm) long.

Identification: The bark is dark reddish-brown and deeply fissured into dark plates. Young trees have a broad bushy base with upswept branches and quite often swept stems. The needle-like, twisted leaves are held in twos and are 2in (5cm) long. Needle color varies along its natural range, from dull, deep green in Oregon and California, to bright yellow-green further north. The cone is pale brown, 2in (5cm) long and points backwards along the shoot.

Distribution: Rocky Mountains from Alaska to California.
Height: 100ft (30m)
Shape: Broadly conical
Evergreen
Pollinated: Wind
Leaf shape: Linear

OTHER SPECIES OF NOTE

Scots Pine *Pinus sylvestris*
Although not native to North America, Scots pine is commonly planted from Quebec to Virginia, and from Saskatchewan to Iowa. It is popular as a Christmas tree. It has bright orange-red bark in maturity, which extends to the branches, where it peels and flakes. The needle-like leaves are borne in twos. They are stiff, twisted, bluish-green, set in an orange-brown basal sheath, and up to 2¾in (7cm) long. Although relatively slow growing it can attain heights around 115ft (35m).

Jack Pine *Pinus banksiana*
This tree, to 90ft (27m), has a natural range which extends from the Yukon to Nova Scotia and south to New Hampshire. It grows further north than any other North American conifer. Jack pine grows extremely well on poor, impoverished soils and will be one of the first tree species to colonize sites of forest fires. The rigid, dark green, twisted, needle-like leaves are borne in twos and are 1½in (4cm) long. The 2in- (5cm-) long cones have a characteristic sweep at the tip and point forward along the shoot.

Knobcone Pine *Pinus attenuata*
Native from Oregon south through California to the Mexican state of Baja California, this medium-size tree, to 65ft (20m), has bright grass-green, needle-like leaves which are borne in threes and are up to 6in (15cm) long. It has upward sweeping branches, which are covered in slender, conical, gray-brown cones that are up to 6in (15cm) long and can remain on the tree for years.

Big-Cone Pine

Pinus coulteri

As the name suggests, this pine produces just about the biggest cone of any pine. They may be up to 12in (30cm) long and weigh over 4½lbs (2kg). Once mature and having released their seed, they may remain on the tree for up to ten years. The seeds are edible and were once considered a delicacy by Native Americans. The botanical name refers to Dr Coulter who in 1831 identified big-cone pine.

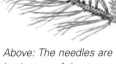

Above: The needles are in clusters of three.

Below: The large cones have hooked spines to the ends of each scale.

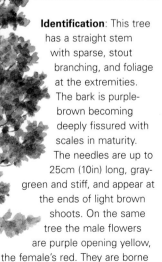

Distribution: Southern California and northwestern Mexico.
Height: 80ft (25m)
Shape: Broadly spreading
Evergreen
Pollinated: Wind
Leaf shape: Linear

Identification: This tree has a straight stem with sparse, stout branching, and foliage at the extremities. The bark is purple-brown becoming deeply fissured with scales in maturity. The needles are up to 25cm (10in) long, gray-green and stiff, and appear at the ends of light brown shoots. On the same tree the male flowers are purple opening yellow, the female's red. They are borne in separate clusters in late spring.

Slash Pine

Swamp pine *Pinus elliottii*

Otherwise known as the swamp pine, this broad, columnar, dark tree inhabits low-lying country on the coastal plains of the Florida Keys. It is also native to the Bahamas, Honduras and eastern Guatemala. It has a tall, tapering trunk, heavy, horizontal branches and, in maturity, a handsome round-topped head. It is much favored for its timber which is extremely hard and durable, being used in construction, and for railroad crossties.

Identification: The bark is smooth orange-brown when young, separating into large, thin scales in maturity. The needle-like leaves are dark green, lustrous, with several bands of silver stomata on both sides. They are 8–12in (20–30cm) long and borne in clusters of three (occasionally two). When crushed, they emit a strong lemon scent. The male flowers are dark purple, the female's pink. Both appear in early spring in separate, short, crowded clusters on the same tree. The ovoid, lustrous rich brown cone is up to 6in (15cm). Each cone scale carries a hard spine.

Distribution: Coast of South Carolina, through Florida to Louisiana, U.S.A.
Height: 100ft (30m)
Shape: Broadly columnar
Evergreen
Pollinated: Wind
Leaf shape: Linear

Left: The slash pine has an open crown.

Right: Large shiny-brown cones carry a hard spine on each scale.

Shortleaf Pine

Pinus echinata

Distribution: Eastern U.S.A. from New York state south to Florida and east Texas.
Height: 100ft (30m)
Shape: Broadly conical
Evergreen
Pollinated: Wind
Leaf shape: Linear

This valuable timber tree is native to 21 American states. It is immediately recognizable by the way the needle-like leaves seem to sprout from everywhere on the tree, including the main branches, and sometimes the trunk. It is rarely seen planted in parks and gardens in North America or elsewhere in the world, for that matter, even though it was introduced to Europe as early as 1720.

Identification: The bark is a gray pinky-orange becoming scaly and shaggy in maturity. The young shoots (which are brittle) are covered in a distinctive blue-white bloom. Ironically considering its name, the shortleaf pine has needle-like leaves, which can be up to 4in (10cm) long; they are fresh green above, paler beneath, with light bands of stomata. The 2in- (5cm-) long, light brown, almost oblong, cones are borne on a short stalk. Each cone scale bears a short prickly spine—the name echinata means "hedgehog-like."

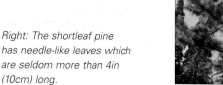

Right: The shortleaf pine has needle-like leaves which are seldom more than 4in (10cm) long.

Left: Each oblong-shaped cone is covered with short prickly spines.

Mexican Pinyon Pine

Pinus cembroides

Distribution: Mexico, Texas, Arizona and California.
Height: 50ft (15m)
Shape: Broadly columnar
Evergreen
Pollinated: Wind
Leaf shape: Linear

Above right: The male flowers are yellow and clustered together towards the tip of the shoot.

Right: As they ripen, the cones turn sandy-brown.

This small bushy tree with a short, quite often twisted trunk, inhabits hot, dry, rocky slopes, particularly in the mountain ranges of central and southern Arizona, where it grows above altitudes of 6,550ft (2,000m). It is probably best known for its edible and tasty seeds that are sold in Mexican markets as "pinones" and elsewhere as "pinyon nuts." It is rare in cultivation.

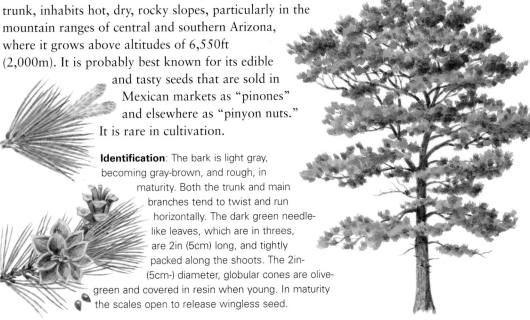

Identification: The bark is light gray, becoming gray-brown, and rough, in maturity. Both the trunk and main branches tend to twist and run horizontally. The dark green needle-like leaves, which are in threes, are 2in (5cm) long, and tightly packed along the shoots. The 2in- (5cm-) diameter, globular cones are olive-green and covered in resin when young. In maturity the scales open to release wingless seed.

OTHER SPECIES OF NOTE

Pitch Pine
Pinus rigida
This hardy, three-needled, medium-size pine grows wild from the northern shores of Lake Ontario south to Georgia. It is distinctive because not only does it have thick, dark yellow-green, 4in- (10cm-) long, rigid needle-like leaves in the main crown, it also has tufts of much finer foliage sprouting from the stem and main branches. The resin of this tree was originally used to make pitch and paint thinner.

Digger Pine *Pinus sabiniana*
Native to the foothills around the Central Valley of California, this light-demanding, medium-size tree has curious, sparse, thin foliage, which gives an almost transparent effect to woodland it grows in. The needle-like leaves are borne in threes, up to 12in (30cm) long, and a pale greenish-gray color.

Gregg Pine *Pinus greggii*
This beautiful rare pine is native to northeast Mexico where it attains heights of up to 100ft (30m). It has bright grass-green, needle-like leaves up to 6in (15cm) long, which are borne in threes, and have a very slight serration along the margins. They feel slightly rough to the skin. Gregg pine has clusters of shiny creamy-brown cones, also up to 6in (15cm) long, which persist on the tree for many years.

Loblolly Pine

Pinus taeda

The loblolly pine is a common tree in southeastern U.S.A., and is quite often seen as a roadside tree. Its timber is valued for construction work and interior joinery, so it is also widely grown in forestry plantations. It is an attractive tree with spreading lower branches, and ascending higher branches, which form a compact, round-topped head. It is sometimes called old field pine because it colonizes disused farmland.

Distribution: Virginia to Texas and south to Florida, U.S.A.
Height: 80ft (25m)
Shape: Broadly conical
Evergreen
Pollinated: Wind
Leaf shape: Linear

Identification: The bark is bright red-brown and irregularly divided by linear fissures, which become scaly in maturity. The shoots are red-brown to pink-yellow, very slender, and covered with pale green to glaucous, stiff, needle-like leaves, up to 6in (15cm) long. The needles are borne in threes and are finely marked on both the upper and lower sides with fine white bands of stomata. Each scale of the cone is armed with a sharp spine.

Below: The gray-brown cones are ovoid, 2–6in (5–15cm) long, and held by short stalks.

FIVE-NEEDLED PINES

Of the 100 different pine species in the world, approximately twenty are five-needled pines and among them are some of the most ornamental of all pines, including the beautiful Mexican white pine, Pinus ayacahuite, *and the Montezuma pine,* Pinus montezumae, *also from Mexico.*

Sugar Pine

Pinus lambertiana

This is the largest pine in the world. It is known, in the past, to have attained heights in excess of 300ft (92m) tall with trunks 20ft (6m) across. It has massive cones, which can be up to 24in (60cm) long. The sugar pine gets its name because of its edible, sugary sap, which was highly prized by native Americans. It has a natural range from the Cascade Mountains down the Sierra Nevada, and across the border into lower California. It thrives in mixed conifer forests. It was discovered in 1826 by David Douglas.

Identification: Young bark is thin, smooth and brown-gray, maturing to orange-pink, with fine fissures. Dried white resin trails are often a feature of the bark. The needle-like leaves are borne in clusters of fives, they are up to 4in (10cm) long, bluish-green and faintly serrated at the margins. Magnificent golden brown cones hang down from the ends of the uppermost branches. They contain 1in- (2.5cm-) long winged seeds, which are edible.

Left: This is the largest pine in the world, reaching heights in excess of 300ft (92m).

Distribution: From Oregon to Baja California.
Height: 235ft (73m)
Shape: Broadly conical
Evergreen
Pollinated: Wind
Leaf shape:
Linear

Right: Each cone may be up to 24in (60cm) long and contains large, edible seeds.

Eastern White Pine

Weymouth pine *Pinus strobus*

Known elsewhere as the Weymouth pine, this is the largest conifer, and the only five-needled pine to grow east of the Rocky Mountains. It was, for many years, one of the U.S.A.'s main timber-producing trees, reliably producing long, straight stems, which were originally used to make ships' masts. It is prone to attack by a fungus that causes the fatal disease known as white pine blister rust.

Distribution: Eastern North America from Newfoundland south to Georgia.
Height: 225ft (70m)
Shape: Narrowly conical
Evergreen
Pollinated: Wind
Leaf shape: Linear

Right: Weymouth Pine cones are pale brown and up to 6in (15cm) long.

Identification: The bark is dark gray and smooth becoming deeply fissured in maturity. The slender, needle-like leaves are up to 4¾in (12cm) long, borne in clusters of fives, blue-green above and silver-gray beneath. Male flowers are yellow; female pink, borne in separate clusters on the same tree in late spring. The eastern white pine has pale brown, hanging, cylindrical cones, which are up to 6in (15cm) long, often curved like a banana, and covered with a sticky white resin.

Left: Slender needles, clustered in fives, may be up to 4¾in (12cm) long.

Montezuma Pine

Pinus montezumae

This pine is named after the early sixteenth-century Aztec emperor, Montezuma II. It is a very variable tree with several different forms, all extremely attractive, mainly because of its long, distinctive foliage. It is a fairly tender species, only surviving in the mildest regions of North America and Great Britain.

Identification: The Montezuma pine has pinkish-gray, rough bark with wide, brownish, vertical fissures, leaving ridges, which are cracked horizontally. The juvenile crown is gaunt, with a few ascending branches; however, as it matures, it develops a huge, low dome, with upturned shoots covered with long, lax, brush-like foliage. Male flowers are purple, ripening to yellow; female flowers are red. The cone is conical and up to 6in (15cm) long.

Distribution: Northeast Mexico and south into Guatemala.
Height: 66ft (20m)
Shape: Broadly spreading
Evergreen
Pollinated: Wind
Leaf shape: Linear

Left: The blue-green needles are up to 12in (30cm) long.

Ancient Pine

Pinus longaeva

This species, allied to the bristlecone pine, *P. aristata*, contains some of the oldest living trees on earth. The oldest tree is reliably recorded at being more than 4,700 years old and is affectionately known as Methuselah. It is found growing 3,475m (11,400ft) up in the White Mountains of California, U.S.A.

Left: Both needles and cones have a scruffy, feather-like appearance.

Distribution: From the White Mountains, eastern California through central Utah and southern Nevada, U.S.A.
Height: 50ft (15m)
Shape: Broadly conical
Evergreen
Pollinated: Wind
Leaf shape: Linear

Identification: This species has scaly, black-gray bark. Young trees are conical in habit, but old trees become gnarled and spreading. The shoot is red-brown and hairy, with needles tightly clustered in fives along its length. Needles are approximately 1¼in (3cm) long, and shiny gray-green on top, with white stomata, and resin canals visible as two grooves on the underside. They persist on the tree for anything up to 30 years. Cones are ovoid, rounded at the base, up to 4in (10cm) long and a rich chestnut-red. This species is particularly hardy, being able to withstand prolonged winter periods with temperatures well below freezing, and long summer periods of drought.

OTHER SPECIES OF NOTE

Mexican White Pine *Pinus ayacahuite*
This beautiful tree attains heights of up to 115ft (35m) in its native Mexico and northern Guatemala. It is extremely hardy and grows high on mountain slopes. It has graceful, drooping foliage with blue-green, slender, lax needles, up to 6in (15cm) long and held in fives. The cone can grow up to 18in (45cm) long and is normally covered with sticky white resin.

Western White Pine
Pinus monticola
This distinctive, handsome tree is native to the eastern Rocky Mountains, from Alberta to Montana, and down the West Coast, from British Columbia to California. It has similar features to its close relative the eastern white pine, *Pinus strobus*; they are both large trees with a slender pyramidal shape, and they both have needles in clusters of five. However, the needles of the western white pine are stiffer and shorter, 3in (7.5cm), and the shoot is covered in dense short hairs.

Bristlecone Pine *Pinus aristata*
This tree is closely related to ancient pine, *Pinus longaeva*, which is confusingly quite often called bristlecone pine. However, they are two different species. *P. aristata* is a small tree with thick, hairy, red-brown shoots. The needle-like leaves are in fives, to 2in (5cm) long and spotted with white resin, which is not the case on *P. longaeva*. It also has longer bristle-like spines on the tip of each cone scale than *P. longaeva*.

SPRUCES

The spruces, Picea, are a group of hardy evergreen conifers that grow throughout much of the colder regions of the Northern Hemisphere. They are different to firs, Abies, in one significant way. On all spruces there is a peg-like stump at the base of every needle. When the needles fall this peg remains, creating a rough texture to the shoot. Firs have smooth shoots.

Brewer Spruce

Picea breweriana

Although relatively rare in the wild, the Brewer spruce has been widely cultivated in parks, gardens and arboreta. Trusses of ribbon-like foliage hang from downward-arching, evenly-spaced, slender branches. This tree comes from a region of high snowfall, and has adapted this weeping habit so that snow can be easily shed, thus protecting the branches from breakage.

Above: The cone is a narrow cylinder, 4–4¾in (10–12cm) long and light red-brown.

Identification: Dull, dark gray-pink bark when young, maturing to purple-gray with prominent roughly circular plates of bark, which curl away from the trunk at the edges. Male flowers are yellow and red, positioned on the ends of hanging shoots. Female flowers are dark red, cylindrical and only found on topmost shoots. Needles are soft, positioned all around the shoot, point forwards, and up to 1¼in (3cm) long. Their upper surface is glossy dark green and dulls with age. The lower surface has prominent, bright white, linear stomatal bands.

Distribution: The Siskiyou and Shasta Mountains bordering Oregon and California, U.S.A.
Height: 15ft (35m)
Shape: Narrowly weeping
Evergreen
Pollinated: Wind
Leaf shape: Linear

Left: Brewer spruce is one of the most beautiful conifers. It has a very graceful, weeping habit.

Sitka Spruce

Picea sitchensis

Distribution: Narrow coastal strip from Kodiak Island, Alaska, to Mendocino County, California, U.S.A.
Height: 165ft (50m)
Shape: Narrowly conical
Evergreen
Pollinated: Wind
Leaf shape: Linear

The largest of the North American spruces, this is a major species within northwest American forests. Valued for its timber, Sitka spruce has been widely planted across the Northern Hemisphere in forestry plantations. The timber is pale pinkish-brown and very strong for its light weight. Originally used for aircraft framing, it is now the major species used in pulp for paper manufacture.

Far left: Male flower.

Left: Female flower.

Right: Cones are pale buff, 4in (10cm) long, have thin papery scales and are pendulous in habit.

Identification: Bark in young trees is a deep purple-brown color. Older trees have large, curving cracks, which develop into plates of lifting bark. The overall shape is an open, narrow cone, with widely spaced, slender, ascending branches. Sitka spruce can easily grow more than 3ft (1m) a year when young. Needles are stiff with a sharp point, blue-green above with two white stomatal bands beneath, and up to 1¼in (3cm) long. They are arranged all around the pale, buff-colored shoot. Male flowers are reddish and occur in small quantities on each tree, shedding pollen in late spring. Female's are greenish-red, only appearing on the topmost shoots.

OTHER SPECIES OF NOTE
Engelmann's Spruce *Picea engelmannii*
This tall tree grows up to 130ft (40m) in height, and is native to the Rocky Mountains, from Alberta to New Mexico. It is a natural survivor, being very hardy, and growing on exposed sites in impoverished soils. It has red-brown bark and a narrow crown with dense, level branching. The needles are bluish-green, ¾in (2cm) long, and when crushed, emit a strong menthol fragrance.

Blue Engelmann's Spruce
Picea engelmannii 'Glauca'
This is a slender, attractive cultivar, which has orange flaking bark and bright glaucous, blue-gray, soft needles, with vibrant white stomatal banding. It has a pendulous cone, which is up to 2½in (6cm) long, thin, papery and found mostly in clusters at the top of the tree.

Likiang Spruce *Picea likiangensis*
A beautiful Chinese spruce widely cultivated as an ornamental species across North America. It has lovely graceful form with widely spaced horizontal branches. However, its most attractive feature is its flowers. Both male and female

flowers are bright red, and in spring are produced in such profusion that, from a distance, it looks as if the tree is covered with burning embers.

Colorado Spruce

Blue spruce *Picea pungens*

Otherwise known as the blue spruce (because of its blue-green needles), the Colorado spruce grows in the Rocky Mountains at altitudes up to 10,000ft (3,050m). It is often found growing as a solitary specimen on dry slopes and beside dried-up stream beds. It was discovered in 1862 on Pike's Peak, Colorado, by Dr C. C. Parry, who sent seeds to Harvard University.

Above: The cone is a pale brown to cream, pendulous cylinder, up to 4in (10cm) long, with thin scales wrinkled at the margins.

Distribution: Montana, Colorado, Utah, Arizona, New Mexico, U.S.A.
Height: 115ft (35m)
Shape: Narrowly conical
Evergreen
Pollinated: Wind
Leaf shape: Linear

Identification: The dark red-brown bark is rough with scales. The tree has a narrow conical form with short, level branches. It has shiny, pale yellow-brown shoots that are slightly hairy, but it is best identified by its foliage. The needles are an attractive blue-gray to gray-green, with a slight glaucous bloom, up to 1¼in (3cm) long, and arranged all around the shoot. Male flowers are red and the female's green. They appear in separate clusters on the same tree in late spring.

Red Spruce

Picea rubens

This widespread tree is found in northeastern North America from Newfoundland down the Appalachian Mountains to northern Georgia, where it thrives on wet, acid soils. The red spruce is a long-lived species, easily reaching 150 years old. It is able to tolerate low light levels, and will grow in shady forest conditions.

Identification: When young, the bark is a rich purplish-red color, peeling away in flakes. In older trees the bark is a dark purple-gray, cracking into irregular concave plates. The crown remains narrowly conical throughout the life of the tree. It has a rather dense form that tapers to a clear spire. The needles are thin, wiry, up to ⅝in (1.5cm) long and lie forwards on the shoot but curve inwards. They are glossy, grassy green and when crushed, emit a fragrance reminiscent of apples or camphor. Male flowers are bright crimson. The cones are 1½–2in (4–5cm) long, pale orange-brown with convex scales, which are crinkled and finely toothed.

Above: Young needles are a rich light green.

Below: The cones hang from the shoots.

Distribution: Nova Scotia to North Carolina, U.S.A.
Height: 82ft (25m)
Shape: Narrowly conical
Evergreen
Pollinated: Wind
Leaf shape: Linear

Left: A female flower.

Right: The distinctive red male flowers gave rise to this tree's common name.

Black Spruce

Picea mariana

This extremely hardy spruce occurs right across the north of North America where it survives in subarctic tundra conditions at the northerly limit for any trees. It is a slow-growing tree, particularly in the far north, and so the leading shoots are always short. This gives the tree a dense, neat appearance, with short branches and short, tightly packed needles. It is this density of foliage, particularly when young, which gives the tree its black appearance, and therefore its name.

Identification: The bark is gray-brown and flaking. The needle-like leaves are slender, to ½in (1.5cm) long, dark blue-green above, blue-white beneath and borne all around pink-brown shoots. When crushed the needles emit the scent of menthol cough drops. Male and female flowers are both red, the male's are carried at the ends of the shoots, and the female's are clustered on the topmost branches. The cones are egg-shaped, shiny red-brown, and less than 2in (5cm) long.

Distribution: Pennsylvania north to Newfoundland and across Canada to Alaska.
Height: 70ft (20m)
Shape: Narrowly conical
Evergreen
Pollinated: Wind
Leaf shape: Linear

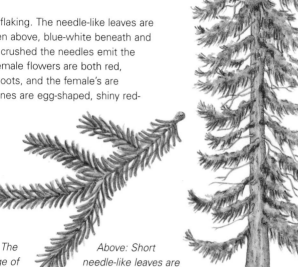

Left: The foliage of this tree is dense.

Above: Short needle-like leaves are blue-green above and blue-white beneath.

Above: The cone is a shiny red-brown egg shape and up to 2in (5cm) long. It matures in one year.

White Spruce

Picea glauca

This tough medium-size tree inhabits land with much the same inhospitable growing conditions as the black spruce, *Picea mariana*. In 1905 Charles Sargent of The Arnold Arboretum, Boston, suggested that the white spruce reached higher latitudes than any other evergreen tree, nearly to the Artic Sea, on ground which only thawed for three to four months each summer. It is not particularly ornamental, but has been widely planted in exposed areas to provide shelter.

Identification: The bark is gray-brown becoming finely fissured and scaly in maturity. The needle-like leaves are positioned mostly on the upper side of the whitish-fawn shoots. They are greenish blue-gray with white bands of stomata on each surface, ½in (1.5cm) long, pointed but not prickly. Male flowers are red opening yellow, and the female's are purple. Both appear in separate clusters on the same tree in spring. The cone is cylindrical, up to 2in (5cm) long, pale, shiny brown with thin and flexible scales.

Distribution: Across Canada from Alaska to Labrador.
Height: 70ft (20m)
Shape: Narrowly conical
Evergreen
Pollinated: Wind
Leaf shape: Linear

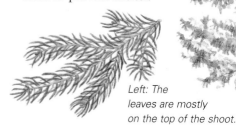

Left: The leaves are mostly on the top of the shoot.

Right: The cone is cylindrical, shiny-brown, up to 2in (5cm) and covered with thin papery scales.

Norway Spruce

Picea abies

The Norway spruce has a regular, symmetrical form with horizontal branching at low levels, gradually becoming upswept towards the top of the tree. It grows naturally in northern Europe up to altitudes of around 4,921ft (1,500m). In America it has been cultivated for its timber, especially in the northeastern U.S.A, southeastern Canada, the Pacific Coast states and the Rocky Mountain states. It is traditionally used to make the bellies of violins and other stringed instruments.

Left: Cones hang downwards.

Identification: The bark in young trees is deep coppery pink; on older trees it becomes dark purple, with shallow, round or oval plates, which lift away from the trunk. The needles are rich dark green with a faint sheen, and are up to ¾in (2cm) long. When crushed, they emit a citrus fragrance, which has become synonymous with Christmas. Male flowers are a golden color, shedding copious amounts of pollen in late spring. Female flowers are purple-red, and frequently confined to the top of the tree. Cones are pendulous, cylindrical, slightly curved and up to 6in (15cm) long.

Left: Male flowers occur in groups at shoot tips.

Right: A female flower.

Distribution: Most of northern Europe (excluding UK), from the Pyrenees to western Russia.
Height: 165ft (50m)
Shape: Narrowly conical
Evergreen
Pollinated: Wind
Leaf shape: Linear

OTHER SPECIES OF NOTE

Oriental Spruce *Picea orientalis*
Sometimes called the Caucasian spruce, this attractive tree originates from the Caucasus Mountains and on into Turkey, where it grows on mountainsides up to 7,021ft (2,140m). In maturity it has a dense, columnar form with short, shiny, fresh green needles ⅓in (8mm) long. Cones have a distinct ash-brown color.

Hybrid American Spruce *Picea x lutzii*
This medium-size hybrid tree was identified in Alaska in 1950, and recognized as a natural cross between Sitka spruce and white spruce. It has the potential to become a major tree within timber plantations because it takes important characteristics from both parents. It has inherited the strength and durability found in Sitka spruce timber, and the hardiness of white spruce, which means it can grow in colder regions of North America, which have not yet been colonized by good timber-producing trees.

Tiger-tail Spruce *Picea polita*
This ornamental, pyramidal-shaped, medium-size spruce originates from central and southern Japan. It is one of the most striking and attractive spruces. Consequently, it has been widely planted in parks and gardens across North America. The needle-like leaves are up to 2in (5cm) long; rigid and spine-tipped—probably the sharpest of any spruce —they are flattened and stand out at right angles to the chestnut brown shoot. The name "tiger-tail" is derived from the appearance of the foliage-covered branch ends, which are pendulous, very much like a tiger's tail.

Serbian Spruce

Picea omorika

The Serbian spruce has a very small natural population and because of this is considered to be endangered in the wild. It is a beautiful, slender, spire-like tree with branches that sweep elegantly downwards, only to arch upwards at their tip. This habit means that it is able to resist damage by efficiently shedding snow rather than collecting it. It is also the most resistant spruce to atmospheric pollution.

Identification: The bark is orange-brown to copper, and broken into irregular to square plates. The shoot is a similar color to the bark and quite hairy. The needles are short with a blunt tip, less than ¾in (2cm) long, glossy dark green above, with two broad, white stomatal bands underneath. The male flowers are crimson and held below new shoots; the female flowers are also red, but confined to the topmost branches. The Serbian spruce's most distinctive characteristic is its spire-like form.

Distribution: Europe: Confined to the Drina Valley in southwest Serbia. In the U.S.A. it grows in hardiness zone 3.
Height: 100ft (30m)
Shape: Very narrowly conical
Evergreen
Pollinated: Wind
Leaf shape: Linear

Above: The cone is pendulous, held on a thick curved stalk, tear-shaped, 2½in (6cm) long and purple-brown in color.

DECIDUOUS LARCHES

This small genus of fewer than a dozen species is confined to temperate regions of the Northern Hemisphere. Deciduous larches are fast-growing conifers, and several species have been widely planted for forestry purposes. Larches are some of the most seasonally attractive conifers. Their needles turn gold and drop in the fall, to be renewed every spring with a flush of lime-green foliage.

European Larch

Larix decidua

This attractive, hardy tree grows naturally at altitudes up to 8,200ft (2,500m) above sea level. It is a long-lived conifer, with some trees in the Alps recorded at over 700 years old. European larch has been widely planted throughout Europe and North America for both forestry and ornamental reasons.

Identification: Bark on young trees is pale gray and smooth. Old trees have heavily fissured, dark pink bark. Whorls of upswept branches are well spaced. Needles are soft, 1½in (4cm) long and bright green, becoming yellow before dropping in the fall. They are carried singly on main shoots and in dense whorls on side shoots. The shoots are pendulous and straw colored. Male flowers are pink-yellow rounded discs, normally on the underside of the shoots. Female flowers appear before the leaves in early spring. They are purple-pink, upright and develop quickly into an immature cone.

Right and left: Cones are 1¾in (4.5cm) long.

Distribution: From the Alps through Switzerland, Austria and Germany to the Carpathian Mountains of Slovakia and Romania. U.S.A. zone 3.
Height: 130ft (40m)
Shape: Narrowly conical
Deciduous
Pollinated: Wind
Leaf shape: Linear

Western Larch

Hackmatack *Larix occidentalis*

Distribution: From British Columbia south to Oregon and east to Montana, U.S.A.
Height: 164ft (50m)
Shape: Narrowly conical
Deciduous
Pollinated: Wind
Leaf shape: Linear

This magnificent tree, otherwise known as hackmatack, is the largest of all the larches reaching, in some instances, 200ft (60m) tall. It grows at elevations up to 7,000ft (2,000m) in both the Rockies and the Cascade Mountains. It is most prevalent around the Flat Head Lake area of northern Montana, which is where the tallest trees are found. It is fast growing, sometimes forming pure forests, although it is more often found growing alongside lodgepole pine, *Pinus contorta* var. *latifolia*. Seedlings will germinate prolifically on bare ground cleared of other vegetation by forest fires.

Identification: The bark is reddish-brown, thick and deeply fissured into large scales in maturity. The needle-like leaves are bright green and soft, to 1½in (4cm) long, borne in dense whorls on slow-growing side shoots and singly on leading shoots. In the fall they turn golden yellow. The male flowers are yellow, the female flowers are red, and both are produced on the same tree in separate clusters in early spring. The cone is ovoid, borne in an upright fashion on the branch, about ¾in (2cm) long, with thin scales from which a papery fawn-colored, tongue-like bract protrudes.

Right: Soft needle-like leaves emerge from winter bud in early spring.

Subalpine Larch

Larix lyallii

Subalpine larch is a tree of the mountains, growing naturally in the northern Rockies and Cascades up to elevations around 8,000ft (2,500m). It quite often demarcates the timberline between bare rock and scree, and the upper limits of tree cover. Its appearance is rather like a short, stunted, drooping western larch, *Larix occidentalis*. It is slow growing, and develops a gnarled windswept appearance from a relatively early age. *L. lyallii* was discovered in 1858 by Scots surgeon David Lyall.

Identification: The bark is thin, smooth and pale gray when young, maturing redbrown with fissures and loosely attached scales. The needle-like leaves are four-angled, pale blue-green, 1in (2.5cm) long, and tufted along densely felted young shoots. Both male and female flowers are dark red to purple, appearing separately on the same tree in early spring. The ovoid, 2in (5cm) long cones have a ragged appearance because of the long, twisted bract, which curls out from beneath each scale.

Right: The deciduous needle-like leaves are pale blue-green and borne in clusters along young shoots, which are covered with pubescence.

Distribution: Alberta, British Columbia, Idaho, Montana and Washington, U.S.A.
Height: 65ft (20m)
Shape: Narrowly conical
Deciduous
Pollinated: Wind
Leaf shape: Linear

Right: Female flowers are dark red to purple and appear on the tree slightly before the leaves appear in early spring.

Tamarack

American Larch, Hackmatack *Larix laricina*

This hardy tree is just as much at home on an exposed mountainside as in a boggy swamp. Although widespread in the wild, it is rare in cultivation. A short-lived tree, it is very slow growing, and colonizes inhospitable ground long before other trees.

Identification: Tamarack is a narrow, thin tree with short, level branches. The branches have a characteristic curled tip, which curls upwards and inwards back towards the crown. Young shoots are pink, turning brown as they mature. Needles are soft, blue-green, 1in (2.5cm) long and have two gray stomatal bands beneath. Male flowers are numerous, small and yellow, growing beneath the shoot. Female flowers are red and held upright on the shoot.

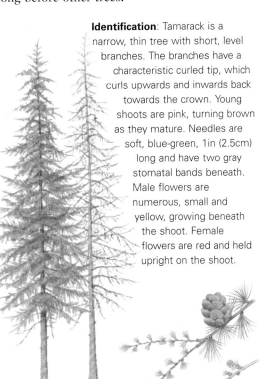

Distribution: Alaska and Canada south to New Jersey and Maryland, U.S.A.
Height: 66ft (20m)
Shape: Narrowly conical
Deciduous
Pollinated: Wind
Leaf shape: Linear

Above: The bark is pinkish orange, flaking into small circular scales.

Left: Cones have few scales and are pale brown, ovoid, erect and up to ¾in (2cm) long.

TULIP TREES AND MAGNOLIAS

The Magnoliaceae family contains 12 genera and just over 200 species. The majority of species are native to North America or Asia. They include some of the most beautiful of all flowering trees. Magnolias are planted in gardens the world over and countless cultivars have been developed. There are magnolias to suit all locations—some are giants, others little more than large shrubs.

Tulip Tree

Yellow poplar *Liriodendron tulipifera*

This magnificent tree is one of the largest and fastest-growing deciduous trees in North America. It stands out from the crowd for several reasons, including its size, its flower, its leaf shape and its ability to withstand atmospheric pollution. It is an adaptable tree, growing in extreme climatic conditions, from severe Canadian winters to subtropical Florida summers.

Identification: The bark is gray-brown and smooth, becoming fissured with age. In maturity, tulip trees have clear, straight stems with broad crowns. The dark green leaves are up to 6in (15cm) long, being lobed on each side with a cut-off, indented leaf tip. The underside of the leaf is almost bluish white. In the fall the leaves turn a butter-yellow color before dropping. Flowers are produced in summer once the tree reaches 12–15 years old. They are upright, 2½in (6cm) long, tulip-shaped and have nine petals: some are green; some are light green to yellowy-orange at the base. Inside each flower is a bright cluster of orange-yellow stamens. Unfortunately, because of the branchless stem of older trees, the flowers are often positioned at the top of the tree, so it is difficult to admire their beauty.

Distribution: Eastern North America from Ontario to New York in the north, to Florida in the south.
Height: 165ft (50m)
Shape: Broadly columnar
Deciduous
Pollinated: Bee
Leaf shape: Simple

Left: As the flowers fade on the tree, the leaves change color giving Liriodendron tulipifera *a second flourish of beauty.*

Cucumber Tree

Mountain magnolia *Magnolia acuminata*

Sometimes called the mountain magnolia because it has the ability to grow at altitudes up to 4,000ft (1,220m) in the Smoky Mountains. This is the largest of the seven magnolias native to North America. The common name "cucumber" is derived from the unripe seed pods, which are up to 7in (18cm) long, green and fleshy.

Identification: The brown-gray bark is unlike that of any other North American magnolia; it is rough and divided into narrow ridges with vertical fissures. The overall form is of a tall, broad tree with a conical crown of mainly upswept branches. The leaf is elliptical to ovate, 10in (25cm) long and 6in (15cm) across, rich green above, blue-green and slightly hairy below. The flowers appear in early to mid-summer; they are blue-green to yellow-green, bell-shaped, 3½in (9cm) long and quite often lost among the foliage. The seed pod ripens from a cucumber-like fruit into an erect, bright red cylinder 3in (7.5cm) long, containing as many as 50 seeds.

Left: The flowers appear in summer but are often difficult to see among the leaves.

Distribution: Eastern North America from Ontario to Alabama.
Height: 100ft (30m)
Shape: Broadly conical
Deciduous
Pollinated: Insect
Leaf shape: Simple ovate

Left: Red cylindrical seed pods appear from the middle of summer onwards.

Bull Bay

Magnolia grandiflora

This magnificent, evergreen, flowering tree is more often than not grown as a wall shrub. However, given a warm, sheltered, sunny position it will develop into a broad-canopied, short-stemmed tree. *Magnolia grandiflora* grows best close to the coast and at low altitudes; it rarely thrives above 500ft (150m). The combination of glossy, dark green, leathery leaves, and creamy white flowers, makes it a very popular garden tree.

Identification: The bark is gray-brown, cracking into irregular small plates. The leaves, which grow up to 10in (25cm) long and 4in (10cm) across, are thick, rigid, glossy dark green above, and either pale green, or covered in copper hairs beneath. Flowers will begin to appear when the tree is only ten years old; they are wide-brimmed and cup-shaped, creamy white to pale lemon and deliciously scented. They can be up to 12in (30cm) across and stand out splendidly against the dark foliage.

Above: The spectacular flowers are like dinner plates, measuring up to 12in (30cm) across.

Left: In the wild, flowers are produced in spring.

Distribution: North American southeast coastal strip from north Carolina to Florida and west along the gulf to southeast Texas.
Height: 82ft (25m)
Shape: Broadly conical
Evergreen
Pollinated: Insect
Leaf shape: Elliptic to ovate

Right: These red seed pods will first appear in midsummer.

OTHER SPECIES OF NOTE

Magnolia 'Charles Raffill'
This is a hybrid between *M. campbellii* and the subspecies *M. campbellii mollicomata*. It is a vigorous, deciduous tree, easily reaching 82ft (25m) in height and, once established, grows up to 24in (60cm) a year. It produces large, deep pink, goblet-shaped flowers in early spring.

Magnolia 'Elizabeth'
This hybrid between *M. acuminata,* and *M. denudata,* is a small, deciduous, conical tree. It produces pale primrose-yellow, fragrant, cup-shaped flowers in early to mid-spring before the leaves emerge from their winter bud. It was raised at the Brooklyn Botanic Garden, and named after Elizabeth Scholtz, director in 1978.

Magnolia 'Samuel Somner'
This magnificent form of *M. grandiflora* produces probably the largest flowers of any magnolia. They are creamy white, very fragrant, saucer-shaped and up to 14in (35cm) across. The leaves are evergreen, thick, leathery, glossy dark green on the top-side and deep brown and hairy beneath. This form is very hardy and wind-resistant and can be grown in the open.

Magnolia 'Wada's Memory'
This lovely deciduous hybrid between *M. kobus* and *M. salicifolia* is broadly conical and grows to about 33ft (10m) tall. It produces white, fragrant flowers, which are cylinder-like as they emerge from the bud in early spring, opening to a lax, saucer shape, approximately 6in (15cm) across. The flowers are held horizontally on the branch.

Sweet Bay

Swampbay *Magnolia virginiana*

This large shrub, or small tree, thrives on coastal plains and in wet swampy conditions. It was the earliest North American magnolia to be introduced to Europe, arriving in Great Britain in 1688. In the wild, the tallest trees tend to grow in the Carolinas and Florida, where heights of 82ft (25m) have been recorded. Elsewhere it seldom achieves 33ft (10m).

Identification: The bark of sweet bay is smooth and gray. The overall form is normally shrubby, with branching low on the stem. Leaves are ovate in shape, up to 4¾ in (12cm) long and 2½ in (6cm) wide. They are deep lustrous green above, and blue-white and downy beneath, especially when young. The flowers are creamy white, maturing quickly to pale yellow. They are cup-shaped at first, opening to a broad saucer. The flowers are short-lived, but produced over a long period, from early to late summer, and are highly scented. The sweet bay rarely sets seed in Europe. This tree used to be known as the beaver tree because early American colonists used its sweet fleshy roots to bait beaver traps.

Distribution: Eastern United States from Massachusetts to Florida.
Height: 82ft (25m)
Shape: Broadly spreading
Semi-evergreen
Pollinated: Insect
Leaf shape: Ovate

Left: Flowers are produced throughout the summer.

Umbrella Magnolia

Magnolia tripetala

This small, hardy tree is native to mountain valleys throughout eastern U.S.A. It grows in woodland shade and quite often beside streams in valley bottoms. It has fragrant flowers and striking foliage, making it an extremely popular ornamental tree in gardens across the U.S.A. It was identified by American plant collector John Bartram in the eighteenth century, and since then, has been widely cultivated across the western world. It requires acid soil to grow well.

Distribution: Eastern U.S.A. from Pennsylvania to Georgia.
Height: 40ft (12m)
Shape: Broadly spreading
Deciduous
Pollinated: Insect
Leaf shape: Obovate to elliptic

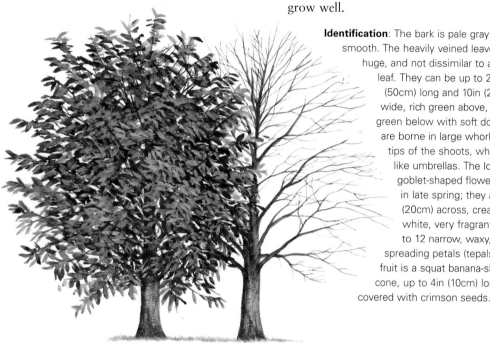

Identification: The bark is pale gray and smooth. The heavily veined leaves are huge, and not dissimilar to a tobacco leaf. They can be up to 20in (50cm) long and 10in (25cm) wide, rich green above, and sage green below with soft down. They are borne in large whorls at the tips of the shoots, which look like umbrellas. The loose goblet-shaped flowers appear in late spring; they are 8in (20cm) across, creamy white, very fragrant, with up to 12 narrow, waxy, spreading petals (tepals). The fruit is a squat banana-shaped cone, up to 4in (10cm) long, and covered with crimson seeds.

Above: After dropping in October, the large leaves take a long time to decompose and skeletal leaf remains will still be evident beneath the tree the following spring.

Campbell's Magnolia

Magnolia campbellii

This majestic tree is capable of attaining heights up to 100ft (30m) in less than 60 years. It is a hardy tree, growing up to 9,850ft (3,000m) above sea level in the Himalayas. It grows well in the warmer states of the U.S.A. It is grown for its dramatic flowers, which only appear after 20 years. They appear as early as mid-winter and are prone to frost damage.

Below: The flowers are up to 12in (30cm) across.

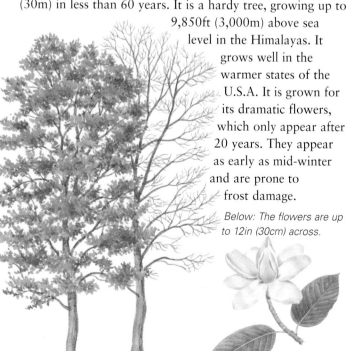

Identification: The bark is smooth and gray, even in old age. The leaves are up to 12in (30cm) long, with a pronounced point, medium green above, sometimes faintly hairy beneath. The flower buds are large, ovoid and covered in gray hairs. They stand out dramatically on the bare branches in late winter. The flowers are even more dramatic, beginning goblet-shaped, but opening to a lax cup-and-saucer shape, up to 12in (30cm) across. The color can vary from deep pink to pale pinkish-white. There is a slight fragrance to the flower. Each flower is held upright on a smooth green stalk. The fruit is a cylindrical, cone-like pod, up to 6in (15cm) long, containing bright red seed.

Right: The huge flowers often appear in profusion, both on cultivated and wild trees.

Distribution: Himalayas from Nepal to Assam and on into southwest China.
Height: 100ft (30m)
Shape: Broadly conical
Deciduous
Pollinated: Insect
Leaf shape: Obovate

Ashe's Magnolia

Magnolia ashei

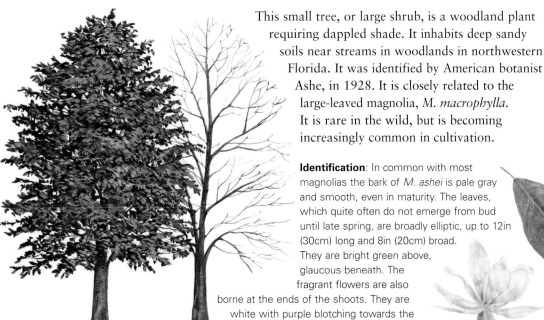

This small tree, or large shrub, is a woodland plant requiring dappled shade. It inhabits deep sandy soils near streams in woodlands in northwestern Florida. It was identified by American botanist Ashe, in 1928. It is closely related to the large-leaved magnolia, *M. macrophylla*. It is rare in the wild, but is becoming increasingly common in cultivation.

Distribution: Northwest Florida, U.S.A.
Height: 33ft (10m)
Shape: Broadly columnar
Deciduous
Pollinated: Insect
   Leaf shape: Elliptic

Identification: In common with most magnolias the bark of *M. ashei* is pale gray and smooth, even in maturity. The leaves, which quite often do not emerge from bud until late spring, are broadly elliptic, up to 12in (30cm) long and 8in (20cm) broad. They are bright green above, glaucous beneath. The fragrant flowers are also borne at the ends of the shoots. They are white with purple blotching towards the base, and arranged in a cup-like fashion.

Left: The leaves are borne in whorls at the ends of the shoots.

Left: The outer petals (tepals) sometimes have a greenish hue. The flowers appear towards the end of spring into early summer.

OTHER SPECIES OF NOTE

Hybrid Magnolia *Magnolia* x *soulangeana*
A hybrid between *M. denudata* and *M. liliiflora*, this has become the most widely planted ornamental magnolia. The deciduous, obovate leaves are up to 8in long (20cm) and 4¾in (12cm) wide. The flowers become cup-and-saucer-like with age. They are creamy-white, with a pink tinge to the base of each thick petal.

Star Magnolia *Magnolia stellata*
This slow-growing, compact Japanese tree, or large shrub, seldom reaches more than 10ft (3m) in height. Its flowers appear on bare branches in late winter and early spring. The flowers are fragrant, pure white, maturing to pale pink, star-shaped, and have 12–18 petals. It was introduced to the U.S.A in the 1860s.

Lily Tree *Magnolia denudata*
Otherwise known as "yulan," this is one of the most beautiful flowering trees. It has been cultivated in Buddhist temple gardens, and around imperial palaces, for 1,300 years. The "water lily-like" flowers are pure white and faintly scented of lemons. It was introduced to the west in 1789 and has become very popular.

Magnolia dealbata
This medium-size Mexican magnolia is related to the *M. macrophylla*. It has large, papery, bright green leaves borne in whorls at the ends of the shoots. The parchment-color, wide-spreading, cup-shaped flowers, which appear in early summer, have a distinctive purple blotch at the base of each petal (tepal).

Large-leaved Magnolia

Magnolia macrophylla

This tree, as the name suggests, has the largest leaves of any magnolia, and possibly the largest entire leaf of any American tree. It is native to southeastern United States, and was discovered in 1759 in the mountains of South Carolina, where it inhabits rich, moist soils, in woodland. Two magnificent specimens grow in front of the museum of the Arnold Arboretum, Boston.

Distribution: Southeast United States.
Height: 50ft (15m)
Shape: Broadly columnar
Deciduous
Pollinated: Insect
Leaf shape: Elliptic to oblong

Identification: The bark is pale gray and smooth. The leaves, up to 36in (90cm) long and 12in (30cm) wide, have pronounced veins, and are smooth, bright green above, and almost white underneath. They are borne in large whorls at the tips of stout olive-green shoots. Large, fragrant creamy-yellow flowers are borne at the ends of the shoots in early to mid-summer. Distinctive, bright red seeds, in irregular clusters, 3in (7.5cm) long, appear in late summer.

Above: The leaves are papery thin.

Below: The flowers are 12in (30cm).

EVERGREEN LAURELS

The Lauraceae family contains more than 40 genera and 2,000 different species, most of which are tropical, originating from Asia and South America. Those that are hardier, and can survive in temperate regions of the world, tend to have several things in common, including aromatic foliage or bark, and evergreen leaves.

Sassafras

Sassafras albidum

Distribution: Eastern North America from Canada to Florida and westwards to Kansas and Texas.
Height: 82ft (25m)
Shape: Broadly columnar
Deciduous
Pollinated: Insect
Leaf shape: Ovate to elliptic

Both the leaves and bark of sassafras are pleasingly aromatic. In the past, both have been used for medicinal purposes. The bark of the root is often used to make a drink not dissimilar to beer. Although fairly widespread in the wild, sassafras has never been widely cultivated in parks and gardens. The leaves, which can be heavily lobed, are similar in outline to those of the common fig.

Identification: A medium-size suckering tree, with wavy or zig-zag branching, which is particularly noticeable when the leaves have fallen in winter. The leaves are 6in (15cm) long, 4in (10cm) across, and variable in shape, sometimes having a pronounced lobe on one or both sides. They are grass-green above and blue-green below. In fall they turn orange-yellow before dropping. The fruit is a dark blue, egg-shape berry, 1cm (½in) across.

Left: Male and female flowers are held on separate trees and produced in late spring. Both are inconspicuous and greenish yellow.

Sorrel Tree

California bay, California olive, Oregon myrtle *Umbellularia californica*

This tree resembles the bay tree in everything but size, being extremely vigorous and capable of reaching 100ft (30m) in height in sheltered, moist valley bottoms. It has a dense, leafy habit, and foliage which, when crushed, emits a very powerful odor, which can induce nausea, headaches, and in some cases unconsciousness. It may also cause skin allergies in some people.

Identification: The bark is dark gray and smooth when young, cracking into regular plates as the tree matures. The leaves are up to 5in (12cm) long, alternately placed on sage-green shoots, elliptic in shape but tapering at both ends, leathery, glossy dark green above and pale beneath. The flowers are inconspicuous, ¼in (5mm) across and yellowy green. They are produced on sage-green upright stalks, 1in (2.5cm) long, in late winter and early spring. The fruit is a pear-shaped berry, 1in (2.5cm) long, green at first, then changing to purple. The timber of Californian laurel is highly prized for veneers and cabinetmaking; also known as "pepperwood" it has pale brown figuring and can be polished to a fine finish.

Distribution: North America, California north to Oregon.
Height: 100ft (30m)
Shape: Broadly spreading
Evergreen
Pollinated: Insect
Leaf shape: Elliptic to oblanceolate

Left: Flowers appear in winter and early spring.

Right: The leaves resemble those of bay.

Bay Laurel

Sweet bay *Laurus nobilis*

This is the laurel used by the Greeks and Romans as a ceremonial symbol of victory; it was usually woven into crowns to be worn by champions. Fruiting sprays were also made into wreaths and given to acclaimed poets, hence the term "poet laureate." Where hardy, it is grown in the U.S.A as a specimen shrub, or in woodland gardens. It may need protecting from winter winds.

Identification: A dense, evergreen small tree or shrub, with aromatic leaves which are commonly used as food flavoring. The bark is dark gray and smooth, even in old age. Leaves are leathery, alternate, dark glossy green above with a central lighter vein, and pale green beneath. They are 4in (10cm) long, 1½in (4cm) across and pointed at the tip. Male flowers appear in late winter; they are greenish yellow, ½in (1cm) across, with yellow stamens, positioned in the axils of the previous year's leaves.

Above: The small male flowers open during late winter. Bay leaves are commonly harvested for use in cooking.

Distribution: Throughout Mediterranean regions. U.S.A zones 8–10.
Height: 50ft (15m)
Shape: Broadly conical
Evergreen
Pollinated: Insect
Leaf shape: Elliptic

Left: The fruit is a rounded berry, ½in (1cm) across, green ripening to a glossy black.

OTHER SPECIES OF NOTE

Wheel Tree *Trochodendron aralioides*
This attractive, evergreen Japanese tree is the sole species in the only genus within the family Trochodendraceae. Its nearest relative is believed to be *Drimys winteri*. It has dark green, shiny, narrow, elliptical, leathery leaves and aromatic bark. Its most interesting feature by far is its wheel-like flowers, which are bright green, ¾in (2cm) across and have exposed stamens radiating outwards from a central disc, rather like the spokes on a cartwheel. They appear on upright slender stalks from early spring to early summer. It survives in U.S.A. hardiness zones 8–10.

Gutta Percha *Eucommia ulmoides*
This Chinese tree is the only member of the Eucommiaceae family. It is the only temperate tree that produces rubber, and is also known as the hardy rubber tree. If the leaf is gently torn in half, the two halves will still hang together, held by thin strands of sticky latex. In China, it has been cultivated for hundreds of years and used for medicinal purposes. Since it has never been found growing in the wild, its origins are unknown. It survives in the U.S.A. in hardiness zones 4–8.

Mountain Laurel

Calico bush *Kalmia latifolia*

Sometimes known as the calico bush, this multistemmed small tree or large shrub, is probably one of the most beautiful evergreens of eastern North America. It grows naturally in the shade of taller trees in woodland, often forming dense impenetrable thickets. It is very popular and cultivated throughout the U.S.A. in parks and gardens as an early summer-flowering ornamental. It grows best on acid soils.

Identification: The bark is a dark red-brown becoming fissured into narrow longitudinal ridges in maturity. Mountain laurel has alternate, glossy, dark green leathery leaves with a distinctive light yellow-green central midrib. They are up to 5in (13cm) long, less than half that broad and tapered at both ends. The dark-green leaves make an excellent foil for the saucer-shaped flowers which are borne in tight clusters in late spring.

Right: The flowers are deep rose-pink in bud opening to bright pink.

Distribution: Eastern U.S.A. from Lake Erie south to Florida and west to Louisiana.
Height: 20ft (6m)
Shape: Broadly spreading
Evergreen
Pollinated: Insect
Leaf shape: Elliptic to lanceolate

Above: Leaf veins are very distinctive, particularly the central midrib vein.

ELMS AND HACKBERRIES

This Ulmaceae family contains about 15 genera and 140 different species of mainly deciduous trees. They thrive in all but the poorest of soils and are widespread throughout most temperate regions of the Northern Hemisphere, including Europe, North America and Asia, except where they have been affected by the fungus Ophiostoma novo-ulmi, *which causes Dutch elm disease.*

American Elm

White elm *Ulmus americana*

Known as white elm because of the timber color, this tree has a wide-spreading crown of pendulous branches. It has been widely planted across eastern U.S.A. for ornament and as a shelter belt tree. Since the 1930s the population has been affected by Dutch elm disease.

Distribution: Saskatchewan south to Florida and Texas.
Height: 115ft (35m)
Shape: Broadly spreading
Deciduous
Pollinated: Wind
Leaf shape: Ovate to obovate

Identification: The bark is ash gray becoming cracked and fissured in maturity. The leaves taper at the tip to a long slender point and are distinctly unequal at the base where they join the leaf stalk (petiole). They are dark green above, lighter green with some pubescence beneath, and rough to the touch.

Right: The leaves are ovate, up to 6in (15cm) long and doubly toothed around the margins.

Hackberry

Nettle tree *Celtis occidentalis*

Distribution: North America.
Height: 82ft (25m)
Shape: Broadly columnar
Deciduous
Pollinated: Wind
Leaf shape: Ovate

Right: The hackberry's other common name seems more appropriate: it is named for its leaves, which resemble those of the stinging nettle.

This medium-size tree, which is closely related to elm, grows naturally right across North America from the Atlantic seaboard to the Rocky Mountains and north into Canada. It produces a profusion of purple, edible, sweet-tasting berries, that are an important food source for birds.

Identification: The bark is light gray, smooth when the tree is young, becoming rough and corky with warty blemishes in maturity. The leaves are ovate, up to 4¾in (12cm) long and 2in (5cm) across, pointed, toothed at the tip and rounded at the base, where there are three pronounced veins. They are glossy rich green and smooth on top; lighter green and slightly hairy on the veining underneath.

Both the male and female flowers are held separately on the same tree. In spring the flowers are small and green, without petals and appear in the leaf axils. The fruit is a purple-black, rounded berry, approximately ½in (1cm) across and borne on a thin green stalk, 1in (2.5cm) long.

Keaki
Zelkova serrata

This large, elm-like Asian tree grows best in its native lands in low-lying river valleys where the soil is deep and rich. It grows at altitudes of 4,000ft (1,220m). Many old Japanese temples are built of its timber, which is strong and extremely durable. In the U.S.A. it is a good replacement for the American elm, *U. americana*, and is strong in urban conditions.

Identification: The bark is pale gray and smooth, like beech. In maturity it peels or flakes, leaving light, fawn-gray patches. Lower branching is light and sweeps upwards, ending in thin, straight twigs. Leaves are ovate, 4¾in (12cm) long and 2in (5cm) broad, with 6–13 sharp teeth on each side. Small, green male and female flowers appear on each tree in spring. The fruit is round and small, ¼in (5mm) diameter.

Right and far right: The leaves are dark green and slightly rough above; pale green with pubescence beneath. In fall they turn an orange-red color.

Distribution: China, Japan and Korea. U.S.A. zone 5–8.
Height: 130ft (40m)
Shape: Broadly spreading
Deciduous
Pollinated: Wind
Leaf shape: Ovate

OTHER SPECIES OF NOTE
English Elm *Ulmus minor* var. *vulgaris*
This large tree, formerly known as *U. procera*, was probably introduced to the U.S.A. from England and Spain. For centuries it was one of the most characteristic features of the English countryside; but in the 1960s, Dutch elm disease wiped out almost the entire population.

Sugarberry *Celtis laevigata*
This handsome, large tree, also known as the Mississippi hackberry, is often planted as a shade and street tree, and is common throughout central and eastern U.S.A. It is often cut back into hedging. It has pale gray bark that sometimes develops a pink tinge with fissured ridges, and narrowly ovate leaves up to 4in (10cm) long. The fruit is a small, rounded orange-red berry which is sweetly edible.

Cedar Elm *Ulmus crassifolia*
This elm is a slow-growing, round-headed, small tree with a short bole and stiff arching branches. It has ovate to oblong leaves, which are hard, and so firmly fixed to the branches that they hardly move. The bark is pinkish-gray becoming very fissured and corky in maturity. Cedar elm is native to southern U.S.A.

Rock Elm *Ulmus thomasii*
A slow-growing, small to medium-size tree, native to east and central North America from Montreal, around the south of the Great Lakes, and south to Missouri. It looks similar to the *U. rubra*, except that the branches develop corky wings and the leaves are up to 5in (12.5cm) long. It is prized for its strong, water-repellent timber.

Slippery Elm
Ulmus rubra

The common name refers to the wet inner bark, which if sucked, is believed to have medicinal qualities that help to cure throat infections. The leaves of this elm were considered the best to eat by the early settlers of New England. Like American elm, *Ulmus americana* (which has a similar natural distribution across eastern North America), slippery elm is susceptible to attack by Dutch elm disease.

Identification: The bark is sooty-gray to brown and vertically fissured into coarse ridges in maturity. In a young tree the overall shape is upright; as it matures it develops a more rounded crown. The rough textured leaves are dark green, up to 8in (20cm) long, heavily serrated around the margin with a long point at the tip. They are borne in profusion on the tree creating a dense, dark canopy when viewed from a distance.

Distribution: From Quebec to South Carolina and west to Texas.
Height: 71ft (20m)
Shape: Broadly spreading
Deciduous
Pollinated: Wind
Leaf shape: Oblong-ovate

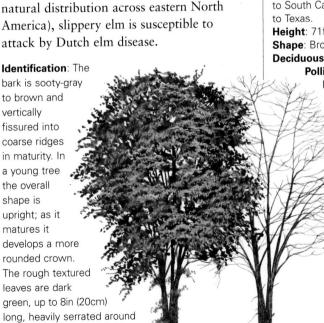

Above: Individual seeds are centrally carried within their own oval-shaped winged membrane.

WALNUTS AND MULBERRIES

One of the main characteristics of these two families is that they both contain trees that produce edible fruits. The mulberry or Moraceae family includes both mulberries and figs, while the walnut or Juglandaceae family includes the common walnut. There are about 800 different species of fig; the majority of them are found in tropical and subtropical regions.

Black Walnut

Juglans nigra

With its pyramidal habit and large pinnate leaves this is a splendid, ornamental large tree. It has long been grown for its lumber and its edible fruit. The lumber is of high quality and has a distinctive deep chocolate-brown color to the heartwood, which is prized for cabinetmaking. The fruit, an edible nut, is not as large as an English walnut, *Juglans regia*, but has the same distinctive flavor.

Distribution: Eastern and central U.S.A.
Height: 100ft (30m)
Shape: Broadly spreading
Deciduous
Pollinated: Wind
Leaf shape: Pinnate

Identification: The bark is dark gray-brown to sooty-ash colored, smooth at first, becoming fissured and ridged in maturity. The leaves are 4in (10cm) long, glossy dark green above, slightly hairy beneath. In the fall they turn a clear butter-yellow before dropping. Both the male and female flowers are catkin-like, yellow-green, and up to 4in (10cm) long when ripe. They are borne separately on the same tree in late spring, early summer. Walnut is late to come into leaf, holding on to bare branches until late May before the leaves appear.

Right: The leaves are pinnate, with up to 17 toothed, pointed leaflets.

Butternut

White walnut *Juglans cinerea*

This handsome, fast-growing tree is common in forests in the Alleghenies, where it stands out in the fall as the leaves turn color earlier than most other trees. The fruit, which gives the tree its name, is a large, sweet and very oily nut encased in a thick shell with four distinct ridges and protected by a pointed, shiny, sticky green husk. The botanical name *cinerea* refers to the fact that the bark is an ash-gray color.

Distribution: From Quebec south to Tennessee.
Height: 80ft (25m)
Shape: Broadly spreading
Deciduous
Pollinated: Wind
Leaf shape: Pinnate

Right: The fruit is a large, sweet, edible nut, contained within a sticky, angular shell.

Identification: The leaves are pinnate, with up to 17 toothed and pointed leaflets, up to 5in (13cm) long. They are all attached directly to the midrib of the main leaf except for the terminal leaflet which is on a short stalk. They are dark grass-green above, paler beneath and covered with slight pubescence. The male and female flowers are borne in pendulous green catkins, up to 4in (10cm) long, and appear on the same tree in late spring.

Southern Californian Walnut

Juglans californica

Distribution: California, U.S.A.
Height: 50ft (15m)
Shape: Broadly spreading
Deciduous
Pollinated: Wind
Leaf shape: Pinnate

Right: The nut has deep, vertical grooves.

Native to the southern Californian coastal region from Santa Barbara to the San Bernardino Mountains, this scrubby, round-headed tree inhabits banks of streams and valley bottoms. Since it is not particularly hardy or attractive, it is rarely found outside its natural region. It was identified in 1899 and plants were sent to Kew Gardens, England, but it never thrived in the damp, cool climate found in that region.

Identification: The trunk of this tree is always short and scrubby with pale gray bark. The leaves are finely serrated around the margin, dull green and attached to the mid-rib of the main leaf by a short hairy petiole. The flowers are green-yellow and borne in catkins, up to 3in (7.5cm) long, in late spring.

Left: The leaves are made up of 11–15 oblong-lanceolate leaflets, each leaflet up to 2in (5cm) long.

OTHER SPECIES OF NOTE

Common Fig *Ficus carica*
Originally from southwestern Asia, this large shrub, or small spreading tree, is now cultivated for its fruit throughout the temperate world. It has smooth, gray bark and distinctive, heavily lobed leaves. The male and female flowers, which are fertilized by wasps, are small and green and borne on separate trees. The delicious fruit is heart-shaped and green, becoming purple-brown when ripe.

Paper Mulberry *Broussonetia papyrifera*
This medium-size, broadly spreading tree is a close relative of the true mulberries and comes from eastern Asia. The paper mulberry has attractive, coarsely toothed, hairy, purple-green leaves, which vary in shape from ovate to rounded, and are deeply lobed. In Japan the tree's inner bark was traditionally used to make paper, hence the common name.

Common Walnut *Juglans regia*
Otherwise known as English walnut, this beautiful tree is native to an area from the Black Sea to China and possibly Japan. It was first introduced into western Europe by the Romans around 2,000 years ago. It has been widely cultivated for its edible fruits ever since. It was brought to America by the early settlers and is found in the east from Massachusetts to Ohio and in the west from British Columbia to New Mexico. Common walnut is the only walnut not to have serrated edges to its leaves.

Osage Orange

Maclura pomifera

Found primarily in wet areas alongside rivers, this tree is best known for its showy orange-like fruit. The fruit is in fact inedible and, when fresh, full of a sour milky juice. The fruit is not always present because the tree is dioecious (male and female flowers are on separate trees) and therefore both sexes are required to be in close proximity for pollination to occur.

Identification: The bark is orange-brown, while the branches are often twisted, and when broken exude a milky sap. The leaves are a glossy rich green above, and pale green beneath. They are ovate, pointed at both ends, untoothed, 4in (10cm) long and 2in (5cm) wide. Sometimes a sharp green spine is present at the base of the petiole. Male and female flowers are yellow-green, ½in (1cm) long and appear in clusters on separate trees in early summer. The fruit is orange-like, green, ripening to yellow and up to 4in (10cm) across. It is actually a cluster of smaller fruits that have fused together.

Below: The fruit of the osage orange looks remarkably like a real orange.

Distribution: Central and southern America.
Height: 50ft (15m)
Shape: Broadly spreading
Deciduous
Pollinated: Insect
Leaf shape: Ovate

PECANS, HICKORIES AND WING NUTS

The Juglandaceae family contains seven genera and over sixty species of tree, which grow throughout temperate regions of North America, Europe and Asia. They include some of the fastest-growing deciduous trees. The leaves of all species are pinnate and the flowers are all catkins. Many of these trees produce edible fruit in the form of a nut.

Mockernut

Big-bud hickory *Carya tomentosa*

Distribution: East of a line from Minnesota to Texas, U.S.A.
Height: 100ft (30m)
Shape: Broadly columnar
Deciduous
Pollinated: Wind
Leaf shape: Pinnate

Right: The lower surface of the leaves is yellow-green and covered with a fine pubescence.

This North American hickory, sometimes called big-bud hickory, is highly prized for its timber, which has several uses. Its strength and ability to withstand impact has made it the ideal material for making tool handles all over the world. It is also used to make sports equipment such as hockey sticks. When the wood is burnt it emits a fragrance used to smoke meats. The pinnate leaves give off a pleasing aroma when crushed.

Identification: The bark is silver-gray and smooth becoming slightly fissured in maturity. The leaves are 12in (30cm) long with up to nine obovate leaflets, the terminal one of which may be up to 8in (20cm) long and 4in (10cm) wide. The upper surfaces of the leaves are dark green. Both the shoots and the leaf stalks are covered in dense short hairs.

Right: Mockernut leaves taper towards the tip and are toothed around the margin.

Bitternut Hickory

Carya cordiformis

Distribution: Similar to Mockernut, east of a line from Minnesota to Texas.
Height: 100ft (30m)
Shape: Broadly columnar
Deciduous
Pollinated: Wind
Leaf shape: Pinnate

As the name suggests, the nuts are not palatable. They do however have a high oil content and were valued because they could be crushed to produce lamp oil. The name hickory comes from the native American *pawcohiccora* meaning nut oil. The species has a similar natural range to that of mockernut, *Carya tomentosa*, but is easily distinguished by its slender, bright yellow winter buds. It is not commonly planted outside its natural range.

Identification: The bark is gray and smooth becoming thick and heavily ridged in maturity. The pinnate leaves have up to nine heavily serrated leaflets which may be up to 6in (15cm) long. They are deep green above and yellow-green beneath. In the fall they turn a rich golden yellow. Both the male and female flowers are carried on catkins; the males in threes, and up to 3in (7.5cm) long, which appear separately on the same tree in late spring. The thin-shelled fruit is an inedible bitter nut.

Right: Bitternut hickory has pinnate leaves that normally bare four pairs of leaflets plus one terminal leaflet. In the fall they turn bright yellow.

Pecan

Carya illinoinensis

This tall tree is known around the world for its delicious nuts. In southern U.S.A. it is extensively cultivated within orchards, and is of great commercial value. The pecan grows naturally in damp soils in forests and river valleys, for example by the Mississippi.

Identification: The bark is gray, corky and deeply fissured and ridged. The leaves are pinnate with up to 17 dark green leaflets, 6in (15cm) long. Each leaflet has a serrated margin and curves slightly backwards at the tip. In the fall the foliage can turn a butter-yellow color. Male flowers are yellow-green, small and clustered on pendulous catkins hanging in threes. They appear in late spring and early summer. The nut is thin-shelled and brown.

Distribution: Southeast and central North America.
Height: 100ft (30m)
Shape: Broadly columnar
Deciduous
Pollinated: Wind
Leaf shape: Pinnate

Left: The pecan nut grows inside a husk 2in (5cm) long. Nuts are harvested in the fall.

Hybrid Wing Nut
Pterocarya x rehderiana
This hybrid, raised at the Arnold Arboretum in 1879, is more vigorous than either of its parents, *P. fraxinifolia* and *P. stenoptera*. It has pinnate leaves, with up to 21 leaflets. The bark is purple-brown, and obliquely fissured. The pendulous catkins are 18in (45cm) long, and contain winged seeds in summer.

Pignut *Carya glabra*
This medium-size, North American hickory has smooth gray bark, which gradually becomes vertically fissured in old age. It has pinnate leaves comprised of five to seven smooth, sharply toothed, taper-pointed leaflets. The nut was traditionally used to feed pigs.

Caucasian Wing Nut
Pterocarya fraxinifolia
This fast-growing, large tree regularly achieves 10ft (3m) growth in one year. As the name suggests it is native to the Caucasus, and the shores of both the Black and Caspian seas. At first glance, it looks similar to black walnut, *Juglans nigra*, however, the fruit is nut-like with semicircular wings and carried in a long hanging "necklace," up to 20in (50cm) long. It is grown in botanic gardens in the U.S.A.

Shagbark Hickory

Carya ovata

Distribution: Eastern North America from Quebec to Texas.
Height: 100ft (30m)
Shape: Broadly columnar
Deciduous
Pollinated: Wind
Leaf shape: Pinnate

This large, vigorous tree differs from other hickories in having flaking, gray-brown bark, which curls away from the trunk in thin strips up to 12in (30cm) long, but stays attached to the tree at the center point. This gives the whole trunk a shaggy, untidy but attractive appearance.

Identification: The leaves are pinnate, with five to seven leaflets on each leaf. Each leaflet is up to 10in (25cm) long, yellowish-green and has a serrated edge for the top two-thirds. In the fall the leaves turn brilliant yellow. In winter, the bud scales curve away from the bud at the tip. Both the male and female flowers are small, yellowish green and borne on pendulous catkins clustered in threes in late spring. In North America, the tree produces a profusion of nuts most years. Elsewhere, crops are not so prolific. The white, sweet-tasting kernel is contained in a green husk.

Right: Fruit occurs at twig ends.

Below: The husk has four ridges.

Right: Leaves appear finger-like before they fill out.

BEECHES

The Fagaceae family contains ten species of true beech, which all occur in temperate regions of the world. They can be found in Asia, North America and Europe, including Great Britain. Beeches are some of the most majestic deciduous trees. They typically have smooth, thin, silver-gray bark and can attain heights in excess of 130ft (40m).

European Beech

Fagus sylvatica

The name "beech" comes from the Anglo-Saxon *boc* and the Germanic word *Buche*, both of which gave rise to the English word "book." In northern Europe early manuscripts were written on thin tablets of beech wood and bound in beech boards. Beech is widely used for hedging because it retains its dead leaves in winter, providing extra wind protection. It is a popular specimen tree in the U.S.A.

Distribution: Europe from the Pyrenees to the Caucasus and north to Russia and Denmark. U.S.A. zone 4–7.
Height: 130ft (40m)
Shape: Broadly spreading
Deciduous
Pollinated: Wind
Leaf shape: Ovate to obovate

Identification: The bark is silver-gray and remains smooth even in maturity. The leaves are up to 4in (10cm) long and 2in (5cm) wide. They have a wavy, but normally untoothed, margin and a rather blunt point at the tip. In spring, juvenile leaves have a covering of hairs and are edible, having a nutty flavor. Older leaves become tough and bitter. Beech flowers are small; female flowers are green and the male's are yellow. Both are borne in separate clusters on the same tree in spring. The fruit is an edible nut, with up to three nuts being contained within a woody husk, covered in coarse bristles.

Right: The husks open in early fall.

Far right: Mature leaves are smooth and have a rich color.

Copper Beech

Fagus sylvatica 'Purpurea'

Neither a true species, or of garden origin, copper or purple beeches are "sports" or "quirks" of nature. Their presence was noted near Buchs, Switzerland, and in the Darney forest, Vosges, eastern France in the 1600s.

Identification: Similar to the European beech, but with the most obvious difference being the purple leaves, which are also more oval. Copper beech may grow more slowly and is not quite as spreading in maturity, but this is more a result of local conditions than a distinct characteristic of the tree.

Distribution: Switzerland and Vosges, eastern France. Northeast North America from Maine to Wisconsin and from Maryland to Missouri.
Height: 130ft (40m)
Shape: Broadly spreading
Deciduous
Pollinated: Wind
Leaf shape: Ovate to obovate

Left: One in 1,000 seedlings collected from European beech may have purple leaves.

American Beech

Fagus grandiflora

This tree is prolific in North America but has never been much of a success elsewhere. In Britain it never really thrives, developing into a rather shrubby-looking tree. Its one distinctive feature is that it can regenerate very easily from root suckers, particularly when coppiced, or badly damaged.

Identification: The bark is slate-gray, thin and smooth, even in old age. The glossy leaves are ovate to elliptic, up to 4¾in (12cm) long and 2in (5cm) wide. They are sharply toothed and taper to a pointed tip. On the underside, they are pale green with tufts of white hair along the midrib and in the vein axils beneath. Young shoots are also covered with fine hair. There are up to 15 pairs of leaf veins as opposed to up to 10 on common beech. Male flowers are yellow; female are green. Both are small and borne in clusters on the same tree in late spring. Fruits are ¾in (2cm) long bristly husks with up to three angular nuts.

Right: American beech nuts (or masts) are held in bristly husks. The leaves are dark green.

Distribution: North America from Nova Scotia to Florida.
Height: 82ft (25m)
Shape: Broadly spreading
Deciduous
Pollinated: Wind
Leaf shape: Ovate to elliptic

OTHER SPECIES OF NOTE

Oriental Beech *Fagus orientalis*
The Oriental beech is native to the forests of the Caspian Sea, the Caucasus, Asia Minor, Bulgaria and Iran. It is similar to common beech, and there is, without doubt, some hybridization between the two species on its western boundary. Oriental beech has larger leaves with more pairs of veining than common beech and will, in good growing conditions, develop into a larger tree. It survives in U.S.A zones 4–7.

Pendulous Beech *Fagus sylvatica* 'Pendula'
Several cultivars of common beech have weeping foliage, but 'Pendula' is the best. It grows into a large tree with enormous pendulous branches, which droop from the main stem like elephants' trunks. Where they touch the ground they sometimes take root, sending up another stem that will in turn begin to weep. Over time a large tent-like canopy can develop around the original tree. It is one of the finest specimen trees available in North America.

Dawyck Beech *Fagus sylvatica* 'Dawyck'
This delightful, narrowly columnar "Lombardy poplar"-shape tree was discovered on the Dawyck Estate in the Tweed Valley, southern Scotland, in 1860. It became an "overnight success" with gardeners and nurserymen, providing the perfect solution for those who wanted a beech tree but did not have the room for the much larger growing kind. It has been widely planted as an ornamental tree right across northeastern North America.

Japanese Beech

Siebold's beech *Fagus crenata*

This species is sometimes called Siebold's beech after the German doctor who was physician to the Governor of the Dutch East India Company's Deshima trading post. It was Siebold who identified the tree in Japan, where it forms considerable forests from sea level to 4,921ft (1,500m). It was first introduced to the West in 1892 and is grown as a specimen tree in the U.S.A.

Identification: Similar to common beech, it differs mainly in its more obovate leaf shape and a small leaf-like structure found at the base of each seed husk in early fall. The bark is silver-gray and smooth, even in older trees. The leaves are up to 4in long (10cm) and 2in (5cm) wide with a wavy, finely pubescent margin and blunt teeth. Leaf veins occur in seven to 11 pairs. The leaf stalk is ½in (1cm) long. Leaves turn an "old-gold" color in the fall. The seed husk is ⅔in (1.5cm) long and covered in long bristles.

Right: A Japanese beech leaf and mast.

Distribution: Japan. U.S.A. zones 4–7.
Height: 100ft (30m)
Shape: Broadly spreading
Deciduous
Pollinated: Wind
Leaf shape: Ovate to obovate

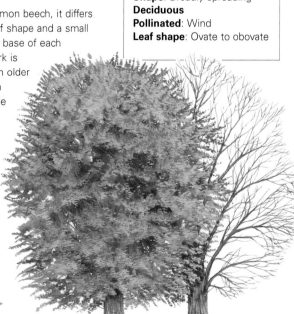

FALSE BEECHES

This relatively little-known group of trees is from temperate regions of the Southern Hemisphere, and is known by the botanical genus Nothofagus. Nothos *comes from the ancient Greek for "spurious" or "false" and* fagus *means "beech"; so the name can be translated as "false beeches." Although these trees are similar to beech there are some differences. Many* Nothofagus *are evergreen and have smaller leaves.*

Antarctic Beech

Nothofagus antarctica

A fast-growing, small to medium-size tree that is extremely elegant, especially when young. It has leaves that, when crushed, or on hot days, emit a sweet, honey-like fragrance. Also known as *nirre* in Chile, it inhabits mountainsides from Cape Horn to northern Chile. In the fall, the leaves turn into a range of glorious colors from scarlet through orange to butter yellow.

Identification: The bark is dark gray, becoming scaly in maturity. The leaves are up to 1½ in (4cm) long, broadly ovate, rounded at the tip and finely toothed around the margin. They are set in two neat rows along the shoot and have a crinkly, shell-like appearance. The flowers are small and pendulous, and appear in late spring, the male borne singly or in twos or threes in the leaf axils. The fruit is a four-valved husk approximately ¼in (5mm) long, each valve containing three nuts.

Distribution: South America: southern Argentina and Chile.
Height: 50ft (15m)
Shape: Broadly columnar
Deciduous
Pollinated: Insect
Leaf shape: Ovate

Left: A flower and fruit.

Right: Leaves are finely toothed.

Rauli

Raoul *Nothofagus nervosa*

Also known as *N. procera*, this large, deciduous forest tree has upswept branches and heavily veined leaves. The name was given by early Spanish settlers who saw its gray, smooth bark and called it after the Spanish word for beech. It is a fast-growing tree, which produces good quality timber and is being planted in temperate regions of the Northern Hemisphere for forestry.

Identification: The bark is dark gray and becomes heavily fissured as the tree matures. The leaves are ovate to oblong, up to 4in (10cm) long and 2in (5cm) across. They are easily distinguished from other *Nothofagus* because they have 14–18 pairs of deep veins, but could at first glance be mistaken for hornbeam. The leaves are positioned alternately along the shoot; they are bronze-green above and paler beneath, with some pubescence on the midrib and veins. The fruit is a four-valved husk about ½in (1cm) long, containing three small nuts.

Distribution: Central Chile and western Argentina.
Height: 82ft (25m)
Shape: Broadly conical
Deciduous
Pollinated: Insect
Leaf shape: Oblong to ovate

Left and right: The long, elegant leaves hang heavily. Unlike those of other members of this genus, they have up to 18 pairs of deep veins.

Dombey's Southern Beech

Nothofagus dombeyi

This large, fast-growing, elegant evergreen tree develops a graceful, broad-spreading habit, not dissimilar to *Cedrus libanii*. It is common in Chilean forests, ranging high into the Andes. In severe winters it may shed its evergreen leaves, replacing them the following spring.

Above: The bark is ash gray, flaking and cracking in maturity.

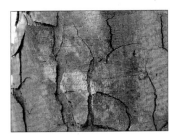

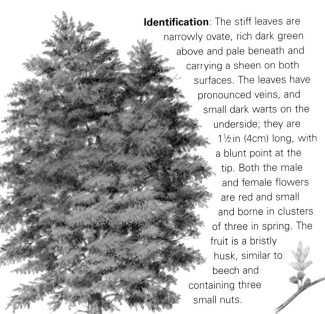

Identification: The stiff leaves are narrowly ovate, rich dark green above and pale beneath and carrying a sheen on both surfaces. The leaves have pronounced veins, and small dark warts on the underside; they are 1½in (4cm) long, with a blunt point at the tip. Both the male and female flowers are red and small and borne in clusters of three in spring. The fruit is a bristly husk, similar to beech and containing three small nuts.

Right: The small husks are visible between the leaves.

Distribution: Chile and Argentina.
Height: 130ft (40m)
Shape: Broadly columnar
Evergreen
Pollinated: Insect
Leaf shape: Ovate

OTHER SPECIES OF NOTE

Black Beech *Nothofagus solandri*
Native to lowland and mountain regions of New Zealand, black beech is a tall, slender, evergreen tree, to 82ft (25m) in the wild. It has small, elliptic, dark green leaves, which are heavily pubescent beneath, and densely borne on wiry shoots, which develop into ascending fan-like branches. It grows in parks across U.S.A.

Silver Beech *Nothofagus menziesii*
Native to New Zealand, where it grows up to 3,280ft (1,000m) above sea level, this evergreen tree reaches 100ft (30m) high. It has a silvery-white trunk, which dulls to gray in maturity. The leaves are ovate to diamond shape, doubly round-toothed and ½in (1cm) long. The petiole and the shoot are covered in a yellowish-brown pubescence. It grows in parks across U.S.A.

Myrtle Tree *Nothofagus cunninghamii*
This medium-size, evergreen Australian tree grows thousands of miles from the majority of the *Nothofagus* genus in South America. It has distinctive, small, diamond-shape leaves which are bluntly toothed in the upper half.

Red Beech *Nothofagus fusca*
This beautiful evergreen tree is native to both islands of New Zealand from 37 degrees latitude south. It reaches large proportions in the wild, but in cultivation, in the Northern Hemisphere, it seldom exceeds 82ft (25m). The leaves are distinctive with their sharply toothed margin. When the old leaves eventually fall they turn coppery red; hence the common name.

Roble Beech

Nothofagus obliqua

Roble is Spanish for oak and in some respects this large South American tree does resemble a European deciduous oak. It also bears oak-like timber, which is tough, durable and over the years has been used for shipbuilding, interior joinery and furniture. It is the most warm-loving of all southern, or false, beeches and thrives in the Mediterranean climate of southern California.

Identification: Roble has gray bark, which becomes cracked and fissured with age. It has dark green, ovate to oval leaves, which are blue-green on the underside, roundly toothed, up to 3in (7.5cm) long, with between eight and eleven pairs of distinct leaf veins. In the fall, the leaves turn golden yellow. Both the male and female flowers are small and green; the males are borne singly and the females in threes, both in late spring.

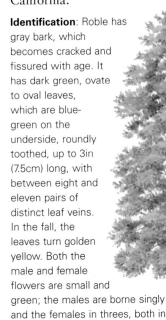

Distribution: Argentina and Chile.
Height: 115ft (35m)
Shape: Broadly columnar
Deciduous
Pollinated: Insect
Leaf shape: Ovate

Above: The fruit is a bristly brown husk, containing three nuts.

CHINKAPINS AND CHESTNUTS

The chestnut genus Castanea *contains just twelve deciduous trees, all of which grow wild in temperate regions of the Northern Hemisphere. They are closely related to both the beech,* Fagus, *and oak,* Quercus, *genera. The majority are long-lived, large trees, which are drought resistant and thrive on dry, shallow soils. All have strongly serrated leaves and edible fruit in the form of a nut.*

American Chestnut

Castanea dentata

Distribution: Eastern North America.
Height: 100ft (30m)
Shape: Broadly columnar
Deciduous
Pollinated: Insect
Leaf shape: Oblong

This majestic tree was once widespread throughout North America, but since the 1930s its population has been devastated by the effects of chestnut blight, *Endothia parasitica*. Today it is rare in the wild, with the species likely to become endangered in the next 20 years. The disease entered North America from east Asia at the end of the nineteenth century.

Identification: The trunk and form of American chestnut is similar to that of sweet chestnut; it has dark gray-brown bark, which becomes spirally fissured with age. Male and female flowers are found in the same yellow, upright catkin. Catkins are up to 8in (20cm) long and ripen in early summer. Fruit is a spiny green (ripening to yellow) husk, up to 2½in (6cm) across.

Right: The oblong leaves are up to 10in (25cm) long and have a margin edged with sharp-toothed serrations. The nuts can be eaten.

Allegheny Chinkapin

Castanea pumila

This small, deciduous American tree is distinguished from other chinkapins by its ability to throw up suckers from the root system. Quite often they will result in a dense thicket around the base of the tree. It is a hardy tree growing up to 4,500ft (1,400m) on dry sandy ridges in the Appalachian Mountains. It produces sweet-tasting nuts, which are sold in the markets of the western and southern States. It is sometimes confused with the trailing chinkapin, *C. alnifolia*, which is a shrub seldom reaching more than 6ft (2m).

Identification: The bark is light brown tinged with red, slightly furrowed and splitting into plate-like scales. The oblong leaves are up to 5in (12cm) long, coarsely serrated around the margin, and taper to a fine point. When the leaves unfold in spring they are tinged with red and covered in a white pubescence which remains on the underside of the leaf throughout the summer. In the fall they turn bright yellow. The fruit is a bristly, spined husk surrounding a dark chestnut-brown nut.

Distribution: New Jersey to Florida and west to Texas.
Height: 50ft (15m)
Shape: Broadly spreading
Deciduous
Pollinated: Insect
Leaf shape: Oblong

Right: The leaves may be up to 5in (12cm) long and carry a white pubescence on the underside.

Sweet Chestnut
Castanea sativa

This fast-growing ornamental is native to warm, temperate areas of the Mediterranean and into southwestern Asia. It has been widely cultivated elsewhere. The Romans introduced it to Europe as a source of food. It is believed to have been introduced into North America in the early seventeenth century.

Castanopsis cuspidata
This is a large, elegant evergreen tree in its native homelands of southern Japan, China and Korea. In cultivation elsewhere, it seldom becomes more than a small, bushy tree. It is hardy to U.S.A. zone 7. The leaves are oval, glossy, dark green and leathery. The fruit is an acorn, borne on a stalk with up to ten others, all encased within rows of downy scales.

Japanese Chestnut *Castanea crenata*
This small tree is native to Japan, but cultivated

elsewhere in botanic gardens. In Japan it is a valuable food source, and the tree is grown in orchards for its small, edible nuts. It is often cultivated in the U.S.A. because of its resistance to blight.

Golden Chestnut

Golden chinkapin *Chrysolepis chrysophylla*

This evergreen tree is quite often referred to as the golden chinkapin, and botanically as *Castanopsis chrysophylla*, although this is incorrect because the flowers on *Castanopsis* are borne on separate catkins, whereas on this tree they are on the same catkin. The name "golden" refers to the underside of the leaf, which is covered with a bright golden pubescence, a feature that quickly distinguishes it from just about any other member of the Fagaceae family.

Identification: The bark is gray, smooth when young, becoming fissured in old age. The leaves are evergreen, lanceolate to oblong, broad in the center tapering to a point at each end, up to 4in (10cm) long and 1in (2.5cm) wide. Glossy dark, almost black-green above and with a rich golden pubescence beneath, they are held on a green petiole ½in (1cm) long. Both male and female flowers are fragrant, creamy-yellow and borne on the same erect, 1½in- (4cm-) long catkin in summer.

Distribution: Oregon and California, U.S.A.
Height: 100ft (30m)
Shape: Broadly conical
Evergreen
Pollinated: Insect
Leaf shape: Lanceolate to oblong

Below: The fruit is a spiny husk, very similar to sweet chestnut, containing up to three glossy brown nuts.

Tanbark Oak

Lithocarpus densiflorus

This evergreen tree is closely related to an oak, but several of the characteristics relating to its flowers are very different from oak. It is native to California and Oregon, where it grows into a pyramidal-shape tree up to 82ft (25m) tall. The leaves are sharply toothed, dark glossy green above and covered with white pubescence beneath. The fruit is an acorn, 1in (2.5cm) long, set in a shallow, pubescent cup with reflexed scales.

Identification: This tender, small tree has smooth gray-brown bark that becomes uniformly fissured with age. The bark is an excellent source of tannin. It has stiff leathery leaves. Both the underside of the leaf and the young shoots are covered with thick gray-white wool. The male and female flowers are creamy yellow and small. They are held in erect, thin spikes, up to 4in (10cm) long, in May.

Distribution: Oregon and California, U.S.A.
Height: 82ft (25m)
Shape: Broadly pyramidal
Evergreen
Pollinated: Insect
Leaf shape: Oval to oblong

Left: Both male and female flowers are long, upright spikes.

Right: The fruit is a small pointed acorn, in a shallow cup.

AMERICAN OAKS

There are almost 600 different species of oak, Quercus, *in the world, the majority of which grow in the Northern Hemisphere. Almost 80 of these grow in North America and at least 60 are large trees. There are oaks native to every region of the North American continent from Alaska to New Mexico. Some play an integral part in the leaf-color spectacle every fall in New England.*

Northern Red Oak

Quercus rubra

Distribution: Nova Scotia and Quebec south to Alabama.
Height: 80ft (25m)
Shape: Broadly spreading
Deciduous
Pollinated: Wind
Leaf shape: Elliptic to obovate

The northern red oak grows further north in eastern North America than any other oak. It is very common in New England and the Allegheny Mountains, and has been widely planted on the West Coast from British Columbia to Oregon. It provides spectacular fall leaf-color, particularly in New England. Its leaves are similar to scarlet oak, but not so glossy on the upper surface.

Identification: The bark is gray and smooth becoming deeply fissured in maturity. The leaves are elliptic to obovate, up to 8in (20cm) long, with distinctive narrow lobes, which run to fine points. They are dull matt green above, and pale green beneath, with tufts of fine brown hair in the vein axils. Male flowers are green-yellow catkins, appearing in late spring.

Left: The fruit is a squat acorn, to 1¼in (3cm) long and seated in a shallow cup.

Pin Oak

Quercus palustris

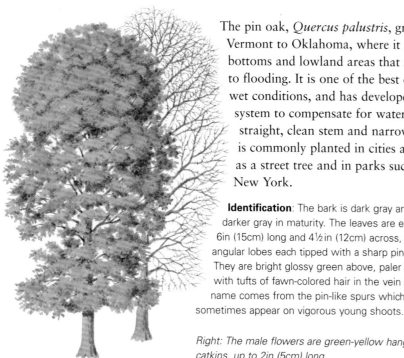

Distribution: From Rhode Island and Vermont to Tennessee.
Height: 100ft (30m)
Shape: Broadly conical
Deciduous
Pollinated: Wind
Leaf shape: Elliptic to obovate

The pin oak, *Quercus palustris*, grows wild from Vermont to Oklahoma, where it grows in valley bottoms and lowland areas that are quite often subject to flooding. It is one of the best oaks for growing in wet conditions, and has developed a shallow rooting system to compensate for waterlogging. Due to its straight, clean stem and narrow, spire-like shape, it is commonly planted in cities across the U.S.A. both as a street tree and in parks such as Central Park in New York.

Identification: The bark is dark gray and smooth becoming darker gray in maturity. The leaves are elliptic to obovate, up to 6in (15cm) long and 4½in (12cm) across, with up to four pairs of angular lobes each tipped with a sharp pin-like bristle. They are bright glossy green above, paler beneath, with tufts of fawn-colored hair in the vein axils. The name comes from the pin-like spurs which sometimes appear on vigorous young shoots.

Right: The male flowers are green-yellow hanging catkins, up to 2in (5cm) long.

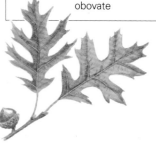

Scarlet Oak

Quercus coccinea

Scarlet oak is one of the most ornamental trees of eastern North America, contributing greatly to the fall leaf-color spectacular. The leaves stay on the trees far longer than those of any of the other fall-color trees. It grows on poor sandy soils up to elevations of 5,000ft (1,520m) in the Appalachian Mountains. It does not grow well in shade.

Identification: The bark is slate gray and smooth, becoming slightly fissured in maturity. Although the leaves are roughly elliptical in shape they are eaten into by several angular lobes, some cutting almost to the midrib. Each lobe point is tipped with a sharp bristle. The upper leaf surface is dark green and glossy, the underside is pale green with tufts of pubescence in the vein axils. Male flowers are borne in yellow, drooping catkins in late spring; the female flowers are inconspicuous, but borne on the same tree. The acorn is 1in (2–3cm) long. Half of it is enclosed in a deep, shiny cup. Although very often confused with red oak, *Q. rubra*, the scarlet oak is a narrower and more open tree, with a rounder and deeper acorn cup.

Distribution: Eastern North America from Ontario to Missouri, but not Florida.
Height: 82ft (25m)
Shape: Broadly spreading
Deciduous
Pollinated: Wind
Leaf shape: Elliptic

Left: The leaves, which have a very ragged appearance for an oak, stay on the tree later than its relatives.

Shingle Oak
Quercus imbricaria
Shingle oak is native to central and eastern U.S.A. from Pennsylvania to North Carolina. The name refers to the fact that early colonial settlers

made roofing shingles from its wood. Shingle oak has deciduous, oblong to lanceolate, untoothed leaves, up to 6in (15cm) long with a wavy margin. The flat acorn cup is covered with overlapping woody scales.

Swamp White Oak *Quercus bicolor*
The swamp white oak is native to eastern North America from Quebec to Missouri. It is a medium-size tree up to 82ft (25m) tall. As the common name suggests it grows best in deep, damp soils and alongside rivers. The species name *bicolor* refers to the fact that the leaf is dark glossy green above, and silvery-gray and covered in soft down beneath.

Willow Oak *Quercus phellos*
This oak is easily recognized by its narrow, willow-like leaves, which are late unfurling from bud, and have a yellow and red tinted center which becomes sage green as the summer progresses. Willow oak is native to an area which extends from Delaware to Texas. This broadly spreading tree is also widely planted in cities, such as New York, as a street tree.

White Oak

Stave oak *Quercus alba*

A large tree, common throughout its range. It grows largest on the lower western slopes of the Alleghany Mountains, and reaches altitudes of 4,500ft (1,400m) in the southern Appalachian Mountains. It is an important timber tree, widely used in cooperage; the close-grained, water-resistant wood is used for making barrel staves.

Identification: The bark is slate gray, smooth at first becoming scaly and fissured with age. The leaves are extremely variable, even on the same tree, but on average they are obovate, up to 8in (20cm) long and 4in (10cm) wide, with between two and four narrow lobes on each side of the leaf, which tapers towards the base. They emerge from winter bud pink and covered in a fine pubescence.

Distribution: From Quebec to Texas and across to the Atlantic coast.
Height: 115ft (35m)
Shape: Broadly spreading
Deciduous
Pollinated: Wind
Leaf shape: Obovate

Left: By midsummer the leaves are bright green above and pale green-gray beneath. In the fall the leaves turn deep purple-red before dropping.

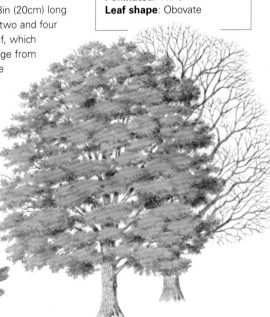

Chestnut Oak

Quercus prinus

The bark of this large American oak, which has chestnut-like leaves, was once used for tanning leather by the early settlers. It grows on mountain slopes and in rocky places, particularly in the Appalachian Mountains, where it is found at elevations up to 4,800ft (1,500m) above sea level. It has been widely planted on the Atlantic coastal plain as an ornamental species in parks and gardens.

Identification: The bark is dark gray, thick, with close, broad ridges and deep fissures in maturity. The leaves are up to 8in (20cm) long and 4in (10cm) wide, with between 10–15 pairs of prominent, parallel veins, which run out to the tip of a rounded tooth. They are dark, glossy green above with a yellow midrib and sage green beneath. The fruit is a shining rich red-brown acorn, which is held in a deep cup that encloses up to one half of the acorn.

Distribution: From Maine southeast to Alabama.
Height: 100ft (30m)
Shape: Broadly spreading
Deciduous
Pollinated: Wind
Leaf shape: Oblong to obovate

Left: The acorns of chestnut oak are borne on the tree either singly or in pairs and attached by a short stout stalk which is seldom more than ½in (1.25cm) long.

Swamp Chestnut Oak

Basket oak, Cow oak *Quercus michauxii*

Distribution: Atlantic coastal plain to the Mississippi basin.
Height: 80ft (25m)
Shape: Broadly spreading
Deciduous
Pollinated: Wind
Leaf shape: Obovate

Also called basket oak because the wood easily splits into thin strips, which were once used to make baskets for carrying cotton. This tree is a close relative of the chestnut oak, *Quercus prinus*, taking over in the south where chestnut oak leaves off. It grows well in wet areas, and is commonly found in valley bottoms and on flood plains. It was also called cow oak because its sweet acorns became a staple food for the cattle of the early settlers.

Identification: The bark differs from chestnut oak in being much lighter and thinner. It is almost creamy gray and much less ridged and fissured. The leaves are also wider, being up to 10in (25cm) long with between 10–14 rounded teeth on each side of the leaf. The leaves are dark green above and almost silver beneath. The fruit is a light brown acorn, up to 1¼in (3cm) long and held in a stout cup.

Above: Swamp chestnut oak is a large round-topped tree with distinctive ascending branches.

Left: When the leaves emerge from bud in spring they are bright yellow-green.

Black Oak

Yellow-bark oak *Quercus velutina*

This large oak is native to dry, gravelly uplands and ridges throughout eastern and central North America. It attains its highest elevations in the southern Appalachian Mountains where it grows up to 4,000ft (1,200m) above sea level. It is also known as yellow-bark oak, a reference to the inner bark which is a deep yellow-orange color. It is full of tannic acid and was once used in tanning of leather and as a yellow dye.

Identification: The outer bark is dark brown and ridged. The leaves, which are tough like parchment, are ovate to elliptic, up to 10in (25cm) long and 6in (15cm) wide. They mostly have seven pointed lobes and a distinct yellow central midrib. They are glossy dark green above and pea-green beneath with tufts of copper-colored hair in the leaf vein axils. The fruit is enclosed in a bowl-shaped cup, which covers about half of the acorn.

Distribution: From Maine to Georgia in the east and Wisconsin to Texas in the west, U.S.A.
Height: 100ft (30m)
Shape: Broadly spreading
Deciduous
Pollinated: Wind
Leaf shape: Ovate to elliptic

Left: The acorn is red-brown and up to 1in (2.5cm) long.

OTHER SPECIES OF NOTE

Oregon White Oak *Quercus garryana*
The only oak that is native to British Columbia and Washington. Its range extends south along the Coast Range through Oregon into California. It is a broadly spreading, medium-size tree, to 80ft (25m). It has dark green, obovate leaves, with two or three deep, rounded lobes on each side.

Post Oak *Quercus stellata*
Widely spread throughout eastern and central U.S.A., this round-headed, medium-size oak has foliage so dark that the tree appears nearly black in the landscape. It has heavily lobed leaves; the lobes are arranged in a way that gives a cross-like appearance to the leaf. Fence posts were once made from the timber, hence its name.

Blackjack Oak *Quercus marilandica*
A medium-size tree native to southeastern U.S.A., from Long Island to Texas and Arkansas, where it grows in dry uplands and on the edge of prairies, and may be little more than a tall, spreading shrub. It has distinctive leaves, which are thick and stiff, almost triangular in shape, and up to 6in (15cm) long and 4in (10cm) wide.

Northern Pin Oak *Quercus ellipsoidalis*
A medium-size tree, which usually has a short trunk and a large spreading crown. It grows naturally from northern Indiana northwards to Minnesota, particularly around the Great Lakes region. The leaves, which are deeply lobed almost to the red midrib, unfurl from bud a pale crimson color, turn shiny dark green in summer and then deep red in the fall.

Valley Oak

Californian white oak *Quercus lobata*

This large, attractive tree, otherwise known as the Californian white oak, grows naturally in the valleys of western California between the Sierra Nevada and the Pacific coast. The oldest trees are to be found in Mendocino county where there are specimens over 600 years old. It has the deepest-lobed leaves of any oak, hence the species name *lobata*; the lobes penetrate deep into the leaf almost to the midrib.

Identification: The bark is light gray, thick and divided into vertical fissures, becoming tinged with orange or brown in maturity. The leaves are up to 4in (10cm) long, deep green above and pale green with some pubescence beneath. They have between five and eleven rounded lobes on each side of the leaf. The acorn is held in a shallow cup that encloses less than a third of the acorn.

Distribution: California from Trinity River to Los Angeles.
Height: 100ft (30m)
Shape: Broadly spreading
Deciduous
Pollinated: Wind
Leaf shape: Oblong to obovate

Right: The fruit is a pointed, slender acorn, up to 2½in (6cm) long.

EVERGREEN OAKS

There are over 30 evergreen oaks that are either native, or commonly cultivated, within North America. Most are medium-size, slow-growing trees and in some cases of great age. They are generally hardy, quite often found growing high up in mountain ranges or on exposed coastline. Their tolerance of exposure and salt spray means they are often used to provide shelter from on-shore winds.

Live Oak

Quercus virginiana

Distribution: Southeast U.S.A.
Height: 50ft (15m)
Shape: Broadly spreading
Evergreen
Pollinated: Wind
Leaf shape: Variable from oblong to elliptic

Right: The acorns are borne in groups of three to five.

This dense, round-topped tree, typically more broad than tall, is native to a coastal belt which runs from Virginia round to southern Texas. In South Carolina it is widely planted as an avenue tree for the long drives leading to the plantation mansions. It is extremely tolerant of salt spray, and is quite often used to provide shelter from onshore winds in coastal areas.

Identification: The bark is dark brown sometimes tinged with red, lightly fissured and separating into small scales in maturity. The evergreen leaves are extremely variable. They may be lobed and toothed around the margin, or entirely smooth and they can vary in length from 2–5in (5–12.5cm). They are dark green and lustrous above, and pale green and pubescent beneath. The shoots and young branchlets are also covered in a gray down. The fruit is a stout chestnut-brown acorn, which is held in a light brown cup to one third of its length.

Canyon Live Oak

Quercus chrysolepis

The canyon live oak is a squat tree with a short trunk, and long, horizontal-spreading branches forming a broad canopy, sometimes 150ft (46m) across. It occurs naturally from Oregon south to the Mexican border, down both the Coast Range and the Sierra Nevada mountains, where it reaches elevations of 9,000ft (2,750m) above sea level. It was identified by Charles Sargent of the Arnold Arboretum, Boston.

Distribution: West Coast U.S.A.
Height: 50ft (15m)
Shape: Broadly spreading
Evergreen
Pollinated: Wind
Leaf shape: Oblong to ovate to elliptic

Identification: The bark is up to 2in (5cm) thick, ash gray, sometimes tinged with red, and covered with small scales in maturity. The leaves are similar to the live oak, *Quercus virginiana*, varying from entire and smooth to lobed and spiny, sometimes on the same tree. They are a bright yellow-green above, and pale green beneath with some pubescence. It has distinctive acorns, which are up to 2in (5cm) long and held in a flat cup, which is as wide as the acorn is tall.

Right: The acorns are usually borne singly and held in a flat cup, which is marked with triangular scales.

Arizona White Oak

Quercus arizonica

This long-lived, slow-growing tree has small, thick, hard evergreen leaves which normally last only one year, falling in spring to be immediately replaced by new ones. It is the most common white oak of southern New Mexico and Arizona and its range extends south to northern Mexico. It grows on hot, sandy hillsides and dry, rocky canyons, up to 10,000ft (3,000m) above sea level. It tends to be a low-spreading tree, with large twisted branches.

Distribution: Texas, New Mexico and Arizona, U.S.A.
Height: 65ft (20m)
Shape: Broadly spreading
Evergreen
Pollinated: Wind
Leaf shape: Oblong-lanceolate

Identification: The bark is ash gray and covered in long, scaly ridges. The leaves may vary from oblong to lanceolate, normally pointed at the tip, but sometimes rounded. They emerge light red in color, quickly turning dull, dark blue-green above, and pale green below and covered in fine pubescence. The fruit is a dark chestnut-brown, oval acorn which is up to 1in (2.5cm) long, and enclosed for half its length in a light brown cup covered with pointed, tipped scales.

Right: The leaves can be entire or toothed.

OTHER SPECIES OF NOTE

Holm Oak
Quercus ilex
This domed, densely branched oak tree is one of the most important trees for shelter in coastal areas throughout Europe. In the wild in

Italy, France and Spain, it grows from sea level to altitudes above 5,000ft (1,520m). It grows across the U.S.A. The bark is charcoal gray, smooth at first, but quickly developing shallow fissures, which crack into small and irregular plates. In more mature trees the narrow, evergreen leaf normally has an entire margin with no serrations.

Turkey Oak *Quercus cerris*
This is a tall, vigorous, deciduous tree with a straight stem, and deeply fissured, gray-brown bark. It is native to central and southern Europe, although its exact range is unknown because it has been planted across the rest of Europe for centuries and naturalizes easily. The elliptic leaves are up to 4in (10cm) long, with irregular lobing, particularly on young trees. The acorn cups are covered in whiskers. It grows in U.S.A. zones 4–7.

Californian Live Oak

Quercus agrifolia

There is a suggestion that the botanical name of this tree should be *aquifolia*, which means "holly-like," rather than *agrifolia*, which means "growing wild on arable land." The leaf is holly-like, and the tree does grow naturally in coastal areas, in some cases directly above the high water mark. This dense foliaged, evergreen tree is an attractive feature of the Pacific seaboard.

Distribution: Southwestern U.S.A.
Height: 80ft (25m)
Shape: Broadly spreading
Evergreen
Pollinated: Wind
Leaf shape: Oval to oblong

Identification: On young trees the bark is smooth and light gray, on older trees it becomes almost black and divided into broad, rounded ridges. The leaves vary from narrow lanceolate to almost round and may taper to a fine point or a blunt end. They are a dark, dull green above and pale sage-green below and sometimes covered with a thick coating of rusty-color down in the leaf axils. The acorn is held in a light fawn-colored cup which extends over a third of the acorn.

Below: The fruit is a light chestnut brown acorn, approximately 1¼in (3cm) long,

BIRCHES

The birches, Betula, are a group of catkin-bearing, alternate-leaved, deciduous trees, native to northern temperate regions of the world. There are more than 60 species in total, spread right across the region, from Japan to Spain and across North America. They are particularly well known for their attractive bark, which, depending on species, can vary from pure white to red.

Yellow Birch

Betula alleghaniensis

Distribution: Eastern North America.
Height: 100ft (30m)
Shape: Broadly columnar
Deciduous
Pollinated: Wind
Leaf shape: Ovate to oblong

Previously known as *B. lutea*, this large, handsome birch has long been a valued timber tree to the US Forest Service. The name is well chosen, for it has several yellow characteristics, including the bark. It has been widely planted as an ornamental species elsewhere in the temperate world.

Identification: The bark is yellowish-brown, peeling in horizontal flakes to reveal more vibrant, yellow-colored bark beneath. The leaves are ovate-oblong, up to 4in (10cm) long and 2in (5cm) across, finely toothed along the margin, tapering to a point, grass green above, paler beneath. In the fall, they turn golden yellow. The male flowers are borne in drooping yellow catkins, 4in (10cm) long; female flowers are borne in shorter, red-brown erect catkins.

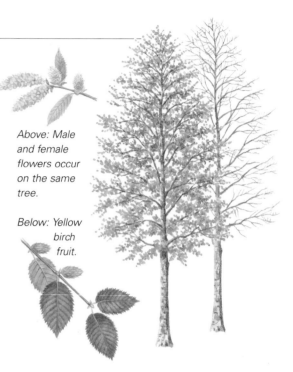

Above: Male and female flowers occur on the same tree.

Below: Yellow birch fruit.

River Birch

Black birch *Betula nigra*

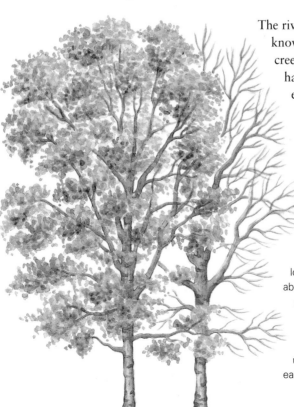

The river birch, or black birch, as it is sometimes known, lives up to its name by growing beside creeks and in low-lying, swampy ground. It has been planted extensively to help control erosion caused by flooding. River birch is one of the few birches to regenerate well from cut stumps and is often coppiced to encourage multiple stems, which display attractive, pink-brown, peeling bark.

Distribution: Central and eastern U.S.A. from Maine in the east to Minnesota in the west and south to Texas.
Height: 100ft (30m)
Shape: Broadly spreading
Deciduous
Pollinated: Wind
Leaf shape: Ovate

Identification: The bark is pink-brown and peeling when young, becoming dark black-purple with orange fissures in maturity. The 4in- (10cm-) long, ovate leaves are edged with sharp, double teeth, which give the leaf a slight lobed appearance. The leaves are deep green above and blue-green beneath with silver-gray pubescence on the leaf veins. Both the male and female flowers are catkins, up to 3in (7.5cm) long. The male catkins are yellow and hang down; while the female catkins are green and upright. Both appear on the same tree in early spring.

Above: Female flowers are upright green catkins which are borne on the tree before the leaves emerge in early spring.

Cherry Birch

Sweet birch *Betula lenta*

This attractive tree is common across central and eastern North America. Its alternative common name refers to the fragrance that the shoots and leaves emit when crushed. Wintergreen oil was distilled from its wood. It has distinctive, dark red bark with purple flakes. In the fall its leaves fleetingly turn vibrant gold.

Identification: The leaves are ovate, to 5in (12cm) long and 2½in (6cm) across. They are edged with small, sharp teeth, and have distinct leaf veins. They are glossy dark green above, and pale green with fine pubescence below, especially when young. The reddish bark is lined with pale horizontal bands of lenticels.

Left: Male and female catkins are borne separately on the same tree in early spring.

Left and right: The leaves taper to a short point.

Distribution: North America from Quebec to Alabama.
Height: 80ft (25m)
Shape: Broadly spreading
Deciduous
Pollinated: Wind
Leaf shape: Ovate

OTHER SPECIES OF NOTE

European White Birch *Betula pendula*
Otherwise known as silver birch, this hardy ornamental tree has long been planted across North America. It is easily distinguished by its white bark, which is marked by black diamond-like patches, and the lax, rather warty, pendulous shoots at the tips of the branches. European white birch is a prolific seeder, and one of the first trees to colonize cleared ground.

Himalayan Birch *Betula utilis*
This Asian birch is one of the most attractive deciduous trees, and has long been planted in parks, gardens and botanical collections across North America. The color of its bark varies from white to pink-brown or orange-red. The bark is paper thin and peels off in long, ribbon-like horizontal strips.

Chinese Red-barked Birch *Betula albo-sinensis*
Discovered in western China in 1901, the Chinese red-barked birch was first planted at the Arnold Arboretum, Boston, in 1905. It has attractive coppery to orange-red bark, which peels to reveal cream-pink bark beneath.

Gray Birch *Betula populifolia*
This North American birch grows wild on the east coast from Nova Scotia and New Brunswick, south to Pennsylvania and Ohio. It is a fast-growing, small species, which seldom reaches 33ft (10m) in height. It has dark green, long, tapering leaves and white bark, which does not peel. It is a common roadside tree throughout its natural range.

Paper Birch

Canoe birch *Betula papyrifera*

Native Americans used the tough, durable bark of this beautiful tree to cover their canoes, having discovered it is impervious to water. It is an extremely hardy tree, growing as far north as Alaska and Labrador. The light, close-grained timber is also used as wood-pulp for paper making. Its peeling bark is one of its most attractive features, varying in color from pure white to pale pink.

Below: The male and female flowers are catkins which are borne separately on the same tree in early spring.

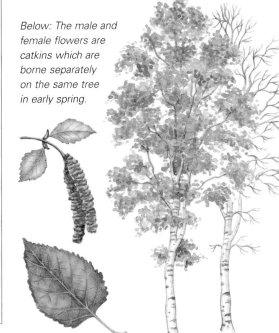

Distribution: Coast to coast northern North America.
Height: 65ft (20m)
Shape: Broadly conical
Deciduous
Pollinated: Wind
Leaf shape: Ovate

Identification: The leaves are ovate, up to 4in (10cm) long, and 3in (7.5cm) wide, with shallow teeth around the margin. Each leaf ends in a tapered point and is dark green and smooth on top, and pale green and pubescent along the veins below. In the fall the leaves turn bright marmalade-orange. Male catkins are up to 4in (10cm) long, drooping and bright yellow. Female catkins are green and slightly shorter. Both ripen and disintegrate on the tree in summer, releasing thousands of seeds, dispersed by the wind.

ALDERS

Alders are a group of 36 species of deciduous trees within the Betulaceae family. They are native primarily to northern temperate regions of the world, where they grow in damp conditions, quite often alongside rivers and watercourses. They are easily recognized by their fruit, which is an egg-shape, pendulous, woody cone containing numerous tiny winged seeds.

Common Alder

Alnus glutinosa

This tree has always been associated with water. It thrives in damp, waterlogged conditions close to rivers and marshy ground, where it creates its own oxygen supply. Alder timber is waterproof, and has been used to make products such as boats and water pipes. It also forms the foundations of many of the buildings in Venice, and is used to make wooden clogs. It was introduced into the U.S.A, and has naturalized, growing alongside streams.

Identification: The bark is dark gray-brown and fissured from an early age. The leaves are obovate to orbicular, finely toothed with up to ten pairs of pronounced leaf veins, and a strong central midrib. Up to 4in (10cm) long and 3in (7.5cm) wide, the leaves are dark green and shiny above and pale grey-green beneath, with tufts of pubescence in the leaf axils. Male and female flowers are catkins: the male is greenish-yellow, drooping and up to 4in (10cm) long; the female is a much smaller, red, upright catkin, which after fertilization, ripens into a distinctive small brown cone. Spent cones persist until the following spring.

Distribution: Whole of Europe into western Asia and south to North Africa. U.S.A. zones 3–7.
Height: 82ft (25m)
Shape: Broadly conical
Deciduous
Pollinated: Wind
Leaf shape: Obovate

Left: Catkins appear before the leaves in spring. The cones grow in summer, by which time the rounded leaves are thick on the branches.

Red Alder

Oregon alder *Alnus rubra*

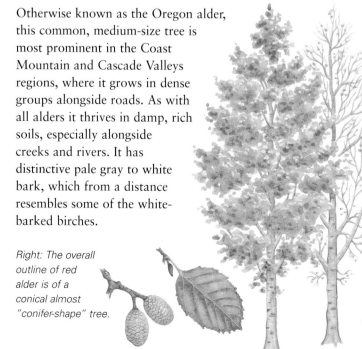

Otherwise known as the Oregon alder, this common, medium-size tree is most prominent in the Coast Mountain and Cascade Valleys regions, where it grows in dense groups alongside roads. As with all alders it thrives in damp, rich soils, especially alongside creeks and rivers. It has distinctive pale gray to white bark, which from a distance resembles some of the white-barked birches.

Right: The overall outline of red alder is of a conical almost "conifer-shape" tree.

Identification: The leaves are ovate to elliptic, up to 4in (10cm) long and 3in (7.5cm) broad, with a slight point at the tip. They are dark green and smooth above, and pale green with rusty-red hairs along the pronounced, straight parallel leaf veins beneath. Both the male and female flowers are catkins, which are borne separately on the same tree in early spring. The male flowers are drooping, orange and up to 6in (15cm) long. The female flowers are much smaller, bright red and borne upright. These ripen into 1in- (2.5cm-) long, egg-shaped woody cones containing numerous seeds.

Distribution: West Coast from Alaska to southern California, U.S.A.
Height: 50ft (15m)
Shape: Broadly conical
Deciduous
Pollinated: Wind
Leaf shape: Ovate

Speckled Alder

Alnus rugosa

Native of North America from Newfoundland to Alaska and ranging south on the east coast to West Virginia, Ohio and Minnesota. It is a hardy small tree, or large shrub, which thrives in cold, wet conditions where other trees would struggle. It is a close relative of the European gray alder, *Alnus incana*. Speckled alder has light, soft, close-grained, fawn-colored wood, which was at one time used for smoking salmon.

Identification: The whole tree has a rather shrubby appearance with branching from ground level intertwining with branches further up the stem. The bark is dark gray and smooth. The leaves are oval to ovate, up to 4in (10cm) long, and may be either rounded or slightly pointed at the tip. They are sharply and unevenly toothed around the leaf margin, bright green and smooth above and pale green with some pubescence beneath. The fruit is a small green cone-like structure that ripens to woody brown and persists on the tree long after leaf fall.

Distribution: Coast to coast from Newfoundland to Alaska.
Height: 30ft (9m)
Shape: Broadly spreading
Deciduous
Pollinated: Wind
Leaf Shape: Ovate

Left: The male catkins are up to 4in (10cm) long and appear before the tree comes into leaf in early spring.

OTHER SPECIES OF NOTE

Gray Alder *Alnus incana*
Native to the Caucasus Mountains of central Europe, this medium-size tree grows up to elevations of 3,280ft (1,000m). It gets its name from the dense covering of gray hairs on the underside of the leaf. The leaves are ovate, up to 4in (10cm) long, double toothed and have a pointed tip. The bark is dark grey and smooth in maturity.

Sitka Alder *Alnus sinuata*
This small, hardy tree is native to western North America from Alaska to California. It grows well at high altitudes and can withstand intense cold and frost. Sitka alder has distinctive yellow male catkins, which can be up to 6in (15cm) long and are borne in great profusion in early spring.

Italian Alder *Alnus cordata*
This handsome, broadly conical tree originates from southern Italy and Corsica, where it grows at up to 3,280ft (1,000m) on dry mountain slopes. It is the largest of the alders, easily reaching in excess of 100ft (30m) tall. Italian alder has large obovate, glossy, dark green leaves, each up to 4in (10cm) across. It has been widely planted in parks, gardens and arboreta across North America since its introduction in the mid-nineteenth century. It is the only alder that will tolerate dry conditions.

White Alder

Alnus rhombifolia

The white alder grows by running streams and watercourses in canyons in the Rocky Mountains from Idaho and Montana south to southern California. To the early settlers its presence was a good indicator of running water. Its botanical name is derived from the almost diamond shape of the leaves; however, they are more commonly ovate or oval to round. It is a rare tree in cultivation.

Identification: The bark of young trees is smooth and pale gray, becoming dark brown, heavily fissured, and scale-like in maturity. The leaves may be up to 4in (10cm) long and 3in (7.5cm) wide. They are unevenly toothed around the edges, dark shiny green above, and pale yellow beneath, with some pubescence. Both the male and female flowers are catkins, which are borne separately on the same tree in early spring, before the leaves appear. The male catkins are reddish yellow and up to 5in (12.5cm) long.

Distribution: Western U.S.A.
Height: 100ft (30m)
Shape: Broadly conical
Deciduous
Pollinated: Wind
Leaf shape: Ovate

Below: When the leaves unfold from the bud they are covered in dense white hair.

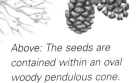

Above: The seeds are contained within an oval woody pendulous cone.

HORNBEAMS, HOP HORNBEAMS AND HAZELS

Hornbeams and hazels are members of the Betulaceae family. They have a strong association with rural communities, although their economic importance has lessened.

American Hornbeam

Blue beech, water beech and ironwood *Carpinus caroliniana*

American hornbeam has an interesting natural distribution, growing wild down the east coast of North America and then in southern Mexico, Guatemala and Honduras. It is not widely planted, yet it has more attractive foliage and superior fall color than the more common European hornbeam.

Below: The male catkins are yellow, drooping and up to 1½in (4cm) long.

Identification: The bark is steel gray and smooth becoming fluted in maturity. The leaves are dark green all over and turn a mixture of orange, purple and red in the fall. Male and female flowers are catkins borne separately on the same tree in spring. The female catkins are green, smaller and borne at the shoot tips. The fruit is a nut attached to two or three bracts; these fruits cluster together in pendulous catkins.

Distribution: From Quebec southwards to Florida and then west to Texas—then a gap and then southern Mexico, Guatemala and Honduras.
Height: 33ft (10m)
Shape: Broadly spreading
Deciduous
Pollinated: Wind
Leaf shape: Ovate

Left: The leaves are ovate, to 4in (10cm) long, edged with coarse double teeth, taper pointed and carry pronounced parallel veins.

Hornbeam

Carpinus betulus

Distribution: Central Europe, including southern Britain to southwest Asia. U.S.A. hardiness zones 4–7.
Height: 100ft (30m)
Shape: Broadly spreading
Deciduous
Pollinated: Wind
Leaf shape: Ovate

Left: The fruit is a ribbed nut.

Hornbeam is sometimes confused with beech because of its silver-gray bark and similar leaf. However, hornbeam bark is far more angular than beech bark. Hornbeam leaves also have obvious serrations around the margin, which are not present on beech. Its timber is dense and hard, and has a clean, white, crisp appearance. It has been introduced into the U.S.A. and is a good shade tree for large lawns.

Identification: The leaves are oval to ovate, up to 4in (10cm) long and 2in (5cm) across, double-toothed around the margin and tapering to a long point. There are normally 10–13 pairs of leaf veins. The upper leaf surface of the leaves is dark green, the underside a paler green. In the fall the leaf turns rich yellow before dropping. Both catkins are borne separately in spring on the same tree. The fruit is a distinctive three-lobed bract with a small, ribbed, brown nut at the base of the center bract. The bract is green in summer, ripening to fawn in the fall and persisting on the tree through to the following spring.

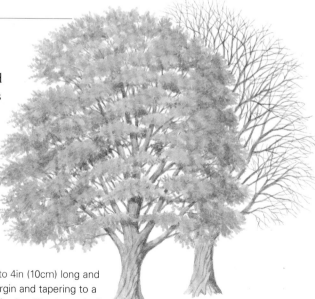

Right: Male catkins are up to 2in (5cm) long. Female catkins (not shown) are smaller.

Hop Hornbeam

Ostrya carpinifolia

This distinctive ornamental tree is primarily known for its hop-like fruit which, when ripe, hangs in clusters of buff-colored, overlapping papery scales, enclosing a small brown nut. Mature trees have long, low, horizontal branches, which seem to defy gravity. It is planted as a street tree in the U.S.A.

Identification: The bark of hop hornbeam is smooth and brown-gray when young, becoming flaky, rather like Persian ironwood, in maturity. The ovate to oblong leaves are up to 4in (10cm) long and 2in (5cm) across. They are sharply pointed and have forward-pointing, double teeth around the margin. They are dark green above and paler beneath, with slight pubescence on both sides. Each leaf has 12–15 pairs of parallel leaf veins and a pronounced midrib. The flowers are catkins: the male's are yellow, drooping and up to 4in (10cm) long; the female's are much smaller and green. The shape in maturity is broadly spreading, with the width quite often exceeding the height.

Distribution: Southern Europe to Iran. U.S.A. zones 6–9.
Height: 66ft (20m)
Shape: Broadly spreading
Deciduous
Pollinated: Wind
Leaf shape: Ovate

Left and above: The hop-like fruit develops in summer from long, drooping catkins.

Eastern Hop Hornbeam

American hop hornbeam, Ironwood *Ostrya virginiana*

This medium-size tree has much the same native range as the American hornbeam, *Carpinus caroliniana*, including southern Mexico. It does not have such a distinctive hop-like flower as the European hop hornbeam, *Ostrya carpinifolia*, but makes up for this with a very distinctive leaf, which has variable teeth around the margin. As one of its other names suggests, the American hop hornbeam has very strong, hard timber which is used to make handles of tools, such as mallets.

Identification: The bark is gray-brown, smooth at first, becoming scaly in maturity. The pointed leaves are ovate, to 5in (12.5cm) long and 2in (5cm) across, with twelve pairs of distinctive leaf veins, and irregular serrations around the leaf margin. They are dark green and smooth above, and slightly paler green with some pubescence in the vein axils beneath. The flowers are catkins, and the fruit is a nut, which is enclosed in a cream, bladder-like husk, which is borne in hanging clusters of up to 20 husks at a time.

Left: Male and female flowers are borne on the same tree.

Right: The dark green leaves look like those of the birch tree.

Distribution: Eastern North America.
Height: 65ft (20m)
Shape: Broadly conical
Deciduous
Pollinated: Wind
Leaf shape: Ovate

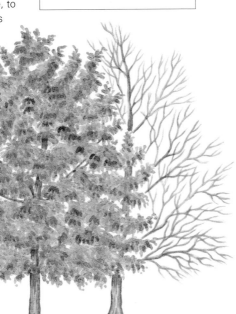

BASSWOODS AND LIMES

There are about 45 different species of lime within the Tilia genus. They are all deciduous and all found in northern temperate regions. Limes are handsome trees, many growing into large, ornamental specimens. Several have been used for urban tree planting, as they respond well to pollarding and hard pruning in residential areas. Limes look good planted in avenues, and within formal vistas.

American Basswood

Tilia americana

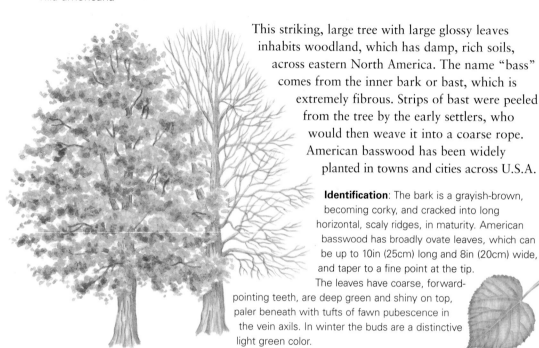

This striking, large tree with large glossy leaves inhabits woodland, which has damp, rich soils, across eastern North America. The name "bass" comes from the inner bark or bast, which is extremely fibrous. Strips of bast were peeled from the tree by the early settlers, who would then weave it into a coarse rope. American basswood has been widely planted in towns and cities across U.S.A.

Identification: The bark is a grayish-brown, becoming corky, and cracked into long horizontal, scaly ridges, in maturity. American basswood has broadly ovate leaves, which can be up to 10in (25cm) long and 8in (20cm) wide, and taper to a fine point at the tip. The leaves have coarse, forward-pointing teeth, are deep green and shiny on top, paler beneath with tufts of fawn pubescence in the vein axils. In winter the buds are a distinctive light green color.

Distribution: From New Brunswick to Manitoba and south to Arkansas and Tennessee, U.S.A.
Height: 80ft (25m)
Shape: Broadly columnar
Deciduous
Pollinated: Insect
Leaf shape: Ovate to round

Right: Clusters of pale yellow, fragrant flowers appear in summer.

White Basswood

Beetree linden *Tilia heterophylla*

White basswood has a similar range to American basswood, *Tilia americana*, and is found growing at its best in the Appalachian Mountains. It differs from American basswood in having many more flowers in each cluster, up to 25, and a white underside to the leaf (caused by a covering of short, white hairs, hence the name white basswood). It is also known as beetree linden, a reference to the thousands of bees that descend on the trees' flowers to collect nectar in summer.

Identification: The bark is silver-gray becoming fissured in maturity. It has silver-backed leaves, variable in shape, and coarsely toothed, with a less pronounced tip than American basswood. The leaves are up to 6in (15cm) long and 4in (10cm) wide. The top side is matt, rather dull, green. The flowers are pale yellow, extremely fragrant, pendulous and borne in clusters of up to 25. The winter buds and shoots are pale green.

Distribution: From New Brunswick to Manitoba and south to Arkansas and Tennessee, U.S.A.
Height: 80ft (25m)
Shape: Broadly columnar
Deciduous
Pollinated: Insect
Leaf shape: Ovate

Left: Each leaf is silver-white on the underside.

Right: Globular fruits are attached to a papery husk.

Silver Linden

Silver Lime *Tilia tomentosa*

This ornamental tree has been widely planted across eastern U.S.A., although it is rarely found in the west. Its richly scented, pale lemon flowers, which emerge later from bud than on most other limes, are a magnet for bees in summer. The bees become intoxicated by the nectar and fall to the ground, where they perish by the thousand.

Above: The fruit is attached to a pendulous papery bract.

Identification: The bark is gray with shallow ridges even in maturity. The leaves are almost rounded, to 5in (12cm) long and 4in (10cm) broad. They are deep green above, silver below and flutter in the slightest breeze. The overall form is slightly broader than other limes with pendulous branching. This pendulous habit has been cultivated to produce an attractive weeping form, *Tilia tomentosa* 'Petiolaris'.

Right: The leaf color creates a silver shimmery effect from a distance.

Distribution: Southwest Asia and Southeast Europe.
Height: 97ft (30m)
Shape: Broadly columnar
Deciduous
Pollinated: Insect
Leaf shape: Rounded

OTHER SPECIES OF NOTE

Small-leaf Linden
Tilia cordata
Native to most of Europe from Portugal to the Caucasus Mountains, this tall, columnar tree has small, cordate leaves. In Britain its presence in woodland indicates the site is ancient. It grows in U.S.A. zone 4. The inner bark or "bast" was once used to make rope. Some coppiced trees are believed to be over 2,000 years old.

Broadleaf Linden *Tilia platyphyllos*
This splendid, large, domed-top tree has a clean, straight trunk and graceful arching branches. It is native to Europe and southwest Asia where it reaches heights in excess of 100ft (30m). It flowers before any other basswood, with pale lemon flowers appearing from late May, in clusters of three to five. It is grown as an ornamental sporadically throughout North America from Ontario to British Columbia and south to Ohio.

Common Lime *Tilia x europaea*
Also known as the European linden, this is a hybrid between the broadleaf linden, *T. platyphyllos* and the small-leaf linden, *T. cordata*, which although vigorous has none of the grace of either parent. It is distinguished by the untidy suckering which appears around the base of the trunk. It is common throughout the U.S.A.

Carolina Basswood

Tilia caroliniana

Carolina basswood is smaller than the other basswoods and also more tender, rarely surviving to any size further north than the Carolinas. It is at its most prevalent in New Hanover County around Wilmington and the Wrightsville Beach area. It was first discovered here by Mark Catesby in 1726. Its most distinguishing feature is its slender red-brown slightly pendulous shoots.

Identification: The bark is silver gray to brown becoming cracked vertically in maturity. The leaves, up to 4in (10cm) long and wide, have a long point at the tip. They are acutely serrated around the margin, dark green above and covered in a pale rusty color pubescence beneath. The creamy-yellow, fragrant flowers appear in June, in clusters of up to 15. After flowering, globular green fruits form.

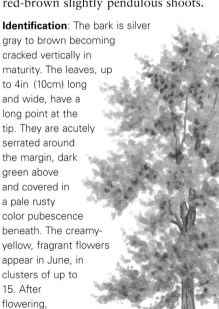

Distribution: Southeastern U.S.A. from North Carolina to Florida and west to Texas.
Height: 65ft (20m)
Shape: Broadly columnar
Deciduous
Pollinated: Insect
Leaf shape: Ovate

Above: Globular green fruits ripen to brown.

Below: The leaves are ovate to slightly heart-shape.

TUPELOS AND MYRTLES

Tupelos are members of the Nyssaceae family, which also includes the dove tree, Davidia involucrata. They are particularly popular in cultivation because of their brilliant displays of fall leaf color, which may vary from purple through red to bright orange. All Nyssas grow best in moist, lime-free soil.

Water Tupelo

Cotton gum *Nyssa aquatica*

As might be expected, considering its name, this is a tree that thrives in swampy ground and may be under water for months on end. In these conditions the stem may develop a distinctive swelling at the base. It has been in cultivation in the U.S.A. since 1735, when it was grown by the English nurseryman Peter Collinson. Its leaves turn brilliant orange in the fall. Water tupelo is sometimes referred to as cotton gum.

Identification: The bark of the water tupelo is light brown and smooth, becoming vertically fissured with age and developing a swelling at the base of the trunk in extreme wet conditions. The leaves are longer and narrower than the black gum tupelo, *N. sylvatica*, reaching 7in (18cm) long. They are held on the shoot by a leaf stalk (petiole) up to 2½in (6cm) long. The flowers are pale green, and develop into fleshy purple berries, about 1in (2.5cm) across, which contain a sharply ridged seed.

Distribution: Southeastern U.S.A. in the coastal plain and the lower reaches of the Mississippi.
Height: 100ft (30m)
Shape: Broadly conical
Deciduous
Pollinated: Insect
Leaf shape: Oblong to lanceolate

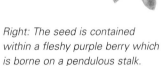

Right: The seed is contained within a fleshy purple berry which is borne on a pendulous stalk.

Tupelo

Black gum, Sour gum *Nyssa sylvatica*

Distribution: Eastern North America.
Height: 82ft (25m)
Shape: Broadly columnar
Deciduous
Pollinated: Insect
Leaf shape: Obovate

Right: Tupelo flowers are green and hard to see against the leaves. The fruit usually appears in pairs.

This slow-growing, medium-size tree has a huge range in North America, stretching from Ontario in the north to Mexico in the south. It has been extensively cultivated elsewhere, primarily for its spectacular fall-leaf coloring, which ranges from yellow and orange through to red and burgundy. Tupelo was introduced into Europe in 1750.

Identification: The bark is dark gray and smooth when young, becoming cracked and fissured into square plates in maturity. The leaves are obovate to elliptic, up to 6in (15cm) long and 3in (7.5cm) across, and have an entire margin and a blunt tip. They are lustrous grass-green above, and glaucous beneath. Both the male and female flowers are small, green and inconspicuous. They are borne in long stalked clusters on the same tree in summer. The fruit is a blueberry-colored, egg-shaped glossy berry, up to ⅔ in (1.5cm) long. It is edible but not particularly palatable, being rather sour.

Chinese Tupelo

Nyssa sinensis

Distribution: Central China.
U.S.A. zones 7–9.
Height: 50ft (15m)
Shape: Broadly conical
Deciduous
Pollinated: Insect
Leaf shape: Oblong to lanceolate

Right: The leaves are pointed.

Closely related to both the black gum and water tupelo, this attractive, small tree grows in woodland and beside streams in central China. It is comparatively rare in cultivation, although under the right conditions, it produces superb fall-leaf colors ranging from red to yellow. It was introduced into the U.S.A. in 1902 by English plant collector E. H. Wilson, working on behalf of the Arnold Arboretum, Boston.

Identification: The bark is gray-brown, smooth, becoming cracked and flaking with age. The leaves are oblong-lanceolate in shape, up to 8in (20cm) long and 2½in (6cm) wide. They emerge from bud a greeny-red color, but quickly fade to deep green. They are shiny above, and paler and matt beneath. Both the male and female flowers are small and green. They are borne in separate clusters in leaf axils on the same tree in summer.

Left: The fruit is a purple-blue berry about 1in (2.5cm) long.

OTHER SPECIES OF NOTE

Swamp Tupelo

Nyssa sylvatica var. *biflora*
This distinctive variety may be considered a separate species. As the name suggests, this tree occupies wetter conditions than the black gum tupelo, *N. sylvatica*, and is found in the coastal plains of southeastern U.S.A. from North Carolina to eastern Florida. Botanically it has a longer leaf, up to 7in (18cm) long, and has female flowers, which cluster in pairs rather than in fours.

Myrtus chequen
This South American, evergreen myrtle is native to Chile, from Coquimbo to Concepcion. It is usually found growing in wet conditions. It is related to the Chilean myrtle, *Myrtus luma*, but does not have the brilliant cinnamon-colored bark. It is also a smaller tree, seldom reaching heights in excess of 13ft (4m). It has a brown felt-like stem, which when young is covered in soft white down.

Myrtus lechleriana
This small evergreen tree has a bushy habit and grows high in the Andes Mountains in Chile, South America. Unlike most myrtles this one flowers in spring rather than late summer. The flowers are creamy-white with yellow anthers. It is hardy and because of its bushy habit it is quite often clipped to create a dense screen or hedge.

Chilean Myrtle

Luma apiculata

This beautiful small tree, which is also known as *Myrtus apiculata*, or *Luma apiculata*, has superb cinnamon-orange colored, thin, felt-like bark, which peels in maturity to reveal cream-color patches beneath. Curiously, no matter how hot the weather, the bark of this tree always feels cold to the touch. The tree is particularly prevalent in the Argentinian tourist resort of Bariloche. It is widely grown in botanic gardens and arboreta across southern states of the U.S.A.

Identification: The leaves are broadly elliptic, up to 1in (2.5cm) long, untoothed with a short point, bronze purple when young quickly becoming dark green and glossy above and sage green beneath. When crushed they emit a strong aromatic fragrance. Chilean myrtle has fragrant, creamy-white flowers with orange-yellow stamens, which are borne singly in the leaf axils of young shoots, in late summer. The fruit is a small round berry that is red when young ripening to purple-black in winter.

Distribution: Chile and Argentina.
Height: 40ft (12m)
Shape: Broadly spreading
Evergreen
Pollinated: Insect
Leaf shape: Elliptic

Below: The dark evergreen leaves of the Chilean myrtle are the perfect backdrop for its creamy-white flowers.

POPLARS

The poplars, Salicaceae, are a genus of over 35 species of deciduous trees found throughout northern temperate regions of the world. They produce small male and female flowers, which are borne in catkins on separate trees and pollinated by wind. Poplars are fast-growing trees, many of which can withstand atmospheric pollution and salt spray from the ocean.

Eastern Cottonwood

American black poplar *Populus deltoides*

This fine tree with its long, clean bole is one of the parents of the most widely planted poplars, *Populus* x *canadensis*, the other parent being *P. nigra*. The botanical name *deltoides* refers to the fact that the leaves are almost triangular.

Identification: When young, the shape of this tree is columnar with a domed top. In maturity it becomes broad and heavily branched. The bark is pale greenish-yellow on young trees, becoming gray and deeply fissured in maturity. The triangular leaves are up to 5in (13cm) long and wide, running to an acute point at the tip. They are medium green and glossy above, and pale green beneath.

Distribution: Across North America east of the Rocky Mountains from Quebec to Texas.
Height: 100ft (30m)
Shape: Broadly columnar
Deciduous
Pollinated: Wind
Leaf shape: Deltoid (triangular)

Left: Male and female flowers are on separate trees.

Black Cottonwood

Western balsam poplar *Populus trichocarpa*

This large, vigorous North American tree is the fastest growing balsam poplar. The first black cottonwood to be planted at the Royal Botanic Gardens, in London, in 1896, reached 56ft (17m) tall in just 13 years. Many fast-growing clones and hybrids of this species have been developed for forestry purposes and are now quite widely planted.

Identification: The bark is smooth and yellow-grey, becoming vertically fissured with age. The young shoots and winter buds are golden-yellow, and covered in a sticky, fragrant balsamic gum. In spring, as the buds open and the leaves unfurl, they emit a delicious balsam fragrance. The leaves are ovate and slightly heart-shaped at the base, up to 10in (25cm) long and 5in (13cm) wide, dark, glossy green above and light sage-green beneath, displaying a network of tiny leaf veins. The male catkins are 2in (5cm) long and the female catkins 6in (15cm). Both are carried on separate trees in early spring.

Left: The elegant leaves have a glossy upper surface.

Distribution: Western North America from Alaska to California.
Height: 130ft (40m)
Shape: Broadly columnar
Deciduous
Pollinated: Wind
Leaf shape: Ovate

Right: Male and (far right) female catkins are produced in early spring on separate trees. Female catkins are three times as long as the male ones.

Balsam Poplar

Tacamahacca *Populus balsamifera*

Until fairly recently this tree was known by the native American name of *tacamahacca*. It is without doubt one of the most distinctive of all American poplars. In spring, woodlands where this tree grows are filled with a heady balsam fragrance, as the leaves unfurl from their long, sticky winter buds. Balsam poplar grows naturally in moist woodlands across northern U.S.A. and Canada. This tree has a tendency to throw up suckers from the roots around its base.

Identification: The bark is gray, smooth at first becoming vertically fissured in maturity. The leaves are ovate, to 5in (12cm) long and 4in (10cm) wide, taper-pointed and finely toothed. When crushed they emit a balsam scent. Both the male and female flowers are in catkins, which are borne on separate trees. The male catkins are 2in (5cm) long and orange-brown when ripe; the female's are 3in (7.5cm) long and yellow-green.

Distribution: From Labrador to Alaska, and south to northern U.S.A. from the east to the west coast.
Height: 100ft (30m)
Shape: Broadly columnar
Deciduous
Pollinated: Wind
Leaf shape: Ovate

Right: The leaves are deep glossy green with a network of white veins.

OTHER SPECIES OF NOTE

Black Poplar *Populus nigra*
Native to western Asia and Europe, the western European subspecies of black poplar is called *P. betulifolia,* and differs from the species in having a pubescent covering to the petiole, shoot, leaf midrib and flower stalk. It is endangered in the wild, mainly because much of the remaining population is male. It is planted as an ornamental and a windbreak across the U.S.A.

Lombardy Poplar *Populus nigra* 'Italica'
This is an upright form of the European black poplar, which has been widely planted as an ornamental species. It is instantly recognizable by its slender, columnar outline and upright branching. Lombardy poplars are predominantly male and are usually propagated by cuttings.

European Aspen *Populus tremula*
Sometimes confused with *P. tremuloides*, this small, ornamental tree, up to 65ft (20m), is native to Europe, from the Atlantic to the Pacific, and south to North Africa. It has gray, smooth bark, broadly ovate leaves up to 3in (8cm) long and wide, flowers that are borne in catkins and seeds that are covered in cotton wool-like hairs.

Chinese Necklace Poplar *Populus lasiocarpa*
This striking tree has the largest and thickest leaves of any poplar. The word necklace in the name refers to the long, pendulous, green seed capsules that appear in midsummer. By late summer these ripen, shedding seed, wrapped in a white cotton wool-like covering, over a wide area. It is widely grown across the U.S.A.

Quaking Aspen

Populus tremuloides

Probably the most widely distributed tree of North America. Quaking aspen has leaves that appear to be in perpetual motion. They flutter or quake in any breeze, and the sound is audible. This motion is caused by slender leaf stalks, which are inappropriate for the size of the leaves, and cause them to flap together. The leaves are one of the easiest ways to identify this species, although this tree can be mistaken for the European aspen, *P. tremula*. It is distinguished by the pale, yellowish bark, which is only found on the American species.

Identification: The leaves are 2in (5cm) long and broad. They can be more round than ovate, with a short, abrupt tip, and a broad, almost flat base. They are finely toothed, dark glossy green above, pale and dull below. The young shoots are reddish-brown. The flowers are in pendulous catkins on separate trees and appear in spring.

Distribution: Across northern U.S.A. and Canada, from Newfoundland to Delaware, and from Alaska south to British Columbia, and down the Rockies.
Height: 100ft (30m)
Shape: Broadly columnar
Deciduous
Pollinated: Wind
Leaf shape: Ovate

Above: The quaking aspen has smaller leaves than its cousin the European aspen.

WILLOWS

There are more than 300 different species of willows in the world, varying from large, spreading ornamental specimens, to diminutive, creeping, tundra-based alpines. The majority are native to northern temperate regions of the world. Willows are mainly deciduous, although one or two subtropical species have leaves that persist into winter. The male and female flowers are normally borne on separate trees.

Weeping Willow

Salix x *sepulcralis* 'Chrysocoma'

Weeping willow is a hybrid between white willow and Chinese weeping willow, and developed naturally where the ranges of these two species met in western Asia. The form 'Chrysocoma' has been selected and cultivated from the hybrid for its golden shoot and more graceful weeping habit. It is the familiar weeping form seen alongside European riverbanks.

Identification: A large, spreading tree with ascending primary branches, supporting long secondary branches, which reach to the ground. The bark is pale gray-brown with shallow, corky fissures. The shoot and young wood is a glorious golden yellow color, as are the long, slender winter buds that hug the shoot. The leaves are up to 5in (13cm) long and up to 1in (2.5cm) wide. Male and female flowers appear as the leaves emerge in early spring.

Left: Catkins grow upwards.

Right: Leaves are long and slender.

Distribution: A hybrid, so not native to anywhere, but widely cultivated throughout temperate regions of the U.S.A. as an ornamental.
Height: 66ft (20m)
Shape: Broadly weeping
Deciduous
Pollinated: Insect, and occasionally wind
Leaf shape: Narrowly lanceolate

Below: The hanging branches make for an unmistakable form.

Black Willow

Salix nigra

This is the largest and probably most frequently seen of all the American willows. It is felled for lumber in the Mississippi delta region where heights up to 130ft (40m) have been recorded. Along the coastal plain it is abundant in roadside swamps where it grows alongside the coastal plain willow, *Salix caroliniana*.

Identification: It has dark, almost black, bark, which becomes deeply furrowed in maturity. The young shoots are yellow at first, gradually turning reddish-brown. The pale green leaves are lanceolate, rounded at the base and narrowing gradually to a long, fine point. They are 5in (13cm) long and finely serrated. The fruit is a small, green capsule that ripens to release large quantities of fluffy seed, dispersed by the wind.

Distribution: Eastern and central North America extending into northeast Mexico.
Height: 100ft (30m)
Shape: Broadly columnar
Deciduous
Pollinated: Insect and occasionally wind
Leaf shape: Lanceolate

Right: Both the male and female flowers appear in catkins on the same tree in early spring.

Peachleaf Willow

Almond willow *Salix amygdaloides*

Otherwise known as the almond willow, this medium-size tree is native from Michigan to Alberta and eastern Oregon, Colorado and Ohio, with outliers stretching along the St Lawrence River. It is commonly found beside creeks, and is the biggest willow west of the prairie states. It has light, soft, close-grained wood that has light brown heartwood, and nearly white sapwood.

Identification: The lanceolate leaves narrow to a long, slender point at the tip and are rounded at the base. They are up to 4in (10cm) long and 1in (2.5cm) wide, light green and lustrous above, pale and glaucous beneath, with a stout yellow or orange midrib. The overall appearance of this tree is broadly spreading, quite often with several stems growing from the base rather than one single bole. Both the male and female flowers are greeny-yellow, upright catkins.

Distribution: Eastern and central U.S.A.
Height: 65ft (20m)
Shape: Broadly spreading
Deciduous
Pollinated: Insect and wind
Leaf shape: Lanceolate

Right: The male and female flowers appear on the same tree in the spring.

OTHER SPECIES OF NOTE

Contorted Willow
Salix babylonica 'Tortuosa'
A peculiar, deformed-looking tree, otherwise known as the dragon's claw willow, or corkscrew willow. It has twisted and contorted branches and shoots, and has become widely cultivated as a garden ornamental. It forms a tangled tree up to 33ft (10m) high. It originates from China, where it was first cultivated more than 100 years ago. Today, cut branches are very popular in flower arrangements.

Coastal Plain Willow *Salix caroliniana*
As the name suggests, this small tree, or large shrub, is native to the coastal plain from Virginia to Texas. It is often seen growing alongside the roads, which are like causeways, with ditches of swampland on each side. It has narrow, lanceolate leaves, which are a distinctive yellow-green on the top side, sage green beneath, and up to 4in (10cm) long.

Pacific Willow *Salix lasiandra*
Otherwise known as the yellow willow, because of its bright yellow new shoots, this medium-size tree, to 65ft (20m) tall, grows naturally from central Alaska south to southern California. It has lanceolate leaves up to 3in (7.5cm) long and ½in (1cm) wide, which are dark green and lustrous above and pale green beneath.

Shining Willow

Salix lucida

This very hardy, tough tree grows further north than any other American willow. It grows beside streams and swamps where it forms a short trunk with erect branches and a broad, round-topped, symmetrical head. The new shoots are a distinctive shiny, dark orange, gradually becoming darker and tinged with red in the second year. The common name is derived from the high-gloss upper surface of the leaves and the shiny, young shoots.

Identification: The bark is thin, smooth, and dark brown but tinged with red. The leaves have a long point at the tip and are rounded at the base. They are a smooth, shiny dark green above and paler beneath, with a pronounced broad yellow midrib. The leaf stalk (petiole) is short, thick and also yellow. Both the male and female flowers are borne in erect, pubescent, greenish-yellow catkins, which persist on the tree from early spring through until early summer.

Below: The 5in- (13cm-) long leaves vary from ovate-lanceolate to narrowly lanceolate.

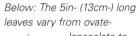

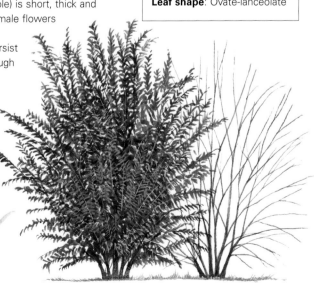

Distribution: From Newfoundland to the shores of Hudson Bay, west to Saskatchewan, and south to Ohio and Pennsylvania.
Height: 33ft (10m)
Shape: Broadly spreading
Deciduous
Pollinated: Insect and wind
Leaf shape: Ovate-lanceolate

PLANES, SYCAMORES AND WITCH HAZELS

The planes are one of the most majestic groups of trees in the world. Their sheer size, form and bark color make them an essential part of any large-scale ornamental landscape. They are able to cope successfully with the rigors of urban city life and provide welcome shade and shelter in return.

Sycamore

Buttonwood *Platanus occidentalis*

This magnificent, large tree has a broad open crown and a trunk, which can be up to 16ft (5m) across. It is a favorite for planting in cities and parks, and provides dense cool shade in the summer months. As with all plane trees (sycamores), this tree is extremely resistant to the air pollution of most industrial cities.

Identification: The bark on the bole is smooth and pale brown, peeling to reveal patches of cream fresh bark beneath. The bark on the branches is almost blue-white, thin and very smooth. The leaves are palmately lobed with three large lobes, rather like a maple, interspersed with broad serrations. They are up to 8in (20cm) long and broad, bright glossy green above and paler beneath. Clusters of new leaves, which appear in summer, are covered in a soft white pubescence. The seed is a pink, spherical dry fruit.

Distribution: Eastern North America.
Height: 115ft (35m)
Shape: Broadly columnar
Deciduous
Pollinated: Insect
Leaf shape: Palmate

Right: The 1in (2.5cm) fruits hang singly on thread-like stalks.

Oriental Plane

Platanus orientalis

The Oriental plane is a majestic tree. Hippocrates, the ancient Greek "father of medicine," is said to have taught his medical scholars under the great Oriental plane tree that still exists on the island of Kos. Another large Oriental plane on the Bosporus, near Büyükdere, is known as "the plane of Godfrey de Bouillon," because tradition states that he and his knights camped under it during the first crusade in 1096. It was introduced to the U.S.A. in the seventeenth century.

Identification: One of the largest of all deciduous temperate trees. It can reach heights in excess of 100ft (30m) tall, with a great spreading canopy and a trunk girth of 20ft (6m). It has attractive, buff-gray bark, which flakes to reveal cream-pink patches. The leaves are palmate, 8in (20cm) long and 10in (25cm) across, deeply cut into five narrow lobes, shiny green above, pale green below with brown tufts of hair along the veins. The leaves are attached alternately to the shoot. In the fall the leaves turn from clear yellow to old gold. The fruit is globular and mace-like, 1in (2.5cm) across, and attached in clusters of two to six on a pendulous stalk.

Distribution: Albania, Israel, Greece, Cyprus, Lebanon, Syria, Crete. U.S.A. zones 7–9.
Height: 100ft (30m)
Shape: Broadly spreading
Deciduous
Pollinated: Insect
Leaf shape: Palmate lobed

Right: Fruit remains on the tree through the winter.

Californian Sycamore

Platanus racemosa

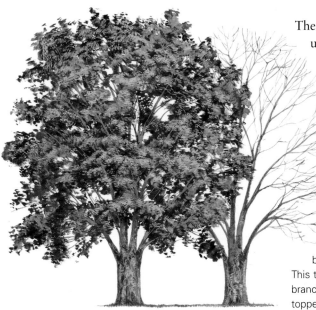

The Californian sycamore grows from the upper Sacramento River, where it grows naturally alongside streams and river banks, along the lower Sierra Nevada, up to altitudes of 4,000ft (1,220m), and into the coastal ranges from Monterey, southwards to Mexico.

Identification: The bark at the base of old trees is dark brown, deeply fissured and up to 4in (10cm) thick. Elsewhere, and on younger trees, the bark is thin, smooth and pale brown becoming almost white on upper branches. This tree is often forked with thick, heavy, spreading branches, which form an open, irregular round-topped head. Young twigs and shoots are reddish.

Distribution: Western California from Sacramento to Mexico.
Height: 100ft (30m)
Shape: Broadly spreading
Deciduous
Pollinated: Insect
Leaf shape: Palmate

Left: The leaves are palmate with three to five deeply cut main lobes and shallow, blunt serrations in-between.

OTHER SPECIES OF NOTE

London Plane *Platanus* x *hispanica*
This tree is a hybrid between the Oriental plane, *P. orientalis*, and the American sycamore, *P. occidentalis*. It is widely planted in cities across the world (including London) because of its ability to withstand atmospheric pollution and severe pruning. The London plane differs from

each parent in being more vigorous, and having leaves with shallower lobes and a lighter colored bark, which peels to reveal cream patches.

Large-leaved Witch Hazel *Hamamelis macrophylla*
This is a rare species, which is closely allied to the American witch hazel, *Hamamelis virginiana*. It is native to southeastern U.S.A. and grows in rich soils by streams or along the borders of forests. It has large, 5in- (13cm-) long, obovate leaves, which are bright green, becoming butter-yellow in the fall. Pale lemon-yellow flowers appear in mid-winter.

Ozark Witch Hazel *Hamamelis vernalis*
A small tree, or large shrub, which is only found growing naturally in the Ozark Mountains of Oklahoma and Arkansas, although it has been cultivated in parks and gardens elsewhere in the U.S.A. The flowers, which appear in January and February, are the smallest of any witch hazel, and also the most fragrant. They vary from pale yellow to red, but are more usually pale orange.

American Witch Hazel

Hamamelis virginiana

This large shrub, or small, spreading tree, grows as an understory to bigger, deciduous trees in forests from Nova Scotia south to central Georgia. It prefers rich, moist soils and is often found on the banks of streams. Outside its native habitat it has been widely cultivated as an ornamental plant in parks and gardens, where winter color and attraction is required. Witch hazel contains an astringent fluid, which is extracted from both the bark and leaves, and used to bring relief from bruising.

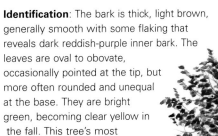

Distribution: Eastern North America.
Height: to 22ft (7m)
Shape: Broadly spreading
Deciduous
Pollinated: Insect
Leaf shape: Oval to obovate

Identification: The bark is thick, light brown, generally smooth with some flaking that reveals dark reddish-purple inner bark. The leaves are oval to obovate, occasionally pointed at the tip, but more often rounded and unequal at the base. They are bright green, becoming clear yellow in the fall. This tree's most distinctive feature is its sulphur yellow, fragrant, spidery-like flowers, which appear in the fall.

Above: A witch hazel leaf.

Right: The flowers appear as the leaves begin to fall and persist well into winter.

SWEET GUMS AND FALL COLOR

Although these trees belong to different families, they have two things in common. They are deciduous, dropping their leaves in the fall before producing replacements the following spring. And, before they lose their leaves, they produce spectacular leaf color. Because of their beauty, many are planted as ornamental trees.

Katsura Tree

Cercidiphyllum japonicum

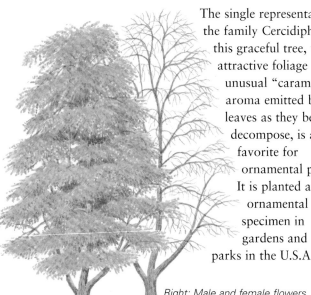

The single representative of the family Cercidiphyllaceae, this graceful tree, with its attractive foliage and unusual "caramel" aroma emitted by the leaves as they begin to decompose, is a favorite for ornamental planting. It is planted as an ornamental specimen in gardens and parks in the U.S.A

Right: Male and female flowers appear on separate trees.

Identification: The bark is gray-brown, freckled with lenticels and becomes fissured and flaking in maturity. The thin leaves are heart-shaped, slightly toothed around the margin, up to 3in (8cm) long and wide, turning a bronzy pink in the fall. The male flowers are bright red, appearing on side shoots before the leaves appear in early spring. Female flowers develop in late spring in clusters of four to six.

Distribution: Western China and Hokkaido and Honshu in Japan. U.S.A. to zone 4.
Height: 100ft (30m)
Shape: Broadly spreading
Deciduous
Pollinated: Insect
Leaf shape: Cordate

Left: Leaves fade to blue-green in summer, and appear in vibrant shades of butter-yellow to purple-pink in the spring.

Oriental Sweet Gum

Liquidambar orientalis

Distribution: South-west Turkey. U.S.A. zones 7–9.
Height: 80ft (25m)
Shape: Broadly conical
Deciduous
Pollinated: Insect
Leaf shape: Palmate

Along with its American cousin the sweet gum, *Liquidambar styraciflua*, the oriental sweet gum is widely planted in parks, gardens and arboreta across the U.S.A. for its magnificent leaf color in the fall. It was discovered, and introduced to Europe, around 1750, but it wasn't until the late nineteenth century that it was cultivated in the U.S.A. Its leaves are more deeply cut into three to five lobes than the sweet gum.

Identification: The bark is orange-brown and thick, cracking in maturity into small plates. The leaves are palmately lobed, to 3in (8cm) long and broad, deep matt green above and paler beneath, turning a brilliant marmalade orange in the fall. Both the male and female flowers are yellow-green and very small. They are borne separately, on the same tree, in spring, at the same time as the leaves emerge from winter bud.

Right: The seed is borne in a 1in (2.5cm), soft, spiky, rounded, hanging fruit.

Sweet Gum

Liquidambar styraciflua

This giant of a tree is known to have reached 150ft (45m) in height and is one of the main constituents of the deciduous hardwood forests of eastern North America. In the fall its leaves turn every shade from orange through red to purple.

Identification: The bark is a dark brown-gray color becoming fissured into long vertical ridges with age. The leaves are up to 6in (15cm) long and broad, normally with five tapering lobes (sometimes seven), the center one of which is normally largest. The margin of the leaf is slightly toothed. The leaf shape sometimes leads to identification confusion with maples; however, maple leaves are in opposite pairs on a smooth shoot, whereas *Liquidambar* leaves are alternately positioned on a corky shoot.

Above: Male and female flowers are both small and round, greeny yellow in color and appear in late spring.

Distribution: North America from Connecticut in the north to Florida and Texas in the south. Also found in Central America.
Height: 130ft (40m)
Shape: Broadly conical
Deciduous
Pollinated: Insect
Leaf shape: Palmate lobed

Left: The seed is contained in clusters of round, brown hanging pods approximately 1½in (4cm) across.

Persian Ironwood

Parrotia persica

A member of the Hamamelidaceae family, it is planted as a specimen tree in the U.S.A. because of its fall color, which turns from copper to burgundy in midseason. In the wild it tends to be a broad, upright tree, but in cultivation it becomes a sprawling mass, seldom attaining a height in excess of 50ft (15m). It is named after the climber F. W. Parrot, who conquered Mount Ararat in 1829.

Identification: Quite often seen in large gardens and arboreta as a dense low-spreading mound, which is quite difficult to penetrate because of criss-cross branching. The bark is dark brown, flaking to reveal light brown patches. The leaves are obovate, sometimes elliptic, 4¾in (12cm) long and 2½in (6cm) wide, becoming progressively shallow toothed and wavy toward the top of each leaf. They are bright glossy green above, and dull green with slight pubescence beneath. The flowers are tiny, clothed in a soft velvet-brown casing, but emerging a startling ruby-red color, which looks dramatic on the bare branches in midwinter. The fruit is a nut-like brown capsule, ½in (1cm) across.

Below: Leaves are darker and glossier on the tops and lighter beneath.

Above: Small ruby-red flowers appear in winter.

Distribution: Mount Ararat, Eastern Caucasus to northern Iran. U.S.A. zones 4–8.
Height: 66ft (20m)
Shape: Broadly spreading
Deciduous
Pollinated: Insect
Leaf shape: Obovate

OTHER SPECIES OF NOTE

Chinese Sweet Gum
Liquidambar formosana
This tender, beautiful small tree was introduced to the U.S.A. in 1911, by plant collector Ernest Wilson, during the time he was working for the Arnold Arboretum, Boston. It has gray-white bark that darkens and becomes fissured in maturity, and palmately-lobed leaves, which are distinctly heart-shape at the base.

Chittamwood
Cotinus obovatus
This small, rare, American tree is otherwise known as the smoke tree because of its smoky-gray, plume-like flowers, which encircle the tree in late summer. It is one of the most brilliantly colored fall trees, with large oval-shape translucent leaves which turn to all shades of orange, red and purple in October.

Weeping Katsura
Cercidiphyllum japonicum 'Pendulum'
This is a beautiful and unusual tree with long pendulous branches that arch gracefully towards the ground. It has long been cultivated in Japan, particularly in temple gardens, but it has been cultivated elsewhere comparatively recently. It is found in botanic gardens across the U.S.A., but should be more widely planted.

MADRONES, PERSIMMONS AND SNOWBELLS

These trees form part of the camellia subclass known as Dilleniidae. They are a mixture of deciduous and evergreen, acid-loving and lime-tolerant species. They have an ornamental appeal, which has secured their place in gardens and arboreta across the temperate world.

Pacific Madrone

Arbutus menziesii

The madrones are the biggest plants of the Heath family, which includes heathers and rhododendrons. The Pacific madrone is the biggest of all, and grows naturally from British Columbia (including Vancouver Island) south to California. It is an attractive, ornamental tree that is widely cultivated in botanic gardens and arboreta across temperate regions of the world.

Above: The fruit in early fall.

Left: The flowers open in March in California, and in May in British Columbia.

Identification: The bark is red-brown, smooth and peels in papery flakes to reveal fresh, green bark beneath. The thick, leathery, evergreen leaves are elliptic, to 6in (15cm) long and 3in (7.5cm) broad. They are glossy, dark green above and pale blue-white beneath. The flowers are creamy-white and small but borne in large, vertical clusters, which may contain in excess of 100 flowers. The Pacific madrone has ½in (1.5cm) rounded, strawberry-like fruits which change from green through orange to red in late summer to early fall.

Distribution: West Coast North America.
Height: 130ft (40m)
Shape: Broadly columnar
Evergreen
Pollinated: Insect
Leaf shape: Elliptic

Persimmon

Possum wood *Diospyrus virginiana*

Also known as possum wood, this large, deciduous, North American tree is one of only three truly hardy members of the ebony family, Ebenaceae. The wood resembles that of ebony, being black, dense and very tough. Traditionally it has been used to make golf clubs. In the fall, persimmon leaves put on a spectacular display, turning rich orange-yellow before dropping from the branches.

Identification: A wide-spreading tree with black-brown rugged bark, cracking in maturity into rough, square plates. The leaves are commonly ovate, up to 5in (13cm) long and 3in (8cm) across, deep glossy green above and light sage-green beneath with an untoothed margin. By far the most distinctive feature of this tree is the fruit, which is quite often described as orange-like but is more akin in looks and size to a small orange tomato. Measuring 1½in (4cm) across, it ripens on the tree in late summer to early fall and contains up to eight brown seeds. The fruit is edible but too sharp for most palates.

Right: Both male and female flowers are pale yellow, bell-shaped, and borne on separate trees in summer.

Distribution: Central-southern United States from Connecticut to Texas.
Height: 100ft (30m)
Shape: Broadly spreading
Deciduous
Pollinated: Insect
Leaf shape: Ovate to oblong

Arizona Madrone

Arbutus arizonica

The Arizona madrone is much smaller than the Pacific madrone, *Arbutus menziesii*, and has thinner, slender leaves. It is native to dry gravel areas in the Santa Catalina and Santa Rita Mountains in southern Arizona, where it grows up to elevations of 8,000ft (2,500m), and in the San Luis and Animas Mountains of New Mexico. It is cultivated in botanic gardens and arboreta across the southern U.S.A.

Left: The small, orange-red, strawberry-like fruits are sweet tasting and edible.

Identification: The bark on young trees is thin, smooth, dark red, and peeling in long, thin strips. Mature trees tend to have thicker bark with vertical fissures and light gray and red patches. The lanceolate, evergreen leaves are thick, leathery, pointed at the tip and rounded at the base, light green above and sage-green beneath. New leaves emerge from the bud with a reddish tinge. The flowers, which appear in May, are very similar to those of the Pacific madrone, *Arbutus menziesii*, except the clusters are rather looser in their formation. The fruit, which ripens in October, is dark orange-red and strawberry-like with a sweet, edible flesh.

Distribution: Arizona and southwest New Mexico.
Height: 50ft (15m)
Shape: Broadly columnar
Evergreen
Pollinated: Insect
Leaf shape: Lanceolate

Right: The flowers are small, creamy-white and borne in loose clusters.

OTHER SPECIES OF NOTE

Mountain Snowdrop Tree *Halesia monticola*
This magnificent spreading tree differs from the silver bell tree, *Halesia carolina*, in its greater size (up to 80ft [25m] tall), and its larger flowers. As the name suggests, it grows wild in upland areas, reaching altitudes in excess of 4,000ft (1,230m) in North Carolina, Tennessee and western Georgia. Due to its beauty, it is widely cultivated elsewhere including in the Arnold Arboretum, Boston, and in Rochester, New York.

Sour Wood *Oxydendron arboreum*
Otherwise known as the sorrel tree, this eastern U.S.A., medium-size tree has leaves that have a bitter taste, similar to that of the herbaceous plant sorrel. They were used by the early American settlers as both a tonic and a cure for fever. It has elliptic 8in- (20cm-) long deciduous leaves that turn scarlet in the fall.

Japanese Snowbell Tree *Styrax japonica*
This is a beautiful, small, spreading tree, which was introduced into North America from Japan in the late nineteenth century. Since then it has been widely planted as an ornamental specimen

in parks, gardens and arboreta across the U.S.A. It has creamy-white, fragrant, open bell-shaped flowers that hang from the tree on long slender stalks in early summer.

Silver Bell Tree

Snowdrop tree *Halesia carolina*

This beautiful small tree, otherwise known as the snowdrop tree, is native to southeast U.S.A., from Virginia south to Florida, and west to Illinois. It is widely cultivated as an ornamental tree in parks and gardens elsewhere in the U.S.A. It favors rich, moist soil and is quite often found growing alongside streams. The botanical name *Halesia* commemorates the English clergyman and botanical author D. Stephen Hales (1677–1761).

Identification: The juvenile bark is pale brown and smooth, becoming darker and scaly in maturity. The leaves are ovate to oblong 8in (20cm) long and 4in (10cm) wide, finely toothed around the margin and running to a long thin tapered point. They are grass-green above and pale green beneath with some pubescence. In the fall they turn clear butter-yellow before dropping. The flowers are bell shape, white, sometimes flushed pink, and have clusters of bright orange stamens at their center.

Distribution: South East U.S.A.
Height: 65ft (20m)
Shape: Broadly conical
Deciduous
Pollinated: Insect
Leaf shape: Ovate to oblong

Above: Husks containing seed.

Below: The flowers appear in spring.

REDBUDS AND LABURNUMS

These two species, redbuds and laburnums, are both members of the Leguminosae (pea) family and as such have beautiful pea-like flowers in springtime. They are popular small trees for cultivation in parks and gardens right across North America. They grow best in full sun with good drainage.

Eastern Redbud

Cercis canadensis

This beautiful small tree is commonly found growing in moist woodlands right across its natural range from New York to Texas. It is also widely cultivated in parks, gardens and as a street tree. Eastern redbud is prone to canker, which can cause leaves to brown and die in summer. An attractive form of this species known as 'Forest Pansy' has deep, purple-red foliage throughout summer and is widely available from nurseries and garden centers.

Identification: The bark is quite distinctive, being dark charcoal brown to almost black. Quite often bright pink flowers will grow directly from the trunk. Eastern redbud has rounded, heart-shape leaves, which are up to 4in (10cm) long and 5in (12cm) wide. There are no serrations around the leaf margin and they emerge bronze-colored from winter bud before quickly turning bright green. They are smooth and papery thin. In the fall the leaves turn bright golden-yellow. The distinctive pea-like pink flowers, ½in (1cm) long, are borne on slender stalks in clusters along old wood in spring to early summer.

Distribution: Central and south U.S.A.
Height: 33ft (10m)
Shape: Broadly spreading
Deciduous
Pollinated: Insect
Leaf shape: Cordate

Left: The seed is contained within a flattened green pod which ripens to brown.

Left: The small pink flowers are borne in clusters.

California Redbud

Western redbud *Cercis occidentalis*

Otherwise known as western redbud, this small tree, or large shrub, is found growing wild in south Utah and Nevada and through Arizona and California. It is fairly uncommon throughout this region and has never been widely cultivated in parks and gardens like its eastern cousin. It has distinctive red-purple shoots, which are particularly prominent in spring, just before the tree comes into leaf.

Identification: This redbud is smaller than the eastern redbud, *Cercis canadensis*, and quite often only attains shrub-like proportions. It also has smaller leaves, which are more rounded and leathery, with a distinctive notch at the tip. It has pea-like flowers that are rose-colored. They are held on short stalks and are produced in clusters on old wood right back to the main stem in spring, just before the leaves emerge from bud.

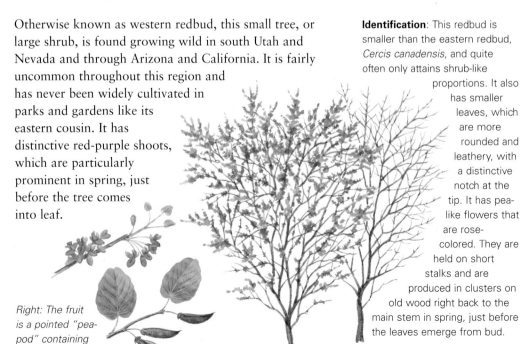

Right: The fruit is a pointed "pea-pod" containing up to 20 seeds.

Distribution: Southwestern U.S.A.
Height: 20ft (6m)
Shape: Broadly spreading
Deciduous
Pollinated: Insect
Leaf shape: Cordate

Voss's Golden Chain Tree

Laburnum x *watereri* 'Vossii'

This stunningly beautiful tree is cultivated in parks and gardens right across North America. It is a form of the hybrid which is a cross between the common laburnum, *Laburnum anagyroides*, and the Scotch laburnum, *L. alpinum*, both of which originate from central and southern Europe. The hybrid was developed at Waterer's nursery, England, before 1864. The form 'Vossii' was raised in Holland late in the nineteenth century and has superseded all other forms of cultivated laburnum.

Identification: The bark is dark gray and smooth becoming shallowly fissured in maturity. The leaves are borne in three elliptic leaflets, each 3in (7.5cm) long. They are grass green above, slightly paler beneath and covered in fine silver pubescence. The flowers, which appear in late spring, are golden yellow, pea-like, 1in (2.5cm) long and borne in dense, hanging racemes, which can be more than 12in (30cm) long. The fruit is a brown, flat seed pod, to 3in (7.5cm) long, normally containing just a few seeds. All parts of this tree are poisonous.

Distribution: A hybrid developed from two European species.
Height: 23ft (7m)
Shape: Broadly spreading
Deciduous
Pollinated: Insect
Leaf shape: Elliptic

Above: The flowers appear in mid to late spring.

Above: Laburnum seeds should not be eaten.

OTHER SPECIES OF NOTE

Texas Redbud *Cercis canadensis* var. *texensis*
This small, shrubby tree is native to Oklahoma and Texas, where it is found on the limestone hills and ridges in Dallas County, and in the valley of the upper Colorado River. It differs from the eastern redbud, *C. canadensis*, in having rich, glossy leaves which are blunt at the tip and shoots, and are smooth with no pubescence.

Judas Tree *Cercis siliquastrum*
Native to western Asia and southeast Europe but has been widely planted in gardens, parks and arboreta in southern U.S.A. It is similar to eastern redbud, *C. canadensis*, except the bark color is lighter, and the lilac-pink flowers bigger. This is allegedly the tree from which Judas Iscariot hung himself after betraying Christ.

Common Laburnum *Laburnum anagyroides*
This beautiful, small tree, which originates from central and southern Europe, is one of the parents of the hybrid form *Laburnum* x *watereri* 'Vossii' which is widely planted across the U.S.A in parks, gardens and streets. It differs from the form in having much shorter, less showy flowers. All parts of this tree are poisonous.

Chinaberry *Melia azedarach*
Otherwise known as the bead tree because of its yellow, bony, bead-like seeds, which are produced in the fall, this attractive, small tree originates from India and China. It is commonly planted in small gardens from Georgia to Texas, and north to Tennessee. It has large, elegant bipinnate leaves and small, fragrant lilac flowers.

Silk Tree

Albizia julibrissin

Sometimes mistakenly called mimosa, this Asian species is extremely popular in areas of the U.S.A. where winters are not too severe. It grows from Long Island, south to Texas, and north to Seattle in the west. As a street tree it develops a wide-spreading, flat-topped shape, and reaches 25ft (8m) tall. When in flower it is a beautiful sight and fills the air with the scent of newly cut hay.

Identification: The bark is dark brown and smooth. The dark green leaves give the tree a "feathery" appearance. They are bipinnate, to 20in (50cm) long, with numerous small, taper-pointed, soft, needle-like, untoothed leaflets about ½in (1cm) long. In the fall the leaves turn yellow and orange before dropping. The fragrant flowers are small but borne in dense, fluffy clusters. They have long salmon-pink stamens evident in summer.

Below: The seed is borne in a brown pea-like pod up to 6in (15cm) long.

Distribution: Southwest Asia.
Height: 40ft (12m)
Shape: Broadly spreading
Deciduous
Pollinated: Insect
Leaf shape: Bipinnate

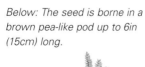

CHERRIES

The cherry genus, Prunus, *contains over 400 different species of tree, the majority of which are deciduous and native to northern temperate regions of the world. They include some of the most beautiful spring-flowering trees, many of which have been cultivated in parks, gardens and arboreta for centuries. The genus is distinguished by having fruit that is always a drupe surrounding a single seed.*

Sargent's Cherry

Prunus sargentii

Sargent's cherry is one of the loveliest of all cherries, producing a profusion of rich pink, single flowers coupled with bronze-colored emerging leaves in spring, and brilliant orange-red leaf colors in the fall. It is named after Charles Sargent, of the Arnold Arboretum, Boston, who obtained a supply of the tree's seed from Japan in 1892.

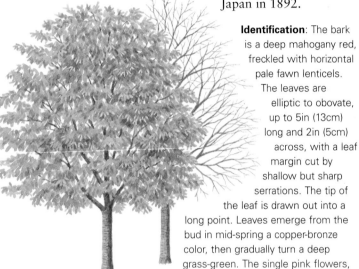

Identification: The bark is a deep mahogany red, freckled with horizontal pale fawn lenticels. The leaves are elliptic to obovate, up to 5in (13cm) long and 2in (5cm) across, with a leaf margin cut by shallow but sharp serrations. The tip of the leaf is drawn out into a long point. Leaves emerge from the bud in mid-spring a copper-bronze color, then gradually turn a deep grass-green. The single pink flowers, which are normally produced in profusion, have five petals and are up to 1½in (4cm) across. They appear just before the leaves emerge. The fruit is a black, egg-shaped drupe.

Distribution: Northern Japan, Korea and Sakhalin island. U.S.A. zones 4–7.
Height: 66ft (20m)
Shape: Broadly spreading
Deciduous
Pollinated: Insect
Leaf shape: Elliptic to obovate

Above left: The blossom of Sargent's cherry is a rich pink color.

Above: Fall leaves turn glorious shades of orange.

Black Cherry

Rum cherry *Prunus serotina*

Also known as rum cherry because its fruits were once used to flavor rum, this willow leaf-like tree has bark that emits a distinctive odor if scratched. It is a member of the birdcherry group and therefore has its flowers borne in spike-like racemes. It is common in woods throughout a region south of Nova Scotia to Mexico.

Distribution: Eastern and central North America, south to Mexico and Guatemala.
Height: 80ft (25m)
Shape: Broadly columnar
Deciduous
Pollinated: Insect
Leaf shape: Elliptic to lanceolate

Identification: The bark is dark gray and smooth becoming horizontally fissured in maturity. The leaves are elliptic to lanceolate, 4¾in (12cm) long and 2in (5cm) wide, glossy dark green and smooth above, paler beneath with some pubescence along the midrib. They taper to a slight point and are finely toothed around the margin. In the fall they turn bright yellow before dropping. The flowers are white, ½in (1cm) across and grouped in racemes, which may be up to 6in (15cm) long.

Above: The fruit is a black, round, edible cherry to ½in (1cm) across.

Below: The flowers are white.

Pin Cherry

Prunus pensylvanica

A hardy, shrubby tree, which reaches 33ft (10m) in height in the wild, but seldom in cultivation. It is able to withstand cold and exposure and is often used to make shelterbelts. It is not widely cultivated because of the sheer number of alternative, more free-flowering cherries, which are readily available. Its most distinctive feature is bright red shoots, which are particularly evident in late winter and early spring.

Identification: The bark is dark brown, smooth but becoming pockmarked with pronounced lenticels in maturity. The leaves are lanceolate and willow-like, up to 3in (7.5cm) long, narrow and tapering to a long, fine point. They are glossy mid-green above and slightly paler beneath, with a bright red leaf stalk coming off red shoots. The flowers are small, ½in (1.5cm) across, white, sometimes with a pink blush, and borne on short racemes in clusters of between four and eight. The fruits are black, pea-sized and quite often borne in profusion.

Below: The fruit has sour flesh.

Distribution: All of Canada south to Georgia and Colorado.
Height: 33ft (10m)
Shape: Broadly columnar
Deciduous
Pollinated: Insect
Leaf shape: Lanceolate

Right: Flowers appear in early May when the leaves are about half grown.

OTHER SPECIES OF NOTE

Tibetan Cherry *Prunus serrula*
A small, spreading cherry, popular throughout North America for its striking, highly polished, deep mahogany-red bark, which becomes a feature in winter. It originates from western China and may attain heights around 50ft (15m), but more often 33ft (10m). The white flowers are relatively inconspicuous and are produced after the lanceolate leaves appear in mid-spring.

Japanese 'Sato' Cherry *Prunus* 'Kanzan'
This colorful cherry, of Japanese garden origin, is probably the commonest cherry in cultivation in North America. It produces masses of bright pink, double flowers, borne in dense clusters throughout the crown. Mature trees develop arching branches that begin by rising strongly from the stem and then droop toward the tip, probably because of the weight of the flowers.

Mazzard *Prunus avium*
This tree, also known as the gean or wild cherry, originates from Europe, but has long been cultivated in America. It has become naturalized in many regions, and is common in southern British Columbia, Vancouver and Seattle. It produces clouds of white, single flowers in late spring and orange and red leaves in the fall.

Pissard's Purple Plum *Prunus cerasifera*
'Pissardii' This is a common variety of the myrobalan plum and is widely grown in suburbs, in western U.S.A. and British Columbia. It is grown for its shiny, distinctive, deep purple leaves. It has delicate, small white flowers, which are pink in bud and open before the leaves emerge.

The Great White Cherry

Prunus 'Tai Haku'

This beautiful tree was cultivated in Japan until the 1700s when it fell from favor and was thought to have become extinct. That was until 1923 when a dying specimen was discovered in a garden in England. The owner had purchased it, along with several other unnamed cherries, from Japan in 1900. Today it has become one of the most widely planted cherries across the world.

Identification: The bark is a warm chestnut brown, becoming fissured in maturity. It has low spreading branches, which in spring are filled with clusters of large, up to 3in (7.5cm) across, pure white, single flowers with central pink stamens. At the same time, bronze-red leaves begin to unfurl from bud. The combination of leaf and flower is spectacular. The elliptic, taper-pointed and finely toothed leaves rapidly turn mid-green and then orange in fall.

Distribution: Of garden origin. U.S.A. zones 4–7.
Height: 33ft (10m)
Shape: Broadly spreading
Deciduous
Pollinated: Insect
Leaf shape: Elliptic

Left: The leaves are bronze in spring, turning green in summer.

Above and below: 'Tai Haku' has the best snow white flowers of any cherry tree.

HAWTHORNS

Hawthorns are members of the Rosaceae family and one of the most numerous genera in North America. There are at least two hundred different species and countless hybrids and varieties. They are among the most adaptable of all trees, tolerating both waterlogged and excessively dry soils, industrial pollution and coastal salt spray.

Downy Hawthorn

Red haw *Crataegus mollis*

Distribution: Central U.S.A.
Height: 40ft (12m)
Shape: Broadly columnar
Deciduous
Pollinated: Insect
Leaf shape: Ovate

Otherwise known as the red haw, the downy hawthorn grows wild from Nova Scotia and Quebec south to Texas and west to Nevada. It is also commonly found in city parks in eastern U.S.A. It is a small tree seldom reaching 33ft (10m) and very tolerant of air pollution, making it an ideal tree for urban areas. There is a specific form of this tree known as the Arnold hawthorn, *Crataegus arnoldiana*, which was developed at the Arnold Arboretum, Boston.

Identification: The bark is red brown, cracking into vertical plates in maturity. The dark green leaves are broadly ovate, approximately 4in (10cm) long, with up to five shallow lobes on each side. The entire leaf margin is sharply toothed, and the texture of the leaf is rough due to hairs on each side. The shoots carry 2in- (5cm-) long spines. The flowers are white with yellow anthers, 1in (2.5cm) across, borne in clusters in late spring. The fruits, which appear towards the end of the summer, are bright red and up to 1in (2.5cm) across.

Right: The leaves are covered with pubescence.

Left: The red fruits are known as haws.

Cockspur Hawthorn

Crataegus crus-galli

One of the most spectacular of all hawthorns because of its long, ferociously sharp spines, which may be up to 4in (10cm) long. It is found growing wild on the edge of woodland, and within open woodland from Quebec south to Florida and west to Texas. It is also planted in towns and cities outside this region. In the fall the leaves turn a fine marmalade-orange color.

Identification: The bark is dark brown and scaly, peeling to reveal fresh orange bark beneath. The obovate leaves are glossy dark green above, paler beneath, with no pubescence. They are 4in (10cm) long and 2in (5cm) across, tapering at the base and rounded at the tip with some serration around the upper half of the leaf margin. The flowers are creamy-white with pink anthers, ½in (1.5cm) across, and carried in dense, rounded heads, in late spring and early summer. The fruits are pea-size, bright red and quite often persist on the tree long after leaf fall.

Distribution: Eastern and central North America.
Height: 26ft (8m)
Shape: Broadly spreading
Deciduous
Pollinated: Insect
Leaf shape: Obovate

Right: The glossy scarlet haws may still be on the tree in mid-winter.

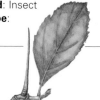

Above: The sharp spine of this species gives the tree its name "Cockspur."

Washington Hawthorn

Crataegus phaenopyrum

An attractive small tree, which grows wild on the banks of streams, in rich soil in woods and thickets, from Virginia to Florida, and is cultivated elsewhere in towns and cities, particularly in the eastern states. It is not common either in the wild or in cultivation and deserves to be better known. It certainly has one of the most attractive forms of hawthorn with a neat, round-headed canopy and glossy, maple-like leaves.

Identification: The bark is red-brown to gray-brown, rather thin, becoming shallowly fissured and scaly in maturity. The leaves are broadly ovate and almost maple-like with three to five sharply toothed lobes, glossy dark green above and sage-green and smooth beneath. The shoots carry long glossy spines up to 2in (5cm) long. In early summer creamy-white fragrant flowers, up to ½in (1.5cm) across are produced in lax clusters. They are followed by a show of dark crimson, pea-size fruit which appears in profusion.

Distribution: Eastern North America.
Height: 40ft (12m)
Shape: Broadly spreading
Deciduous
Pollinated: Insect
Leaf shape: Ovate

Right: The glossy round haws are some of the latest to ripen.

Right: The glossy maple-like leaves are a distinctive feature of this tree.

OTHER SPECIES OF NOTE

Black Hawthorn *Crataegus douglasii*
This small, hardy tree, with long drooping branches, grows naturally from Alaska and British Columbia southward to California, and grows at heights in excess of 6,000ft (1,800m) above sea level in the Rocky Mountains. David Douglas, who identified the tree, recorded that its thorns were used for fish hooks.

One-seed Hawthorn *Craetagus monogyna*
This European tree has been cultivated across North America since its introduction by the early settlers, who used it to create hedges to contain their stock. It has now naturalized across wide areas of North America from Quebec to North Carolina and in the west across Oregon and British Columbia.

Arkansas Thorn *Crataegus arkansana*
An elegant, small tree, up to 20ft (6m) tall, which grows wild in the White River area near Newport, Jackson County. It has relatively few thorns on its orange-brown, lustrous shoots, and is cultivated as far north as eastern Massachusetts, for its large, bright red fruits, which can be up to 1in (2.5cm) across, and persist on the tree well into early winter.

Crataegus arnoldiana
A beautiful small tree with large red fruits the size of cherries, and shallowly lobed leaves. It was found growing wild in the area of the Arnold Arboretum, Boston, and is cultivated in parks and gardens in eastern U.S.A. and recognized in winter by its upright "zigzag" branches.

Paul's Scarlet Thorn

Crataegus laevigata 'Paul's Scarlet'

This lovely tree is a cultivar of the Midland hawthorn, *Crataegus laevigata*, which gets its name from the English Midlands, where it is common and a good indicator of ancient woodland. The cultivar 'Paul's Scarlet' was produced as long ago as 1858, and since then has become a favorite ornamental species for parks and gardens.

Identification: The bark is gray and smooth, becoming shallowly fissured in maturity. It has ovate to obovate glossy dark green leaves that are 2in (5cm) long and wide, with shallow lobes around the upper half of the leaf. The double, almost rose-like flowers are its main feature, being a bright, deep pink color and produced in dense clusters all over the tree in late spring and early summer. These are followed in late summer by bright red, oval-shape fruits, up to 1in (2.5cm) long, which persist long into the fall.

Distribution: Of garden origin.
Height: 33ft (10m)
Shape: Broadly spreading
Deciduous
Pollinated: Insect
Leaf shape: Ovate to obovate

Right: Beautiful clusters of rose-like vibrant pink flowers are borne from late spring into early summer.

Right: The ovate leaves are dark green above and pale green beneath.

FLOWERING CRAB APPLES

The flowering crab genus, Malus, *contains over 25 species, native mainly to northern temperate regions. They are hardy, small to medium-size deciduous trees, widely grown as garden ornamentals for their profusion of spring flowers and late summer fruit. The flowers are similar to a cherry's, but have five styles presenting the female stigma for pollination instead of just one.*

Sweet Crab Apple

Malus coronaria

The sweet crab apple grows wild along streams and woodland edges from New York and Illinois south to Arkansas and Georgia. Although cultivated in parks and gardens elsewhere, the form 'Charlottae', which has strong violet-scented, double flowers, is planted in preference to the true species. It has easy to work, soft, decorative timber, with pink-red heartwood and yellow sapwood.

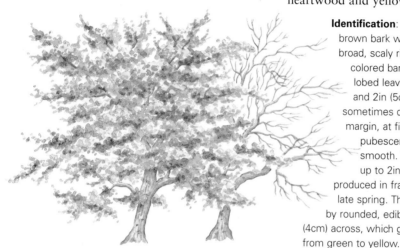

Identification: The sweet crab apple has red-brown bark which is shallowly fissured into broad, scaly ridges that flake to reveal lighter colored bark beneath. The deep green lobed leaves are ovate, to 4in (10cm) long and 2in (5cm) broad. They are sharply and sometimes double-toothed around the leaf margin, at first covered in a fine pubescence but soon becoming smooth. The flowers are single, pink, up to 2in (5cm) across and produced in fragrant clusters in late spring. These are followed by rounded, edible fruits 1½in (4cm) across, which gradually ripen from green to yellow.

Distribution: Eastern North America.
Height: 30ft (9m)
Shape: Broadly spreading
Deciduous
Pollinated: Insect
Leaf shape: Ovate

Right: Hard, bitter fruits are borne on short stalks.

Prairie Crab Apple

Malus ioensis

Distribution: Central U.S.A.
Height: 26ft (8m)
Shape: Broadly spreading
Deciduous
Pollinated: Insect
Leaf shape: Ovate

This is the midwestern sweet crab apple, which grows wild from Indiana and Wisconsin south to Oklahoma and Arkansas, where it inhabits moist stream banks and wood margins. The form of this tree known as 'Bechtel's Crab' is more popular than the species, because it reliably produces a profusion of semi-double pink, fading to white, flowers every spring.

Left: The pink-white flowers are borne in clusters of up to six but more commonly three to four.

Identification: The prairie crab apple is a low, bushy tree with level branches, which have gray bark, unlike the bark on the stem, which is purplish-brown and flakes in long narrow strips. The leaves are broadly ovate and borne on dark red shoots covered in gray pubescence. The single flowers are pink fading to white, each with five petals and borne in clusters of three to four. They are followed by round, smooth fruit which is pale green, or green flushed with red. It is up to 2in (5cm), very hard and bitter to taste.

Malus 'Dartmouth'
This North American cultivar was raised in New Hampshire before 1883. It bears pure white, single flowers, 1in (2.5cm) across, in profusion in mid-spring against a backdrop of fresh green leaves. These are followed in the fall by deep crimson, slightly angular fruits, up to 2in (5cm) across, which are covered in a purple bloom and persist long after the leaves have fallen.

Hueph Crab Malus hupehensis
This hardy Chinese tree is one of the most beautiful of all small deciduous trees. It grows wild in the mountains of central China where local people use the leaves to make a drink called "red tea." Since 1900, when it was introduced to America, it has become increasingly popular for planting in parks and gardens, and in spring it produces a mass of white flowers that are flushed with soft pink.

Willow-leaved pear Pyrus salicifolia
This eastern European and Asian tree is the most ornamental of all the pears. It is a firm favorite for planting where a small tree with silver foliage is required. It was introduced into North America over 150 years ago and has been widely planted since. It makes a very good centerpiece for a lawn and is easily recognizable by its long, narrow, silver-gray leaves and creamy-white flowers. The fruit is a small, hard green pear 1¼in (3cm) long.

Japanese Crab Apple

Malus floribunda

Distribution: Japan. U.S.A. zones 4–8.
Height: 17ft (5m)
Shape: Broadly spreading
Deciduous
Pollinated: Insect
Leaf shape: Elliptic

Believed to be a hybrid, but cultivated in Japan for centuries. It was introduced into America in 1862. Since then it has become popular and is now commonly found from Ontario to California. It is one of the first crab apples to come into leaf, and the whole crown is smothered in flowers in May. It has an extremely spreading habit and will quite often be wider than it is tall.

Identification: The bark is purple brown, flaking into thin, vertical plates in maturity. The dark green leaves are elliptic, 4in (10cm) long and 2in (5cm) broad, sharply toothed around the margin and running to a long tapered tip. They are smooth on top, but carry some pubescence beneath. The flowers are followed by pea-size, rounded yellow fruits that are clustered together on long slender stalks.

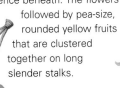

Above: Fruit.

Right: The flowers are 1in (2.5cm) across, deep red in bud, gradually opening pale pink, and then fading to white.

Pillar Apple

Malus tschonoskii

This slender Japanese tree has become extremely popular for planting in streets and town squares across America (hardiness zones 4–8) because of its narrow, fastigiate form and its ability to grow on impoverished soils. In Japan it grows on shallow, rocky soils that have little nutrient content. It hardly has any fruit, which is a bonus in streets. It does, however, produce stunning leaf color in the fall.

Distribution: Japan.
Height: 50ft (15m)
Shape: Broadly conical
Deciduous
Pollinated: Insect
Leaf shape: Ovate

Identification: The bark is at first purple-brown and smooth, but becomes increasingly fissured and rough in maturity. The leaves are broadly ovate, to 5in (12cm) long and 3in (7.5cm) across, sharply toothed and running to a tapered point at the tip. They are grass green, smooth and glossy above and slightly hairy beneath. The flowers are 1in (2.5cm) across, white, flushed pink with yellow anthers and produced in clusters in mid-spring. The fruit is rounded, green flushed with red, and covered with brown lenticels.

Right: When the leaves emerge from bud they are covered with gray hair.

Right: The fruit is speckled with light brown lenticels.

ROWANS, SERVICEBERRIES AND LOQUATS

The rose family, Rosaceae, is one of the largest plant families. It encompasses an incredibly diverse range of plants, including cherries, apples, quinces, loquats, cotoneasters, rowans and roses. It is also one of the most commonly seen families within cultivation, because of the excellent flowers and beautiful fruit. The Rosaceae include the following diverse and beautiful group of trees.

American Mountain Ash

Roundwood *Sorbus americana*

This small tree, or large shrub, grows into a round-topped, spreading, low tree, which seldom exceeds 33ft (10m). It has a natural distribution that extends from Newfoundland south to Georgia, and westward into Michigan and Wisconsin. It is not widely planted as an ornamental, preference in parks and gardens being given to its European cousin *Sorbus aucuparia*, which has creamy-white spring flowers.

Identification: The bark is pale gray, smooth at first, becoming scaly in maturity. The leaves are pinnate, to 10in (25cm) long, with up to 15 lanceolate, slightly toothed and pointed leaflets, which are 4in (10cm) long and 1in (2.5cm) across. In the fall the leaflets turn orange and the leaf stalks bright red. Creamy-white flowers appear in dense clusters in late spring to early summer. These are followed by bright orange-red berries that last well into the fall, if not eaten first by birds.

Distribution: Eastern North America.
Height: 33ft (10m)
Shape: Broadly spreading
Deciduous
Pollinated: Insect
Leaf shape: Pinnate

Showy Mountain Ash

Sorbus decora

The showy mountain ash is a northern and high-altitude form of the American mountain-ash, *Sorbus americana*, and may be of hybrid origin. It gets its name from its large showy bunches of bright red berries, which first appear in late summer, and may last well into winter. It covers much of the same range as the American mountain ash, but occurs further north in Quebec, Ontario and Labrador.

Identification: The bark is pale gray and smooth, becoming slightly fissured and scaly in maturity. The flowers are creamy white and borne in early summer in dense, pungent-smelling clusters. The flowers are followed by berries in large heads of up to 6in (15cm) across, orange at first, maturing to deep red.

Right: The leaves are pinnate, to 10in (25cm) long, with up to 17 lanceolate, sea green-color leaflets, each 3in (7.5cm).

Right: Each berry is up to ¼in (6mm) across.

Distribution: Northeast North America.
Height: 33ft (10m)
Shape: Broadly spreading
Deciduous
Pollinated: Insect
Leaf shape: Pinnate

American Serviceberry

Amelanchier laevis

Quite often known simply as serviceberry, this small, round-topped tree is native to northeastern North America, from Newfoundland west to Wisconsin, and south along the Appalachian Mountains to northern Georgia, where it occurs naturally in cool ravines and hillside woodlands. It is beautiful in early May when masses of white fragrant flowers appear alongside emerging leaves that are the color of light bronze.

Identification: The bark is gray-brown and smooth even in maturity. The leaves are elliptic to ovate or sometimes obovate; up to 2½in (6cm) long and 1in (2.5cm) across. They are finely serrated around the leaf margin and run to a point at the tip. Initially bronze-red, they turn deep-green in summer and then bright orange-red in the fall. The flowers are pure white, with five narrow petals and are held in upright, spreading racemes up to 3in (7.5cm) long.

Distribution: Eastern North America.
Height: 40ft (12m)
Shape: Broadly spreading
Deciduous
Pollinated: Insect
Leaf shape: Elliptic to ovate

Left and right: The spring flowers are followed by small, round, purple-black berries.

OTHER SPECIES OF NOTE

Rowan
Sorbus aucuparia
This small, hardy tree is native right across Europe and temperate Asia. It survives in U.S.A. hardiness zone 4. It is also known as the mountain ash; appropriate, because it does have bright green, ash-like leaves and is found growing high up on mountainsides: sometimes it seems to be growing out of bare rock. The flowers, which are creamy-white and slightly pungent, emerge in mid-spring, and clusters of bright red berries appear in late summer.

Chinese Rowan *Sorbus hupehensis*
This is a beautiful small tree, native to much of temperate China and cultivated throughout the temperate world as a garden ornamental. It has ash-like, deep green leaves and a display of delightful white berries, slightly flushed with pink.

Snowy Mespilus *Amelanchier lamarckii*
Otherwise known as *Amelanchier canadensis*, this beautiful small tree is believed to have originated in northeastern North America from where it was introduced into Europe as early as the seventeenth century. It is widely planted as an ornamental species because of its attractive white star-shaped flowers. They appear in spring alongside leaves that emerge from the bud a warm copper-bronze color. These are followed by purple-black, sweet-tasting, globular fruits which are quite often used as a pie filling.

Loquat

Eriobotrya japonica

This magnificent large shrub, or small tree, has probably the most distinctive leaves of any ornamental species grown in America. They are thick, leathery, glossy dark green, with a corrugated appearance and deeply veined. It is grown as a popular ornamental throughout warm, frost-free areas of U.S.A., from Charleston to California, where it is frequently seen in small gardens, courtyards and growing up walls. It produces round, golden-yellow, edible fruits in spring.

Identification: The bark is gray-brown and smooth becoming heavily fissured in maturity. The shoots are stout and covered in a slight pubescence. Each shoot carries several large leaves up to 5–12in long, (13–30cm) which are dark glossy green above, with some pubescence beneath. Loquat has small white hawthorn-like flowers, which carry the scent of almonds, and are borne in dense flowerheads up to 6in (15cm) across. These are followed by golden-yellow, round fruits that contain several glossy brown seeds.

Distribution: China and Japan.
Height: 30ft (9m)
Shape: Broadly spreading
Evergreen
Pollinated: Insect
Leaf shape: Elliptic to ovate

Left: The leaves are rigid, thick, leathery and up to 12in (30cm) long.

Left: The golden-yellow fruits of the loquat are sweet and edible.

LOCUST TREES AND PAGODA TREES

The pea family, Leguminosae, contains more than 15,000 species of trees, shrubs and herbaceous plants in 700 genera. They are found growing wild throughout the world in both temperate and tropical conditions. Most have compound leaves, pea-like flowers and seed pods, and root systems which have the ability to use bacteria to absorb nitrogen from the soil.

Pagoda Tree

Sophora japonica

Despite its botanical name *japonica*, the pagoda tree is not thought to be a native of Japan. However, it has been widely cultivated there for centuries, particularly in temple gardens and places of learning. In China the flower buds were used to make a yellow dye and all parts of the tree, if taken internally, create a strong purgative effect. In the U.S.A. it is grown as a lawn tree. On trees grown from seed the flowers can take 30 years to appear.

Identification: The bark is greenish brown, becoming vertically fissured and ridged in maturity. The overall shape is rounded, with branching starting low on the stem. The leaves are pinnate and up to 10in (25cm) long, with up to 15 opposite, untoothed, ovate, pointed leaflets, which are dark green above and glaucous with some pubescence beneath. The flowers are white, pea-like, fragrant and borne in terminal panicles in summer. The fruit is a seed pod up to 3in (8cm) long, containing up to six seeds. It ripens from green to brown.

Distribution: Northern China but could be more widespread. It survives to U.S.A hardiness zone 5.
Height: 66ft (20m)
Shape: Broadly spreading
Deciduous
Pollinated: Insect
Leaf shape: Pinnate

Left: The white flowers of the pagoda tree are produced in summer in open sprays.

Black Locust

Robinia pseudoacacia

This locust tree originates from the Appalachian Mountains from Pennsylvania to Georgia; however, it is now naturalized over most of the U.S.A. It was once valued for ships' masts because of its strong, durable timber, and clean straight trunk. Native Americans used the lumber to make bows. Black locust has the habit of suckering from the root system and on mature trees suckers can be found up to 33ft (10m) away from the base of the tree.

Identification: The leaves are pinnate to 12in (30cm) long, with 11 to 21 ovate to elliptic untoothed, thin leaflets, each 2in (5cm) long and ending in a sharp point at the tip. They are grass-green above and blue-green below. Quite often there are two sharp spines at the base of each leaf. The fragrant flowers are pea-like, white, with a pea-green blotch in the throat.

Left: The fruit is a dark brown bean pod up to 4in (10cm) long.

Distribution: Eastern U.S.A.
Height: 80ft (25m)
Shape: Broadly columnar
Deciduous
Pollinated: Insect
Leaf shape: Pinnate

Honeylocust

Gleditsia triacanthos

This remarkable tree is probably best known for its armory of ferocious thorns that cover its trunk and main branches; this could be considered a reason for not planting it. However, honeylocust is widely planted in city streets because it is able to withstand heat, dust, drought and airborne pollutants. Unlike other members of the pea family it does not have the ordinary "wing and keel" pea flower.

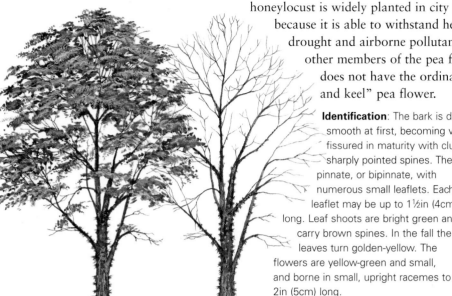

Identification: The bark is dark gray, smooth at first, becoming vertically fissured in maturity with clusters of sharply pointed spines. The leaves are pinnate, or bipinnate, with numerous small leaflets. Each leaflet may be up to 1½in (4cm) long. Leaf shoots are bright green and carry brown spines. In the fall the leaves turn golden-yellow. The flowers are yellow-green and small, and borne in small, upright racemes to 2in (5cm) long.

Distribution: From New England to Texas, U.S.A.
Height: 100ft (30m)
Shape: Broadly spreading
Deciduous
Pollinated: Insect
Leaf shape: Pinnate

Right: The seed is contained in a large, up to 18in (45cm) long, often twisted, brown hanging pod, in late summer.

Rose Acacia *Robinia hispida*
Otherwise known as moss locust, this beautiful small tree, or large shrub, native to Virginia and Kentucky south to Georgia, is widely planted because of its delightful rose-pink flowers, which are produced on bristly branches in late spring and early summer. It makes an ideal tree for a small location, but has a habit of suckering for some distance away from the main stem.

Robinia pseudoacacia 'Frisia'
This cultivated form of the black locust is now one of the most popular trees for ornamental planting in the U.S.A. It was first raised at the Jansen Nursery, Holland, in 1935, and since then has been widely planted both in town and country. It has striking yellow pinnate foliage throughout the spring and summer months. The wood is quite brittle and in exposed conditions breaking branches are a possibility.

Tree of Heaven *Ailanthus altissima*
This Chinese tree has been planted as an ornamental street tree in just about every North American city from Montreal to Los Angeles. It

has naturalized in areas such as the Allegheny Mountains where it self-seeds and suckers at an incredible rate. It has a very distinctive, broadly columnar form, and long, graceful, pinnate leaves.

Kentucky Coffee Tree

Gymnocladus dioica

This tree is widely planted in parks and gardens as an ornamental tree even outside its natural range, which extends from New York and Pennsylvania to Nebraska. It is said that the seeds of this tree were roasted to make into a type of coffee by early European settlers in North America. In fact raw seeds of this species are poisonous. It is easily distinguished by its huge bipinnate leaves which may be up to 40in (1m) long and carry up to 140 leaflets.

Distribution: Central and eastern U.S.A.
Height: 80ft (25m)
Shape: Broadly columnar
Deciduous
Pollinated: Insect
Leaf shape: Bipinnate

Identification: The bipinnate leaves have ovate leaflets, each to 3in (7.5cm) long, which are thin, untoothed and emerge from winter bud a bronze color, before turning dark green above and sea-green beneath. The flowers are greenish-white and fragrant, 1in (2.5cm) across, and borne in conical panicles up to 4in (10cm) long.

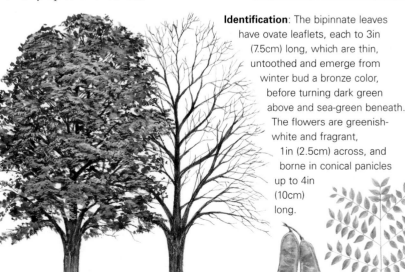

EUCALYPTUS

There are more than 400 species of eucalyptus, or gum tree, native to the Southern Hemisphere. They are abundant in Australia, Tasmania, New Guinea, the Philippines and Java. Most eucalyptus are evergreen and fast-growing, with attractive bark, luxuriant foliage and white flowers. They have been widely cultivated for their ornamental qualities, and lumber, in other warm temperate regions.

Cider Gum

Eucalyptus gunnii

The cider gum is native to the island of Tasmania, where it grows in moist mountain forests up to 4,265ft (1,300m) above sea level. It is one of the hardiest of all eucalyptus species and one of the most widely planted around the world. Cider gum has attractive glaucous-colored, round, juvenile foliage, which is prized by flower arrangers and florists. Trees that are regularly coppiced maintain juvenile foliage. Wild trees grow up to 98ft (30m) tall.

Right: If left to mature, cider gum leaves become long and slender, and hang from the branches.

Identification: This potentially large, fast-growing tree has smooth, gray-green to orange bark, peeling to reveal creamy fawn patches. The juvenile leaves are round, 1½in (4cm) across, glaucous to silver-blue and borne opposite in pairs. Mature leaves are lanceolate, up to 4in (10cm) long, sage-green to silver-colored and borne alternately on the twig. Flowers are white with numerous yellow stamens, borne in clusters of three in the leaf axils during summer. The fruit is a green, woody capsule, open at one end and contains several seeds.

Right: After pollination in summer, the flowers develop into woody fruit.

Distribution: Tasmania. Thrives in the Pacific Northwest. U.S.A. zones 8–10.
Height: 100ft (30m)
Shape: Broadly columnar
Evergreen
Pollinated: Insect
Leaf shape: Juvenile leaves are rounded, and the mature leaves are lanceolate

Tasmanian Blue Gum

Eucalyptus globulus

This fast-growing, but rather tender Australasian tree, is the floral emblem of Tasmania. It was introduced into the San Francisco area of the U.S.A. as a lumber-producing species in 1875, but since then, it has escaped from cultivation and taken over extensive areas in the hills to the south where it grows at elevations in excess of 2,000ft (600m). In good growing conditions the blue gum will grow more than 8ft (2.5m) in one year.

Left: Mature leaves are lanceolate, glossy green and up to 16in (40cm) long.

Identification: The bark is a patchwork of blue-gray, yellow and brown, at first smooth, but becoming shaggy in maturity, and peeling in long ribbons. The juvenile leaves are an attractive glaucous gray-green color and rounded. Quite often trees are pruned back hard to encourage juvenile foliage which is used in floral arrangements. The adult leaves are ovate to lanceolate, waxy to the touch, glossy green and up to 16in (40cm) long. The flowers are creamy-white with golden yellow stamens. They grow singly in the leaf axils in spring.

Right: The leaves are arranged opposite each other on the twigs.

Distribution: Tasmania and the State of Victoria, Australia.
Height: 195ft (60m)
Shape: Broadly columnar
Evergreen
Pollinated: Insect
Leaf shape: Lanceolate

Longbeak Eucalyptus

Eucalyptus camaldulensis

The longbeak eucalyptus has a natural range which extends right across northern Australia. Consequently it is not as hardy as the blue gum, *Eucalyptus globulus*, and has not become naturalized in the wild, in California, to such an extent. It is found in profusion in the Bay area and further east into Arizona, where it is common in towns and cities as an ornamental species. Elsewhere, further northward, it is kept in check by winter frost. The longbeak eucalyptus has a much more open crown than that of the blue gum.

Identification: The bark is a mixture of light fawn, yellow and gray-red, smooth at first, becoming straggly, and peeling in narrow strips in maturity. The adult leaves are pale green with a white midrib, 6in (15cm) long and 1in (2.5cm) across. At first glance there is a similarity in the leaf with weeping willow, *Salix babylonica*. The hard seed capsules ripen to a five-pointed star shape.

Distribution: Northern Australia.
Height: 80ft (25m)
Shape: Broadly columnar
Evergreen
Pollinated: Insect
Leaf shape: Lanceolate

Left: The white flowers grow in clusters of five to six. The flower buds have a distinctive, stout, beak-like tip, hence the name.

OTHER SPECIES OF NOTE

Mountain Gum *Eucalyptus dalrympleana*
This handsome tree is native to Tasmania, New South Wales and Victoria in Australia. It is also known as the broad-leaved kindling bark because it sheds large, dry patches of pale cream bark. It grows on steep, rocky slopes at elevations of up to 4,921ft (1,500m) above sea level. It has gray-green lanceolate leaves that are bronze-colored when juvenile.

Small-leaved Gum
Eucalyptus parviflora
This hardy, medium-size gum tree originates from New South Wales, but has been grown as an ornamental in parks, gardens and arboreta across southern states of U.S.A. since the 1930s. It has attractive, smooth, gray, peeling bark, gray-green ovate juvenile leaves, and blue-green, ovate, mature leaves up to 2in (5cm) long.

Alpine Ash *Eucalyptus delegatensis*
This is one of the tallest of all eucalyptus, regularly attaining heights in excess of 197ft (60m) in the mountains of Tasmania. In cultivation, in the U.S.A., it is more likely to reach heights of around 100ft (30m). It has a straight, clean trunk and sparse airy crown. The juvenile bark is smooth, bluish-gray and shed in narrow, vertical ribbons; in maturity it becomes rough and fibrous. The adult leaves are lanceolate, dull sage-green and up to 6in (15cm) long.

Silver Dollar Tree

Eucalyptus polyanthemos

This tender gum is native to New South Wales and Victoria, Australia. It was introduced into the U.S.A. in the late nineteenth century. It is the only eucalyptus to be seen growing in the eastern states outside southern Florida. It is cultivated in parks and gardens from Atlanta to west of New Orleans, inland Georgia and Alabama, as well as in California. Although relatively hardy, it is often cut to the ground by frost and regrows as a shrubby bush rather than a tree.

Identification: The bark is orange red and fibrous, becoming shaggy in maturity. Both the juvenile and adult leaves are almost round and a bright glaucous, silvery blue-white color, hence the name silver dollar. The juvenile leaves are borne opposite on the shoots, and the adult leaves are alternate. From a distance this tree is very distinctive with its light silvery coloring. The flowers are creamy-white, small and borne in clusters in early spring.

Distribution: Australia.
Height: 100ft (30m)
Shape: Broadly columnar
Evergreen
Pollinated: Insect
Leaf shape: Orbicular

Above: Small clusters of creamy-white fragrant flowers are borne in early spring.

DOGWOODS AND HANDKERCHIEF TREE

The flowering dogwoods are some of the most beautiful trees in North America. They have been widely cultivated as ornamental specimens in parks and gardens from the eastern seaboard to the west coast. Their small insignificant flowers are surrounded by colored bracts which act as protection for the flowers.

Flowering Dogwood

Cornus florida

This beautiful small tree is common in North America. It has a natural range that extends from Portland, Oregon, east to Maine and south to Texas. It has distinctive bark that becomes deeply fissured into small, square, red-brown blocks. It is slow-growing and eventually makes a bushy, upswept tree with a low crown. The cultivar 'Cherokee Chief' that has deep pink flower bracts is common in cultivation.

Identification: Flowering dogwood has untoothed and taper-pointed leaves that are ovate to elliptic, up to 4in (10cm) long and 2in (5cm) across. They are dark green with a slight sheen above, paler with some white soft pubescence beneath. In the fall they turn through pink to a stunning rich, burgundy-red. The flowers have a distinct notch at the tip. These are followed by glossy, bright red berries.

Distribution: North America.
Height: 40ft (12m)
Shape: Broadly spreading
Deciduous
Pollinated: Insect
Leaf shape: Ovate

Left: The flowers are tiny, green and produced in a dense cluster that is surrounded by four 2in- (5cm-) long, white bracts.

Pacific Dogwood

Cornus nuttallii

Distribution: British Columbia south to California.
Height: 80ft (25m)
Shape: Broadly conical
Deciduous
Pollinated: Insect
Leaf shape: Elliptic

The Pacific dogwood grows naturally in lowland forests beneath larger trees, such as the Douglas fir, from Vancouver Island along the Coast Range to south California and the western flanks of the Cascade Sierra Nevada. It has been widely cultivated as an ornamental tree outside this region in parks and gardens. In late spring it produces some of the biggest bracts of any dogwood. In cultivation it rarely attains its full potential height, more often growing as a multistemmed, large shrub, or small tree.

Identification: The bark is smooth, gray, becoming cracked into irregular plates in maturity. The untoothed, pointed leaves are elliptic, sometimes obovate, to 6in (15cm) long and 3in (7.5cm) across, dark green above, paler beneath, with some pubescence. In the fall they turn bright red. After flowering, small oval-shaped, shiny red berries appear in clusters.

Far left: The flowers are small, green and borne in dense, hemispherical clusters. Four to seven large creamy-white (sometimes blush-pink) bracts, to 3in (7.5cm) long, surround each cluster.

OTHER SPECIES OF NOTE

Alternate-leaved Dogwood *Cornus alternifolia*

As the name suggests, this species of dogwood is unusual in having leaves that are borne alternately on the shoot; most dogwoods have opposite leaves. This large shrub, or small multistemmed tree, is native to eastern North America from Newfoundland to Florida. It is sometimes known as the pagoda dogwood because of the tiered effect created by its horizontal branches.

Cornus 'Eddie's White Wonder'

This is an extremely popular ornamental hybrid between the two main American dogwoods; flowering dogwood, *Cornus florida*, and the Pacific dogwood, *C. nuttallii*. It has large white bracts, which appear consistently year upon year, and leaves that turn a brilliant orange-red color every fall. It was first developed in America in the 1960s.

Japanese Strawberry Tree *Cornus kousa*

This beautiful small tree, native to Japan and Korea, was introduced into North America in the 1870s and has since become widely cultivated in parks and gardens across the U.S.A. It differs from the American dogwoods in having showy, pointed creamy-white, or pink-blushed, bracts, and red, edible strawberry-like fruits, which hang from the branches in late summer, early fall. The variety *chinensis* is a taller, more open form with larger leaves. It was introduced into America in 1907.

Handkerchief Tree

Dove tree, Ghost tree *Davidia involucrata*

This beautiful tree was introduced into the West from China in 1904, by the plant collector Ernest Wilson, who had been commissioned by Veitch's nursery to collect propagation material from "this most wondrous of species." All of the tree's common names refer to the white hanging leaf bracts that appear in late spring.

Identification: The bark is orange-brown with vertical fissures, creating flaking, irregular plates. The leaves, up to 6in (15cm) long and 4in (10cm) wide, are sharply toothed with a drawn-out, pointed tip. They are glossy bright green above and paler with some hairs beneath. In times of drought they roll into a cigar shape in an effort to reduce water loss by transpiration. The flowers appear in late spring. They are small, numerous, clustered into a ball and have conspicuous lilac anthers. The fruit is a green-purple husk containing a single, hard nut, inside which are up to five seeds.

Distribution: Western China. U.S.A. zones 6–8.
Height: 82ft (25m)
Shape: Broadly conical
Deciduous
Pollinated: Insect
Leaf shape: Cordate

Above: Surrounding the flowers are two large white bracts of unequal size, up to 8in (20cm) long, which flutter in the breeze.

Golden Raintree

Koelreuteria paniculata

This Asian tree, sometimes called "pride of India" or "China tree," is particularly valued for its golden-yellow flowers, which appear in the height of summer. It has long been planted as an ornamental species in parks, gardens and streets throughout the U.S.A. After flowering, three-sided papery, pink, bladder-shaped capsules develop, which contain three hard black seeds.

Identification: The bark is pale brown, smooth, becoming shallowly fissured, in maturity. The large, attractive leaves are pinnate, sometimes bipinnate, to 18in (45cm) long, and divided into 4in- (10cm-) long, toothed, dark green leaflets, which turn butter-yellow in the fall. This tree has golden-yellow flowers, ½in (1cm) across, which are carried in conical-shaped panicles up to 18in (45cm) long, at the tips of the growing shoots. After flowering, bladder-like seed capsules develop.

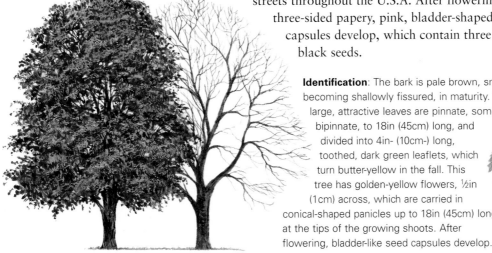

Distribution: China and Korea. U.S.A. zones 5–9.
Height: 40ft (12m)
Shape: Broadly spreading
Deciduous
Pollinated: Insect
Leaf shape: Pinnate

Above: The flowers are greenish-pink, gradually fading to pale brown. In China the seeds they contain were made into decorative necklaces.

HOLLIES AND BOX

*There are more than 400 species of temperate and tropical, evergreen and deciduous, trees and shrubs in
the Aquifoliaceae family; the majority belong to the holly, or Ilex, genus. Hollies are dioecious (either
male or female). The leaves occur alternately on the shoot and the fruit is a berry. Holly has long been
associated with the Christmas season.*

Common Holly

Ilex aquifolium

Holly is one of the most useful and ornamental trees of the temperate world. It is extremely
hardy, and its dense foliage provides better shelter in exposed coastal and mountainous
localities than just about any other tree. Holly has long been considered an integral part of
Christmas celebrations and its bright berries cheer up the dullest of winter
days. Holly timber is dense and hard and has been used for making
just about everything, from piano keys to billiard cues. The common
holly has given rise to numerous attractive garden cultivars.

Identification: The bark is silver-gray and smooth even in maturity. The leaves
are elliptic to ovate, up to 4in (10cm) long, glossy dark green and waxy above,
and pale green beneath. They are extremely variable: some leaves have
strong spines around the margin; others are spineless. Both the male
and female flowers are small and
white with a slight fragrance; they
appear on separate trees clustered
into the leaf axils in late spring and
early summer. The fruit is a round,
shiny, red berry up to ½in (1cm)
across, borne in clusters along
the shoot in winter.

*Right: The dense foliage of holly
makes it a useful hedging plant.*

Distribution: Whole of
Europe, western Asia and
North Africa. It survives in
U.S.A. hardiness zones 6–8.
Height: 66ft (20m)
Shape: Broadly columnar
Evergreen
Pollinated: Insect
Leaf shape: Elliptic to ovate

*Right: Holly flowers are
scented and
appear from
spring into
summer.*

American Holly

Ilex opaca

This native American tree grows wild in eastern
U.S.A., from Long Island south to Florida, and is
common as a planted roadside tree in Tennessee,
Louisiana, Arkansas and eastern Texas. In the
wild it is most prevalent on coastal sandy soils.
It is similar to the common holly, *Ilex
aquifolium*, except the leaf is less
glossy above and it has a more
pronounced yellow-color beneath,
and there is less variability in
the number of spines on the
leaf margin. It produces
brilliant red berries in winter.

*Left: There are several cultivars
and varieties of* Ilex opaca *in
North America including the
form xanthocarpa which has
bright yellow fruits.*

Identification: The bark is
gray and smooth,
becoming finely lined in
maturity, with dark
yellow-green fissures.
The leaves are elliptic,
to 4in (10cm) long and
2in (5cm) across.
They are matt
dark green above,
yellow-green
beneath, with
spines at the tip
and around the
leaf margin. Both
the male and
female flowers are
small, dull white and
borne in leaf axils on
separate trees in late spring.
The fruit is a red, shiny spherical
berry to ½in (1cm) across.

Distribution: Eastern North
America.
Height: 66ft (20m)
Shape: Broadly conical
Evergreen
Pollinated: Insect
Leaf shape: Elliptic

Japanese Holly *Ilex crenata*
Native to both Japan and Korea, this attractive evergreen plant is more a tall shrub than a tree, seldom attaining heights in excess of 13ft (4m). It has stiff, deep green, glossy, small leaves, which are ½in (1cm) long and more akin to those of common box than holly. These are densely borne on reddish brown shoots, which also carry globular, glossy black berries in winter. It survives in the warmer areas of zone 5.

Chinese Holly *Ilex cornuta*
Also known as horned holly because of its horn-like spines, this small evergreen tree is native to China and Korea, and rare in cultivation. It has slightly larger red berries than common holly and a rectangular-shaped leaf with a large spine at each corner, plus smaller intermediate spines. It is slow-growing with a neat compact habit.

Highclere Holly *Ilex* x *altaclarensis*
The term Highclere holly has come to represent a whole group of ornamental holly cultivars developed from the original *Ilex* x *altaclarensis* hybrid between the common holly, *I. aquifolium*, and the Madeira holly, *I. perado*. The original hybrid was developed at Highclere Castle, England in the late 1800s. Most of the cultivars have broad, rounded, glossy leaves. One of the most popular cultivars is 'Golden King'.

Yaupon

Ilex vomitoria

This small tree, or large shrub, grows naturally on the Coastal Plain from Virginia to Texas. It gets its botanical name *vomitoria* from the fact that at one time native Americans would make an infusion of the leaves, which they then drank in large quantities causing severe vomiting. They continued to drink the infusion for two or three days until they had sufficiently cleansed themselves. This species is tender and although widely planted in southern United States it is seldom seen growing successfully in northern states. It has become naturalized in Bermuda.

Identification: Yaupon has smooth pale gray bark and shoots that arise from stout, horizontal branches. It is a densely branched small tree with a central trunk rarely more than 18in (45cm) in diameter. The leaves, which persist for two years, are glossy dark green above and pale yellow-green beneath, narrowly oval or ovate, tapered at the base and blunt at the tip with irregular, small spines. Both male and female flowers are small, white and borne in clusters in the leaf axils on separate trees in spring. The fruit is a bright orange-red berry.

Distribution: Southeastern U.S.A.
Height: 20ft (6m)
Shape: Broadly spreading
Evergreen
Pollinated: Insect
Leaf shape: Oval

Above: The leaves are up to 4in (10cm) long and 2in (5cm) broad.

Right: The flowers are borne in the leaf axils.

Common Box

Buxus sempervirens

This small tree or spreading shrub has dense foliage and has been grown for centuries in gardens for hedging, screening and topiary. It is a favorite for use in defining knot gardens and parterres, and clips well. It withstands dense shade and will happily grow beneath the branches of other trees. It has hard, cream-colored wood, which has been extensively used for wood engraving and turnery.

Identification: The bark is fawn or buff-colored, smooth at first, then fissuring into tiny plates. The leaves are ovate to oblong, 1in (2.5cm), rounded at the tip with a distinctive notch, glossy dark green above, pale green below and borne on angular shoots. Both male and female flowers are produced in mid-spring; they are small, pale green with yellow anthers and carried separately in the same clusters on the same trees.

Far left: The fruit is a small woody capsule holding up to six seeds.

Right: Male and female flowers are produced separately in the leaf axils.

Distribution: Europe, North Africa and western Asia. It survives in U.S.A hardiness zones 5–10.
Height: 20ft (6m)
Shape: Broadly conical to spreading
Evergreen
Pollinated: Insect
Leaf shape: Ovate

BUCKEYES AND HORSE CHESTNUTS

The horse chestnut genus, Aesculus, *contains some of the most popular and easily recognizable ornamental trees in the world. There are just 15 species, all native to northern temperate regions, where they are widely grown in parks, gardens and arboreta for their stately habit, and attractive flowers and fruit. All horse chestnuts have compound, palmate leaves and large flowers borne in upright panicles.*

Californian Buckeye

Aesculus californica

There are six different species of American buckeyes, or horse chestnuts, as they may be known, five of them are native to eastern U.S.A., and this one, which is native to California. It is found in the low, dry foothills from Shasta to the Coast Ranges and south along the western slopes of the Sierra Nevada. It is low-growing, with branches emerging from the trunk 12in (30cm) from the ground. The flowers have the strongest fragrance of any buckeye.

Identification: The juvenile Californian buckeye has pale gray, smooth bark that becomes scaly, thick and a pale pink-gray color in maturity. The winter leaf buds are large, red-brown and very resinous. The leaves are palmately compound with five to seven oblong, toothed leaflets, to 6in (15cm) long and 3in (7.5cm) broad. They are yellow-green above and sage green beneath. The small flowers are white, or pale pink, and are borne in dense upright columnar panicles, up to 8in (20cm) long. These are followed by glossy brown pear-shaped seeds, individually protected in pink-green casing.

Distribution: California, U.S.A.
Height: 33ft (10m)
Shape: Broadly spreading
Deciduous
Pollinated: Insect
Leaf shape: Compound palmate

Right: Fall leaf color is not significant.

Left: The flowers appear in early summer.

Yellow Buckeye

Sweet buckeye *Aesculus flava*

Sometimes referred to as *Aesculus octandra* or sweet buckeye, this handsome, round-headed tree was introduced from North America into Europe as early as 1764. *Flava* means yellow and refers to the yellow flowers that appear in early summer. This is one of the best horse chestnuts for fall color because the leaves turn a stunning orange-red in early fall.

Identification: The bark is brown-gray, flaking in maturity into large irregular-shaped scales. Branches tend to be horizontal or even drooping with a characteristic sweep upwards towards the tip. The leaves are compound and palmate, with five sharply toothed, dark-green leaflets, each up to 6in (15cm) long, all joining a pea-green leaf stalk at a common point. The flowers are yellow with a pink blotch and borne on upright panicles up to 6in (15cm) long in late spring and early summer. The fruit, two brown nuts or "conkers," are encased in a smooth, round husk, up to 2in (5cm) across.

Distribution: U.S.A.: From Pennsylvania to Tennessee and Georgia, and west into Ohio and Illinois.
Height: 100ft (30m)
Shape: Broadly conical
Deciduous
Pollinated: Insect
Leaf shape: Compound palmate

Left: The yellow buckeye is named for its flowers.

Right: The fruit is smooth.

Red Buckeye

Aesculus pavia

Red buckeye is native to the Coastal plain from North Carolina to Florida and east to the Mississippi River valley, where it grows in moist woods and thickets. It is a small tree, sometimes little more than a shrub, with a slightly weeping, pendulous habit to the outer branches. It is one of the parents of the hybrid red horse chestnut, *Aesculus* x *carnea*, to which it gives the red color of its flowers. Red buckeye has been in cultivation in parks and gardens since the eighteenth century.

Distribution: Southeast U.S.A.
Height: 17ft (5m)
Shape: Broadly spreading
Deciduous
Pollinated: Insect
Leaf shape: Compound palmate

Identification: The bark is dark gray and smooth, becoming cracked in maturity. The leaves are palmately compound, with five elliptic, sharply toothed and pointed, shiny dark green leaflets, to 6in (15cm) long. The flowers are, without doubt, the best red color of any buckeye, and far better than that of its hybrid offspring. They are slender, bright red, borne in upright panicles to 8in (20cm) long in early summer. These are followed by small pear-like fruits that open to reveal one or two glossy mahogany brown seeds.

Left: The flowers are at their best in June and July.

Right: The fruits resemble small unripe pears.

OTHER SPECIES OF NOTE

Red Horse Chestnut *Aesculus* x *carnea*
This popular tree is a hybrid between *A. hippocastanum* and *A. pavia*. It is not known where this hybrid originated, but it is likely that it occurred naturally in Germany in the early 1800s. It is a round-headed, spreading tree, seldom reaching heights in excess of 66ft (20m). The flowers are deep pink to red and borne in upright panicles in late spring.

European or Common Horse Chestnut
Aesculus hippocastanum
Native to Greece and Albania, but planted as an ornamental tree throughout Europe and North America, this is a stunning parkland tree, reaching heights in excess of 100ft (30m) tall. The flowers are creamy-white, blotched with yellow and pink, and borne in large, upright conical panicles to 10in (25cm) long in mid-spring.

Japanese Horse Chestnut
Aesculus turbinata
Similar to the European horse chestnut, but with much larger leaves. Each leaflet can be up to 16in (40cm) long, and turns bright orange in the fall. It was introduced into North America in the late nineteenth century.

Ohio Buckeye

Aesculus glabra

This tree has the largest natural distribution of any North American buckeye. Its range extends from Pennsylvania to Tennessee in the Allegheny valley bottoms, and westwards into Texas. It is also widely planted as an ornamental tree in parks and gardens throughout this range because of its beautiful yellow flowers, which appear early every summer.

Identification: Ohio buckeye has smooth gray bark at first, becoming very rough and flaky in maturity. The leaves are palmately compound with scarcely any leaf stalk. There are five elliptic leaflets, up to 8in (20cm) long, glossy green above, paler beneath, turning a good orange-yellow in the fall. The flowers are pale lemon-yellow, 1in (2.5cm) long, and densely borne in upright conical panicles to 6in (15cm) long. Most years the flowers are borne in profusion right across the whole canopy, producing a magnificent sight in early summer.

Distribution: Southeast and central U.S.A.
Height: 33ft (10m)
Shape: Broadly spreading
Deciduous
Pollinated: Insect
Leaf shape: Compound palmate

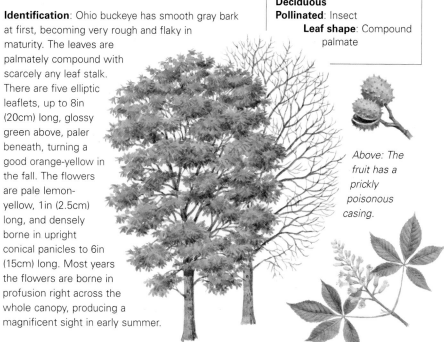

Above: The fruit has a prickly poisonous casing.

MAPLES

There are more than 100 species of maples, Acer, in the world and countless cultivars, particularly of the Japanese maples. They are mainly deciduous and predominantly found throughout northern temperate regions, with a few extending into subtropical Asia. They range in size from mighty American giants to slow-growing Japanese bonsai. Many are cultivated for their attractive foliage and graceful habit.

Ash-leaved Maple

Box elder *Acer negundo*

This variable small to medium-size maple is found growing wild across North America, particularly alongside rivers and in moist soils. The leaves do not resemble those on the Canadian flag, but are pinnate with up to seven leaflets that individually resemble the leaves of elder, *Sambucus*. The name "box" is derived from the timber, which is white and dense, like boxwood.

Identification: The bark is brown to silver-gray, thin and smooth. The leaves are pinnate, with each leaflet approximately 4in (10cm) long and sometimes lobed. Leaflets are arranged opposite in pairs, with a terminal leaflet that is usually slightly bigger than the rest. They are rich green above and lighter green with some hair beneath. Both male and female flowers are small, yellow-green and borne on separate trees in spring, just as the leaves are emerging. The male flowers are tassel-like with long drooping stamens; the females soon develop the familiar seed wings. The fruit is the classic, downward-pointing, two-winged seed.

Distribution: North America.
Height: 66ft (20m)
Shape: Broadly columnar
Deciduous
Pollinated: Insect
Leaf shape: Pinnate

Left: Flowers hang, tassel-like, from the outer twigs. The seeds each have two wings to catch the wind and spin as they fall from the tree. The leaves are different from those of most maples.

Red Maple

Acer rubrum

One of the most striking of all American maples, from its bright red showy flowers in spring, until its stunning fall color, this is a tree not to be missed. It has a natural range that extends from eastern Newfoundland to Ontario in the north, south to Florida and westwards into Texas. Red maple grows particularly well in wet lowland areas. It is a common tree in parks, gardens and cities right across its natural range.

Identification: The bark is dark gray and smooth, even in maturity. The leaves are palmate, to 4in (10cm) long, and broad, with three or five coarsely serrated lobes. The upper surface is dark matt green; the underside is sage-green to almost white with yellow pubescence around the leaf veins. Small red flowers appear on bare branches in early spring. Both male and female flowers are bright red and they appear on slender red stalks in dense clusters in early spring. These are followed by red two-winged seeds, each about 1in (2.5cm) long.

Distribution: Eastern and central North America.
Height: 100ft (30m)
Shape: Broadly columnar
Deciduous
Pollinated: Insect
Leaf shape: Palmate

Right: The winged seeds.

Left: The leaves turn scarlet in the fall.

Silver Maple
Acer saccharinum

This is one of the fastest-growing North American maples, and is widely planted as an ornamental specimen for parks and gardens. It is altogether more refined than sycamore, having a light, open crown with bicolored leaves, which catch the light as they flutter in the breeze. It does have rather brittle wood, which means that it has a tendency to drop its branches—sometimes with no warning.

Identification: The bark is gray and smooth when young, becoming flaky with epicormic growth in maturity. The leaves are palmate, up to 6in (15cm) long and wide, and have five sharply toothed lobes, each ending in a sharp point. They are light green above and glaucous with some hair beneath. The leaves are borne on lax stalks up to 6in (15cm) long, allowing them to flutter in even the lightest breeze. Both male and female flowers are small and greenish-yellow. They are clustered together on the young shoots as the leaves begin to emerge. Each winged seed is up to 1in (2.5cm) long.

Distribution: Eastern North America from Ontario to Florida.
Height: 100ft (30m)
Shape: Broadly columnar
Deciduous
Pollinated: Insect
Leaf shape: Palmate

Left: In mid-fall the leaves turn yellow before dropping.

OTHER SPECIES OF NOTE
Black Maple *Acer nigrum*
This maple is considered by some to be a sub-species of the sugar maple, *A. saccharum*. It is certainly closely related, but has larger, darker leaves and a more open pattern of growth. In the fall the leaves become a rich yellow. It has a similar natural range to that of sugar maple, but is not as common in cultivation.

Canyon Maple *Acer grandidentatum*
The canyon maple is also considered to be a subspecies of sugar maple. It may be referred to as bigtooth maple because of its large lobed leaves. It is native to damp canyons in the southern parts of the Rocky Mountains, where it grows up to altitudes of 8,000ft (2,500m). It is a much smaller tree than the sugar maple, seldom attaining heights in excess of 33ft (10m).

Norway Maple *Acer platanoides*
Native to northern and central Europe, Norway maple was introduced into North America over a century ago. Since then, it has become a common tree in cultivation across much of northern North America, particularly in cities and towns. At first glance it is similar to sugar maple, but it has a much smoother bark in maturity and more prominent yellow flowers in spring.

Paperbark Maple *Acer griseum*
This beautiful small tree was discovered in China, in 1901. It has striking, cinnamon-colored, wafer thin, peeling bark, which flakes away to reveal fresh orange bark beneath. It has distinctive trifoliate leaves which turn burgundy-red and orange in the fall.

Sugar Maple
Acer saccharum

The sugar maple has the most striking scarlet-orange, fall leaf colors. It has a natural range from Quebec and Nova Scotia, south to North Carolina, and west to Missouri, but is commonly cultivated throughout eastern and central North America. This tree is the source of maple syrup, which is produced from its boiled sap. Its lumber is hard and resistant to wear and has been used for dance floors.

Identification: The bark is brown-gray, smooth at first, becoming shallowly fissured and flaking in maturity. Each leaf is mid to dark green above and paler beneath, with some pubescence in the vein axils. The flowers are small, yellowish-green and borne in drooping open clusters in early spring just as the leaves emerge from bud.

Below: The fruit is a two-winged seed up to 1in (2.5cm) long.

Distribution: Eastern North America.
Height: 100ft (35m)
Shape: Broadly columnar
Deciduous
Pollinated: Insect
Leaf shape: Palmate

Below: The palmate leaves have five prominent tapered lobes that run to long points.

Right: Each leaf may be up to 6in (15cm) long and broad.

Smooth Japanese Maple

Acer palmatum

Smooth Japanese maple was discovered in 1783 and introduced to the West in 1820. Surprisingly though, it was almost another 80 years before it became popular and began to be widely planted. The famous acer glade at Westonbirt Arboretum in England was not planted until 1875. Today there are hundreds of cultivars of smooth Japanese maple. In the wild the species grows within, or on the edge of, mixed broad-leaved woodland, providing dappled shade and shelter.

Identification: The bark is gray-brown and smooth, even in maturity. The overall shape of the tree is like a large natural bonsai, with horizontal, spreading, meandering branches forking from the main stem quite close to the ground. The leaves are palmate with between five and seven deep, pointed lobes that have forward-facing serrations around the margin. They are up to 4in (10cm) across. The flowers are burgundy-red with yellow stamens. They are borne in upright or drooping clusters as the leaves emerge in spring. The fruit is green to red winged seeds carried in pairs; each wing is up to ½in (1cm) long and clustered together on the branch with up to 20 other seeds.

Below left: In the fall, the leaves turn red and gold before dropping.

Distribution: China, Taiwan, Japan and Korea. U.S.A. zones 5–8.
Height: 50ft (15m)
Shape: Broadly spreading
Deciduous
Pollinated: Insect
Leaf shape: Palmate

Right: New leaves emerge a bright green color.

Oregon Maple

Bigleaf maple *Acer macrophyllum*

The big leaves are the main characteristic of this handsome North American species, which inhabits riverbanks, moist woods and canyons. In fact everything about this tree is big; its trunk, flowers and fruit are also among the largest for the genus. The lumber of Oregon maple is highly valued in America, where it is used to make furniture.

Identification: The bark is gray-brown and smooth, becoming vertically fissured in maturity. The leaves are palmate with large, coarsely toothed lobes cutting deep into the leaf center. They are up to 10in (25cm) long and 12in (30cm) across, grass-green, and carried on long, buff-colored leaf stalks. The flowers are green-yellow, fragrant and hang in conspicuous clusters up to 8in (20cm) long as the leaves unfurl in spring. The fruit has paired wings, each up to 2in (5cm) long, covered in fawn bristles and containing one seed at its base.

Distribution: Western North America from British Columbia to California.
Height: 82ft (25m)
Shape: Broadly columnar
Deciduous
Pollinated: Insect
Leaf shape: Palmate

Below: The flowers appear in spring as the new leaves emerge.

Below left: The winged seeds are held on the tree in small bunches.

Fullmoon Maple *Acer japonicum*
Native to Japan, this tree is cultivated in U.S.A. zones 5–7. However, it has produced some of the finest and most popular ornamental cultivars, including the vine-leaved 'Vitifolium', 'Aconitifolium' and the golden-leaved 'Aureum', which is now considered a species in its own right with the name *A. shirasawanum*.

Cappadocian Maple *Acer cappadocicum*
Native to the Caucasus Mountains, this round-headed, large tree has palmate leaves with five to seven taper-pointed, untoothed lobes. The leaves are borne on long stalks which, when cut, exude a milky white sap. In fall the leaves turn a brilliant butter-yellow color before dropping.

Nikko Maple *Acer maximowiczianum*
A delightful, round-headed, medium-size Japanese tree with trifoliate leaves, the undersides of which are covered with soft blue-white hairs. It is one of the finest maples for fall color and thrives in U.S.A. zones 4–8. Leaflets gradually change from green through yellow and orange to red, before dropping.

Rocky Mountain Maple *Acer glabrum*
Otherwise known as rock maple, this small, bushy tree is native to western North America, from Montana to New Mexico, where it grows on riversides and in moist woodlands. It has variable leaves, with three or five lobes. It has dull red shoots that are prominent in winter.

Moosewood

Striped maple *Acer pensylvanicum*

In North America moose eat the bark of this tree; however, striped maple is far more descriptive because of the way the gray-brown bark is beautifully striped with vertical, wavy white lines. This species thrives in moist woodlands. There is a popular cultivated garden form of moosewood called 'Erythrocladum', which has bright crimson shoots and winter buds.

Distribution: Eastern North America.
Height: 33ft (10m)
Shape: Broadly columnar
Deciduous
Pollinated: Insect
Leaf shape: Oblong

Identification: The striped bark develops at a young age; immature shoots are green, ripening to reddish-brown before developing vertical white lines (within three years). The leaves are up to 6in (15cm) long, oblong with three triangular, taper-pointed, toothed lobes cutting into the top half of the leaf. They are deep green and crinkly with pronounced veining above and some rust-colored pubescence beneath. The inconspicuous green flowers are borne in weeping clusters in spring. The fruit is a small two-winged seed; each wing is 1in (2.5cm) long.

Left: The distinctive striped bark.

Right: The winged seeds.

Norway Maple

Acer platanoides

This fast-growing, handsome, hardy maple has been cultivated as an ornamental species for centuries. It has a large, spreading crown with upswept branches and is as much at home in parkland settings as in woodland. Recently, smaller cultivars have been developed, which are being planted in great numbers alongside roads.

Identification: The bark is gray and smooth when young, becoming vertically ridged and fissured in maturity. The leaves are rather like the leaf on the Canadian flag, palmately lobed, with five lobes, each ending in several sharp teeth and a slender point. Each leaf is up to 6in (15cm) in length and width, bright green and borne on a long, slender, pink-yellow leaf stalk. The flowers are bright yellow, sometimes red, and borne in conspicuous drooping clusters in spring as the leaves emerge.

Distribution: Southwest Asia and Europe, north to Norway. U.S.A. zones 3–7.
Height: 100ft (30m)
Shape: Broadly columnar
Deciduous
Pollinated: Insect
Leaf shape: Palmate

Right: Flowers may be either yellow or red.

Left: The fruit is a pair of green-yellow winged seeds borne in clusters. Each wing is up to 2in (5cm) long.

Right: Fresh foliage is a light green color.

ASHES AND CATALPAS

There are about 65 species within the ash genus, Fraxinus. All have pinnate leaves and are found within temperate regions of the world, primarily North America, Europe and Asia. They are hardy, fast-growing deciduous trees that tolerate exposure, poor soils and atmospheric pollution. The catalpas make up a genus of eleven species of beautiful flowering trees, mainly native to North America and China.

White Ash

Fraxinus americana

The white ash is a common North American tree that has a natural range extending from Nova Scotia east to Wisconsin, and south to Texas and Florida. It was first introduced into cultivation in 1724 and is now widely planted in parks and cities throughout this region. White ash produces clean, straight, strong flexible timber, which is used to make baseball bats, polo mallets, hockey sticks and rowing oars.

Identification: The bark is gray, with prominent narrow fissures which become deep in maturity. The winter leaf buds are rusty brown and borne on green shoots. The leaves are pinnate, to 14in (35cm) long. Each has up to nine short-stalked, ovate to lanceolate, sparsely toothed, taper-pointed leaflets, each 4¾in (12cm) long, which are dark green above and pale green to white beneath. Male and female flowers are purple, small and appear in spring on separate trees before the new leaves emerge.

Distribution: Eastern North America.
Height: 94ft (28m)
Shape: Broadly columnar
Deciduous
Pollinated: Insect
Leaf shape: Pinnate

Right: White ash flower.

Right: The fruit is a winged seed, 2in (5cm) long, borne in dense pendulous clusters.

Black Ash

Brown ash *Fraxinus nigra*

Black ash, or brown ash, as it is sometimes known, grows further north than any other American ash. It occurs naturally from Manitoba to Newfoundland and south to West Virginia. It is also planted as a street tree in northern cities. It gets its name from its lumber which has dark brown to black heartwood, surrounded by a ring of almost white sapwood. Black ash thrives in wet, swampy areas, and on the banks of streams and lakes.

Identification: The bark is gray, slightly tinged with red, becoming thick with corky scales in maturity. Winter buds are dark brown to black and slightly velvety to the touch. The pinnate leaves are up to 16in (40cm) long, with up to eleven 4in- (10cm-) long, oblong to lanceolate, long-pointed, toothed leaflets, which are dark green above and paler beneath, with tufts of pubescence along the midrib. Dark purple male and female flowers appear on separate trees in early spring, before the leaves appear. These are followed by pendulous clusters of green, single-winged seeds, which ripen to pale brown in fall and remain on the tree well into winter.

Distribution: Southern Canada and northern U.S.A.
Height: 94ft (28m)
Shape: Broadly columnar
Deciduous
Pollinated: Insect
Leaf shape: Pinnate

Left: The green seeds ripen to pale brown in the fall.

Below: The pinnate leaves have up to five pairs of opposite leaflets and one terminal leaflet.

Green Ash

Fraxinus pennsylvanica

This is the most widespread of all American ashes. Its natural range extends from Nova Scotia to Alberta, and south to the Gulf Coast, Texas. It prefers rich, moist soils, but has been planted as a street tree in towns, both within and to the west of its natural range. It is a fast-growing tree, quick to establish on reclaimed land and widely used for wind protection.

Identification: The bark is gray-brown with narrow, interlacing ridges. The winter leaf buds are chocolate-brown and slightly pubescent. It has pinnate leaves, to 12in (30cm) long, with up to nine ovate to lanceolate, taper-pointed leaflets, 4in (10cm) long, sharply toothed around the margin, but sometimes untoothed. The flowers appear in early spring before the leaves. They are small, usually purple and carried in clusters. They are followed by single-winged seeds, up to 2in (5cm) long, which are borne in pendulous clusters.

Far right: Male and female flowers are borne on separate trees.

Distribution: Central and eastern North America.
Height: 80ft (25m)
Shape: Broadly columnar
Deciduous
Pollinated: Insect
Leaf shape: Pinnate

Right: The leaves are glossy dark green above, and pale, almost sage green beneath.

OTHER SPECIES OF NOTE

Blue Ash *Fraxinus quadrangulata*
This small tree gets its name from its square, four-angled young shoots which are slightly winged. Blue ash has a natural range from Ohio west to Missouri, and south to Georgia. The blue in the name refers to the inner bark which early settlers used to make blue dye.

Oregon Ash *Fraxinus latifolia*
This ash is native to the West Coast from Washington State south to central California along the flanks of the Sierra Nevada. It has been widely planted as a shade-giving tree in towns and cities in the southwest. It produces much valued timber and has large leaves, up to 12in (30cm) long.

European Ash, Common Ash
Fraxinus excelsior
This large, fast-growing tree is widespread throughout Europe from the western Mediterranean eastward into Russia. It has been grown in North America for over 100 years. It is similar in form to white ash, *Fraxinus americana*.

Narrow-leaved Ash *Fraxinus angustifolia*
This large, elegant, fast-growing tree, native to southern Europe and North Africa, is better

known in cultivated form rather than as a species. There are several cultivars including 'Pendula' and 'Raywood', which are widely planted throughout U.S.A.

Velvet Ash

Fraxinus velutina

This small, pretty tree, which is sometimes known as the Arizona ash, grows wild from Texas west to California and south into Mexico. It gets its common name from the dense covering of gray velvety down which regularly covers the leaves, stalks and shoots. Velvet ash is planted as a shade-giving street tree, particularly in California.

Identification: The bark is thick, gray, sometimes tinged with red, and deeply fissured when mature into broad, flat, broken ridges. Velvet ash has dark brown winter buds. The leaves are 4in (10cm) long, with up to five ovate leaflets, although more commonly three. Each leaflet is up to 2in (5cm) long and normally covered with soft, dense gray-white hairs. They are dark green above and paler beneath. The flowers are deep purple colored and appear on the tree in March and April before the leaves appear. Male and female flowers are borne on separate trees.

Right: Purple flowers appear in early spring.

Below: The seeds are narrow, oblong and 1in (2.5cm) long.

Right: The leaflets run to a long even point.

Distribution: Southwest U.S.A.
Height: 40ft (12m)
Shape: Broadly columnar
Deciduous
Pollinated: Insect
Leaf shape: Pinnate

Western Catalpa

Northern catalpa *Catalpa speciosa*

Sometimes known as the northern catalpa, this large, vigorous tree is native to the lands around the Mississippi and Ohio rivers in Illinois, Indiana, Missouri, Arkansas and Kentucky. It is also widely cultivated in parks and gardens elsewhere including on the West Coast in British Columbia, Washington State and Oregon. It is a much taller and tougher tree than its southern cousin *Catalpa bignonioides*. This vigorous tree is not for small gardens. In North America the wood is prized for its natural durability and ability not to degrade or rot in wet conditions. It is quite often used to make untreated fence posts, which are then sunk into moist soil.

Identification: The bark is dark gray and coarsely ridged. The leaves are broadly ovate, to 12in (30cm) long and 8in (20cm) wide, tapering at the tip to a long point. They are glossy dark green above, slightly lighter beneath, quite thin and lax. The flowers are bell-shaped, 2in (5cm) long, white, spotted with yellow and purple, and borne in upright open panicles in summer. These are followed by pendulous slender, bean-like pods, up to 18in (45cm) long, which persist on the tree well into winter.

Distribution: Southeastern U.S.A.
Height: 130ft (40m)
Shape: Broadly columnar
Deciduous
Pollinated: Insect
Leaf shape: Ovate

Below: When young the leaves are covered with slight pubescence.

Right: The seeds are contained within long, pendulous bean-pods.

Right: This large tree is perfect for parks and arboreta.

Crape Myrtle

Lagerstroemia indica

Although native to China and Korea, this beautiful, upright, bushy little tree is widely planted as an ornamental throughout the southern states of the U.S.A. in parks and gardens. Elsewhere it is rather tender and requires a sheltered, sunny position. The main attraction of crape myrtle is its lilac, deep pink flowers which appear from late summer well into fall.

Identification: Crape myrtle has pretty bark, which is smoothly ribbed and mottled gray, pink and cinnamon. The leaves are opposite, alternate or in whorls of three; they are privet-like, obovate, untoothed around the leaf margin and up to 2in (5cm) long and 1in (2.5cm) wide. The flowers are borne in terminal panicles, up to 6in (15cm) long, with crinkly deep pink petals, which contract at the base into a slender claw. A distinctive feature of this tree is its multi-stemmed habit, with several stems rising from the base through 360 degrees.

Distribution: China and Korea.
Height: 20ft (6m)
Shape: Broadly spreading
Deciduous
Pollinated: Insect
Leaf shape: Obovate

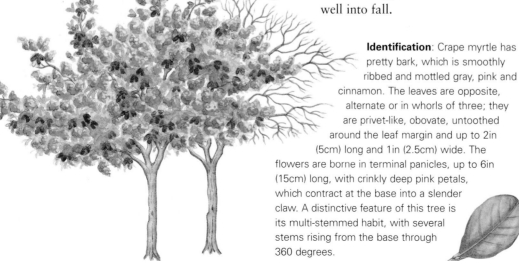

Right: The deep pink flowers of the crape myrtle are borne in late summer to mid fall.

Left: The leaves are thick, tough and reminiscent of privet.

Foxglove Tree

Paulownia tomentosa

This beautiful flowering tree is native to the mountains of central China. It takes its genus name from the daughter of Czar Paul I of Russia, Anna Paulownia. The spectacular pale purple, foxglove-like flowers appear on spikes in late spring. The lumber has a certain resinous quality and was used in China and Japan to make a stringed instrument similar to a lute. Quite often *Paulownia* is coppiced for its foliage, which on juvenile shoots can be up to 18in (45cm) across.

Identification: The bark is rather like beech, being gray and smooth, even in maturity. The leaves are ovate, up to 18in (45cm) wide and long, heart-shaped at the base, with two large, but normally shallow, lobes on each side. They are dark green, with hair on both surfaces and shoots. The shoots are soft and pithy. Each trumpet-shaped, pale purple flower, blotched inside with dark purple and yellow, is 2in (5cm) long. Flowers are on upright panicles up to 18in (45cm) tall.

Distribution: Central, eastern China. U.S.A. zones 5–9.
Height: 66ft (20m)
Shape: Broadly columnar
Deciduous
Pollinated: Insect
Leaf shape: Ovate

Left: The fruit is a green, pointed, egg-shaped, woody capsule containing several winged seeds. The purple flowers resemble foxgloves.

Indian Bean Tree

Catalpa bignonioides

The Indian part of the name refers to the Native Americans, who used to dry and paint catalpa seeds and wear them as decoration. This is one of the last trees in its region to flower, and is normally at its best in midsummer. It tolerates atmospheric pollution well, and has become widely planted in towns and cities, despite its broad, spreading crown.

Identification: Catalpa has gray-brown bark, becoming loose and flaking in patches in maturity. The leaves are broadly ovate, up to 10in (25cm) long and 6in (15cm) wide, rarely lobed, and heart-shaped at the base. On emerging from the bud they are bronze, gradually turning grass-green with some hair beneath. Each leaf is borne on a long, lax leaf stalk. The branches are quite brittle and prone to breakage in summer.

Distribution: Southeast U.S.A.
Height: 66ft (20m)
Shape: Broadly spreading
Deciduous
Pollinated: Insect
Leaf shape: Ovate

Right: The seed pods are 16in (40cm) long.

Below: Each trumpet-shaped flower is up to 2in (5cm) long.

PALMS AND YUCCAS

There are almost 150 genera within the Arecaceae (Palm) family. The majority of these are indigenous to tropical or subtropical regions of the world. However, one or two are native to the United States and others are cultivated for their fruit or for ornamental purposes in many temperate parts of the world.

Canary Island Date Palm

Phoenix canariensis

This is the most majestic and stately of all palms that thrive outside the tropics. Although only native to the Canary Islands, it is widely planted as an ornamental species in warm temperate regions throughout the world. In the U.S.A. it is commonly planted on sea fronts, and along avenues from Florida west to California. Many of the best specimens in Florida were blown over by Hurricane Andrew in 1992.

Right: The leaves are up to 16ft (5m) long evergreen fronds.

Identification: The Canary Island date palm has a long, straight, golden-brown fibrous stem with reptilian-like scales, formed by the shedding of previous fronds. It may be up to 5ft (1.5m) in diameter at the base, which tends to splay out just above ground level. The leaves are pectinate (comb-like) fronds, which gracefully arch skywards before drooping towards the tip. Golden-yellow flower spikes, up to 6.5ft (2m) long are borne in the spring, followed in warm climates on female trees by bunches of purple-brown fruits.

Distribution: Canary Islands.
Height: 40ft (12m)
Shape: Broadly spreading
Evergreen
Pollinated: Insect
Leaf shape: Pectinate

California Washingtonia

Washingtonia filifera

The California washingtonia is native to Palm Springs and south to the Mexican border. It has, however, been planted as an ornamental species further north in California and, to a lesser degree, in Florida. A distinctive characteristic of this tree is the way it carries its old, dead, fan-shape leaves around the stem, below the live crown of evergreen leaves. The species is named, appropriately enough, in honor of the former president and has nothing to do with the state.

Identification: This attractive palm has a light-brown, stout, columnar stem, sometimes broadening towards the base. The leaves are fan-shaped, and divided nearly to the middle into up to 70 slender, pointed lobes and carried on 5ft (1.5m) long, spine-edged stems. Panicles of yellow flowers up to 10ft (3m) long are borne in summer, persisting dead on the tree long into fall. The fruit is an erect, short-stalked black berry with thin dry flesh.

Left: The fruit of California washingtonia is an ovoid brown-black berry.

Right: Attached to each fan-shape frond are thin straw-like threads.

Distribution: California, U.S.A.
Height: 75ft (23m)
Shape: Broadly columnar
Evergreen
Pollinated: Insect
Leaf shape: Flabellate (Fan-shaped)

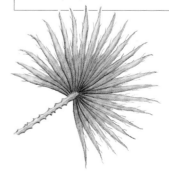

Cabbage Palmetto

Sabal palmetto

The cabbage palmetto grows naturally throughout peninsular Florida, the Florida Keys, coastal Georgia, and South Carolina. Elsewhere in southern U.S.A. it has been widely planted in parks, gardens, and streets near the coast. It is also cultivated in Hawaii. The seeds of the cabbage palmetto are buoyant and salt resistant. Near coastal areas, water is an important means of seed dispersal. In some areas seeding is so successful that "pure forests" of the plant may cover 25 acres (10ha).

Identification: An erect, unbranched tree with a uniform stem diameter of 12–24in (30–60cm). The gray trunk is covered with interlacing leaf stubs, known as boots, which persist before breaking off to give the stem a smooth appearance. The leaves are fan-shaped, palmately divided and spineless, with a prominent arching midrib. Cream to yellowish-white flowers, borne in drooping clusters up to 6ft (2m) long, are produced between April and August.

Left: The leaves may be up to 10ft (3m) long.

Distribution: Southeastern U.S.A.
Height: 82ft (25m)
Shape: Broadly columnar
Evergreen
Pollinated: Insect
Leaf shape: Flabellate (Fan-shaped)

Right: The black, fleshy fruits contain a single seed.

OTHER SPECIES OF NOTE

Blue Hesper Palm *Brahea armata*
This beautiful tree has the bluest leaves of any palm. It is native to Baja California, Mexico, where it inhabits dry canyons. It reaches heights of 40ft (12m), but is slow-growing and takes a long time to reach this height. The flowers are creamy-white and are borne in profusion in distinct, long, weeping inflorescences.

Jelly Palm *Butia capitata*
Otherwise known as the pindo palm, this beautiful small palm is native to Brazil, but has been widely cultivated in southern coastal areas of the U.S.A. It has gray-green to silver arching fronds, and fragrant yellow flowers, which are tinged with purple. These are followed by yellow fruits which can be used to make jelly or wine.

Mexico Fan Palm *Washingtonia robusta*
The Mexican fan palm grows taller than its Californian cousin and has a thinner trunk. Although not native to the U.S.A., it is widely cultivated as a single-trunked street palm in the southwest. It has dense gray-green fan-shaped foliage and leaf stalks that are tinted red.

Chilean Wine Palm *Jubaea chilensis*
Otherwise known as honey palm, or syrup palm, this spectacular tree, with its straight, symmetrical, elephant-gray trunk, has become a rarity in its native Chile largely because of over-felling for its sugary sap content, which is used to make wine. Chilean wine palms are widely planted as an ornamental species in warm coastal areas of U.S.A. Each gray-green pinnate leaf may be up to 13ft (4m) long.

Joshua Tree

Yucca brevifolia

The Joshua tree is one of the most characteristic trees of the Mohave Desert. It has a natural range from southern California, Mexico, and western Arizona, eastward into southern Nevada and south western Utah. It is named after Mormon Brigham Young, who led a group of Mormons to Utah. As they crossed the Salt Lake Desert, Young is said to have pointed at a yucca tree's outstretched arm-like branches and said, "There is Joshua welcoming us to the Promised Land."

Identification: The bark is soft and cork-like, rough and fissured, reddish-brown to gray with trunks up to 4ft (1.2m) in diameter, quite often single-stemmed but sometimes two or three-stemmed. Erratic branching may begin as low as 3ft (1m) from the ground. The branches are erect, ascending or spreading and in maturity form a dense, compact, rounded top. The flower is contained within a big ovoid bud that unfolds to a stout 10in-(25cm-) long, greenish-white flower.

Distribution: Southwest U.S.A.
Height: to 49ft (15m)
Shape: Broadly spreading
Evergreen
Pollinated: Insect
Leaf shape: Pectinate

Above: The leaves are short, sharply pointed and closely set spines.

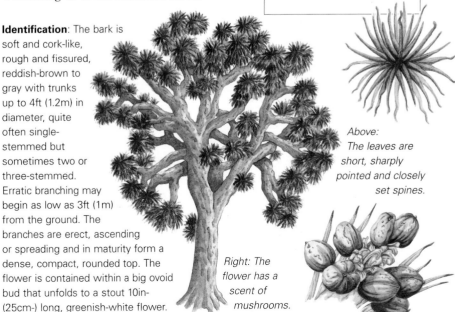

Right: The flower has a scent of mushrooms.

TREES OF TROPICAL AMERICA

Within the tropical and subtropical area is a range of diverse habitats.
These include ferociously hot dry deserts, humid and windless lowland
forests, cool, temperate-like montane areas and coastal mangrove
swamps. Understandably, the trees that inhabit these areas vary
enormously. The main factors are the high light intensity and day length,
which fluctuates by around 12 hours throughout the year, and the
similarity of the seasons. The majority of the trees are evergreen, but if
they are deciduous, it is often only fleetingly, or to advertize glamorous
flowers. Numerous tropical flowers are large and intoxicatingly
beautiful. Many tropical trees demonstrate cauliflory, whereby flowers
and fruit emerge directly from the trunk, enabling easier access for
pollination by wind, insects, bats and birds.

California

Texas

Florida

Gulf of California

Mexico

Gulf of Mexico

Cuba

Jamaica

Haiti

Puerto Rico

Belize

Honduras

Guatemala

Dominican Republic

El Salvador

Nicaragua

Venezuela

Guyana

Suriname

Costa Rica

Panama

Columbia

French Guiana

Ecuador

Peru

Brazil

Bolivia

Paraguay

Pacific Ocean

Chile

Uruguay

Argentina

Atlantic Ocean

Falkland Islands

Key
Trees that thrive in the area colored green are featured in the following chapter. In this area trees that are suited to a tropical climate thrive.

CONIFERS

Conifers belong to a botanical grouping of plants known as gymnosperms, where the naked seeds are held within a cone. The majority are evergreen trees with leaves reduced to needles or scales. Many of them live to a great age. There are about 840 species of gymnosperms, in 86 genera.

Caobilla

Podocarp, Wild pine *Podocarpus coriaceus*

This evergreen tree, belonging to the Taxaceae family, grows in mountain forests on certain islands in the Caribbean, notably on Puerto Rico. In Trinidad it is known as wild pine. The wood is soft and easily carved, and has been used for making furniture, partly as a result of which, mature trees are now scarce. Mature specimens may reach 30ft (9m) with a narrow or spreading crown.

Identification: An evergreen tree with scaly bark that peels off in strips. The inner bark is pink, and the heartwood yellow or brown. The young twigs are green when young, becoming brown with age, and bear alternate, almost stalkless, leaves, which are yellow-green on the underside. The leaves are crowded on the twigs and are long and narrow, with a leathery surface. Male and female trees are separate. The male cones are yellow-green, turning brown, occur singly at the base of the leaves, and are unstalked. The naked seeds are small and gray, becoming pointed and with a bright red base as they ripen.

Distribution: Puerto Rico, St Kitts, Montserrat, Guadeloupe, Dominica, Martinique, St Lucia, Trinidad and Tobago.
Height: 30ft (9m)
Shape: Variable
Evergreen
Pollinated: Wind
Leaf shape: Linear, unstalked

Left: Seeds develop on a fleshy red or purple base.

Left: The stalkless leaves are alternately arranged on the twig.

Mexican Swamp Cypress

Taxodium mucronatum

This species, closely related to the bald or swamp cypress (*T. distichum*), is common in parts of Mexico and also occurs in a few places in Guatemala. It grows besides streams or in shallow water, at altitudes of up to 2,200ft (1,400m). The wood is light to dark brown or yellowish and polishes well, but is weak and soft. Even so, it is used in Mexico for construction as it is resistant to decay and insect attack. It is a decorative tree, particularly attractive at the turn of the year when the leaves become yellow and red.

Identification: It is a large tree with a tall, straight trunk, enlarged at the base, and covered with light brown or brownish-red bark. The leaves, ¼–½in (5–10mm) long, are arranged in two ranks on the branches, and are thin and soft in texture. The male flowers appear in slender, drooping panicles, and the female ones are solitary, or in pairs, near the branch ends.

Distribution: Mexico and Guatemala.
Height: 100ft (30m)
Shape: Tapering
Deciduous
Pollinated: Wind
Leaf shape: Linear

Far left: The cones are about 1in (2.5cm) in diameter.

Left: The flowers appear in panicles

Norfolk Island Pine
Araucaria heterophylla
From Norfolk Island but not a pine, this beautiful, fast-growing conifer reaches 200ft (60m) and grows successfully throughout the tropics. In Hawaii, plantations provide timber for ships' masts. It is a very symmetrical, formal-looking tree. It stands upright and is conical with a regular branching pattern. The soft, curved leaves are bright green and glossy. This tree will thrive in deep sand and is wind tolerant. As a result, it is often planted in coastal locations. It is tolerant of low light levels and is sold as a houseplant in temperate climates.

Mexican White Pine *Pinus ayacahuite*
A native of the moist mountain regions of Mexico, Guatemala, El Salvador and Honduras, this species can grow to a height of 147ft (45m) in the wild, but is usually shorter in cultivation. Its bark is grayish-white and smooth on young trees, later becoming light brown or copper, and broken up into thin, rectangular plates. The leaves are in bundles of five, pale green to silvery, and the resinous cones are narrow and up to 18in (45cm) long. This is one of Central America's most attractive pines, with foliage that glistens in the sunlight.

Ocote Pine *Pinus oocarpa*
This pine grows wild in the mountains from Mexico south to Nicaragua. It is probably the most abundant pine in Guatemala where it is an important source of timber. Its bark is thick, rough and gray, and deeply fissured into broad plates. It has a dense, rounded crown, particularly in older trees. The stiff needles are in bundles of three to five, are olive- or grass-green, and up to 12in (30cm) long. The cones are broadly ovoid and up to 4in (10cm) long. The wood is pale and yellowish, and is used for building work and also for furniture.

Smooth-barked Mexican Pine
Pinus pseudostrobus
A pine of moist forests, this species is widely distributed in mountain regions from Mexico to Nicaragua (the southern limit for mountain pines in Central America). It forms a medium to large tree with whorls of branches spreading horizontally, and has a dense, rounded crown. Its bark is smooth and gray, darkening to brownish-gray or blackish. Its leaves are in fives, light to dark green, flexible, drooping, and are up to 14in (35cm) long.

Caribbean Pine

Cuban pine *Pinus caribaea*

Also commonly called the Cuban pine, this conifer is grown commercially for its timber, which is resinous, and for the making of turpentine. The mature, open, broad crown is rounded and consists of heavy, spreading branches.

Identification: The bark varies from gray to brown and naturally sheers off in large, flat plates. The winter buds at the branch tips are cylindrical, producing the leaves, which have adapted into thin needles. Each leaf is 12in (30cm) long, deep green and glossy. Leaves occur in bundles of three to five. The male cones consist of many catkins bunched together, producing large amounts of pollen. The female cones may be oval or conical and are 4–5in (10–13cm) long by 2–2½in (5–6cm) wide. They are covered in glossy, reddish-brown scales with a prickle at the end of each, and contain black, triangular seeds.

Mexican Cypress

Cupressus lusitanica

This native of Mexico and Central America has been introduced to many other places such as Florida, Puerto Rico, and from Colombia to Chile. It is an attractive, aromatic tree useful as an ornamental and also in forestry, and has a dense, narrow crown with dark green foliage. It takes cutting and pruning well, and is therefore useful as a hedge tree. A number of varieties exist, with various shapes, including a long, narrow form and one with weeping or drooping branches.

Identification: Naturally grown specimens have a tall, straight trunk with reddish-brown, somewhat scaly bark. The twigs are slender, and covered with tightly pressed, scale-like, pointed leaves. The male cones develop at the ends of short branches, and are greenish-yellow and cylindrical. The female cones are brown when fully ripe, and open to release the winged seeds.

Distribution: Central America, southeast United States, Honduras and Cuba.
Height: 100ft (30m)
Shape: Domed
Evergreen
Pollinated: Wind
Leaf shape: Needle

Right: The foliage and cones easily identify this tropical pine.

Distribution: Mexico, Guatemala, El Salvador, Honduras.
Height: 45ft (13.5m)
Shape: Slender
Evergreen
Pollinated: Wind
Leaf shape: Scale-like

Above: Female cones have six to eight scales.

Below: The foliage is delicate, with closely pressed, scale-like leaves.

ANNONAS

Annona is a large genus of more than 100 species within the family Annonaceae. The species are all similar: they are tropical and subtropical trees, usually evergreen, with large, simple, oblong, smooth-margined and aromatic leaves. The fruit-scented flowers are fleshy, emerging directly from old wood. The fruit is made of many fused segments and is normally edible.

Custard Apple

Annona squamosa

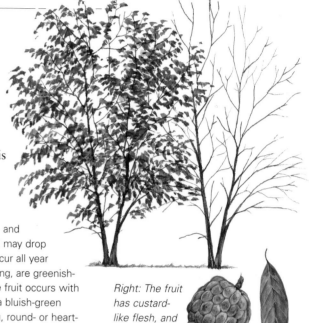

The custard apple is grown for its delicious fruit, sometimes described as tasting like strawberries and cream. The fruit is eaten fresh or processed into confectionery and drinks. The tree has an open crown of zigzagging branches and needs high humidity, and is only seen in very humid tropical areas.

Distribution: North of South America and West Indies.
Height: 20ft (6m)
Shape: Spreading
Semi-deciduous
Pollinated: Beetle
Leaf shape: Lanceolate to oblong

Identification: The leaves, which are fragrant when crushed, vary in shape and may be from 3½–6in (9–15cm) long. They are dull, pale green and smooth with minute dots on both surfaces, and may drop in dry spells. The pleasantly scented flowers occur all year round. They have three fleshy petals 2in (5cm) long, are greenish-yellow and found singly or in small clusters. The fruit occurs with the flowers. They are greenish-yellow but with a bluish-green surface bloom. Each fruit is 2–5in (5–13cm) long, round- or heart-shaped and made up of prominent lumps which, when ripe, may be pulled apart. The white flesh has a smooth texture and is sweet.

Right: The fruit has custard-like flesh, and the leaves are scented.

Soursop

Annona muricata

The soursop is the easiest *Annona* to grow in the tropics and carries the largest fruit, weighing up to 2lbs (1kg). The prolifically produced fruit appears throughout the year. It is not sour as the name suggests, but has unpleasant smelling skin and is often rather fibrous. It is rarely eaten fresh, but instead is processed into refreshing drinks and ices.

Distribution: West Indies and north of South America.
Height: 23ft (7m)
Shape: Columnar
Evergreen
Pollinated: Beetle
Leaf shape: Ovate, obovate, elliptic to lanceolate

Identification: Sometimes seen as a multistemmed tree, the branches are sharply ascending and begin low on the trunk; young growth is covered in silky brown hairs. The leaves are 6in (15cm) long, slightly curved, variable in shape, bright, glossy dark-green above and rusty below, with an unpleasant aroma if crushed. The rather peculiar flowers appear year-round from the trunk and branches. They have three very thick, cardboard-like petals, are 2in (5cm) long, pale greenish-yellow and fragrant. The fruit is yellow when ripe, often oval, yet distorted in shape, being 12in (30cm) long and covered in short, fleshy spines. The skin of the fruit is thin. The flesh is firm, white, juicy, pleasantly fragrant and embedded with black seeds.

Right: The simple, glossy soursop foliage smells unpleasant.

Left: The flowers of the soursop are stiff and the fruit prickly.

Cherimoya

Annona cherimola

Distribution: Peru and Ecuador.
Height: 26ft (8m)
Shape: Spreading
Briefly deciduous
Pollinated: Beetle
Leaf shape: Ovate, elliptic or lanceolate

Found in mountain valleys in its native Andes, the cherimoya is suited to cooler, drier conditions than many others in this genus. It forms an attractive, low-branched, spreading tree with nicely scented leaves. The cherimoya is grown in various parts of the world for its tasty, slightly acidic fruit.

Right: The fruit grows slowly, ripening in mid- to late spring.

Identification: The leaves, which drop briefly in the spring, are rather variable in shape. They are a dull, deep green with velvety undersides, 10in (25cm) long and strongly scented. The fragrant, hanging flowers are produced in the middle of summer. They consist of three thick, fleshy petals, are 1in (2.5cm) long and vary from greenish-yellow to reddish-brown on the outside, and pale yellow or off-white with a purple central blotch on the inside. The ripe fruit is yellow, 6 x 4in (15 x 10cm) and covered in large overlapping scales, each with a small black spot on it. The flesh is white and pulpy.

OTHER SPECIES OF NOTE

Ilama *Annona diversifolia*
This spreading tree from lowland areas of western Mexico and Central America reaches 23ft (7m) in height. It has tasty fruit, but may not produce it in great quantity. Although grown only on a local scale, many varieties are raised. Some have fruit with rich red flesh, with others it is white, pink or purple. The 1in (2.5cm) flowers are maroon with furry petals and are held on long stalks. The aromatic leaves are glossy green above, dull below and 6in (15cm) long. The fruit is variable in shape and texture, and may be light green, deep pink or even purple.

Pond Apple *Annona glabra*
Occurring in swampy and mangrove areas of southern Florida, northern South America, Peru and West Africa, the pond apple tree grows to 40ft (12m) tall. Its evergreen leaves are glossy above, paler and hairy below, and vary in shape and size. The large, thick flowers grow in pairs in summer. They are maroon inside and yellow with red spots on the outside. The round, ovoid or cone-shaped fruit is greenish-yellow, 3in (8cm) long and inedible.

Poshte *Annona scleroderma*
Reputed to be one of the tastiest of all annonas, the poshte is unfortunately rarely seen outside its native Mexico, Belize, Guatemala and Honduras. It is grown in Guatemala on a local scale, but being a 66ft- (20m-) tall evergreen tree, it is difficult to harvest and causes excessive shade over other crops. The leathery, lanceolate, shiny leaves are 10in (25cm) long and 3in (8cm) wide. The tough-skinned fruit may be green, green with brown spots or reddish. The flesh is smooth and either creamy or gray.

Bullock's Heart

Annona reticulata

The fruit takes time to develop, and is less pleasantly flavored than other annonas. Nonetheless, the bullock's heart is grown locally for its fruit in the tropics. Depending on location, it may drop its leaves for part of the year or stay evergreen.

Identification: The 8in (20cm) long leaves are dark green, smooth, pointed, and dotted on the surface. If crushed they release an unpleasant odor. The fragrant flowers hang in clusters from the leaf axils on new wood. They are yellow or yellowish-green with a purplish blotch or tint inside, 1in (2.5cm) long and have narrow, fleshy petals. The fruit may be heart-shaped, oval or conical, weighing up to 2lbs (1kg), but often less, and 3–6½in (8–16cm) across. It is greenish-yellow, becoming attractively reddish-brown or rosy on the side that is facing the sun. The surface is smooth and lined. The flesh of the fruit is creamy-white and pulpy.

Distribution: West Indies and northern South America.
Height: 33ft (10m)
Shape: Spreading
Semi-evergreen
Pollinated: Beetle
Leaf shape: Oblong-lanceolate

Above: Bullock's heart's flowers appear near the growing tips.

Above: The fruit may contain hard or grainy sections within the flesh.

LAUREL FAMILY

The Lauraceae family is made up mostly of aromatic, evergreen, tropical and subtropical trees and shrubs. The leaves are often irregularly spaced and clustered at the branch tips. They are generally elliptical and glossy with smooth margins—typical rainforest leaves. The six-lobed flowers are small, greenish or yellow and appear singly along stalks in clusters. The fruit is a one-seeded berry or drupe.

Avocado Pear

Persea americana

Avocados naturally grow in wet lowlands, but have been planted extensively throughout the tropics. They are grown for their tasty and highly nutritious, savory fruit, which is rich in minerals, oils and sugars. This fast-growing tree initially forms a round head but may become spreading in maturity. As the plants need to cross-pollinate to produce fruit, two or more are usually grown together.

Identification: The trunk is short with dark fissured bark. The leaves are leathery, elliptical, heavily veined, and up to 18in (45cm) long. They are dark green and glossy above, and coated with a bloom below. The green, branched racemes of fragrant flowers arise in the axils from the fall to the spring. Each flower measures ½in (1cm). The fruit may weigh up to 2lbs (1kg) but is usually smaller, measuring about 4–6in (10–15cm) long. It is pear-shaped and purple to greenish-brown with leathery skin.

Left: The fruit has a buttery texture and is often eaten with spices and sugar.

Distribution: Mexico and West Indies.
Height: 60ft (18m)
Shape: Domed
Evergreen
Pollinated: Insect
Leaf shape: Elliptic

Right: The leaves carry a pale bloom on their undersides.

Slugwood

Guajón, Aguacatillo, Laurier madame *Beilschmiedia pendula*

This Caribbean tree is known by several different names —including guajón, aguacatillo, and laurier madame. Slugwood is its usual name in Jamaica. The fruit consists of fleshy berries, ripening from green to black, and is rather olive-like, with a single large seed, borne from spring to fall. It is not eaten by people, but is apparently consumed by pigs and other livestock in Cuba. This is a timber tree, used for carpentry, furniture, flooring and shipbuilding; the wood is quite hard, strong and heavy, and good for shaping, planing and sanding.

Distribution: Caribbean: Cuba, Jamaica, Dominican Republic, Puerto Rico, St Thomas, Lesser Antilles (St Kitts to St Vincent).
Height: 75ft (23m)
Shape: Variable
Evergreen
Pollinated: Insect
Leaf Shape: Broad, elliptic

Right: A twig, showing development from flower to young and mature fruit.

Identification: Medium-size evergreen tree with dark brown, smooth, slightly fissured bark. The broad leaves (green above, paler beneath) are mostly almost hairless, alternate and untoothed, with a short stalk. The foliage, bark and twigs have a spicy aroma. The flowers develop in clusters and are yellow-green when open, on slightly hairy branches. The fruit consist of fleshy, single-seeded green berries, which turn black when ripe, and they resemble olives or small avocados.

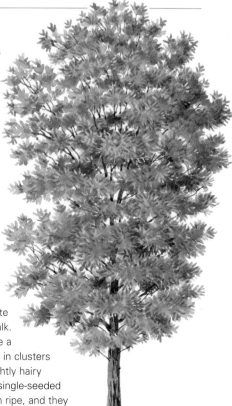

Sweetwood

Misanteco, Gulf licaria, Laurel blanco *Licaria triandra*

This a rare native tree in southern Florida, where it is called Gulf licaria. It is also found locally in Cuba, Jamaica, Haiti, the Dominican Republic, Puerto Rico, and Martinique. Sweetwood is its name in Jamaica, while in Cuba it is known as laurel blanco. Like several members of the laurel family, its foliage, bark and twigs are spicy. In Puerto Rico it favors moist forests on limestone, in the north of the island.

Identification: This small, evergreen tree develops a broad, rounded crown, and has potential for planting as a shade tree. The bark is dark brown and scaly. Its strong timber is used for posts and general construction. It has slender twigs that are rather reddish when young, and these have fine hairs and raised lenticels. The alternate, stalked leaves have broad blades and are shiny dark green, mostly with a long, tapering point. The flowers are small and white, in branched clusters, and develop into green fruit, ripening to dark blue.

Distribution: Southern Florida, Greater Antilles, Martinique.
Height: 30ft (9m)
Shape: Rounded
Evergreen
Pollinated: Insect
Leaf shape: Broad, elliptic, pointed

Left: The white flowers develop in clusters.

Far left: Each fruit sits in a thick red cup, rather like an acorn.

OTHER SPECIES OF NOTE

***Persea* cultivars**
Avocado cultivars are selected for many fruiting characteristics, including non-stringy flesh, small seeds, good storage (which is important) and firm attachment to the tree. The trees must produce steady yields, remain small, and have a spreading habit. Each cultivar has different characteristics. Fruit can vary from 2in (5cm) to 2ft (60cm) long, and the skin can be light green, dark green, brownish, purple or red. The flesh may be fiberless, thick and creamy, or watery, insipid and fibrous. The most popular are the Mexican and Guatemalan crosses: 'Fuerte' matures in winter and spring with smooth, green skin, but fruits in alternate years; 'Hass' has a purple to black warty skin, and is produced in spring and summer.

Laurel Espada *Ocotea floribunda*
This is a medium-size evergreen tree, growing to 60ft (18m), with smooth, light brown bark and long, spreading branches. Like many members of the family, its twigs, bark and leaves are, in fact, quite spicy. The greenish-white flowers are borne in branched clusters, and the fruit is small and black. Flowering is normally from October through to December, and the fruit appears from February through to July. It grows in forests from Cuba, Jamaica and Puerto Rico through the Lesser Antilles to Trinidad. In Jamaica it is known as black sweetwood. This genus contains about 350 species.

Jamaica Nectandra

Laurel avispillo, Sweetwood, Black torch

Nectandra coriacea

This small tree is often planted for shade in southern Florida and in Cuba, and its clusters of fragrant flowers scent the air and provide a source of food for insects, including bees. It is rather a small tree, with attractive, shiny, dark green, leathery leaves, and smooth gray bark. In the wild it grows in the moist limestone forests of Puerto Rico, and is also found from the Florida Keys and right through the West Indies from the Bahamas and Cuba to Tobago, as well as on the Yucatán Peninsula (Mexico), Guatemala, and Honduras. In Jamaica it is called sweetwood, and black torch or sweet torchwood in the Bahamas.

Identification: A small tree with a trunk about 1ft (30cm) in diameter. The twigs are slender, green and slightly hairy, and the alternate leaves are shiny, with obvious veins on both surfaces. The small, white flowers appear in clusters.

Distribution: Mexico and West Indies.
Height: 25ft (8m)
Shape: Narrow
Evergreen
Pollinated: Insect
Leaf Shape: Elliptic

Right: The white panicles develop into dark blue or blackish fleshy fruits (above), each containing a red-brown seed.

BUCKWHEAT AND POKEWEED FAMILIES

The buckwheat family, Polygonaceae, contains mostly temperate plants from the Northern Hemisphere. Their small flowers are usually held in spikes and produce one-seeded fruit. The majority of plants in the pokeweed family, Phytolaccaceae, are tropical, from South America and Africa. Many have succulent leaves, some are spiny and many have poisonous sap.

Sea Grape

Coccoloba uvifera

Distribution: Coastal tropical America and West Indies.
Height: 30ft (9m)
Shape: Variable, domed
Evergreen
Pollinated: Insect
Leaf shape: Kidney (reniform)

The beautiful sea grape is completely salt tolerant and will grow right on the beach. It has been planted in coastal locations throughout the tropical and warmest temperate regions of its range. Tree shape and size vary immensely, and are dependent on climatic factors. The sea grape can be dense and domed, or many-stemmed, sprawling and untidy. Whatever its shape, this tree's distinctive leaves make it easy to recognize.

Identification: The thick trunk has gray, fissured bark. The leaves are very tough, leathery and stiff. Olive green and veined in red, pink or white, they are 8in (20cm) across. The leaves turn a rich orange or maroon before dropping. The scented, greenish-white flowers are produced year-round, but are particularly abundant in the spring and summer. They are held in dense, erect clusters, 10in (25cm) long. The purple fruit occurs in long, hanging bunches like grapes— each fruit is ¾in (2cm) wide. The fruit has an acidic flavor and is used to make jellies.

Right: Male and female flowers are separate. Female flowers produce the grape-like bunches of edible fruit.

Bella Sombre

Phytolacca dioica

Distribution: South Brazil, Uruguay, Paraguay and north Argentina.
Height: 66ft (20m)
Shape: Domed
Semi-evergreen
Leaf shape: Elliptic

Bella sombre is Spanish for "beautiful shade," and this tree is often planted for shade in villages. The wonderfully sculptured, buttressed and spreading surface roots create natural seating up to 6½ft (2m) high, and spread across an area up to 60ft (18m) in diameter. The bella sombre tree is often multistemmed, and stores large amounts of water in its massive trunks. It is a fast-growing species native to grassy plains, and is fire and wind resistant. The tree is very highly revered in Argentina, and often lives to a very great age.

Identification: The bark of the sturdy trunks and surface roots is white. The soft, thick leaves are smooth and 4in (10cm) long with a prominent midrib that is red when the leaves are young. Before falling, the leaves turn yellow and then purple. The small, white flowers are held in pendulous clusters 4in (10cm) long. The fruit is a small berry, ripening through yellow and red to black. When ripe, it is fleshy with reddish-purple juice.

Right: Trees may drop their leaves in the fall or during cold or dry spells. Each tree is male or female, with only the female trees producing berries.

NETTLE AND CASUARINA FAMILIES

The nettle family, Urticaceae, is mainly tropical and includes only a few trees, many of which have stinging hairs. Their small flowers are usually green, and when the pollen is ripe, it is released when the anthers suddenly uncoil. The casuarina family, Casuarinaceae, contains four genera, and the best is featured below.

Flameberry

Urera caracasana

This unusual tree is armed with stinging hairs on its leaves; presumably it evolved as an anti-grazing device, and indeed it is often known as "stinging nettle." The dangerous hairs are mainly on the undersides of the leaves, on the midrib, and lie flat, only injecting their poison (formic acid) if brushed in one direction. A small tree, it has stout, rather fleshy twigs and large leaves. Partly because of its deterrent properties, it is sometimes planted as a hedge, or living fence. In the wild, it tends to grow scattered in the understory of mountain forests.

Identification: The large leaves have long stalks and shallowly toothed margins. There are also stinging hairs on the stalks and on the branches of the flower clusters. The latter have a good supply of very small, greenish or pink flowers. The fruit is juicy and orange-red.

Right: The toothed leaves are large and nettle-like.

Left: The fleshy fruits grow in clusters.

Distribution: Broad range in tropical America, in the Caribbean islands, and from Mexico to Peru, Brazil, Paraguay and Argentina.
Height: 30ft (9m)
Shape: Variable
Evergreen
Pollinated: Insect
Leaf shape: Cordate

Australian Pine

Casuarina equisetifolia

This elegant, wispy tree looks like a pine, hence its common name. However, it is not a true pine. Fast-growing, this species has the ability to fix nitrogen into the soil by its roots, and is tolerant of wind and some salinity. It is used for windbreaks, soil stabilization and dune reclamation in coastal regions. It is also grown for its timber, which is used for making boats, furniture and houses. This species may live for several hundred years. Though not native in the region, this species is established in Hawaii, Puerto Rico, the Bahamas, Caribbean islands, and coastal Florida.

Identification: The short trunk has thick, brown, peeling bark, while the long, weeping branches are silvery gray. From the branches arise 4–8in (10–20cm) long, extremely narrow, downy branchlets. These branchlets resemble long pine needles and are coated in minuscule triangular leaves. The flowers appear in May and June. Male flowers are red, tufted, catkin-like and measure 1½ x ¼in (4cm x 5mm). Smaller female flowers are grayish-brown and globular. The cone-like greenish-gray fruit takes five months to develop.

Right and far right: The tiny scale leaves are adapted to coastal conditions.

Left: The compound, cone-like fruit is highly misleading as an identifying feature, as this tree is not a conifer.

Distribution: Coastal regions of northeast Australia, Southeast Asia and Polynesia.
Height: 115ft (35m)
Shape: Columnar
Evergreen
Pollinated: Wind
Leaf shape: Reduced to tiny scales

PAPAYA AND RELATIVES

The papaya family (Caricaceae), the Flacourtiaceae, the Moringaceae, and the Elaeocarpaceae are all related within the subclass Dilleniidae. The Caricaceae has about 30 species, which have large fruits, with a fleshy coat. The Flacourtiaceae has many tropical species, but the Moringaceae has only a single genus with a dozen species, while the Elaeocarpaceae has 540 species—mainly tropical trees and shrubs.

Wild-coffee

Guassatunga *Casearia sylvestris* (Flacourtiaceae)

This is a widespread tree typical of open sites such as roadsides, coastal forests and in the forest understory. Although often only a small tree or large shrub, it does sometimes grow taller, up to 65ft (20m). The fragrant flowers are particularly attractive to honeybees.

Identification: The alternate leaves are long with wavy margins and are rather shallowly toothed. The clusters of tiny yellowish- or greenish-white flowers appear at the base of each leaf close to the point of insertion on the twig. From these the red fleshy seed capsules develop, each with usually three brown seeds. The bark is gray and smooth. The seeds are a source of oil, used for treating leprosy, while the leaves are used traditionally for fever and snakebite.

Above: The fruits are fleshy.

Right: The flower clusters grow from the base of the leaves.

Distribution: Cuba, Jamaica, through Antilles to Trinidad and Tobago, Mexico, Peru, Brazil, Argentina, and Uruguay.
Height: 15ft (4.5m)
Shape: Spreading
Evergreen
Pollinated: Insect
Leaf Shape: Lance-shaped to elliptic

Horseradish Tree

Drumstick tree *Moringa oleifera* (Moringaceae)

This ornamental tree is planted widely in tropical regions, often in gardens, or along roadsides or in hedgerows. It withstands pruning well, and grows back vigorously. It also produces large numbers of clustered, fragrant white flowers, and in Florida gardens, for example, flowers throughout the year. The thick roots, which have a taste not unlike horseradish, are used as a condiment in some places, and extracts of the bark and resin have medicinal properties. The large seeds from the bean-like pods yield oil used as a lubricant, and also in perfume. Honeybees find the flowers attractive.

Left: The young leaves and flowers are edible, and are sometimes cooked as a vegetable.

Right: The seed pod splits open when ripe.

Distribution: Southeast Asia, East Indies, India, but now widespread in tropics.
Height: 30ft (9m)
Shape: Spreading
Deciduous
Pollinated: Insect
Leaf shape: Compound, pinnate

Identification: A small tree with rather fragile branches, feathery foliage and clusters of prominent white, perfumed flowers. The seeds develop in pods, to 14in (36cm) long, which hang down from the twigs. These split to release several winged seeds.

Motillo

Sloanea berteriana (Elaeocarpaceae)

This is a large tree found in the wild in tropical mountain forests of certain Caribbean islands, where it is patchily dominant and may appear above the main forest canopy. The trunk grows straight and tall and develops obvious buttresses or flanges at the base—a common growth habit of rainforest trees, which gives support and stability in shallow, damp soils. The wood is very hard and finds a use as durable timber, although it is said to be attacked by termites.

Identification: The bark is smooth and dark gray with reddish warty lumps, and the alternate dark green leaves are large, elliptic and tapering. The flowers, which are pale yellow, are arranged in clusters (racemes). The fruit is a capsule that splits into four to release the seeds when ripe.

Distribution: Caribbean: Hispaniola, Puerto Rico, Lesser Antilles.
Height: 100ft (30m)
Shape: Straight
Evergreen
Pollinated: Insect
Leaf Shape: Elliptic

Top left: Pale yellow motillo flowers appear in clusters.

Left: The large elliptic leaf tapers towards the tip

Papaya

Carica papaya

The popular papaya fruit is tasty, juicy and has a distinctive flavor. It is grown throughout the tropics, and the fruit is exported to temperate regions. It is very fast growing, easy to cultivate and crops heavily, even from a young age. This herbaceous "tree" has a single stem or may branch a little into a flat crown when older, and the leaves only ever remain on the growing tips. The stem always remains soft, becoming woody only at the base even when mature. The enzyme papain is contained within the leaves and fruit and is used for tenderizing meat.

Above: Deep indentations in the trunk remain where the leaf stems were once attached.

Distribution: South America.
Height: 20ft (6m)
Shape: Columnar or spreading
Evergreen
Pollinated: Insect
Leaf shape: Round (orbicular) but heavily lobed

Identification: The stem remains light with old leaf scars evident. Leaves are 24in (60cm) long, dark green and heavily incised into five to seven lobes, each further incised. Leaf stems are 24in (60cm) long. The fleshy flowers appear year round, borne on the stem, and are creamy or greenish white, and 2in (6cm) across. Trees may be either sex or both. The fruit is orange-yellow when ripe, pear shaped or round, smooth and up to 12in (30cm) long but usually 8in (20cm) long.

Left: Papaya leaves may help to aid digestion when taken medicinally.

Above: The papaya is a popular, yet short-lived, cropping tree.

Left: Papaya fruits are common in the tropics. They hang close to the stem among the leaf stems.

Elephant Apple

Dillenia indica (Dilleniaceae)

This spectacular tree is common in cultivation. It is grown for the combination of stunning, unusual foliage, beautiful, scented flowers and large, edible fruit. The fruit consists of heavily swollen overlapping sepals, rolled into a ball containing a sticky green mass of seeds. It is musk-scented, tasting like an unripe apple, and is used to make cooling drinks and jellies. The fruit are apparently popular with elephants! The tree has an open broad crown above a short, dark trunk, with leaves concentrated towards the branch tips.

Identification: The trunk has rich orange-brown bark and few branches. The leaves are heavily corrugated, up to 30in (75cm) long, toothed, leathery and smooth on the upper surface but rough below. The flowers appear in late spring and early summer, and are fragrant, 8in (20cm) across, creamy yellow to pure white with a mass of central golden stamens. The fruit reach 6in (15cm) across and are green.

Distribution: East India and Southeast Asia. U.S.A. hardiness zone 9.
Height: 60ft (18m)
Shape: Domed
Semi-evergreen
Pollinated: Insect and beetle
Leaf shape: Elliptic-oblong

Left: The enormous solitary flowers face downwards; they are the largest of all Malaysian flowers and last only a day. The leaves are altogether rather unusual for a tropical tree.

Far left: The ripe fruit is huge and edible and hangs down from the tree. Unripe fruit is made into chutneys.

Left: The leaves are toothed and leathery.

Jamaica-cherry

Muntingia calabura (Tiliaceae)

Distribution: Cuba, Jamaica, Hispaniola, Trinidad and Tobago; also from southern Mexico to Venezuela, Peru, Bolivia and Brazil. Introduced to southern Florida and Hawaii.
Height: 25ft (7.5m)
Shape: Variable
Evergreen
Pollinated: Insect
Leaf shape: Lanceolate

A small, rapidly growing tree native through much of Central and South America, this species has a fibrous inner bark, the silky fibers of which have been used traditionally for making baskets and rope. It is also used as a shade tree and is commonly planted for this purpose. Its rapid growth and ability to spread have turned it into something of a weed in certain areas. It flowers and fruits throughout the year, and the flowers have been used medicinally, while the berries are edible and juicy, with a slightly sweet flavor.

Identification: This small evergreen tree has smooth brown bark and stringy, pale, inner bark, and gray twigs which turn brown with age. The leaves are alternate and toothed, green and softly hairy. The flowers are quite large, with five rounded white petals. The fruit is a yellowish or reddish berry containing tiny brown seeds.

Below left: The cherry-like fruit is rounded.

Right: The flowers arise from the leaf bases.

Sandpaper Tree

Chaparro *Curatella americana* (Dilleniaceae)

This shrub or small tree is distributed throughout the subarid regions of Central America, Cuba, and South America. It is known by a number of different names, including chaparro and lengua de vaca (meaning cow's tongue), a reference to the abrasive nature of the leaves which contain a considerable amount of silica and are commonly used as a substitute for sandpaper to polish articles of wood and metal, and to clean kitchen utensils. In Brazil, a decoction of the leaves is used to treat wounds. The wood is hard and heavy, difficult to cut and plane, but very durable. It is used for a variety of purposes, including fuel, charcoal, fence posts, raddle frames and even cabinet making. In some regions the bark, which is rich in tannin, is used for curing skins.

Identification: The white or pinkish flowers, arranged in clusters, are unpleasantly scented. These are followed by hairy fruits containing black seeds that have been used for flavoring chocolate.

Distribution: Western Mexico to Panama, Cuba, and tropical South America.
Height: 20ft (6m)
Shape: Spreading
Semi-evergreen
Pollinated: Insect
Leaf shape: Oval or elliptic

Left: The hairy fruit contains two seeds.

Left: The white flowers grow in clusters and have an unpleasant smell.

Florida Trema

Jamaican nettle-tree, guacimilla *Trema micrantha* (Ulmaceae)

A small, evergreen, fast-growing tree, with a spreading crown and drooping branches and leaves. It grows naturally in open forests and clearings, but has been widely naturalized and indeed become invasive in some areas. The timber is rather soft and light and is used mainly for posts, tea-chests and matches, and also as a fuel, and the pale brown bark yields a strong fiber. The tree has also been used to provide shade in coffee plantations.

Identification: The trunk, which grows to a diameter of 12in (30cm), is covered with light brown, smooth or slightly fissured bark. The open crown has horizontal or slightly drooping branches. The leaves are alternate, toothed and hairy, and the fresh foliage is poisonous to wild animals and livestock. The flowers, which are small and green, grow in clusters near the leaf bases and usually consist of both male and female flowers. The female flowers develop into tiny rounded, fleshy fruit, each with a single black seed. Seed dispersal is mainly via birds, which eat the fruits, then pass the seeds in their droppings. Flowering and fruiting occurs throughout the year.

Distribution: Central and southern Florida, Cuba and West Indies to Trinidad and Tobago, Mexico, Argentina, Brazil.
Height: 40ft (12m)
Shape: Spreading
Evergreen
Pollinated: Wind
Leaf shape: Lanceolate, long-pointed at apex

Left and right: The alternate leaves show distinct toothed margins, and the flowers develop in small clusters, arising from the leaf stalk bases.

ELM FAMILY

The elm family (Ulmaceae) has about 175 species of trees and shrubs, mainly in the Northern Hemisphere, from tropical to temperate regions. Their flowers are small and wind pollinated, and many species are important as timber trees. The leaves are simple, and often arranged spirally on the twigs.

Mexican Elm

Ulmus mexicana

Elms are found wild only in the Northern Hemisphere, and this species is native throughout Central America. It is a large tree of wet forest regions, with a crown as much as 66ft (20m) high and almost as broad. The trunk, that can be over 3ft (1m) in diameter, is covered with scaly, gray bark. The branches grow upwards at an angle, and bear leaves in two rows along the branchlets. The wood is heavy, hard and strong, and varies from light to dark brown. The bark is astringent, and in some areas is used as a treatment for coughs.

Distribution: Mexico to Panama.
Height: 130ft (40m)
Shape: Crown broadly spreading
Deciduous
Pollinated: Wind
Leaf shape: Lanceolate or narrowly ovate to ovate-oblong

Identification: The leaves are small, only 1½–5in (4–12cm) long and 1–2in (2–5cm) wide. The inflorescences emerge from buds in the axils of fallen leaves, and are composed of yellow flowers in whorls of three or four. Each dry fruit has one seed.

Left: The leaves are very unequal at the base, often rough on both surfaces and with a sharply toothed margin.

Almez

Celtis trinervia

This small or medium-size deciduous tree is found in some of the islands of the Caribbean and also in southern Mexico and Guatemala. On Puerto Rico it is rare, and grows mainly in thickets and forests near the coast, especially in the southwest, in moist limestone valleys, from sea-level up to about 300ft (90m). It flowers and fruits rather irregularly throughout the year. The wood is very hard and yellowish in color.

Distribution: Greater Antilles, Virgin Islands, Mexico, Guatemala.
Height: 50ft (15m)
Shape: Variable
Deciduous
Pollinated: Insect
Leaf shape: Narrowly ovate

Identification: The leaves are alternate in two rows, and each leaf has three main veins (hence the specific name), and toothed margins towards the pointed tip. The flowers are very small, yellow-green and clustered near the leaf bases. The fruit is single, black, and fleshy. The light brown or gray, smooth bark has fine fissures, and the twigs are slightly hairy when young.

Far left: The three main veins in the leaves are characteristic.

Left: This tree has long-stalked leaves.

HIBISCUS FAMILY

Most members of the Malvaceae family are herbaceous shrubs, many from temperate areas. The trees are fast growing and have soft wood. Mallow flowers have five petals, are usually asymmetrical and are often showy; many of the family are grown as garden ornamentals. The fruit is usually a capsule, more rarely a berry.

Sea Hibiscus

Seaside majoe *Hibiscus tiliaceus*

Distribution: Brazil, Peru, Mexico, Caribbean region, Florida. Throughout the tropics; probably native to the Old World.
Height: 20ft (6m)
Shape: Broad-crowned
Evergreen
Pollinated: Insect
Leaf Shape: Rounded, cordate

A beautiful small tree often found growing in coastal, swampy soils, it is also commonly grown as a garden ornamental. It often has a mangrove-like habit in saline swamps, rooting freely in the mud. The flowers are large and showy, yellow at first, turning orange and then reddish as they age. The tree grows vigorously and resprouts well after cutting, even from fence posts. It has a number of uses: the stringy bark for rope, matting, and coarse cloth; various parts in medicine; and the flowers attract bees and are a source of honey.

Identification: The leaves, which are alternate, have long stalks, and prominent veins, and are a shiny yellow-green above, densely hairy beneath. The young twigs and the seed capsules are also hairy. The bark is gray and smooth, and fibrous internally.

Right: The five-petaled flowers produce pointed fruit capsules, which split to release dark brown or blackish seeds.

Portia Tree

Thespesia populnea

This tree is often confused with the mahoe, and there are numerous similarities between them. The portia tree is very salt tolerant, growing on seashores and in sandy places, and has a dense, spreading crown. The trunk, although sometimes contorted, has good, hard timber with chocolate-brown heartwood, which is used for furniture.

Distribution: Coastal throughout all tropics.
Height: 66ft (20m)
Shape: Rounded, spreading
Evergreen
Pollinated: Insect
Leaf shape: Cordate to ovate

Above: A portia can be mistaken for a mahoe but has rugged bark and yellow flower stigmas.

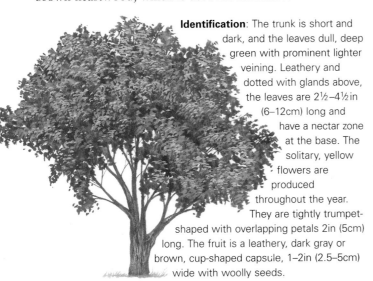

Identification: The trunk is short and dark, and the leaves dull, deep green with prominent lighter veining. Leathery and dotted with glands above, the leaves are 2½–4½in (6–12cm) long and have a nectar zone at the base. The solitary, yellow flowers are produced throughout the year. They are tightly trumpet-shaped with overlapping petals 2in (5cm) long. The fruit is a leathery, dark gray or brown, cup-shaped capsule, 1–2in (2.5–5cm) wide with woolly seeds.

Above and left: The flowers open in the evening attracting night-flying moths. From daybreak they fade to orange, pink or maroon to attract day-flying insects. They stay on the tree for a few days.

KAPOK FAMILY

The kapok family of tropical trees is especially well represented in South America, and includes some outstanding species. Many have thick or swollen trunks for water storage and spectacular flat-topped, spreading crowns. Their leaves are often lobed and clustered towards the tips of the thick branches. Bombacaceae flowers, with five petals and many stamens, are usually large and showy.

Pochote

Ceiba aesculifolia

This tree is closely related to kapok, and indeed it has been planted in some regions, such as in Guatemala, for its cotton-like fibers, which are used for similar purposes to those of kapok. It is also sometimes planted as an ornamental and to provide shade.

Identification: Pochotes are medium or large deciduous trees, with conical spines on the otherwise rather smooth trunk and twigs. The alternate leaves have five to eight toothed leaflets, and long, slender stalks. The leaflets are pale green beneath, and pointed toward both the tip and the base, and have short, hairy stalks. The flowers are large, with yellowish, hairy, spreading petals to 6in (15cm) in length, and long, protruding stamens. The fruit consists of large oblong capsules.

Right: Inside the brown fruit, the seeds are protected by masses of brownish-white, cotton-like hairs.

Distribution: Southern Mexico, Guatemala, Honduras, El Salvador; introduced more widely.
Height: 165ft (50m)
Shape: Spreading
Deciduous
Pollinated: Bat
Leaf shape: Palmate

Left: The large bronze flowers open in late evening.

Kapok

Ceiba pentandra

This tree was sacred to the ancient Maya of Central America, and today is often seen in market places. It probably originated in South America but has become so widespread that it is difficult to be certain. The kapok has a distinctive outline; its huge, thick trunk is heavily buttressed and often covered with thick spines. The thick, heavy branches are held at right angles to the trunk, and the tree eventually becomes as wide as it is tall. Kapok fruit yields fine silky filaments, which are used to stuff pillows and life jackets.

Distribution: Throughout tropics (America, Africa and Asia).
Height: 200ft (60m)
Shape: Conical
Semi-evergreen
Pollinated: Bat
Leaf shape: Round (orbicular) and divided

Right: Mature trees yield up to 900 fruits. They are harvested and laid out in the sun until they open.

Identification: The bark is gray. The leaves are 12in (30cm) wide and divided into between five and seven mid-green leaflets, each lanceolate and 6in (15cm) long. The fragrant flowers appear in spring, when the tree is leafless (if deciduous). The flowers are 6in (15cm) across, woolly and white, creamy pink or yellow. The fruit pod is 6in (15cm) long, narrowly elliptical, leathery and dark.

Water Chestnut

Pachira aquatica

The seeds of this tree are eaten raw or roasted. Although they are called water chestnuts, they are completely unrelated to the water chestnuts used in Chinese cooking. This species occurs on damp ground and along watercourses. It has a very dense canopy and a heavy, buttressed trunk.

Identification: The bark is gray. The leaves are divided into between five and nine leaflets. They are smooth, 4–12in (10–30cm) long and bright green with lighter midribs and veins. The flower buds are obvious, solitary, thick, brown, velvety spikes poking out from the leaf axils. The flowers have five narrow petals up to 14in (35cm) long, pale buff on the top and brown underneath. They encircle hundreds of 6–8in- (15–20cm-) long stamens, which may be red, purple, pink or white. The fruit pod is up to 15in (38cm) long x 5in (3cm) across, velvety, reddish-brown and contains the seeds in pulp.

Distribution: Tropical America and West Indies.
Height: 60ft (18m)
Shape: Spreading
Evergreen
Pollinated: Bat
Leaf shape: Round (orbicular) and divided

Left: The flowers are fragrant and showy but open at night, each lasting for only 24 hours.

OTHER SPECIES OF NOTE
Wild Chestnut *Pachira insignis*
The edible seeds in the pod of this tree are the "chestnut." This buttressed tree from the West Indies and Mexico grows to 60ft (18m). It has large leaves divided into five to seven egg-shaped to oblong, glossy leaflets. The spidery-looking flowers are fleeting. They have five fleshy, pale pink, crimson or brownish petals, which are long and narrow, and elegantly curl back in on themselves. Held within the petals are many pale, delicate stamens. The fruit pods are 8–10in (20–25cm) long. It is sometimes planted as an ornamental or shade tree, and is also a honey plant. The seeds, which are eaten raw or toasted taste like the sweet chestnut.

White Floss Silk Tree *Chorisia insignis*
This fast-growing tree from Peru and northeastern Argentina has an open, sprawling crown and grows to 40ft (12m) tall. The smooth trunk has green to gray bark, with a few thick spines, and is swollen. It may measure up to 6ft (1.8m) in diameter. The deep green, deciduous leaves comprise five to seven broad overlapping leaflets, each 6in (15cm) long. In the fall the 6in- (15cm-) wide, trumpet-shaped flowers appear in clusters at the branch tips. The flowers have five waxy petals and are pale yellow when they open but change to orange or purple before finally becoming white. They may have brown markings but are highly variable. The old pale flowers hang on the tree after they have died. The woody fruit contains seeds in kapok floss.
  The closely related floss silk tree, *C. speciosa*, is considered to be one of the most beautiful of flowering trees. Its pink flowers are large and showy and appear before the leaves.

Red Silk Cotton Tree

Bombax ceiba

Now found throughout the tropics, this tree is popular for its dramatic flowering display, and in India the thick flower petals are added to curries. The seed pod contains kapok but of an inferior quality to that of the real kapok tree. The tree is fast growing and has soft wood. The trunk is heavily buttressed and may have thick spines when young, as may the branches, which form in whorled tiers.

Identification: The bark is gray. The glossy leaves are divided into between three and ten leaflets, each 10in (25cm) long, dark green above and paler below. The flowers appear along the branches in late winter while the tree is briefly leafless. They are 11in (28cm) across and have five succulent, curved petals that are bright shining scarlet, pale red or vermilion, and surround many bright red stamens. The fruit develops in late spring. It is a brown pod, 6in (15cm) long and contains kapok fibers and seeds.

Distribution: Tropical South America.
Height: 120ft (36m)
Shape: Spreading
Deciduous
Pollinated: Bird
Leaf shape: Round (orbicular) and divided

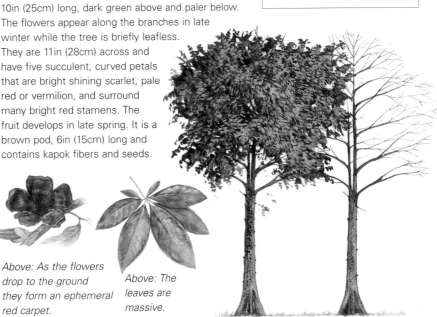

Above: As the flowers drop to the ground they form an ephemeral red carpet.

Above: The leaves are massive.

Balsa Wood

Ochroma lagopus

Distribution: Central and north South America.
Height: 70ft (21m)
Evergreen
Pollinated: Bat
Leaf shape: Cordate

Balsa is renowned for its incredibly light wood, which is used for floats, rafts, aircraft construction and insulation, among other things. Balsa wood is the lightest wood known, weighing just 7lb per cubic foot (9kg per cubic meter). The tree is incredibly fast growing and is common in its native haunts, colonizing secondary rainforest in dense patches.

Identification: The straight trunk has smooth, brown bark. The leaves are easily recognized, as they are immense—24in (60cm) long with leaf stems equally long. Rough textured and weakly divided into angular lobes, the leaves occur in groups of five to seven. Each leaf is pale green with toothed margins, and downy below. The solitary flowers are funnel-shaped, pale brown or yellow. The semi-woody fruit is produced in spring, and is rather curious: brown, velvety and 7in (18cm) long, it is ridged longitudinally and stands erect on the branches. When the fruit splits open it reveals floss, making it look like a soft, brown brush.

Above: The fast-growing, short-lived balsa can prove a weed in some localities. In Spanish, the name translates as raft or dinghy.

Left: Each giant flower lasts only one night, and may produce up to 4 tsp (20ml) of nectar to attract bats during that time.

Left: The huge leaves are unusual within the forest canopy. The largest leaves are seen on young trees.

Garrocho

Swizzle-stick tree *Quararibea turbinata*

The natural habitat of this small tree is a deep shady site in a moist forest, where it typically forms part of the understory. It has a straight trunk with gray-brown bark, and branches arranged characteristically in distinct whorls of four or five. The inner bark is yellow. The leaves taper to a point, and produce a strong smell, especially when dry. Flowering is mainly from February through May. The wood makes sturdy sticks, and the rings of branches make very good coat hangers or hat-racks.

Identification: The leaf-bases have a pair of gray, scale-like stipules which fall off as the leaves age, leaving behind distinct scars. The flowers grow close to the twigs, and each has five pale whitish petals. The fruit is round, fleshy and orange, supported at the base by the calyx, and each containing one or two large seeds.

Distribution: Mainly Caribbean—from Haiti and the Dominican Republic to Puerto Rico and Lesser Antilles; Surinam.
Height: 20ft (6m)
Shape: Rather straight, with whorled branches
Evergreen
Pollinated: Insect
Leaf shape: Short-stalked, elliptic

Right: Note the tapering leaf and the flowers inserted close to the twig.

Left: Swizzlesticks are traditionally made from the twigs and used for stirring drinks.

Floss Silk Tree

Chorisia speciosa

The floss silk tree is grown for its beautiful and delicate cup-shaped flowers, which are quite different from those of other members of this family. It is thought that no two floss silk trees have identical flowers. This species grows quickly and has soft wood. The trunk is swollen at the base and has thick thorns; the number and density of thorns varies between trees. The branches are angular and sprawling.

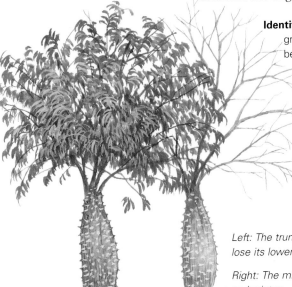

Identification: The bark is green when young and turns gray as the tree ages. The leaves are divided into between five and seven leaflets, each long and narrow with a toothed margin and a long leaf stalk. The flowers appear in the leaf axils through the fall and winter. They are 3in (8cm) across and may be red, pink, white or yellowish with gold or white throats, and purple or brown dots and striations. The large, capsular fruit is pear-shaped and contains cotton-like silky white kapok.

Left: The trunk swells as it matures, and may lose its lower spines with age.

Right: The mid-green leaves drop in the fall and winter.

Distribution: Brazil.
Height: 50ft (15m)
Shape: Spreading
Deciduous
Leaf shape: Round (orbicular) and divided

Above: Speciosa means "showy," describing the beautiful flowers.

Shaving Brush Tree

Pseudobombax ellipticum

This fast-growing tree is grown for its beautiful winter flowers, which open at night, and its colorful reddish-bronze young leaves, which contrast well with the pale green branches in spring. This species may have one or many short stout trunks.

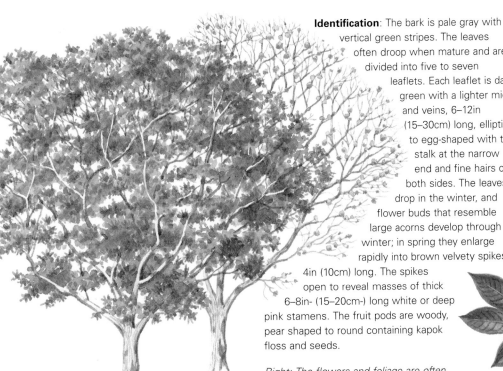

Identification: The bark is pale gray with vertical green stripes. The leaves often droop when mature and are divided into five to seven leaflets. Each leaflet is dark green with a lighter midrib and veins, 6–12in (15–30cm) long, elliptic to egg-shaped with the stalk at the narrow end and fine hairs on both sides. The leaves drop in the winter, and flower buds that resemble large acorns develop through the winter; in spring they enlarge rapidly into brown velvety spikes 4in (10cm) long. The spikes open to reveal masses of thick 6–8in- (15–20cm-) long white or deep pink stamens. The fruit pods are woody, pear shaped to round containing kapok floss and seeds.

Right: The flowers and foliage are often mistaken for those of the water chestnut tree.

Distribution: Guatemala, southern Mexico and the West Indies.
Height: 30ft (9m)
Shape: Spreading
Deciduous
Pollinated: Bat
Leaf shape: Round (orbicular) and divided

COCOA FAMILY

The Sterculiaceae family is found mainly in the tropics and includes trees, shrubs, climbers and herbs, with about 1,500 species. The flowers have three to five sepals and may have either five or no petals. The fruit may be fleshy, leathery or woody, and the seed may or may not have an outer covering. This family includes some important crop and timber trees.

Cacao

Theobroma cacao

Cacao originated and was first harvested in Central America. Today it is also cultivated in the West Indies, tropical Africa, Java and Sri Lanka for its beans, which are the source of cocoa, the key ingredient in chocolate. Cocoa bean pods are harvested and opened to collect the beans, which are fermented for a few days and then dried in the sun to cure them. These cured beans are roasted, ground and heated to extract the cocoa butter and cocoa solids.

Distribution: Central America.
Height: 30ft (9m)
Shape: Domed
Evergreen
Pollinated: Insect
Leaf shape: Oblong-elliptic

Identification: The deep green, leathery leaves are smooth, often with dry, crispy edges or tips, and are 10in (25cm) long. Flowers emerge directly from the trunk and older branches all year round and are abundant in spring. Creamy yellowish or pinkish, they are ½in (1cm) wide and have five petals. The fruit is an ovoid, longitudinally ribbed pod 8in (20cm) long. It may be brown, maroon or orange.

Right: The fruit contains 50–100 beans. The ¾ in- (2cm-) long beans are set in a slimy white pulp, which has a lemony flavor. The fresh beans may be deep royal purple inside.

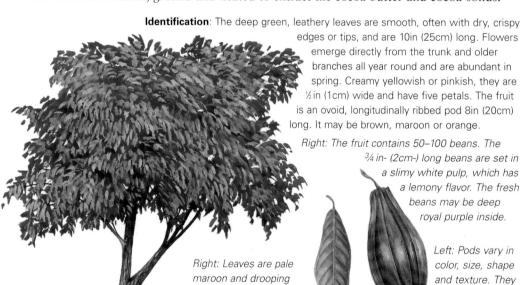

Right: Leaves are pale maroon and drooping when young; this is thought to deter pests.

Left: Pods vary in color, size, shape and texture. They may have smooth or warty skin.

West Indian Elm

Guazuma ulmifolia

A small to medium-size tree characteristic of stream banks and clearings. It grows rapidly in both dry and moist areas. The light pink-brown wood is used to make fence posts, furniture, boxes and barrels, tool handles and violins. The flowers attract honeybees.

Right: After the flowers have withered, hard, warty, rounded fruits develop.

Identification: The trunk, up to 2ft (60cm) in diameter, has gray or gray-brown bark. The branches are horizontal and end in long, slender twigs. The thin leaves are up to 5in (13cm) long, with long-pointed tips and finely toothed margins. At night the leaves hang down vertically. The small, slightly scented flowers have yellow petals and are in clusters at the base of the leaves.

Distribution: West Indies, Central and South America.
Height: 50ft (15m)
Shape: Rounded crown
Evergreen: except in areas with a very dry season
Pollinated: Insect
Leaf shape: Ovate-lanceolate

Castaño *Sterculia mexicana*

This is one of 150 species of the genus distributed throughout the tropical world. It grows in moist or wet forests in Mexico, Guatemala and Honduras. It grows up to 100ft (30m) tall. The trunk is often buttressed at its base and grows to about 3ft (1m) in diameter. The bark is slightly rough at the base of the trunk but is smooth elsewhere. The many-flowered panicles are about 12in (30cm) long, and composed of flowers that lack petals. Color is, however, provided by the sepals, which are pale pink, cream or red. The fruits are dry pods, dull orange on the outside and red within. Lining the fruits are stiff hairs, which are said to cause intense irritation.

Devil's-hand Tree *Chiranthodendron pentadactylon*

Wet forests high on the mountains of Mexico and Guatemala are the native habitat of this curious tree, which is unusual in several ways. First, there is doubt whether it should be placed in the cocoa or the hibiscus family. Second, it is the only species in a genus found nowhere else in the world. It grows up to 100ft (30m) or more in height, and with a trunk 3–6ft (1–2m) in diameter. The leaves are up to 12in (30cm) long. The flower has no petals, and looks like a small, blood-red hand with long, claw-like, outstretched fingers, hence the tree's common name.

Panama Tree

Sterculia apetala

This species is the national tree of Panama, which is found in tropical and subtropical forests and alongside rivers, where it thrives. It is grown in gardens and as a street tree, and has become naturalized in the West Indies. The Panama tree is fast growing and has many uses in addition to its fine stature as an ornamental, shade-bearing tree. It is a useful species for reforestation and erosion control.

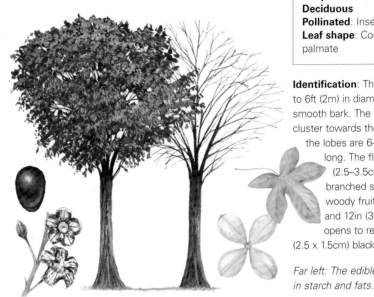

Distribution: Central America, northern South America and the West Indies.
Height: 130ft (40m)
Shape: Rounded
Deciduous
Pollinated: Insect
Leaf shape: Compound palmate

Identification: The trunk can be up to 6ft (2m) in diameter and has gray, smooth bark. The five-lobed leaves cluster towards the branch ends; the lobes are 6–20in (15–50cm) long. The flowers are 1–1½in (2.5–3.5cm) wide, in branched structures. The woody fruit is yellow to grey and 12in (30cm) long, and opens to reveal the 1 x ½in (2.5 x 1.5cm) black seeds.

Far left: The edible seeds are rich in starch and fats.

Cola Nut

Cola acuminata

"Cola" is a world-renowned drink, yet few people know that it is also a tree. The "nuts" (really seeds) of this tree are two percent caffeine, and were originally used in the cola drink. The tree is cultivated in Sri Lanka, the West Indies, Malaysia and west Africa. In the tropics its seeds are chewed for medicinal purposes, for their stimulating effects and to enable people to undertake feats of endurance. They are no longer used in the drink to which they gave their name and are now little used in the West. The tree grows in humid lowlands.

Distribution: Tropical west Africa. U.S.A. zones 11–12.
Height: 40ft (12m)
Shape: Spreading
Evergreen
Pollinated: Insect
Leaf shape: Oblong-ovate

Identification: The leaves are leathery, dark green and 4–6in (10–15cm) long. The flowers are found in clusters of 15 throughout the year, or, on some trees, only in winter. The flowers are ½in (1.5cm) across and have no petals. However, they do have five pale yellow sepals, each with central purple markings. The green, warty fruit is a 5–7in- (13–18cm-) long pod.

Below: The ugly cola fruit contains the "cola nuts." White nuts are popular for chewing, and command the best price.

Right: The long-lived cola tree may yield fruit for 100 years.

ANNATTO FAMILY

This small family consists of a handful of shrubs and small trees. Members of the Bixaceae have large leaves that are often lobed. They have resin cells within them and small appendages (stipules) at the base of the long delicate leaf stem. The flowers have four or five petals, many yellow stamens and are held in branched clusters. The fruit is a many-seeded capsule, which splits into sections when ripe.

Annatto

Bixa orellana

Tribal peoples use bright red dye from the annatto's greasy seeds cosmetically, and plantations have been set up to supply the export market to Europe and North America, where the pigment is used for lipstick and coloring foods, such as cheese. This densely crowned tree or shrub with multiple branching has pretty flowers, and is popular in tropical gardens, where it is grown as an ornamental or hedging plant.

Identification: The alternate, glossy leaves are light green with prominent veins, 8 x 6in (20 x 15cm) and a reddish tone when young. The bark is light brown. The flowers occur in clusters at the ends of twigs or small branches. Each flower is pink or white with purple tones, 2in (5cm) across and has masses of fluffy, central stamens. The fruit is a flattened ovate capsule, 2in (5cm) long. Coated in dense, soft spines, it may be white, red, pink or brown. The seeds inside are deep red.

Distribution: Tropical America and West Indies.
Height: 23ft (7m)
Shape: Domed
Evergreen
Pollinated: Insect
Leaf shape: Broadly ovate

Left: Attractive, dense foliage makes Bixa *ideal for hedging in tropical gardens.*

Right: The lovely flowers appear for most of the year. Although they are short-lived, they appear in continual succession, soon followed by attractive seed pods.

Buttercup Tree

Wild cotton tree *Cochlospermum vitifolium*

This fast-growing tree with soft, brittle branches is grown for its intense yellow flowers, which are borne on bare branches. It is sometimes grown as a hedge, and there are varieties with double flowers. The buttercup tree is also commonly called the wild cotton tree due to the white floss that covers the seeds. This floss is used like kapok to stuff cushions and soft toys. The buttercup tree has a rather open, sparsely branched canopy. Some botanists consider it to be the sole genus in its own family, Cochlospermaceae.

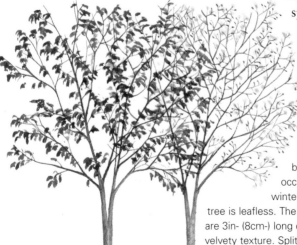

Identification: The 12in- (30cm-) wide, vine-like leaves are deeply divided into between five and seven lobes, each toothed along the edges. Held in erect, branched clusters, the flowers occur for three months in late winter and spring while the tree is leafless. The brown, elliptic fruits are 3in- (8cm-) long capsules with a velvety texture. Split into five sections, they contain kidney-shaped, dark brown seeds covered in floss.

Distribution: Tropical America.
Height: 40ft (12m)
Shape: Spreading
Deciduous
Leaf shape: Round (orbicular) and lobed

Left: The flowers are 4½in (11cm) across, golden yellow, and have masses of central stamens.

CECROPIA FAMILY

These plants have prominent stilt roots and sheaths or caps protecting their growing tip. They often have palmate, lobed leaves and produce brown latex in the shoot tips. The cecropia family (Cecropiaceae) is very closely related to the fig family, Moraceae, and also to the nettle family, Urticaceae. This family contains 180 species of trees, shrubs and lianes, in six genera.

Guarumo

Cecropia insignis

This fast-growing, softwood species inhabits wet lowland rainforest, and is a pioneer species, colonizing open or recently disturbed places with plenty of light. The guarumo grows into a large, open-crowned tree with branches radiating in tiers. Its trunk and thick branches are hollow, providing a home for aggressive ants which defend it from leaf-cutting ant species. The large, umbrella-like leaves of this species are very eye-catching.

Identification: The trunk is pale in color and produces milky sap: the twigs are reddish-brown. Each of the dramatic leaves is round, up to 36in (1m) across and heavily lobed, usually with seven separate lobes. Lobes are oblong to egg-shaped, with the narrow end nearest the leaf stalk. The tiny flowers are densely clustered on spikes: the male and female flower spikes are similar, 2½–4½in (6–12cm) long x ½in (1cm) wide, initially enveloped in a pink to brownish-red spathe (a modified leaf), pale green and generally erect. The tiny green fruit is a dry nut with one seed, held on a spike up to 8½ x ½in (21 x 1cm).

Above: The leaves are rough on the upper surface.

Distribution: Costa Rica.
Height: 80ft (25m)
Shape: Irregularly domed
Deciduous
Pollinated: Insect
Leaf shape: Orbicular, deeply lobed

Right: Each spike carries numerous tiny seeds, which are popular with birds.

OTHER SPECIES OF NOTE
Amazon Grape *Pourouma cecropiifolia*
This tree is grown for its enormous leaves, and for the fruit that it produces prolifically over three months, from the age of three years. It has a light tan trunk, characteristic stilt roots and short, very wrinkly branches, often containing brown latex. It grows on damp ground, exploiting the light from gaps in the forest canopy. The beautiful circular leaves consist of 10–13 lobes. When young, they are burgundy and droop, but they flatten out as they mature. The yellowish-green fruit is ovoid, 1in (2cm) long and covered in dense, velvety hair. Each contains a large seed and sweet, juicy pulp with a gummy, sticky texture. The pulp is used to make sweet wine, jam and jellies.

Trumpet-tree

Guarumo *Cecropia peltata*

This medium to large tree has a spreading crown formed from upwardly curving branches. Usually evergreen, in areas with a pronounced dry season it is deciduous. The branches and twigs are often hollow and frequently inhabited by colonies of ants.

Identification: Notable for its large lobed leaves, up to 2½ft (75cm) in diameter. The bark is smooth and gray, and the young branches are green and hairy. Individual trees are either female or male (tree is dioecious), and the clusters of tiny flowers and fruits develop at the leaf bases.

Distribution: Venezuela, Colombia, Guyana, Surinam, French Guiana, Mexico, Costa Rica, West Indies from Jamaica and Cuba to Trinidad and Tobago.
Height: 70ft (21m)
Shape: Spreading
Evergreen or dry-deciduous
Pollinated: Insect
Leaf shape: Large, peltate, lobed

Above left: The fruits are liked by bats, which are a major agent of seed dispersal.

MULBERRY FAMILY

The diverse family Moraceae includes mostly tropical trees, shrubs, herbs, climbers and stranglers. All members have milky sap and distinctive conical caps that cover the growing tips of twigs. The leaves are simple and often large. Flowers are of one sex, generally small and clustered in spikes, discs or hollow receptacles. The fruit is fleshy with a single, hard stone, and often many are grouped into one body.

Panama Rubber

Castilla elastica

A large tree with a trunk up to 3ft (1m) in diameter supported by buttresses, which form at the base of mature specimens. The bark is light brown with fine fissures, and when cut it oozes latex which coagulates on exposure to the air. In the past it was an important source of rubber, both from wild trees and from plantations. Nowadays most rubber comes from the para rubber tree (*Hevea brasiliensis*), an unrelated species, although some latex is still collected from wild trees. The tree is fast growing and is occasionally planted beside roads for shade. The wood is fairly soft and not durable, but can be used for fuel.

Identification: The long, slightly drooping hairy twigs have hairy leaves in two rows. The leaves are up to 18in (45cm) long and 8in (20cm) wide, heart-shaped at the base and with a short, blunt point at the tip, and minute tufts of hairs along the edges. Male and female flowers are in separate clusters on the same tree, and are yellow-green. The clusters of female flowers develop into multiple fruits, which are disc-shaped and 2in (5cm) across.

Right: The ripe fruit is red and juicy, with a sour taste. Each contains one white oblong seed.

Distribution: Mexico to northern South America.
Height: 70ft (21m)
Shape: Crown spreading
Evergreen
Pollinated: Insect
Leaf shape: Oblong-obovate

Breadfruit

Artocarpus altilis

It was the lavish attention received by breadfruit saplings that caused the infamous mutiny on the *Bounty*. The trees now thrive in the West Indies and are grown throughout the humid tropics for their valuable and plentiful fruit. The fruit is rich in carbohydrate, and tastes and is cooked like potato. The cooked seed is also eaten and tastes like chestnut.

Left: Breadfruit leaves are huge and glossy green.

Identification: These fast-growing trees have smooth bark, ascending branches and a dense bushy crown. The leaves are very dramatic looking. They are 24–36in (60–90cm) long, ovate and deeply cut into six to nine lobes. Deep glossy green above, they have a rougher texture and are paler below. The minute green flowers are found on a round organ, which looks like a developing young fruit. The compound fruit is round or ovoid, 4–8in (10–20cm) long, weighs up to 10lbs (4–5kg) and is green with a bumpy surface. Breadfruit does not usually have seeds—those that do produce seeded fruit are called breadnuts.

Distribution: Malaysia, Indonesia, Pacific Islands.
Height: 66ft (20m)
Shape: Columnar to domed
Evergreen
Pollinated: Wind and insect
Leaf shape: Ovate

Above: The compound fruit oozes white sticky latex when cut, but is a popular, tropical staple food.

Jackfruit

Artocarpus heterophyllus

Jackfruit trees are grown for their gigantic compound fruit, which measures up to 36in (90cm) long x 20in (50cm) across and weighs up to 40lbs (18kg). The fruit varies enormously between trees. It is full of starches—23 percent of the sticky, pink to golden yellow, waxy flesh is carbohydrate. Jackfruit flesh has a strong, unpleasant smell but a sweet taste. The seeds within the flesh are also eaten. These fast-growing trees are cultivated throughout the wet tropics.

Identification: The reddish-brown, straight trunk carries a dense crown. Juvenile leaves are often lobed, whereas mature leaves are oblong to egg shape with the leaf stalk at the narrow end, dark green, leathery, 4–8in (10–20cm) long and downy beneath. The flowers are minute, greenish and emerge directly from the trunk and older branches. The fruit contains numerous 1¼in- (3cm-) long seeds with a gelatinous covering.

Distribution: India to Malaysia.
Height: 66ft (20m)
Shape: Domed, columnar
Evergreen
Pollinated: Wind and insect
Leaf shape: Obovate

Left: The yellowish-green fruit has short fleshy spines, and hangs from the trunk.

Right: The leaves are arranged alternately.

Fustic

Mora *Chlorophora tinctoria*

This relative of the osage-orange of the southern United States is widespread in tropical America. It was once an important source of yellowish (khaki) dye, which was exported to Europe and other places. The tree is spreading and often spiny, and its timber is used for many things, including boats, sleepers, flooring, furniture and veneers. The bark is also used in tanning, and the resinous latex for waterproofing boats, and in medicine.

Below: The leaves are pointed and alternately arranged on the twigs.

Distribution: Caribbean islands; Mexico to southern Brazil, Peru, Bolivia and Argentina.
Height: 50ft (15m)
Shape: Spreading
Deciduous
Pollinated: Insect
Leaf shape: Elliptic

Identification: The bark is smooth, light gray or yellowish, with raised lenticels; the inner bark is orange with creamy latex. The yellow-green alternate leaves are arranged in double rows on the twigs, and are pointed and often slightly hairy, with toothed margins. The male and female flowers are on separate trees (the tree is dioecious). Male flower clusters droop from the leaf bases, while the female flowers are crowded into globular clusters. The latter develop into multiple fruits which are juicy, sweet and edible.

FIGS

This large genus of plants, also in the mulberry family, has around 750 species growing predominantly in the tropics and subtropics. Figs are enormously varied, and range from small-leafed climbers to huge trees and epiphytes (plants that grow on others). The infamous "strangling" figs begin their lives as small epiphytes. Fig flowers are tiny and enclosed within a fleshy receptacle. This receptacle is the fig itself.

Shortleaf Fig

Ficus laevigata

Distribution: Southern Florida and West Indies.
Height: 60ft (18m)
Shape: Crown spreading
Evergreen
Pollinated: Insect
Leaf shape: Elliptic-oblong

Right: The long leaves are shiny.

A small to medium-size tree which, like some other related species, probably starts as a young plant high in the fork of another tree where a bird has dropped a seed. The young tree puts out aerial roots which grow to the ground, usually uniting to form a trunk. The tree then grows rapidly, often overwhelming the host plant. This species has smooth, whitish bark that becomes slightly fissured with age. When cut, white latex oozes out. Although the wood is tough it is not durable, and is subject to attack by termites. Nevertheless it is suitable for boxes and crates, interior construction, light carpentry, and even for making guitars. Since cuttings root readily, it is also excellent for making live fence posts.

Identification: The green-gray twigs have alternate leaves, varying in shape and size. They can grow to 6in (15cm) long and 3in (7.5cm) broad, with a short point at the tip, and are rounded or slightly heart-shaped at the base. The upper side is slightly shiny with numerous tiny dots, raised on dry leaves. The multiple fruit is ½in (1cm) in diameter and tasteless.

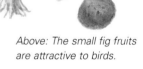

Above: The small fig fruits are attractive to birds.

Amate

Ficus obtusifolia

This fig species grows into a medium-size evergreen tree with a smooth trunk and light brown bark, and the familiar milky white latex. A typical habitat for the wild tree is coastal forest, from sea level to about 400ft (120m).

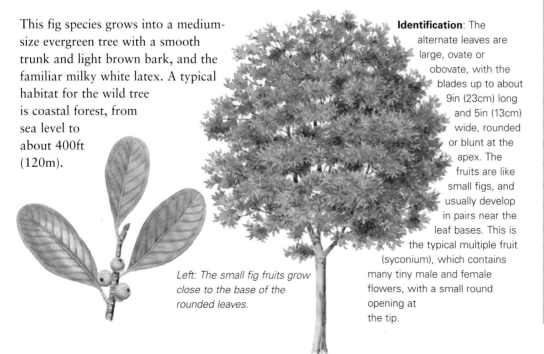

Left: The small fig fruits grow close to the base of the rounded leaves.

Identification: The alternate leaves are large, ovate or obovate, with the blades up to about 9in (23cm) long and 5in (13cm) wide, rounded or blunt at the apex. The fruits are like small figs, and usually develop in pairs near the leaf bases. This is the typical multiple fruit (syconium), which contains many tiny male and female flowers, with a small round opening at the tip.

Distribution: Virgin Islands (only on St Croix), Lesser Antilles; also mainland tropical America from central Mexico and Honduras to Colombia, Venezuela and northern Peru.
Height: 45ft (13.5m)
Shape: Variable
Evergreen
Pollinated: Insect
Leaf shape: Ovate, elliptic or obovate

Bo Tree

Ficus religiosa

It is said that the Buddha was sitting beneath a bo tree when he attained enlightenment. This type of fig is incredibly long lived, with specimens thought to be more than 2,000 years old. It is sacred to Buddhists and Hindus, and is regularly seen growing in the grounds of temples. A strangling climber, it may start its life on house roofs or gutters. Despite the problems this can cause, it is rarely removed because of its sacred status.

Identification: The great trunk has slight buttressing and dark brown bark. Most mature specimens have only a few aerial roots and some surface roots. The open crown, which is as wide as the tree is tall, consists of heart-shaped leaves with long, elegant tails. Each leaf is 8in (20cm) long x 6in (15cm) wide and blue-green with a pale midrib. The leaves have long stalks on which they move in the slightest breeze, and drop briefly in late winter. The tiny dark purple or brown figs grow in pairs in leaf axils along the branches.

Distribution: India, Burma, Thailand and Southeast Asia. Bo tree grows in tropical areas of the U.S.A.
Height: 100ft (30m)
Shape: Spreading
Deciduous
Pollinated: Wasp
Leaf shape: Cordate

Right: The elegant, wispy-tailed leaves of the bo tree are used in arts and crafts in the West.

Indian Rubber Tree

Ficus elastica

A mature specimen is an impressive sight. Curtains of aerial roots form a veritable forest of high-buttressed trunks, while the surface roots swarm over the soil. The tree lives wild in tropical and subtropical forests, but is grown throughout Asia for shade and ornament. In temperate countries this species is known as the rubber plant and is grown in pots indoors. The milky latex tapped from the trunk was the traditional rubber of commerce until *Hevea* rubber was discovered.

Identification: Each leaf measures more than 12in (30cm) long and 6in (15cm) wide and has a single, prominent midrib. Young leaves are tinged pink, and a long pink or red sheath protects the growing tip. The leaves form a dense crown at the end of clear branches. The oval, ¾in- (2cm-) long, greenish-yellow figs are crowded in pairs in the leaf axils towards the ends of twigs on trees over 20 years old. Figs are produced all year round.

Below: The spirally arranged foliage is simple, dark green, very smooth, thick and leathery.

Distribution: East Himalayas, northeast India, Burma, north Malay Peninsula, Java, Sumatra. Tropical areas of the U.S.A.
Height: 200ft (60m)
Shape: Spreading
Evergreen
Pollinated: Wasp
Leaf shape: Oblong to elliptic, tip pointed

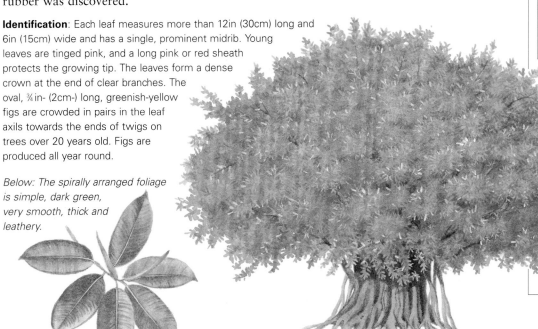

RUBBER FAMILY

A large family of more than 300 genera, the Euphorbiaceae includes herbs, climbers, shrubs and trees, many with white poisonous sap. The leaves are highly variable, and the small flowers are often without petals. The flowers are either male or female and occur on individual stalks in bunched clusters called cymes, or on branched structures known as panicles.

Rubber

Hevea brasiliensis

This erect, fast-growing tree is the source of natural rubber. When the tree reaches five or six years old it is "tapped" by cutting a long, slanting channel into the bark at about 3ft (1m) from the ground. A white, milky latex flows from the channel and is collected in cups. The latex is then strained, standardized to a set density and coagulated by the addition of acetic acid. The resultant white spongy material, rubber, may be processed in a number of ways and is smoked for preservation.

Identification: The bark is patchy, pale brown or gray and smooth. The spirally arranged leaves have long stalks and smooth, elliptic, dark green leaflets, each 8in (20cm) long. During a dry period, they turn orange and fall off, to be followed by the appearance of the flowers. Small, greenish-white and scented, they are held on panicles, which grow from the axils. The fruit is a smooth, greenish-brown, 1¼in- (3cm-) long, three-sectioned capsule.

Distribution: Amazonian (Brazil) and Orinoco (Venezuela) river basins.
Height: 130ft (40m)
Shape: Variable
Semi-evergreen
Pollinated: Insect
Leaf shape: Trifoliolate

Left: The trees are tapped with diagonal cuts in the bark.

Right: The three-sectioned fruit explodes when ripe.

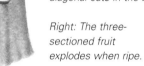

Sandbox Tree

Hura crepitans

Distribution: West Indies, Mexico, Central America and northern South America.
Height: 200ft (60m)
Shape: Spreading rounded
Deciduous
Pollinated: Insect
Leaf shape: Cordate

Every part of this tree is highly poisonous, and the sap may cause blindness if it contacts the eye. The fruit resembles a miniature brown pumpkin, and when ripe it bursts open explosively, discharging its seeds over quite some distance. In the past, these fruits were harvested then filled with sand and used as quill stands. Now they are occasionally filled with molten lead and sold as paperweights.

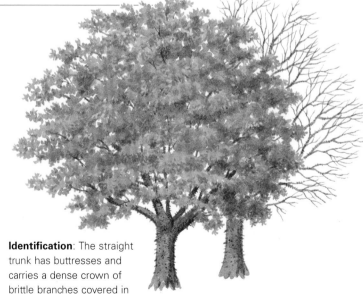

Identification: The straight trunk has buttresses and carries a dense crown of brittle branches covered in thick, dangerous spines. Held on long leaf stems, the thick, glossy leaves are dark green, up to 12in (30cm) long, with light veining on the upper surface. The female flowers are carried on a thick, pendulous spike 6in- (15cm-) long, and the male ones on a structure resembling an ear of corn. The 3in- (8cm-) wide fruit has a grooved surface and is made up of 15–20 sections, each containing a flat, pale brown seed.

Right: The flowers are small and dark red.

Far right: The fruit is pumpkin-like.

Candleberry Tree

Aleurites moluccana

This fast-growing native of hillside forests has been cultivated for hundreds of years, and is now naturalized throughout the tropics. Annually each tree produces up to 100lbs (46kg) of poisonous nuts, which are 50 percent oil and burnt for light, hence the tree's common name. The nutshells are used as beads and yield a dye, while the timber is a popular choice for canoe- and house-building.

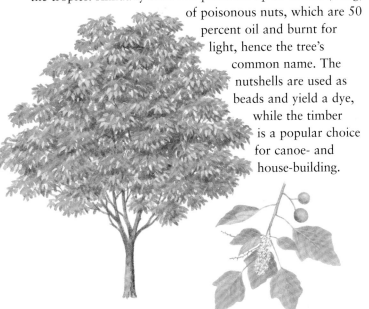

Identification: The thick, straight trunk has relatively smooth gray bark. Leaves are clustered toward the branch tips, have oil glands and are slightly scented if crushed. Each leaf is 4–8in (10–20cm) long, divided into three or five lobes and has pale rusty down on the underside. Young leaves and shoots are coated in fine, white down. Tiny, white, bell-shaped flowers are produced throughout the year in long, terminal panicles. The rough-skinned, hard, pale green fruit is a 2in- (5cm-) wide ball.

Left: The fruit contains one seed and is poisonous when raw, but can be eaten cooked.

Left and right: The juvenile and mature leaves differ in shape.

Distribution: Moluccas and South Pacific Islands. Tropical U.S.A.
Height: 60ft (18m)
Shape: Domed
Evergreen
Pollinated: Insect
Leaf shape: Broadly ovate

OTHER SPECIES OF NOTE

Coral Plant *Jatropha multifida*
This little tree from South America reaches 20ft (6m) tall, and has amazing leaves and colorful flowers. The leaves are round and up to 12in (30cm) across, but heavily divided into up to 12 leaflets, each of which has many incisions towards its tip. The leaves and seeds are poisonous but used locally for medicine. The small, red flowers appear throughout the year in flat-topped clusters above the tree. Each cluster stands on a long, upright stem.

Manchineel, Poison-guava
Hippomane mancinella
This tree is deadly poisonous, and all the more dangerous because it bears attractive, apple-like juicy fruit which is sweet-scented and palatable. Eating it causes nausea, diarrhea, muscular weakness, and sometimes death. The plant is also poisonous to livestock. Nevertheless, it is an attractive evergreen tree, to 40ft (12m), with a spreading crown. It is widely distributed on tropical shores, the fruit drifting in ocean currents, and this partly explains why it was notorious for poisoning marooned sailors. The milky sap is irritating to the skin and dangerous if it contacts the eyes, causing blistering and blindness. Legends abound: sleeping beneath it was reputed to be dangerous. Some indigenous people tipped poison arrows with its sap. It may be found in southern Florida, from the Bahamas to Trinidad and Tobago, and also on Pacific and Atlantic coasts of Mexico, Venezuela, Colombia, and Ecuador, as well as the Galapagos Islands.

Peregrina

Jatropha integerrima

This tree is grown for its continuous display of vibrant, intense cerise or scarlet flowers. In the wild it often grows as a multistemmed tree, and it may be pruned or trained in gardens to retain its young, shrub-like habit or force it to grow as a single-stemmed specimen. In temperate countries it is sold as a houseplant.

Identification: The bark is dark brown and fissured. The glossy leaves alternate on each side of the stem, are deep green with paler veining and have a pair of glands near the base. They are 1½–6in (4–15cm) long, vary from elliptic to egg-shaped, have smooth margins and may be partially and irregularly lobed with a long, slender point. The flowers are in long cymes protruding from the axils or the ends of branches. Each is either male or female, 1–2in (2.5–5cm) wide and has five petals; the male flowers have yellow anthers. The fruit is nearly round in shape, ½–⅔in (1–1.5cm) wide and split into three sections when ripe.

Right: The flower cymes bear many more male than female flowers.

Distribution: Cuba, West Indies and Peru.
Height: 20ft (6m)
Shape: Columnar
Evergreen
Pollinated: Insect
Leaf shape: Irregular

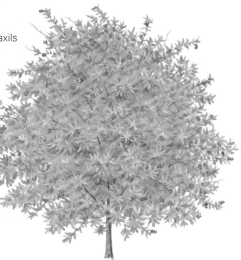

BRAZIL NUT FAMILY

Lecythidaceae includes shrubs and trees—many of the latter being large, rainforest, emergent species. The plants have a characteristic odor, tough fibers in their stems and leaves with toothed margins. The family is closely related to the myrtle family, and this is reflected in the flowers, which have numerous stamens, and are often large and showy. The fruits are large berries or capsules, and the seed is nut-like.

Cannonball Tree

Couroupita guianensis

A mature cannonball tree with fruit and flowers is an impressive sight. The large, waxy flowers hang the full length of the trunk and are interspersed with tough, sinuous cords holding large, cannonball-like, reddish-brown fruit.

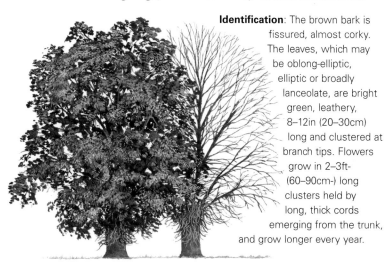

Identification: The brown bark is fissured, almost corky. The leaves, which may be oblong-elliptic, elliptic or broadly lanceolate, are bright green, leathery, 8–12in (20–30cm) long and clustered at branch tips. Flowers grow in 2–3ft- (60–90cm-) long clusters held by long, thick cords emerging from the trunk, and grow longer every year.

Above and right: The spherical fruit is 10in (25cm) wide. When ripe, it falls to the ground, exploding and releasing its foul-smelling red pulp.

Distribution: Northern South America including the Amazon basin.
Height: 100ft (30m)
Shape: Columnar
Deciduous
Pollinated: Bat
Leaf shape: Variable

Right: Flowers are 3–4½in (8–12cm) wide, and strangely scented.

Brazil Nut Tree

Bertholletia excelsa

This emergent rainforest tree has a small crown topping a trunk that is clear of branches for much of its height. The fruit holds 10–15 Brazil nuts, and is a favorite food of cat-size rodents called "agoutis." Agoutis, which live on the ground, open the fallen fruit to feed on the nuts. Like squirrels, they have the habit of burying some for later; a few are never dug up again, and they take root and grow. These trees do not fare well in plantations, and nuts are still collected from the wild.

Below: The hard fruit takes about 15 months to develop. A large tree may yield 300 fruits in one season.

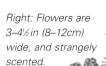

Distribution: Amazon basin.
Height: 100ft (30m)
Shape: Oval
Evergreen
Pollinated: Bee
Leaf shape: Oblong

Identification: The alternate leaves are dark green, leathery and large. Before dropping they turn brownish-red. The flowers appear on thick branches above the foliage in long, branched clusters. Each individual flower is yellow and 1in (2.5cm) wide. The fruit is attached to a long woody stem. It is round, brown, hard and 4in (10cm) across. The fruit contains the hard-shelled, angular seed, which is the edible Brazil nut.

Far left: Brazil nut trees require cross-pollination (with another tree) to produce fruit.

Left and right: The leaves have wavy edges.

Barringtonia

Barringtonia asiatica

This handsome tree is native to tropical Asia, but is planted as an ornamental and shade tree in the New World. It is quite often seen in parks and botanical gardens. In its native habitat it forms stands close to the shore, and its cork fruit can float and spread via the sea, like the coconut. The large, fragrant flowers open in the evening and are mainly pollinated by bats. In its native region, the trunks are used to make canoes, the buoyant fruits are fashioned into fishing floats, while the bark, fruit and seed are used as fish poison and traditional medicine.

Identification: The large leaves are shiny and dark green, and tend to be crowded towards the ends of the branches. The flowers are very large with whitish petals about 3in (7.5cm) long. The hard, heavy fruit has a thick, corky, fiber-rich husk. Inside is the large rounded fruit, about 2in (5cm) in diameter.

Distribution: Native to south Pacific region, but planted in southern Florida, Hawaii, Puerto Rico, Jamaica, Dominica and Trinidad.
Height: 30ft (9m)
Shape: Spreading
Evergreen
Pollinated: Bat
Leaf shape: Large, obovate

Far left: The flower has protruding stamens.

Left: The husk germinates within the fruit.

OTHER SPECIES OF NOTE
Stinkwood *Gustavia augusta*
This evergreen timber tree or shrub from Guyana and the Amazon grows up to 73ft (22m). The leaves vary from egg- to teardrop-shaped, with the stalk at the narrow end. They grow in tufts from the branch tips. They measure 19in (48cm) long x 5in (13cm) wide, and are pink when young. The scented flowers have six to nine white petals tinted pink below, and appear in clusters, each up to 8in (20cm) across. The fruit is spherical and 3in (8cm) in diameter.

Paradise Nut *Lecythis zabucajo*
This tree is closely related to the Brazil nut, but is much less well known outside its native range. The nut has a delicate flavor and is said to be superior to Brazil nuts. However, they are more difficult to collect than Brazil nuts as the seed drops from the shells, and they are therefore more expensive. Once the nuts have fallen they must be gathered quickly before they rot. Often, the nuts are extracted from the fruit while still on the tree, by birds or monkeys. The tree provides good timber and has become quite rare.

Cream nut

Lecythis pisonis

This tree is grown ornamentally for the stunning effect created when the purple flowers and new young pink leaves unfurl, turning the entire crown pink and mauve. It is also highly regarded for its tasty nuts, which can be hard to find because monkeys and other animals are fond of eating them too.

Identification: The trunk carries ascending branches and a dense crown. It has gray bark with deep vertical fissures. The smooth, leathery leaves have specks on them, and have toothed margins and a prominent midrib. The flowers form in clusters at the ends of the twigs and branches. The hard fruit is cinnamon colored, 8in (20cm) long, and contains the delicious, red to brown, elliptical seeds, each of which is 2in (5cm) long.

Distribution: Eastern tropical America.
Height: 100ft (30m)
Shape: Domed
Deciduous
Pollinated: Insect
Leaf shape: Oblong-elliptic

Right: The rough-skinned fruit has a closely fitting lid and contains delicious seeds.

Below: The large, purple to white flower has a dense central disc of stamens surrounded by six petals.

CHICLE TREE FAMILY

These tropical and subtropical trees and shrubs of the Sapotaceae family are an ecologically important part of the South American rainforest. They all have milky sap and leaves with smooth margins. The small flowers are whitish, greenish or tan and have four to eight petals fused into a tube at the base. The often edible fruit is fleshy, and the seeds are big, shiny and dark brown with a lighter colored scar.

Chicle Tree

Manilkara zapota

Distribution: Mexico, Belize, Guatemala, northern Colombia.
Height: 115ft (35m)
Shape: Domed
Evergreen
Pollinated: Insect
Leaf shape: Elliptic

The sweet fruit of this tree is very popular in tropical America, where it is eaten raw and made into syrups and preserves. The trunk produces a gum, which may be tapped every two or three years. Called "chicle," this was the original base for chewing gum, but it is now rarely used. Chicle trees are grown in plantations in tropical America and the Far East. The thick branches, closely set in tiers, have incredibly dense foliage.

Identification: The bark is gray to brown and made up of small, interlocking plates. The 5–6in- (13–15cm-) long, leathery leaves are glossy dark green with a prominent midrib and are clustered towards the branch tip. The flowers are small, greenish or creamy white, tubular and found in the leaf axils, while the 3in- (8cm-) wide fruit is spherical to egg-shaped and has rough, matt brown skin. The flesh varies in color from cream to yellowish or even reddish-brown.

Left: The leaves are glossy and attractive.

Right: The fruit is produced all year and has a grainy, pear-like texture.

Sapote

Mamey Pouteria sapota

Distribution: Southern Mexico, Central America to Nicaragua. Planted from southern Florida and Bermuda, throughout the West Indies.
Height: 60ft (18m), occasionally 100ft (30m)
Shape: Rounded crown
Evergreen or deciduous
Pollinated: Insect
Leaf shape: Lanceolate

This medium-size or large tree is one of the best known native fruit trees in the region, and it is sometimes cultivated. It bears large, edible fruit which is brown and egg-shape, about 6in (15cm) long, and with a sweet, pinkish flesh and milky sap. These are either eaten raw, or made into various preserves and jellies, or used to flavor ice cream. The seed is also ground as a flavoring, though some reports claim it is poisonous. The seeds yield oil, which the Aztecs used to apply to their hair. The flowers are attractive to honeybees. The wood is moderately hard and strong, and is sometimes used in carpentry.

Identification: The bark is red-brown and rather shaggy, and the stout twigs have rust-red hairs towards their tips. The leathery leaves are alternate but clustered towards the ends of the twigs, and their blades are up to 14in (36cm) long, tapering towards the base. The flowers grow close to the twigs and have pale yellow corollas.

Below: The fan-like clusters of leaves are at the end of a twig.

Right: The egg-shape fruit is large and edible.

Star Apple

Chrysophyllum cainito

This slow-growing tree occurs in wet lowlands and foothills. The fruit, which is found only on mature trees, is eaten when soft to the touch and has a cool, refreshing, sweet flavor. The name "star" refers to the shape of the fruit—in cross-section the seed chambers radiate from the center like a star. The tree has a short trunk and may be as broad as it is tall. Its thick, pendant branches have weeping tips and carry a dense mass of foliage.

Distribution: Central America and West Indies.
Height: 100ft (30m)
Shape: Domed to columnar
Evergreen
Pollinated: Insect
Leaf shape: Oblong-elliptic

Left: The delicious fruit has white or purple flesh and dark brown to black seeds.

Identification: The bark is gray-brown and becomes deeply fissured as the tree ages. The 4–6in- (10–15cm-) long leaves are deep shiny green above and lustrous with copper-colored velvet below. The young branches also have a copper-colored down. Small, white, purplish or yellow flowers appear in summer and are barely visible, due to the thick foliage. The smooth-skinned, round fruit ripens in spring and is up to 4in (10cm) across. The fruit ripens to either a dark purplish-red or to white, depending on the variety.

Right: The fruit's skin must not be eaten, because it contains bitter latex.

OTHER SPECIES OF NOTE

Balata *Manilkara bidentata*
This evergreen tree from the West Indies, Panama and South America produces gum balata, a latex similar to, and sometimes used as a substitute for, gutta percha. It also has hard, dense, durable wood. It has a short trunk and a massive oblong crown, and may reach 100ft (30m) tall. The narrowly oblong leaves are 10in (25cm) long, leathery, shiny and deep green above and grayish and velvety below. They have prominent yellow midribs. The small flowers are white and form in clusters in the leaf axils. The yellow spherical fruit is ¾in (2cm) across.

False Mastic *Sideroxylon foetidissimum*
This evergreen tree is native in Florida, throughout the West Indies, and is also found in southeast Mexico and Honduras. It grows to 49ft (15m) high, although 78ft (24m) has been recorded. It has a straight trunk, up to 12in (30cm) in diameter, and a dense, irregular crown. On young trees the bark is smooth, with only small fissures and horizontal cracks, but on older, larger trees it becomes deeply furrowed, splitting into plates. The alternate leaves are elliptic-oblong, slightly shiny, and yellowish-green. The numerous flowers are yellow, about ½in (1cm) across, usually in small clusters along the stems, and have a curiously pungent, cheesy smell. The fruits are yellowish, ¾in (2cm) long, and contain one large brown seed. The wood is hard, heavy and strong, excellent for making boats, planks, furniture and fences. The tree is suitable as an ornamental because of its abundant flowers, and it is also said to be a useful honey plant.

Damson Plum

Satin Leaf *Chrysophyllum oliviforme*

This slow-growing, long-lived tree has particularly attractive foliage. The leaves have shimmering velvety red or copper undersides, leading to its other name, "satin leaf." It is grown in towns to form an avenue or as a shade tree, and has edible fruit, which varies in flavor from plain and insipid to quite tasty.

Distribution: West Indies and southernmost Florida.
Height: 40ft (12m)
Shape: Oval
Evergreen
Pollinated: Insect
Leaf shape: Ovate-oblong

Identification: The trunk is reddish-brown, scaly, sometimes thorny and carries weeping branches. The glossy, 4–8in- (10–20cm-) long leaves are dark green above and a rich tone below, while the ¼in- (5mm-) long, five-petaled flowers are white, cream, gray or grayish-green. The latter appear in clusters in the leaf axils throughout the year, and are particularly abundant in late summer and early fall. Like the flowers, the fleshy fruit is well hidden among the leaves. When ripe, the fruit is dark purple, shiny, up to 1½in (4cm) long and contains one seed.

Above: Although naturalized in Hawaii, the damson plum has become endangered in its native Florida.

Left: The name Chrysophyllum, meaning "gold leaf," alludes to the coppery underside of the leaf.

CLUSIA FAMILY

The trees in the Guttiferae family have oil glands and ducts on their leaves, which give a clear spot effect. Many also yield resins. Most are tropical trees or shrubs, and some are semi-epiphytic, using other plants to support them. They often produce latex, which may be white, yellow or even orange, and many have stilt roots. This family includes several useful timber trees, and some species grown for their fruit.

Autograph Tree

Clusia rosea

This tree earns its name from its leaves, which are so thick that one can carve words into them—historically, they have even been used as playing cards. The tree may start life on rocks or as an epiphyte, becoming a strangler with aerial roots forming many trunks. It grows quickly into a sprawling, irregular tree with horizontal branches and a dense crown. Being adapted to salt spray, high winds and sandy, saline soil, and with surface wandering roots, it occurs naturally and is planted in coastal locations.

Distribution: Caribbean, Florida Keys, and southeast Mexico.
Height: 50ft (15m)
Shape: Spreading
Evergreen
Pollinated: Insect
Leaf shape: Obovate

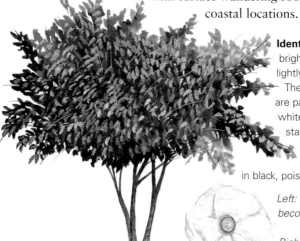

Identification: The tree has yellow sap and thick, bright green leaves 3–8in (7.5–20cm) long. The lightly scented flowers have thick, waxy petals. They appear intermittently throughout the year, but are particularly abundant in late summer. Solitary and white, ageing to pink, they have many bright yellow stamens and are 2–3½in (5–9cm) across. The fruit is round, pale green, 2–3½in (5–9cm) across, and bursts open to reveal red seeds embedded in black, poisonous resin.

Left: The lovely scented flowers are short-lived, becoming brown after only a few days.

Right: The thick, tough, waxy leaves are designed to withstand harsh coastal conditions.

Cupeillo

Clusia krugiana

Distribution: Puerto Rico and Dominican Republic.
Height: 40ft (12m)
Shape: Crown spreading
Evergreen
Pollinated: Insect
Leaf shape: Obovate

Right: Several light brown seeds are embedded in the orange pulp.

This small or medium-size tree has a trunk up to 12in (30cm) in diameter bearing a crown of thick branches, sometimes supported by a few prop roots. If its smooth, gray bark is damaged, the yellow or orange latex seeps out, coagulating on exposure to the air. Flowering and fruiting is thought to continue through the year. The light brown wood is hard and heavy, but has little value as lumber, and is used mainly for fuel.

Right: The yellow flowers are attractive.

Identification: The stout, brownish twigs, ringed at the nodes, bear very thick, leathery, dark green leaves, up to 5in (13cm) in length, 4in (10cm) in width, with scarcely visible veins. The small, yellow flowers are arranged in branched clusters at the ends of the stems, male and female flowers on separate trees. The female flowers develop into round, green fruit, which retains the enclosing calyx at the base, and also the five blackish stigmas at the apex.

Palo de Cruz

Rheedia portoricensis

This small tree is found growing wild only in the forests and thickets of the coastal regions of Puerto Rico and on the neighbouring island of Vieques. Its trunk, only about 4in (10cm) in diameter, has smooth or slightly fissured brown bark and bears a crown of horizontal or slightly drooping branches with dark green foliage. A pale yellow latex is found in the inner bark, twigs, leaves and fruit. Characteristic of this species are the green or gray twigs which occur in pairs opposite each other, at right angles to the main axis. This regular, cross-like branching has given rise to the local Spanish name for the tree. The light brown wood is very hard and heavy, but as the trees are small it is mainly used for posts. It is regarded as a handsome tree, and may therefore have some potential ornamental value.

Identification: The small, spine-tipped leaves are arranged opposite each other along the stems. They are stiff, thick and shiny, and grow up to about 3in (7.5cm) long and 2in (5cm) broad, dark green on the upper surface and light green beneath. The small flowers, less than ½in (1cm) across, are pale yellow with a tinge of pink. They grow singly or in small groups at the base of the leaves.

Distribution: Puerto Rico, Vieques.
Height: 20ft (6m)
Shape: Crown narrow
Evergreen
Pollinated: Insect
Leaf shape: Elliptic-obovate

Left: The yellow elliptical fruit, is about 1¾in (4cm) long.

Barillo

Symphonia globulifera

A large tree, common at sea level in wet or swampy forests along the Atlantic coast of Central America, barillo resembles the American elm (*Ulmus americana*) in general appearance. The stout trunk, occasionally more than 3ft (1m) in diameter, is sometimes supported by stilt roots. The rough, dark bark contains yellowish resin, from which this tree derives its Spanish name of *leche amarillo*. On exposure to the air, this resin becomes black and pitch-like, and in some regions is used for waterproofing boats. The hard, heavy timber is used for building purposes, carpentry, crates and boxes, railroad crossties, and fuel. Small quantities have been exported to North America and Europe, mainly for use as veneers.

Identification: The branches of this tree spread out horizontally, or droop slightly, and bear short-stalked, leathery leaves. The flowers, with round, red petals, are followed by small, ovoid, dark green, berry-like fruit that become brownish or yellowish with age.

Distribution: Atlantic coast of Central America, from Guatemala to Panama; West Indies; coastal South America; tropical Africa.
Height: 100ft (30m)
Shape: Crown rounded
Evergreen
Pollinated: Bird
Leaf shape: Lanceolate

Above: Each leathery fruit contains one to three seeds.

MIMOSA SUBFAMILY

The Mimosoideae are a subclass of the large pea family, the Leguminosae. There are almost 3,000 species, including trees, shrubs and some herbs, most have finely divided leaves, and the acacias are probably the most familiar members. The flowers tend to be small and are often in eye-catching clusters. There are 1,200 species of Acacia, 900 of which occur in Australia.

Guaba

Inga vera

Distribution: Jamaica, Cuba, Haiti, Dominican Republic, Puerto Rico, and possibly Mexico.
Height: 60ft (18m)
Shape: Spreading
Evergreen
Pollinated: Insects, birds, and bats
Leaf shape: Alternate, pinnate

The range of this medium-size, spreading tree has been considerably extended due to its use as a shade tree in coffee plantations, and this has blurred its natural distribution somewhat. The genus is a large one, with 350 species. The flowers open at different times and are pollinated by insects and birds, and possibly also by bats at night. The timber is used for posts and furniture.

Identification: The pinnate leaves have three to five pairs of large, drooping, hairy leaflets. The trunk may reach 3ft (1m) in diameter, and the bark is gray-brown and smooth at first, becoming fissured with age. The fruit is a brown, hairy, slightly curved pod.

*Left:
The whitish flowers have long, protruding stamens, giving them a feathery appearance. Each flower opens only for a short period of just a few hours.*

Ice Cream Bean

Inga edulis

This fast-growing tree is used in its native home to provide shade in coffee plantations. It is also grown for its seed pods, which contain sweet, white pulp that tastes like vanilla ice cream.

Identification: The trunk has smooth, gray bark and may be multistemmed. The spreading branches are heavily clothed with leaves, providing dense shade. The branches are somewhat brittle and occasionally break under their own weight. The leaves are 24in (60cm) long, and have three or four pairs of dark green leaflets with lighter veining. Each leaflet is 4in (10cm) long, rough textured and elliptical. The stem between each pair of leaflets is winged. The flowers appear sporadically throughout the year, but are most common in the spring and summer. They have small, brown petals and long, white stamens, and are clustered together like tight powder-puffs. The greenish-brown pods are 12–24in (30–60cm) long, oblong in cross section and velvety.

Distribution: West Indies, Central America and northern South America.
Height: 40ft (12m)
Shape: Spreading
Evergreen
Pollinated: Hummingbird and bee
Leaf shape: Pinnate

Above right: Seeds are encased in soft pulp.

Left: Winged leaf stems are typical for the Inga genus.

Right: The ice cream bean forms a dense mass of foliage.

Sweet Acacia

Aroma *Acacia farnesiana*

This tree spreads rapidly and is naturalized in Florida and Louisiana, as well as being occasionally planted in gardens. It is the source of perfume, which is distilled from its flowers—these being known in the trade as "cassie flowers"—and is also grown for this purpose in southern Europe, where it is sometimes called "mimosa." Not surprisingly, the flowers attract bees, and this is a good honey plant. The foliage and twigs of this multi-use species are eagerly browsed by livestock, and the pods and bark are used in the tanning industry. Bunches of dried flowers retain a pleasant perfume, and are sometimes used to scent and freshen linen.

Identification: A small tree with dark brown, rather smooth bark, and paired spines at the base of its feathery leaves. The flowers are arranged in tight, bright yellow balls on hairy stalks, and are pleasantly perfumed. The fruits are typical legume bean-like pods, each with several brown seeds, and they remain on the tree long after ripening.

Distribution: California, Texas, Arizona, Mexico, West Indies, through Central and South America to Chile and Argentina.
Height: 10ft (3m)
Shape: Spreading
Deciduous
Pollinated: Insect
Leaf shape: Feathery (twice-pinnate)

Left: The globular flowerheads are sweet-scented and golden yellow.

Mesquite

Algarobbo *Prosopis juliflora*

This spiny tree has a wide distribution—from California right through to Central and South America—and it is also widely naturalized in the tropics elsewhere. It is a multi-use species, yielding durable, rot-resistant timber, fuelwood, and high-quality charcoal. Its bark is used for tanning leather, and its flowers attact honeybees. Native Mexican and American people traditionally used the pods to grind into a kind of flour, for use in cooking. Mesquite pods are nutritious, and are also eaten by animals, including cattle.

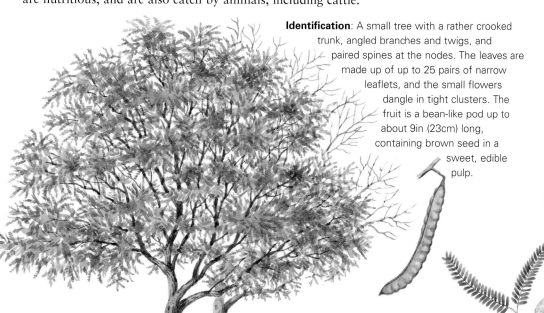

Identification: A small tree with a rather crooked trunk, angled branches and twigs, and paired spines at the nodes. The leaves are made up of up to 25 pairs of narrow leaflets, and the small flowers dangle in tight clusters. The fruit is a bean-like pod up to about 9in (23cm) long, containing brown seed in a sweet, edible pulp.

Distribution: Southwest U.S.A., through Mexico and the Caribbean islands, to Colombia, and Venezuela; naturalized in Hawaii and elsewhere.
Height: 30ft (9m)
Shape: Broad-crowned, spreading, flat-topped
Deciduous
Pollinated: Insect
Leaf shape: Feathery (twice-pinnate)

Left: The catkin-like cylindrical flower clusters attract insects including honeybees.

Manila Tamarind

Pithecellobium dulce

This plant has thorns on all its branches and, when kept pruned as a shrub, makes a good spiny hedge. The Manila tamarind has several other uses: yellow dye is made from its bark, a drink is made from the fruit pulp, and its pods are collected for animal fodder. It is suited to dry conditions, and has a light and airy canopy with ascending branches.

Identification: The pale gray bark has longitudinal ridges. The leaves have one pair of side stalks, each with only a single pair of leaflets. Each leaflet is 1–2in (2.5–5cm) long, blunt-ended and matt grayish-green when mature. The young leaflets are dull maroon. The overall effect of the leaves makes the tree look congested. The tiny, greenish flowers are packed into round heads ¾in (2cm) wide, which are held on branched clusters springing from the leaf axils. The pods are 4½–6in (12–15cm) long, ½in (1cm) wide, lobed and spirally twisted.

Distribution: Mexico and Venezuela.
Height: 50ft (15m)
Shape: Domed
Evergreen
Pollinated: Insect
Leaf shape: Bipinnate

Right: As the pods mature they twist up. They contain three to nine shiny black seeds in pink and white edible pulp.

Yellow Rain Tree

Albizia saman

The grass underneath this tree is often green when the surrounding grass has dried out and died. This was once attributed to the tree making rain overnight, hence its name. In reality the leaves close at night and during showers, allowing rain to fall on to the grass below when that beneath other trees receives far less or none. The yellow rain tree is widely planted in the tropics for shade—its crown, which has a symmetrical form with ascending branches, attains a spread of 200ft (60m). The pods contain a sugary pulp, which is favored by cattle and used for fodder.

Identification: The bark is gray and lightly fissured. The leaves are 12in (30cm) long with three to six pairs of side stalks, each carrying six to eight pairs of leaflets. Each leaflet is 1–2in (2.5–5cm) long, mid-green above, pale green below and oblong to diamond-shaped. The delicate flowers occur throughout the year and are particularly common from spring to summer. They have small petals but long stamens, which together give the look of an airy, pink-tipped powder-puff. The pods are 6–10in (15–25cm) long, flat, black and contain brown seeds.

Distribution: West Indies, Central America.
Height: 115ft (35m)
Shape: Spreading, domed
Semi-deciduous
Pollinated: Insect
Leaf shape: Bipinnate

Right: The leaves close up an hour or more before sunset, and open an hour or so after sunrise. It is thought that this allows moisture through the canopy, and enables numerous epiphytes to live on the tree's trunk and branches.

Powder-puff

Calliandra haematocephala

This plant is grown for its amazing flowers—large, soft powder-puffs of intense scarlet or the darkest pink. It may be grown as a large shrub or pruned to give it a more tree-like shape. The branches droop and sprawl somewhat, but are amply covered with thick foliage. The flowers first appear when the plant is quite small.

Identification: The leaves are composed of two pinnae, each 10in (25cm) long and consisting of five to ten pairs of leaflets. Each leaflet is oblong to sickle-shaped, deep green when mature and 1½in (4cm) long. When young, the foliage weeps and is a soft coppery pink. The 4in- (10cm-) wide flower clusters contain hundreds of individual flowers with their petals obscured by the numerous, 2½in- (6cm-) long, red stamens. The flowers appear mostly in the fall and winter months.

Distribution: Bolivia.
Height: 30ft (9m)
Shape: Spreading
Evergreen
Pollinated: Hummingbird and insect
Leaf shape: Bipinnate

Left: The tight flower buds are reminiscent of small-berried fruit, and burst open to reveal the long stamens.

Right: The flowers are short-lived, lasting only a day or two.

Ear Pod Tree

Enterolobium cyclocarpum

This upright tree is grown for the novelty value of its pods, which look uncannily like human ears. These pods may be eaten when young and are often collected for animal fodder. The bright red seeds are used for jewelry and the lumber is of high quality. The ear pod tree can grow as wide as it is tall and has thick, ascending branches.

Identification: The bark is light gray and smooth, while the leaves are bright green and feathery, consisting of four to eight pairs of pinnae, each with 12–24 pairs of leaflets. The leaflets are ⅔in (1.5cm) long and oblong to sickle-shaped. The tree blossoms in spring, producing sprays of tiny white flowers clustered into balls. Each flower has greenish-white, ¼in- (5mm-) long petals and longer, white stamens. The seed pods often appear in the dry season, when the tree is leafless. They are deep russet brown, shiny and 3–6¼ in (8–16cm) long.

Distribution: Venezuela.
Height: 100ft (30m)
Shape: Spreading
Deciduous
Pollinated: Insect
Leaf shape: Bipinnate

Left: The pods are produced in large numbers and contain a dry, sugary pulp, a valuable fodder at the end of the dry season.

Right: The leaves are fine and feathery.

CAESALPINIA SUBFAMILY

The legumes include well over 600 genera spread across the globe, and they are particularly common in the tropics. The family includes annuals, herbaceous plants, shrubs, trees and climbers. The trees play an important role in the forests of South America and Africa. The Caesalpinia subfamily is distinguished by flowers with five petals, and one odd-sized petal is enclosed by the others.

West Indian Locust

Hymenaea courbaril

An attractive forest tree, with a trunk at least 4ft (1.2m) in diameter, sometimes supported by buttresses, and covered by a thick layer of smooth, gray bark. This is an important timber tree, being used for furniture, wheels and cogs, railroad crossties, veneers and cabinet work, etc. The tree is commercially important as the source of South American copal, used in varnishes. A good shade tree, but not for planting near houses because of the odor of the fruits.

Left: Each leaf has two shiny green leaflets, each up to 4 x 1¾in (10 x 4cm) and narrowing near the base.

Identification: The stout branches forming the crown terminate in sturdy brown twigs bearing compound leaves. The flattened flower clusters stand upright at the ends of the branches, and consist of numerous whitish flowers. The pods contain pockets of gum, and large, dark red seeds embedded in thick, pale yellow pulp. The pulp is edible.

Distribution: West Indies; Central and South America.
Height: 65ft (20m)
Shape: Crown rounded and spreading
Evergreen
Pollinated: Insect and bat
Leaf shape: Oblong, but unequal-sided

Left: The flowers develop into rough, dark brown pods, up to 4 x 2in (10 x 5cm).

Flame of the Forest

Flamboyant tree *Delonix regia*

Also called the flamboyant tree, the flame of the forest flowers in late spring and early summer when it becomes one mass of intense vermilion blossoms, completely obliterating from sight any foliage across its incredibly wide, flat-topped crown. The tree is also eye-catching in fruit, when hundreds of long pods hang from its horizontal branches. Even when it is in leaf the tree has a pleasant, airy appearance. It has been planted in considerable numbers throughout the tropics including the U.S.A., but with its spreading, shallow roots and eventual buttresses, it has not proved popular as a street tree.

Identification: The smooth bark is light brown or gray, and the trunk carries thick branches, which are never straight. The leaves are delicate, 24in (60cm) long, bright green above and lighter below. The flowers have four red petals, and one larger white petal with yellow and red streaks. The dark brown, flattened seed pods are up to 24in (60cm) long.

Distribution: Madagascar.
Height: 66ft (20m)
Shape: Spreading
Deciduous
Pollinated: Bird
Leaf shape: Bipinnate

Above: Profuse, beautiful flowers give rise to masses of hard, woody pods, which remain on the tree even when splitting open.

Right: This fast-growing tree may grow to 25ft (7.5m) in four years.

Rose of Venezuela

Brownea grandiceps

Distribution: Northern
Venezuela.
Height: 60ft (18m)
Shape: Domed
Evergreen
Leaf shape: Pinnate

This slow-growing, handsome tree is notable for its
display of impressive flowers and fine foliage. Despite
being the largest flowering member of its genus, it is
not heavily planted in the tropics. The leaves display
an interesting piece of behavior—they cover the
flowers by day to protect them from the sun, then
move aside to reveal them at night. The rose of
Venezuela grows naturally in mountain
forests.

Identification: The dense crown has leaves up
to 36in (90cm) long divided into five to eleven pairs
of long, narrow leaflets. Young leaves are translucent
pink or bronze and hang; when mature they are bright
green, leathery and flat. The delicate flowers are bright
red and tubular with long, protruding anthers. They occur
in clusters of about 50, in large hanging balls towards the
branch tips. Each cluster is 10in (25cm) wide. The wide,
flattened seed pods are 10in (25cm) long.

*Left: Flowers appear year round
and are particularly abundant in
spring and early summer.*

OTHER SPECIES OF NOTE

Pink Shower Tree *Cassia grandis*
The thick canopy of coral pink flowers this tree
produces falls quickly in early spring to form a
pink carpet below. This species comes from
Central America. It has a spreading crown and
grows to 60ft (18m) tall. The leaves are pinnate,
12in (30cm) long and mid-green. The black,
cylindrical pods may be up to 15in (38cm) long,
and contain flat, yellow seeds.

Jerusalem Thorn *Parkinsonia aculeata*
This spiny shrub or small tree is native to the
southern United States and Mexico, but has
been extensively planted elsewhere as a hedge
plant or ornamental. Nowadays it is found from
California to Florida, southwards to Central and
South America and the West Indies, and even in
the Old World tropics. It grows to about 20ft
(6m), often branching near the ground, and has
an open crown of spreading branches. The
smooth, thin bark is at first yellowish or bluish-
green, but becomes brown and fissured on
larger, older trunks. The slender, slightly zigzag
green stems bear specialized leaves, consisting
of a ¾in- (2cm-) long spine and two or four
dangling axes, up to 12in (30cm) long, each
edged by 20–30 pairs of tiny, oblong, deciduous
leaflets. At the base of each leaf is a pair of short
spines. The colorful, fragrant flowers have five
bright yellow petals, the upper one often tinged
red, 10 stamens with green filaments and
orange-brown anthers, and a reddish ovary and
style. The leathery, brown, pointed pods, up to
3in (8cm) long, are pinched between the seeds.
The wood is too brittle to be used for construction,
and is useful only for fuel. Leaves and pods are
eaten by livestock, and an infusion of the leaves
has been used in domestic medicines.

Dividivi

Caesalpinia coriaria

This small deciduous tree is native mainly in
the Caribbean but has been widely planted
elsewhere, partly as a source of tannin from
its pods. The bark is also rich in tannin. The
tree has feathery foliage and an irregular,
spreading crown, often flattened at the top,
and the flowers are fragrant, attracting bees.

Identification: The light green leaves have finely
hairy axes, and each branch (secondary axis) carries
up to 24 tiny leaflets, giving an almost fern-like
appearance. The flowers have yellow or whitish
petals, and are arranged in clusters. The fruit is
a thick, hard pod, at first light brown, but
turning reddish and twisting into a circular or
S-shape. The wood is very heavy and hard, and
takes a polish well.

Distribution: Greater and
Lesser Antilles; Mexico to
Colombia and Venezuela.
Bahamas and Trinidad
(introduced).
Height: 25ft (7.5m)
Shape: Variable
Deciduous
Pollinated: Insect
Leaf shape: Bipinnate

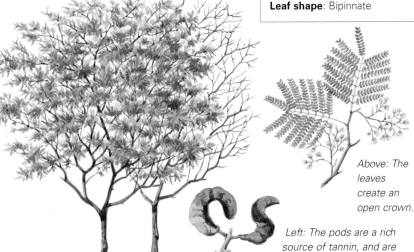

*Above: The
leaves
create an
open crown.*

*Left: The pods are a rich
source of tannin, and are
also used to produce a black dye.*

BEAN SUBFAMILY

There are more than 12,000 species in this legume subfamily (Faboideae). It contains mainly herbs (such as clovers and vetches), but also some shrubs (such as Broom) and some trees, including Laburnum. The flower structure is the typical pea flower, with a large standard petal, lateral wing petals, and a keel formed by two fused petals, adapted to pollination by insects and sometimes by birds.

Common Coral Tree

Erythrina crista-galli

This fast-growing plant has soft wood, and is grown as a multistemmed tree in tropical regions and as a herbaceous plant in warm temperate areas, where it is cut to the ground by the cold each winter. The stems are covered in thick, ⅜in- (1cm-) long, curved thorns, and even the leaf stems carry spines. The large, long-lasting flower panicles are produced throughout the year, and are the showiest in the genus.

Left: As it matures, the tree gains rough fissured bark and contorted branches.

Above and below left: These stunning flowers are adapted to pollination by birds through their red color, tubular shape, copious amount of nectar and sturdiness.

Distribution: Brazil.
Height: 30ft (9m)
Shape: Spreading, irregular crown
Evergreen
Pollinated: Bird
Leaf shape: Trifoliate

Identification: The trunk has ridged bark and grows into a gnarled form. The leaves are deep green, smooth and leathery with elliptic leaflets each measuring 3in (7.5cm) long. The flowers are scarlet to deep pink, and 2–3in (5–7.5cm) long. They form an inflorescence containing up to 100 flowers, which often hangs down. The flowers appear in cycles of six weeks. The smooth pods are up to 12in (30cm) long and contain gray seeds.

Cabbage-bark

Dog-almond *Andira inermis*

This is a striking, beautiful tree, especially when it is in full bloom, when it boasts clusters of purple or pink, pea-shaped flowers, which attract insects, notably honeybees. It is sometimes planted as a shade tree or ornamental in parks and gardens. Its strange name derives from the distinctive smell of the cut bark—not unlike cabbage. The bark is poisonous, as are the seeds, but it is also reputed to have medicinal properties, killing parasitic worms. The heartwood is attractively patterned and is consequently suitable for furniture.

Far right: The fruit is rounded, fleshy and olive like.

Right: The leaves are arranged opposite on the twig.

Identification: This much-branched tree has scaly bark and rather sturdy twigs which are covered in fine hairs when young. The pinnate leaves have shiny, pointed green or yellow-green leaflets. The flowers are pink or dark red, and develop in branching clusters, while the fruit has a rounded, fleshy outside and is hard on the inside.

Distribution: Mexico, Peru, Bolivia, Brazil, southern Florida (introduced), west tropical Africa.
Height: 50ft (15m)
Shape: Rounded
Deciduous
Pollinated: Insect
Leaf shape: Pinnate

Left: The pea-like flowers are stunningly pretty.

Pea-tree

Quick-stick, Mother-of-cocoa *Gliricidia sepium*

This small tree has pretty pea-like flowers arranged in clusters mainly close to the wood of older branches, and opening between December and May. The timber is strong and heavy, and has been used as railroad crossties, and to make sturdy posts. One name is "mother-of-cocoa," referring to its use as a shade tree in cocoa plantations, where it also enriches the soil. Many parts of this tree are poisonous, and have been used to kill rodents, although the flowers attract honeybees.

Identification: The pinnate leaves have numerous elliptic leaflets with hairy stalks and green or grayish blades. Each flower has a spreading, butterfly-shaped corolla with pink or purplish-white petals, and resembles that of a sweet-pea. The fruit pods are yellow-green at first, ripening to brownish-black, and contain blackish seeds.

Distribution: Mexico, Colombia, Venezuela; introduced in Caribbean islands from Cuba to Trinidad, and also in southern Florida, Brazil, and in Africa and south Asia.
Height: 25ft (7.5m)
Shape: Variable
Deciduous
Pollinated: Insect
Leaf shape: Pinnate

Left: This tree is well-named as the individual flowers are like those of the sweet-pea.

OTHER SPECIES OF NOTE

Swamp Immortelle *Erythrina fusca*
This tree is found across a very wide natural range that includes the tropics of America, Africa and Asia. It is a deciduous tree with a rounded crown that may grow to 80ft (24m) tall and have a spread almost equally large. The swamp immortelle is grown for its scarlet flowers, which are densely crowded into 10in- (25cm-) long sprays. The flowers appear in spring and summer, and have a brick-red upper petal and brownish-maroon to cream wings and keel. The tree grows with a crooked, buttressed trunk, which loses its thick curved spines when mature. The leaves have three deep green, smooth and leathery elliptic leaflets, each 3in (8cm) long. The narrow pods are 12in (30cm) long.

Mountain Immortelle *Erythrina poeppigiana*
From eastern Peru and Brazil, this tree has been widely introduced into the Caribbean and Costa Rica. Growing up to 80ft (24m) tall, it is sometimes used as a shade tree in cocoa plantations. In spring, and occasionally in late summer, it can be seen from a long way off due to the abundant scarlet to deep pink flowers covering its dome-shaped crown. The flowers are pollinated by small birds. The mountain immortelle has thorny bark covering a soft-wooded trunk, which usually exceeds 3ft (1m) in diameter. The leaves have three leaflets: the lower two are 4in (10cm) across, and the terminal leaflet is 6in (15cm) wide. The pods are 4½in (12cm) long and contain two seeds.

Pride of Bolivia

Tipuana tipu

The pride of Bolivia is a fast-growing tree that forms a thick, straight trunk with buttresses. This tree is common in Bolivia, and one valley there has so many of them that it is known simply as Tipuana. Once it has passed through a young, ungainly stage, the pride of Bolivia normally grows into a wide, spreading tree with horizontal, zigzagging branches. It has been planted around South America, in North America and in the south of France for its spring and summer flowers, attractive shape and abundant shade.

Identification: The dark brown trunk is usually short in cultivated trees. The leaves are 12in (30cm) long and composed of 13–21 leaflets, each dark to yellowish green and oblong. The butterfly-like flowers vary from pale yellow to orangey yellow. They are in terminal clusters. The fruit appears in the fall and is a winged key, 2–4in long (5–10cm) and brown.

Distribution: South America.
Height: 100ft (30m)
Shape: Spreading
Semi-evergreen
Pollinated: Insect
Leaf shape: Pinnate

Below: This drought-tolerant species produces its flowers in spring and summer.

Fish-poison Tree

Piscidia carthagenensis

A medium-size tree common on coasts and coastal hills, often in seasonally dry regions. It is also planted in gardens and parks. In some regions, including the West Indies, the root bark, young branches and crushed leaves were thrown into the water to assist in fishing. The effect on the fish is to render them temporarily helpless (hence the tree's common name). They float to the surface where they are easily caught, but they apparently recover and swim off if left alone. The wood is hard and heavy.

Identification: The pinnate leaves typically have seven or nine elliptic, gray-green, fine-haired leaflets. The flowers are pea-like, pink and arranged in clusters (panicles), often appearing before the leaves. The fruit is a rather unusual pod, with four broad, papery wings along the sides. Inside the fruit are several bean-like, brown seeds.

Distribution: Islands of the Caribbean; coasts of Venezuela, Colombia, Ecuador, northwest Peru, Panama along Pacific coast to southern and western Mexico.
Height: 35ft (11m)
Shape: Variable
Deciduous
Leaf shape: Pinnate

Above: The attractive pink flowers are arranged in clusters on the tree.

Left: The fruit is highly unusual in shape, with distinct flanges.

Right: Like many members of the subfamily, the fish-poison tree has pinnate leaves.

Geno-geno

Lonchocarpus domingensis

This deciduous tree is native to southern and western Puerto Rico and some other Caribbean islands. In Tobago it can be found in semi-deciduous forests at the northern tip of the island. Here the canopy is about 49ft (15m), and it is co-dominant with other trees such as *Bursera simaruba*. The pale or yellowish wood is fairly strong and is used mainly for posts. It flowers mainly in the spring, and the fruit ripens in summer. The bark has been used for rope. It is planted occasionally as a shade tree or ornamental, and is also attractive to honeybees.

Identification: The leaves have seven to eleven untoothed leaflets, usually pointed. The flowers are pea-shaped, pale rose or violet and appear in clusters (racemes or panicles). The fruit is a pod covered in fine brown hairs, and contains several flat, dark brown seeds. The bark is brown, with pale dots.

Below: The leaves have a medicinal use.

Distribution: Cuba, Hispaniola, Puerto Rico, Guadaloupe, Martinique, Tobago.
Height: 70ft (21m)
Shape: Spreading
Deciduous
Pollinated: Insect
Leaf shape: Pinnate

Right: The flattened pods contain dark brown seeds.

MACADAMIA FAMILY

The Proteaceae are found in warm regions of the Southern Hemisphere, and are well represented in Australia and South Africa. Many species produce showy, long-lasting flowers used in the cut-flower industry. The leaves are often thick and waxy or hairy—adaptations for water retention. There are 1,600 species belonging to 77 genera in this family.

Silk Oak

Silky oak *Grevillea robusta*

This pretty, medium-size tree is native to Australia, but is widely planted in other tropical and subtropical regions, including the West Indies and Central and South America. It has divided, almost fern-like leaves, and showy flowers which produce copious nectar—attracting birds as well as insects. Often planted for shade, for example along roads, it also propagates readily and grows rapidly. It is also drought resistant and cold hardy, but can become ragged with age, and the branches tend to break rather easily. The timber is used for furniture, and has prominent rays.

Identification: The bark is smooth, gray, becoming furrowed with age. The leaves are rather delicate and fern-like, and the yellowish flowers are crowded together in unbranched clusters. The fruit is pod-like, broad and flattened and split open on one side to release the winged seeds.

Left: Silk oak flowers appear orange-yellow in mid spring.

Distribution: Australia; introduced and naturalized in the West Indies, and from Mexico to Brazil, Argentina and Peru; also in southern Florida, southern California and southern Arizona.
Height: 70ft (21m)
Shape: Variable
Evergreen
Pollinated: Insect and bird
Leaf shape: Pinnate

OTHER SPECIES OF NOTE
Queensland Nut
Macadamia ternifolia
This is a medium-size tree, related to *M. integrifolia*, and likewise produces edible seeds. A native of Queensland and New South Wales in Australia, it is also grown in the Caribbean area, notably in Puerto Rico, mainly as an ornamental tree. It has whorled, narrow, oblong leaves, and short-stalked whitish flowers in drooping clusters. The rounded fruit is about 1in (2.5cm) in diameter and splits into two when ripe to release the single, hard, thick-shelled, edible nut.

Macadamia Nut

Macadamia integrifolia

The delicious nuts for which this species is famous are found inside the fruit. Macadamia nut trees are grown throughout the tropics, particularly in Australia and Hawaii, where they were introduced in 1890. The trees grow naturally in eastern Australia's rainforests, but most grown commercially are selected, grafted varieties. The wild tree is handsome with a dense, wide crown.

Identification: The leaves are leathery, glossy, dark green and up to 12in (30cm) long. They appear in whorls, have wavy-toothed margins and yellowish midribs. The tiny flowers form dangling tassels, 4–12in (10–30cm) long in winter and spring. Each flower is white, cream or pale pink. The fruit is usually ready in late summer, when it hangs in long clusters. Each fruit is spherical, 1in (2.5cm) across and green, with a broad scar revealing the inner husk. The shell and husk are hard to break and poisonous.

Distribution: Queensland and northern New South Wales, Australia. Hawaii.
Height: 69ft (21m)
Shape: Domed
Evergreen
Pollinated: Insect
Leaf shape: Oblanceolate

Above: The fruit takes up to nine months to mature.

GUAVA FAMILY

Many Myrtaceae are evergreen trees and shrubs, having leaves with a distinctive, spicy scent. They usually have smooth margins, and grow opposite one another on the stem. The bark is often papery, peeling or splotched with pale and reddish patches. The flowers are arranged in various ways but often have many stamens, giving them a powder-puff look.

Weeping Paperbark

Melaleuca quinquenervia

This tree occurs naturally in swampy ground, but is very adaptable to even dry soils and has been planted throughout the tropics. In the Everglades of Florida in the U.S.A., the tree has become naturalized and is proving a threat to the local, indigenous species. In Hong Kong, the weeping paperbark has a different reputation. There it is widely planted by the government to stabilize swampy farming ground, and considered invaluable in land reclamation.

Identification: The thick, shaggy, peeling bark is pale cinnamon-brown to white. The tree emits volatile oils that deter insects. The smooth, shiny, hard leaves are a bluish gray-green, flat, 1½–4in (4–10cm) long and have parallel veins. The leaves are distilled to produce an essential oil with many uses.

Right: The white flowers form bottlebrush-like inflorescences 4in (10cm) long. The flowers release large amounts of pollen, causing problems for hay fever sufferers.

Distribution: Eastern coastal Australia, New Guinea and New Caledonia. Florida, U.S.A.
Height: 60ft (18m)
Shape: Columnar to spreading
Evergreen
Pollinated: Bird
Leaf shape: Elliptic-lanceolate

Allspice

Pimenta dioica

The fruit, sold as allspice, is often mistakenly thought to be a mixture of different spices. This error is understandable quite apart from the fruit's name, because allspice has a scent similar to a combination of clove, nutmeg and cinnamon. Allspice trees are widely grown in Jamaica, from where the spice is exported. The fruit is collected before it is completely ripe and dried in the sun for up to ten days. After drying, the fruit looks similar to pepper, so the genus is named *Pimenta*, from the Spanish for "pepper." The berries are an essential part of Caribbean cuisine and have medicinal properties.

Identification: This dense-crowned tree is aromatic in every part. The trunk is short and has pale gray peeling bark. The leaves are glossy, mid-green with prominent veining below, and are 6–8in (15–20cm) long. The flowers appear in spring and early summer in short panicles, which are in axils near the branch tips. Each flower is white or pale green, scented and tiny. The valuable fruit, ¼in (5mm) across, is produced in summer, and is picked when green and is black when ripe.

Distribution: Caribbean, southern Mexico and Central America.
Height: 40ft (12m)
Shape: Oblong
Evergreen
Pollinated: Insect
Leaf shape: Oblong-elliptical

Left: The allspice tree's stems, bark, leaves and flowers are all scented, filling the air around with a thick aroma. The tree also yields an oil used in perfumes and liqueurs.

Guava

Psidium guajava

This fruit tree is grown extensively throughout the tropics and into temperate areas, where it has proved itself capable of surviving slight frosts. It is popular because it is such an accommodating, undemanding tree and readily produces tasty fruit. Although it has a slightly unpleasant, grainy texture, the fruit is eaten raw and is highly nutritious, containing large amounts of vitamin C.

Above: Guava fruit is made into drinks, conserves and confectionery.

Distribution: West Indies to Peru.
Height: 33ft (10m)
Shape: Domed
Evergreen
Pollinated: Insect
Leaf shape: Oblong-elliptic

Identification: The distinctive, brown bark flakes off leaving mottled, green patches on the trunk and branches. The leathery leaves form a dense crown. They are up to 6in (15cm) long, downy below, yellowish-gray-green and heavily veined. The white flowers have hundreds of stamens and appear mostly in spring and early summer. They are slightly scented, about 1in (2.5cm) wide and occur in the axils. The fruit is a yellowish-green or pinkish tone when ripe.

Left: The round, lumpy fruit is heavily scented and measures 2¾in (7cm) across.

Strawberry Guava

Psidium littorale

A narrow, leggy, upright shrub or small tree, the strawberry guava has a dense crown and produces small fruit in large quantity. The fruit is juicy and has a similar taste and texture to strawberries, although it is a little more acidic and grainy. The strawberry guava is a slow-growing tree cultivated in tropical and warm temperate regions. In the latter it may be severely cut back by the winter cold, whereas in the former it may become naturalized and a serious problem.

Distribution: Eastern Brazil.
Height: 20ft (6m)
Shape: Columnar
Evergreen
Pollinated: Insect
Leaf shape: Oblong-obovate

Identification: The tree has smooth, reddish or deep brown bark that flakes to reveal a mottling of grayish green below. The short-stalked leaves are smooth, glossy, thick and tough. Bright green, they have lighter midribs, are downy below and measure 3–4in (7.5–10cm) long. The single white or yellow flowers are 1in (2.5cm) across and scented. The round fruit is smooth-skinned, 1–2in (2.5–5cm) across, red or yellow when mature and has white flesh containing many seeds.

Right: The fruit may be eaten raw, but is usually used to make jams and jellies.

CREPE MYRTLE FAMILY

The Lythraceae family includes herbaceous plants, trees and shrubs but only a few are well known, and only a handful are used in horticulture. The trees have simple, smooth-edged leaves positioned opposite one another on the stem. The star-shaped flowers have petals that are crumpled up when in bud and appear in panicles, racemes or cymes. The fruit is a capsule or berry containing many seeds.

Queen's Crepe Myrtle

Pride of India *Lagerstroemia speciosa*

This tree is grown as an ornamental plant for its large panicles of showy, pink flowers—the name *speciosa* actually means "showy." It grows wild in humid forests and along forested waterways. The queen's crepe myrtle has a dense crown that loses its leaves in the cooler winter months. The tree flowers in summer.

Identification: The unusual bark is pale gray and often flakes off in large chunks, leaving concave indentations and resulting in the trunk having a yellowish mottling. The leaves have prominent veining and may have scalloped margins. They are 7in (18cm) long and 2¾in (7cm) wide, dark green and rough. The flowers form in erect panicles up to 24in (60cm) tall on the top of the tree. Each individual flower is 3in (8cm) across and has six crinkled, pink petals, which fade to purple as they mature. The small fruit sits in a star-shaped structure formed by the sepals, and the ovoid woody capsule has six sections. Each section of the fruit contains a winged seed.

Distribution: India, Sri Lanka, Burma, southern China and southeast Asia. U.S.A. hardiness zones 10–11.
Height: 80ft (24m)
Shape: Spreading and round
Deciduous
Pollinated: Insect
Leaf shape: Elliptic

Above left: Leaves turn bright red before dropping.

Left: Cultivated forms have flowers in different hues.

Tulip-wood

Physocalymma scaberrima

This tree is the only species in its genus, and it is native to the tropical regions of northern South America. The timber is used mainly for making furniture. It is fairly straight-grained, moderately hard, and easy to work, and becomes smooth and lustrous when polished. It is also durable, though may be subject to insect attack. Characteristic of the species are the oil or resin canals that are present both in the bark and in the wood. The oil is used in perfumery.

Identification: It is tall, but has rather a slender, columnar trunk. There are no branches until about 16½ft (5m) from the base, and then they continue, wide-spreading, to the top of the tree. The bark is pinkish-brown and scaly, the sapwood is pinkish-brown or yellowish and the heartwood purplish-red or dark brown. The leaves are rough, leathery, shiny and up to 4in (10cm) in length. The showy flowers, with a dark purple calyx and a bright pink corolla, are arranged in clusters.

Far right: The beautiful flowers of this tree produce sweet nectar which attracts forest birds.

Right: The buds appear at the end of the twigs.

Distribution: Northern South America.
Height: 80ft (25m)
Shape: Crown spreading
Evergreen
Pollinated: Bird
Leaf shape: Obovate

RED MANGROVE FAMILY

Many of the trees and shrubs in the Rhizophoraceae family are mangroves, living in brackish and salty water along tropical coasts. Several allow their seeds to germinate while still attached to the branches, giving them a better chance of getting established inbetween the tides. Leaf shape and size varies considerably, but flowers are star-shaped, and either solitary or produced in groups in the axils.

Red Mangrove

Rhizophora mangle

Distribution: Coastal tropical America and West Africa.
Height: 100ft (30m)
Shape: Domed or irregular
Evergreen
Pollinated: Wind or self
Leaf shape: Elliptic

Right: The thick, waxy leaves are well adapted to harsh coastal conditions.

The red mangrove is an incredibly important species ecologically. Able to withstand saline conditions, it grows right down to the low tide mark, forming dense, often storm-proof thickets along coastlines and providing shelter for young fish and nesting sites for birds. The red mangrove is able to survive where it does by excreting excess salt, and by having pores on its roots that allow gaseous exchange when exposed to the air. This species is incredibly slow-growing and forms distinctive, branching stilt roots. As time passes, the main trunk dies until eventually the aerial roots alone support the plant.

Identification: The bark is pinkish-red when young and gray when mature. The leaves sit opposite one another on the branch, and are deep green with a prominent paler midrib. Thick, succulent and glossy, they may be up to 8in (20cm) long. The flowers appear throughout the year in groups in the axils. They are cream, ¾in (2cm) wide and have four thick petals. The fruit is 1in (2.5cm) long, brown and contains a single seed. The seedling may grow to 12in (30cm) before dropping from the tree.

Goatwood

Cassipourea guianensis

While most mangrove species inhabit coastal saltmarshes and swamps, goatwood prefers damp forests, from sealevel up to about 3,000ft (915m). It is widespread, but not always common on many of the Caribbean islands, or in parts of Central America and northern South America. This shrub or small tree has dark gray bark and horizontal branches. Its wood is fairly hard and is used for poles, posts, and carpentry.

Identification: The hairless leaves are opposite, spreading in two rows, with thin blades, shiny green above and yellow-green beneath. The flowers develop at the leaf bases, and are small and bell-shaped, with white petals. Flowering is throughout the year, and irregular. The fruit is berry-like with three to four cells and the seed has a yellow covering.

Below: The fruit in the axils.

Distribution: Greater and Lesser Antilles, Trinidad; Mexico, through Central America (not El Salvador), to Guyana, Brazil, Peru and Ecuador.
Height: 20ft (6m)
Shape: Variable
Evergreen
Pollinated: Wind and insect
Leaf shape: Elliptic to ovate

Left: The small flowers of goatwood are inconspicuous, at the bases of the leaf stalks.

SOAPBERRY FAMILY

The Sapindaceae family contains a large number of very diverse but mostly tropical trees, shrubs and climbers. The leaves may be simple, pinnate, bipinnate or even tripinnate. The small flowers, normally with three to five petals, form in branched clusters or in bunches with each flower on an individual stem. The fruit is also highly variable but is always composed of three sections.

Ackee

Blighia sapida

The tasty fruit of the ackee is a popular ingredient in West Indian cooking, but extreme care must be exercised when preparing it. The thick, creamy flesh can be fried or boiled as a vegetable, but it contains highly poisonous seeds, which must be removed before cooking.

Identification: The tree is fast-growing and forms a handsome, dense crown. The trunk is short and thick with gray bark. The leaves consist of three to ten egg-shaped to oblong leaflets, each of which is glossy, mid-green above and paler below, 6–12in (15–30cm) long with prominent veining. The scented flowers are hairy, white and hang from the tree. The smooth-skinned fruit is spherical to pear-shaped, and triangular with rounded corners in cross-section. When ripe, it turns rosy pink, apricot, or red and measures 3–4in (7.5–10cm) long. The fruit divides into three sections, each containing a shiny black seed surrounded by white flesh.

Distribution: West Africa. Introduced to the Caribbean islands and Florida.
Height: 50ft (15m)
Shape: Rounded
Evergreen
Pollinated: Insect
Leaf shape: Pinnate

Left: The fruit is deadly both before ripening and soon after bursting open.

Guayo

Talisia oliviformis

A tree of medium height that grows wild in wooded ravines or thickets at low altitudes, and is often planted near dwellings. It is one of 40 species of *Talisia*, all of which are confined to the tropical regions of America. It is best known and cultivated for its fruit, which is rounded and about 1in (2.5cm) across, with a firm texture and sage-green rind. It becomes yellowish on maturity and encloses a considerable amount of orange-red pulp, which has an agreeably acid flavor.

Identification: The leaves are composed of four leaflets, arranged in opposite pairs, thin and leathery, and 2–4⅔in (5–12cm) in length. The inflorescences spring from the axils of the leaves, and are often clustered at the ends of the branches. They are usually small, shorter than the leaves, and densely hairy. The tiny flowers, only ⅛in (3–4mm) long, have white petals fringed with hairs.

Distribution: Mexico, Guatemala, Honduras, Colombia and Venezuela.
Height: 60ft (18m)
Shape: Crown spreading
Evergreen
Pollinated: Insect
Leaf shape: Elliptic to lanceolate-oblong

Left: The fruit is eaten fresh and made into juice and jam, and the seeds are eaten roasted.

Guara

Candlewood-tree *Cupania americana*

In the wild this medium-size tree grows typically on moist sites near the coast, or in forests along rivers. Because of its broadly spreading crown and large leaves it is also sometimes planted as a shade tree. The light brown wood is subject to attack by termites. It is however, used for posts, poles, general construction, and in shipbuilding. The leaves and also the seeds are said to possess medicinal properties, and the flowers attract insects, including honeybees.

Identification: In young trees the gray bark is fairly smooth, but with age this becomes rough and broken into plates. The stout, hairy twigs bear alternate leaves. They are pinnate, with up to eight large leaflets, which are rounded and with a notch at the tip, with wavy, toothed margins. On the underside they are covered in dense, soft hairs, and above are shiny, with hairy veins. The small, white flowers are arranged in branched clusters, and develop into round, reddish-brown seed capsules, opening in three parts to reveal the shiny black seeds.

Right: The leaves are a characteristic shape, with large, rounded leaflets, notched at the tip.

Distribution: Greater and Lesser Antilles, Barbados, Trinidad and Tobago, Venezuela and Colombia.
Height: 50ft (15m)
Shape: Rounded crown
Evergreen
Pollinated: Insect
Leaf shape: Pinnate

Soapberry

Sapindus saponaria

A small to medium-size tree, that grows wild or is cultivated in many regions, including tropical areas in the Old World. The yellow or light brown wood is hard and heavy, and is used for posts and in carpentry. The common name refers to the fruit being used as a substitute for soap. Since the fleshy part is up to 30 percent saponin, it produces abundant suds when placed in water. A medicinal oil can be extracted from the seed, and the roots and leaves are used in home medicines. It is also useful as a honey plant and as a shade tree.

Identification: The trunk grows to more than 12in (30cm) in diameter, and is covered with light gray or brown bark, fairly smooth though warty at first, becoming finely fissured and scaly with age. The stout twigs have pores which appear as raised, reddish-brown dots. They bear alternate leaves 8–16in (20–40cm) long, composed of three to six pairs of stalkless leaflets, 6in (15cm) long and 2¾in (7cm) broad, with sometimes a single terminal one, and a characteristic winged stalk. The male flowers are produced in vast quantities, raining down and littering the ground beneath. The shiny brown globular fruits contain a yellow, sticky, poisonous flesh.

Distribution: California and Florida, throughout Central America and the West Indies, to Peru, Brazil, and south to Paraguay and Argentina.
Height: 60ft (18m)
Shape: Crown broad
Evergreen
Pollinated: Insect
Leaf shape: Pinnate, with elliptic-lanceolate leaflets

Center left: The seeds can be used whole as necklace beads and, when crushed, as a fish poison or insecticide.

Left: The tiny flowers have a feathery appearance.

CASHEW FAMILY

The Anacardiaceae family includes a number of economically important tropical trees. It also contains shrubs and some temperate plants. Many members of the family have resinous bark and poisonous leaves with a strong odor. Leaves are pinnate or simple and arranged alternately or in whorls. Flowers are five-petaled stars, held in branched clusters, while the fruit has firm flesh surrounding a single seed.

Mango

Mangifera indica

Distribution: India to Malaysia. Introduced into Florida and Brazil.
Height: 98ft (30m)
Shape: Domed
Evergreen
Pollinated: Insect
Leaf shape: Lanceolate

Right: The fruit varies greatly in shape, size and color.

The mango is thought to have been cultivated for more than 4,000 years. Mangoes are most widely grown in India, where legends surround the tree, and numerous varieties have been developed. The genus name comes from a mixture of Hindi and Latin; "mango" is the original Hindi name for the tree and *fera* is the Latin verb "to bear." The fruit of the mango tree is juicy.

Identification: The trunk is buttressed when mature and carries a dense crown. The drooping leaves are red when young, and deep green and glossy when mature. The flowers appear at the ends of twigs in late winter in loose, branched clusters. Each cluster contains thousands of tiny blossoms, which may be pink, yellow, green, brown or white.

Right: The leaves reach up to 12in (30cm) long.

Cashew Nut

Anacardium occidentale

The tasty, kidney-shaped cashew nut is produced individually inside a fleshy husk. The husk contains an extremely acrid, resinous sap, which can burn human skin. Once the husk is removed, the nuts are roasted, explaining their relatively high price.

The stem from which the nut hangs swells into a 4in- (10cm-) long, fleshy, pear-shaped organ, which is red when ripe. Called the "cashew apple," this can also be eaten.

The cashew nut tree is fast growing and untidy-looking, and can bear fruit from a young age. The cashew tree favors areas with long, hot dry seasons.

Identification: The bark is light gray to brown. The smooth, leathery leaves are 6in (15cm) long, mid-green and blunt-ended or notched at the tip. The tiny yellow flowers occur early in the wet season in erect, branched clusters at the ends of twigs and branches. They are fragrant at night, and fade to pink when mature. The fruit, which contains a single nut, is gray or brown and 1½in (4cm) long.

Distribution: West Indies and tropical America.
Height: 33ft (10m)
Shape: Spreading, irregular
Evergreen
Pollinated: Insect
Leaf shape: Oval-obovate

Right: The cashew apple grows above the nut. It is eaten raw and is used in a fermented drink.

Brazilian Peppercorn Tree

Christmas berry tree *Schinus terebinthifolius*

All parts of this tree have a spicy scent, and may cause irritation if they come into contact with the skin. The small, pink to red fruit is the pink peppercorn which is often mixed with green and black peppercorns for taste and decorative effect. The fruit appears at Christmas time, giving the species its other common name, the Christmas berry tree. The tree is fast growing and forms a dense crown of brittle branches, which may naturally ooze sap. It grows readily from seed and has become naturalized in many parts of the world, including Hawaii and Florida, where it is now an invasive weed.

Identification: The leaves are 4–7in (10–18cm) long, dark green and divided into seven blunt-ended, elliptical leaflets (three pairs and one terminal). Each leaflet is 1–2in (2.5–5cm) long and has pale veins. The tiny white or greenish-white flowers form in dense, erect, branched clusters 2–6in (5–15cm) long. The fruit is spherical and ¼in (5mm) across.

Distribution: Tropical Central and South America.
Height: 30ft (9m)
Shape: Rounded
Evergreen
Pollinated: Insect
Leaf shape: Pinnate

Left: The pink "peppercorn" fruit is produced in abundance. It does not have a peppery flavor, rather a sweet, subtle taste, but looks very similar to peppercorns.

OTHER SPECIES OF NOTE
Pepper Tree *Schinus molle*
Native to the deserts of Peru's Andean region, this tree thrives in sandy, dry places in tropical and temperate regions, and may become a pest. It grows quickly to 50ft (15m) tall and has a rounded crown, graceful weeping branches and fine blue-green, pinnate foliage. The small, pink fruit may be substituted for peppercorns.

Hog Plum *Spondias mombin*
This handsome tree occurs wild in rainforest areas of the West Indies, Central America and northern South America. The orange to yellow fruit forms in clusters and tastes acidic, often with an unpleasant flavor similar to the smell of paint thinner. The tree has thick, fissured, pale cinnamon bark on a heavy trunk and a spreading crown of light green, pinnate foliage.

Yellow Mombin *Spondias dulcis*
This tree reaches just 30ft (9m) tall and may grow as a large, sprawling shrub. It comes from tropical America and the West Indies and has 4–10in- (10–25cm-) long, light green, pinnate leaves. The branched clusters of tiny pink or purple flowers appear in spring and produce small, yellow, orange, red or purple fruit with an acidic, plum-like flavor.

Purple Mombin

Purple-plum *Spondias purpurea*

This is a small tree, with edible fruit that resembles small plums in both appearance and flavor. It is widely distributed in tropical America, and commonly planted in southern Florida, and also throughout most of the Caribbean. The fruit can be eaten raw, or cooked, or incorporated into wine or other alcoholic drinks. In some parts of Central America, including Mexico, this is one of the major fruits. It is a handsome tree, with spreading branches and clusters of pink or red flowers.

Distribution: Mexico, Peru, Brazil; naturalized through the West Indies; introduced to Florida and parts of the Old World tropics.
Height: 30ft (9m)
Shape: Spreading
Deciduous
Pollinated: Insect
Leaf shape: Pinnate

Below: The small, plum-like fruit is edible, but has a rather sour taste.

Identification: The bark is gray or brown and smooth, turning rougher on older wood, and the branches are large, but somewhat brittle. The alternate leaves are pinnate and have up to 25 thin, yellowish-green leaflets. Flowers develop in clusters (panicles), and are small, five-lobed and red or pink.

MAHOGANY FAMILY

This family includes many important lumber trees, some with sweetly scented wood. It also contains trees and shrubs with edible fruit or valuable seeds. The Meliaceae are tropical or subtropical trees and shrubs with pinnate or bipinnate leaves. The flowers have four or five petals and appear in branched clusters. The leathery-skinned fruit often contains seeds with wings.

Mahogany

Swietenia mahagoni

Distribution: Central America and West Indies.
Height: 66ft (20m)
Shape: Rounded
Evergreen
Pollinated: Insect
Leaf shape: Pinnate

This very slow-growing, long-lived tree is famous for its hard, red, glowing lumber, which polishes to a high shine. It has been a favorite choice of cabinetmakers ever since it was first discovered in the seventeenth century, and is now threatened in the wild due to over-collection. In some places it is grown as a shade or avenue tree as it spreads out when fully mature. It is cultivated throughout the tropics and flourishes in drier climates, such as that of India.

Identification: The buttressed trunk has dark, reddish-brown, scaly bark and carries a crown that becomes open when the tree reaches maturity. The leaves have five to seven pairs of 2¾in- (7cm-) long, ovate to sickle-shaped, dark green leaflets. The insignificant flowers are greenish-yellow or white, scented and form in branched clusters from the leaf axils in spring and summer.

Right: The fruit is an oval, woody capsule, 4in (10cm) across, and contains 45–55 winged seeds.

Chinaberry

Bead tree *Melia azedarach*

In India this tree is venerated and grown for its pretty, honey-scented flowers, which are used as temple offerings. It is often called the "bead tree," as its poisonous seeds have a hole through them, making them ideal for threading. It was once grown in Italy specifically for the making of rosaries. The chinaberry is a short-lived tree that grows quickly and easily in dry tropical and subtropical areas. In some places it is considered a weed.

Identification: The trunk has smooth, thin, dark purplish or grayish-brown bark and carries brittle branches crowded with 20in- (50cm-) long leaves. The leaves have three to five pairs of pinnae, each with three to five pairs of leaflets. The leaflets are mid- to light green, ovate and have toothed margins. The flowers appear in large, branched clusters, which sprout from the leaf axils in spring. Each flower is pale pink with a dark purple tube at the center and up to ¾in (2cm) wide. The abundant fruit appears in the fall; it is oval, pale yellow or orange and 1in (2.5cm) long.

Distribution: From Iraq to Japan down to Australia. Naturalized in the southeastern U.S.A.
Height: 40ft (12m)
Shape: Spreading
Deciduous
Pollinated: Bee
Leaf shape: Bipinnate or tripinnate

Right: Toothed leaves.

Left: The chinaberry may produce its fragrant flowers all year round, and from a very young age.

American Muskwood

Trompillo *Guarea trichilioides*

One of the commonest trees in moist forests of Puerto Rico, where it is also found in coffee plantations. It has been introduced to southern Florida, where it serves as a useful shade tree. It regenerates quickly and also withstands the shade of taller trees. The timber has a pretty grain and takes polish well, and is used for furniture, as well as for general building.

Right: The seed capsules (above right) grow close to the flower clusters.

Identification: A large tree with a dense crown, and large leaves with up to 20 dark green, rather glossy leaflets. The bark is brown or reddish and rough, with longitudinal fissures. The lateral flower clusters (panicles) consist of many, small, fragrant greenish-white flowers, maturing into red-brown, followed by rounded seed capsules which dangle rather like bunches of grapes.

Distribution: Cuba, Hispaniola, Trinidad, Costa Rica, Panama, Brazil and Argentina. Introduced to Florida.
Height: 75ft (23m)
Shape: Spreading
Evergreen
Pollinated: Insect
Leaf shape: Pinnate

OTHER SPECIES OF NOTE

Honduran Mahogany
Swietenia macrophylla
Once an important timber tree in Central and South America, the Honduran mahogany is incredibly valuable. It grows in lowland rainforests but huge areas have now been depleted due to over-collection. Unfortunately, this species is difficult to establish in plantations, due to pests. It grows with a straight, buttressed trunk to 150ft (45m) tall and has rough, brown bark. The pinnate leaves are 15in (38cm) long and have up to six pairs of leaflets. The flowers are insignificant, but the woody, brown fruit is 6in (15cm) across and hangs on 12in (30cm) stems.

Broomstick *Trichilia hirta*
This is a small deciduous tree with a dense rounded crown, and alternate, pinnate leaves. It grows on the islands of the Caribbean and in Mexico, Ecuador, Peru, Brazil and Venezuela, and like many tropical species has also been introduced to Florida, where it provides both shade and honey. In Venezuela the wood was used for making paddles and oars. It grows to about 50ft (15m), and the trunk has rough, furrowed bark. The alternate, pinnate leaves are shiny and green, and slightly hairy beneath. The fragrant flowers are small and greenish-white, in narrow clusters (panicles) towards the ends of the twigs, and the fruits are rounded and greenish-brown.

Cigar Box Cedar

Jamaican cedar *Cedrela mexicana*

This tree produces a mahogany-like timber, which is used for cabinets and cigar boxes. The wood is light reddish brown, aromatic and termite-resistant. The cigar box cedar is sometimes called the Jamaican or Honduran cedar, and has been over-exploited in its native forests. The genus name *Cedrela* was given because of the similarity of the wood's scent to that of true cedars, *Cedrus*. The cigar box tree is fast growing, has brittle branches and forms an untidy, thin, open crown.

Identification: The trunk has pale brown bark and reaches 36in (90cm) wide. The leaves are up to 24in (60cm) long and divided into between six and eight pairs of leaflets. Each leaflet is oblong to elliptic, smooth, pale green and up to 4½in (12cm) long. The small, white flowers appear at the ends of twigs and branches in pyramidal branched clusters 12in (30cm) long. The fruit is hard, brown, oblong, 1¾in- (4.5cm-) long pods, which split open to release winged seeds.

Distribution: West Indies and Central and South America.
Height: 115ft (35m)
Shape: Narrow
Evergreen
Pollinated: Insect
Leaf shape: Pinnate

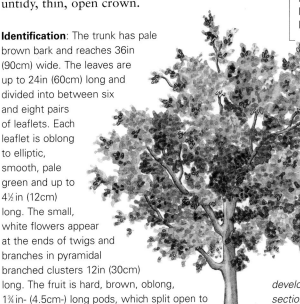

Above: The woody fruit takes nine to ten months to develop. When ripe it splits into five sections revealing a woody, central core and numerous winged seeds.

CITRUS FAMILY

Many of these plants are strongly scented, often with a citrus-like aroma, and yield valuable oils. The oils are found in translucent glands, often visible in the flowers, fruit, leaves and bark. The Rutaceae family is comprised mostly of trees and shrubs, a number of which have thorns, but throughout the family botanical features are highly variable.

Satinwood

Yellowheart *Zanthoxylum flavum*

A medium-size tree found mainly in the Caribbean region, and highly valued for its decorative wood, which has a satiny sheen, and is used for making fine furniture, veneers and paneling. Exploitation for its timber has sadly diminished stocks, to the point where native stands are increasingly rare. It is, however, also planted for shade, and as a honey source.

Below: The leaves are arranged opposite on the twig. The flowers and fruit grow in clusters.

Identification: The bark of this tree is thin and gray and rather smooth, and the inner bark has a distinct citrus taste. The young twigs are hairy, and the branched flower clusters (panicles) are made up of small, yellowish, five-lobed, fragrant flowers. Male and female flowers are borne on separate trees (the tree is dioecious). The fruit is a small, stalked pod containing a single shiny black seed.

Distribution: Bermuda, Bahamas, Cuba, Hispaniola, Puerto Rico, Lesser Antilles, Jamaica. Also reported from Florida Keys, where it is very rare and restricted to just a handful of locations.
Height: 50ft (15m)
Shape: Spreading
Evergreen
Pollinated: Insect
Leaf shape: Pinnate

Lime

Citrus aurantifolia

This familiar citrus tree is best known for its small, green fruit which is widely used in flavoring, and for making drinks, and in cooking, and also for dyeing and in medicine. Oil from the rind and seeds is also used for making soap. Lime fruit is sharp, but sweeter than lemon. Although it is native to the East Indies, it was introduced to the New World (especially the Caribbean) more than 400 years ago, and this is now the main area of production, along with southern Florida. The fruit is picked and shipped young, and travels well. The flowers are attractive to honeybees.

Distribution: East Indies (native); introduced in Mexico, West Indies, Florida and parts of South America.
Height: 20ft (6m)
Shape: Variable
Evergreen
Pollinated: Insect
Leaf shape: Elliptic

Identification: A small spiny, aromatic tree or shrub with shiny, leathery green leaves and small (compared with other citrus fruits) green fruits, turning yellowish when fully ripe. The whitish flowers are softly fragrant, and each has four or five petals.

Left: The lime fruit is similar to a lemon, but smaller and with a greener coloring.

LIGNUM VITAE AND INCENSE-TREE FAMILIES

The lignum vitae family (Zygophyllaceae) contains about 285 species of mostly tropical trees, shrubs and herbs, many found in arid areas. Their stems are often swollen at the nodes. The 540 species of the incense-tree family (Burseraceae) are tropical trees or shrubs, mostly from the Americas, or found in northeast Africa. Their bark is usually rich in resins.

Lignum Vitae

Guaiacum officinale

The wood of this pretty, extremely slow-growing tree has outstanding characteristics. It is possibly the heaviest wood in the world, weighing 67lb per cu ft (1,307kg per cu m). It even sinks in water. It is the hardest wood used commercially and has a high content of oily resin. The latter gives a good level of lubrication, lending the wood resistance to rot, termites, fungus, borers and harsh chemicals. It is particularly favored for use on boats, where bearings of this wood will outlive metal. The name *lignum vitae* translates as "wood of life"; in sixteenth-century Europe the tree was thought to have great healing properties. Due to over-harvesting these trees are now facing a very high risk of extinction in the wild.

Identification: The short trunk has dark gray bark and may ooze greenish resin. The crown is dense. The 4in- (10cm-) long leaves are composed of four to six obovate, blunt-ended, 1in- (2.5cm-) long leathery leaflets. The beautiful, fragrant, felty flowers appear twice a year, and are 1in (2.5cm) across with four or five petals. The fruit is often seen with the flowers, and is yellow or orange, heart-shaped with a moist leathery skin and 1in (2.5cm) across.

Distribution: West Indies, Panama, Colombia and Venezuela.
Height: 30ft (9m)
Shape: Spreading
Evergreen
Pollinated: Insect
Leaf shape: Pinnate

Far left: The deep blue flowers fade to silvery blue.

Left: The colorful fruit holds up to five hard, oblong seeds.

Incense Tree

Gumbo-limbo *Bursera simaruba*

A fine, spreading tree with aromatic foliage and a smooth, coppery bark which characteristically peels off in flakes, revealing the newer bark beneath, which is greenish-brown. The bark exudes a gray resin which smells of paint thinner. This resin is used in making glue, varnish, and incense. It has also been used as a traditional medicine. An attractive tree, it is often planted along roads or as an ornamental, notably in Florida. The lumber is used for light carpentry, plywood and matches.

Identification: A thick-trunked tree with sturdy, spreading branches. The small, whitish or yellow-green flowers are five-lobed and arranged in terminal or lateral clusters (panicles). The angled, pointed fruit splits into three when ripe, to release the pale seeds.

Right: The leaves, which also smell when crushed, are pinnate, and about 8in (20cm) long.

Left: The small flowers develop into pointed fruits.

Distribution: Southern Florida, West Indies from Bahamas and Cuba to Trinidad and Tobago; Mexico to Colombia, Venezuela, Guyana.
Height: 40ft (12m)
Shape: Spreading
Deciduous
Pollinated: Insect
Leaf shape: Pinnate

BUTTONWOOD FAMILY

The Combretaceae family includes trees, climbers and shrubs. Its members vary significantly and have few consistent features. Many of the trees have large yet narrow buttresses and yellow inner bark, and the flowers usually have greatly reduced petals and protruding anthers. The fruit, which is dry, is dispersed by water or wind, and has wing-like structures protruding from it.

White Buttonwood

White-mangrove *Laguncularia racemosa*

Distribution: Coasts of tropical America, from Mexico to Ecuador, Peru, and Brazil, southern Florida, Bermuda, and most of West Indies; also in west Africa.
Height: 40ft (12m)
Shape: Variable
Evergreen
Pollinated: Insect
Leaf shape: Elliptic

Like other mangroves, this tree grows mainly in salt or brackish water on muddy and silty shorelines. It is fast growing, often reaching maturity and flowering in less than two years. It also sprouts vigorously after cutting, and trees may therefore develop rather tangled shapes. The strong, heavy timber is used for making tool handles, posts, and in general construction. The fleshy, rapidly germinating fruit floats when it falls into water, and this is its main means of dispersal.

Left: Like those of many species growing in salty conditions, the leaves are tough and leathery.

Identification: The bark of this mangrove is gray-brown and rough, with a paler, bitter inner bark. The leaves are opposite, leathery and rounded, being yellow-green, with reddish stalks. The pale, bell-shaped flowers develop in clusters (panicles), and are fragrant. The rather fleshy fruit is green, turning brown when ripe, and each one has a single large seed.

Tropical Almond

Terminalia catappa

The nuts of this tree are incredibly hard and popular with humans and animals. The tree is highly tolerant of salt, and is often grown along beaches to provide shade and help stabilize the soil. Its reddish timber is used for boat construction. The tropical almond is a good-looking tree with horizontal tiers of foliage that spread out to make it wider than it is tall. It thrives in tropical cities throughout the U.S.A.

Distribution: Tropical coastal Asia.
Height: 80ft (24m)
Shape: Spreading
Deciduous
Pollinated: Insect
Leaf shape: Obovate

Identification: The trunk is short and dark, and the smooth, glossy leaves cluster towards the branch tips. The leaves are deep green turning bright orange, red or purple before dropping at any time of year. The flowers occur mostly in summer on 9in- (23cm-) long spikes, produced near the branch tips. The fruit is greenish-yellow or red, almond shaped and 2in (5cm) long.

Above: The inconspicuous but fragrant flowers are greenish-white to cream.

Left and right: Leaves are leathery and 12in (30cm) long.

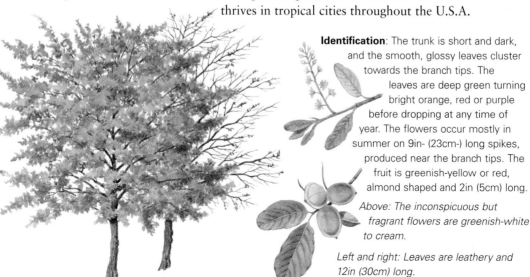

IVY FAMILY

*The ivy family, Araliaceae, spans temperate and tropical regions and encompasses trees, shrubs, climbers
and herbs. Some are prickly, and in tropical countries may be epiphytic or semi-epiphytic. They are
grown for their foliage yet often have an unpleasant scent. Their alternate leaves vary immensely, whereas
flowers are more distinctive, small and usually in umbels. The fruit is often a small, black berry.*

Matchwood

Morototo *Didymopanax (Schefflera) morototoni*

A distinctive, rather umbrella-
shaped tall tree of wet tropical
forests, it has a smooth, gray,
unbranched trunk topped by
a crown of radiating branches
bearing large, palmately
compound leaves. Although the wood is
used for building, it is susceptible to termite attack,
and is therefore more suitable for crates, plywood,
or matchsticks.

Identification: The bark bears faint horizontal markings, and
the inner bark has a distinctive spicy flavor. Each leaf has
a long, strong stalk and has usually 10 or 11 oblong leaflets,
each about 12in (30cm) in length. The leaves are alternate
and grow close together. The flowers, which have white,
somewhat pointed, petals, grow in broad, umbel-like
panicles. The fruit is a flattened berry, containing a pair
of brown, flat seeds.

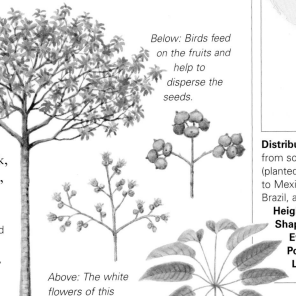

*Below: Birds feed
on the fruits and
help to
disperse the
seeds.*

Distribution: Widespread
from southern Florida
(planted) through West Indies
to Mexico, Guyana, Bolivia,
Brazil, and Argentina.
Height: 60ft (18m)
Shape: Spreading
Evergreen
Pollinated: Insect
Leaf Shape: Linear

*Above: The white
flowers of this
tree grow in
spreading clusters.*

*Left: The leaves are large
and long-stalked, with
spreading leaflets.*

Pollo

Angelica tree *Dendropanax arboreus*

Distribution: Widespread
from southern Florida
(planted) through West Indies
to Mexico, Colombia,
Venezuela, Peru, and Bolivia.
Height: 40ft (12m)
Shape: Spreading
Evergreen
Pollinated: Insect
Leaf Shape: Ovate

This widespread, medium-size tree is
typically found in lower
mountain tropical forests,
but is also planted,
sometimes to give shade
to crops of coffee. In
some areas the leaves and
roots have been used in
traditional medicine.
Extracts have been
found to be cytotoxic,
and this species is being tested
for anti-cancer compounds. The
flowers are attractive
to honeybees and
other insects.

Identification: The bark is gray,
and often warty, and the
green twigs turn gray
with age. The leaves are
alternate, and have
long, green stalks
with blades to 8in
(20cm) long and
3½in (9cm) in
width. The flowers
are tiny, with yellow
petals, in tight clusters
(a raceme of umbels).
The fruit, a rounded, fleshy
berry, is pale green at first,
gradually ripening
to black.

*Right: The flowers are
small and in dense
clusters.*

*Left: The seeds are mainly
dispersed by birds.*

FRANGIPANI FAMILY

This family is renowned for its toxic properties. Plants contain a large quantity of poisonous, milky latex, which, in some species, is of value to humans. The family is also valuable for its contribution to ornamental horticulture. Most of the Apocynaceae are tropical, and many are shrubs. The simple leaves are usually opposite, the five-petaled flowers are funnel-shaped and the fruit is usually dry and in pairs.

Frangipani

Plumeria rubra

The legendary frangipani is regarded as one of the world's most beautifully scented flowers. It is thought a botanist named Frangipani first distilled the perfume in the sixteenth century, hence the common name. The trees are found growing in temple grounds of Buddhists, Hindus and even Muslims, and the flowers are used as offerings. In Hawaii garlands made of these flowers are used on special occasions, and to greet visitors. Although the flowers may be white, red, yellow or pink, the form *P. rubra* f. *acutifolia* with white flowers with golden centers is most widely planted.

Identification: The fleshy round stems are rubbery and green when young, woody and pale gray when mature. Branching is sparse and candelabra-like. The thick, 12in- (30cm-) long leaves with paler midribs cluster at the branch tips. The 3in- (8cm-) wide twisted flowers form in terminal clusters. The fruit grows in pairs of 6in- (15cm-) long leathery pods.

Distribution: Southern Mexico to Panama.
Height: 26ft (8m)
Shape: Domed
Semi-evergreen
Pollinated: Insect and self
Leaf shape: Elliptic-obovate

Above left: The leaves are long and tapering.

Left: Each funnel-shaped flower has five waxy petals and an intoxicating perfume.

West Indian Jasmine

Milk tree *Plumeria alba*

This small tree gets one of its common names from the abundant milky juice that exudes when it is cut. It is found wild only on some of the islands of the West Indies, and does not appear to be much cultivated, despite its attractive appearance. The white, or cream species that is often grown, is in fact a color variant of *P. rubra*. The light brown wood is hard, heavy, and tough. It is usually used only as fuel, but where the trunk is of sufficient size it can be useful for carpentry.

Identification: The trunk rarely exceeds 4in (10cm) in diameter, and with only a few branches it often resembles a shrub. The stout, yet soft, rather brittle branches end in a cluster of think, leathery leaves, up to 15in (38cm) long but only about 2in (5cm) wide. They are shiny green above, white and densely hairy beneath, with downturned margins. The flower stalks, up to 8in (20cm) long, bear a flattened cluster of very fragrant, waxy, white flowers. The fruit is about 6in (15cm) long and ½in (1cm) wide, and contain numerous flat, winged seeds.

Distribution: Puerto Rico; Lesser Antilles.
Height: 16½ft (5m)
Shape: Variable
Evergreen
Pollinated: Insect
Leaf shape: Narrow, tapering

Left and right: The flowers can be 2in (5cm) long and broad, and if successfully pollinated they develop into a pair of brown pod-like follicles.

White Frangipani

Plumeria obtusa

One of the most popular frangipanis is this 26ft- (8m-) tall evergreen tree from Mexico and the Caribbean islands. It is endowed with intensely fragrant, pure white blossoms. The fragrant, waxy, flower clusters appear on long stalks between the terminal bunches of leaves. As with other frangipanis, the flowers develop all year round in constantly wet areas, or in the wet season only in monsoon areas. The attractive leaves are dark green, glossy, obovate and 6–12in (15–30cm) long. Dwarfing varieties have been developed to be more shrub-like. Although not seen as often in cultivation as *P. rubra*, it is an attractive shrub or tree.

Identification: The trunk grows to a diameter of about 10in (25cm), and has gray, smooth or slightly furrowed bark. The green twigs, which turn gray as they age, produce abundant milky white latex, which is sometimes irritating to the skin.

Distribution: Mexico (Yucatán), Honduras, Bahamas, Cuba, Hispaniola, Puerto Rico, Jamaica.
Height: 15–40ft (4.5–12m)
Shape: Variable
Evergreen
Pollinated: Insect
Leaf shape: Obovate, notched at tip

Left: Each flower produces two long pods which split open to release many flat, winged seeds.

Palo Rosa *Aspidosperma polyneuron*
This magnificent tree, native to central Brazil, Paraguay, and northeast Argentina, grows to 140ft (42m) tall, with a straight trunk for the first 66–100ft (20–30m), and a diameter of 5ft (1.5m). Its thick bark is ash-gray or slightly reddish, with deep, more or less parallel fissures. This is topped by a crown of twisted branches, that divide repeatedly down to the smallest branchlets. The evergreen leaves are simple, rather leathery, and very variable in shape. The small whitish or yellowish flowers are followed by woody fruit containing numerous winged seeds. The wood is hard, fairly heavy, strong and resistant, and is used for furniture and building.

Quebracho Blanco *Aspidosperma quebracho-blanco*
This tree can grow to about 85ft (25m), and like the previous species it has a straight lower trunk, but in this case branching occurs from about half way up, ending in an irregular conical crown. The leaves are evergreen, lanceolate and spine-tipped. The scented yellowish-white flowers develop in clusters from September to January, and produce gray-green woody capsules, 2¾–4½in (7–12cm) in length, containing numerous roundish seeds. The wood is heavy and hard, and the bark contains tannin and other medicinal substances.

Yellow Oleander

Thevetia peruviana

The sap and fruit are extremely poisonous, and yet the deadly poisonous seeds contain beneficial chemicals that are extracted for use in heart medicines. Curiously the seeds are also thought to be lucky, and are carried as charms or worn as pendants. In addition to the typical yellow flowers, forms exist with white, orange or apricot flowers. In some plants they are pleasantly scented, while others have no scent. Often used as a fast-growing hedge or screen, the foliage gives an unusual, soft appearance.

Distribution: Southeast Mexico, Belize and the West Indies.
Height: 30ft (9m)
Shape: Domed
Evergreen
Pollinated: Insect
Leaf shape: Lanceolate

Above and right: The foliage is evergreen, and the flowers appear all year round.

Identification: The brown trunk is often multistemmed and rarely upright. The bright green, glossy leaves cluster at the tips of the branches forming a dense crown. Each leaf is 4–6in (10–15cm) long. The terminal clusters of a few flowers appear throughout the year. Each flower is tubular-shaped and 3in (8cm) long. The fruit is a rounded, four-sided, 1½in- (4cm-) wide, hard, fleshy pod. When ripe it is black.

POTATO FAMILY

The important potato family, Solanaceae, is very large and contains nearly 3,000 species; it is found worldwide, but especially in South America. It contains trees, shrubs, lianes and herbs, including the familiar potato and tomato. Although parts of certain species may be edible, it's worth stressing that many contain poisons.

Lady-of-the-Night

Brunfelsia americana

This shrub or small tree is very popular with gardeners, chiefly because of its masses of attractive cream flowers, which are some of the most fragrant of the family. The scent develops in the evening, and lasts all through the night, attracting moths. It thrives and flowers best in humid conditions, and the perfume is reported to be detectable from 100ft (30m) away. Flowering is in cycles, with hundreds opening together. Growth is straight, with moderate branching and pruning is unnecessary, making this an ideal garden shrub or tree. In the wild it is found in moist, coastal forests, from sea level to about 2,000ft (600m).

Identification: The alternate leaves are borne on short side twigs, and are shiny above. The flowers are solitary, the large corolla emerging from the bell-shaped calyx as a narrow tube 2in (5cm) in length, with five rounded, spreading lobes about 1½in (4cm) across. The fruit (reputedly poisonous) is round, yellow, and contains brown seeds.

Right: The enormous flowers are a spectacular feature of this tree.

Distribution: Hispaniola, Puerto Rico, Virgin Islands, Lesser Antilles; planted in southern Florida, Colombia and Venezuela.
Height: 15ft (4.5m)
Shape: Variable
Evergreen
Pollinated: Insect
Leaf shape: Elliptic to obovate

Tree Potato

Solanum wrightii

This incredibly fast-growing tree has been recorded at 30ft (9m) high with an equal spread in only two years. Inevitably this cannot last, and trees are said to lose their condition after only four years. The flowers open as deep purple and fade to white over a couple of days. As they are in clusters and appear throughout the year, the tree almost always has a colorful collection of purple, mauve and white flowers. In some gardens it is kept pruned as a shrub; this treatment inhibits flowering but extends the life, and encourages the hairy, ornamental leaves to become huge.

Identification: The soft-wooded, pale gray trunk is often multistemmed. The bright green leaves vary enormously in size depending on the way the plant is grown; as shrubs they can reach 18in (45cm) in length, but as trees they are more normally 10in (25cm) long. Each is deeply incised into angular lobes and covered in coarse hairs. The midrib and main veins carry thorns. The round fruit is 2in (5cm) across, and orange-yellow to brown when ripe. It contains four cavities filled with pulp and flat seeds.

Distribution: Bolivia and adjoining area of tropical Brazil.
Height: 40ft (12m)
Shape: Domed
Evergreen
Pollinated: Insect
Leaf shape: Ovate

Left: The flowers are crumpled up in bud. When open they are 3in (8cm) across and have a cluster of central golden stamens. They have five petals and form in small clusters.

BORAGE FAMILY

The majority of the Boraginaceae family are herbs with just a few trees, shrubs and climbers included. Many of the woody species are tropical. They have simple, hairy leaves, usually alternately arranged and smooth edged. Stems are often covered in stiff hairs, too. The five-petaled flowers are occasionally solitary, but more often in cymes. The fruit has one to four seeds and is usually dry and hard.

Salmwood

Cordia alliadora

This attractive, fast-growing yet long-lived pioneer species is often found on disturbed land within humid and dry regions. It is grown throughout its native range for its quality timber, used in numerous products including veneers, furniture, and boat and housing construction. The flowers are a major source of nectar for beekeeping, producing a thick, pale honey. The crushed leaves have a distinctive onion-like odor. Some trees have hollow, swollen nodes which are inhabited by ants.

Identification: The thin trunk, which may have small buttresses, has smooth, pale gray or brown bark, and carries a thin, open crown. The dark green leaves reach 7in (18cm) and are covered in hairs below. Flowers appear mostly in summer, and a large tree may produce as many as 10 million in one season. They are ½in (1cm) long and in 4–12in- (10–30cm-) long inflorescences. The dry, brown fruit is up to ½in (1cm) long with a parachute formed from the expanded petals.

Distribution: Northern Mexico through to northern Argentina and Paraguay and the islands of Cuba to Trinidad.
Height: 130ft (40m)
Shape: Oblong
Evergreen
Pollinated: Insect
Leaf shape: Elliptic

Left: Trees can flower from as young as two years, although viable seed is only produced from five-year-old trees. In mature specimens, up to one million seeds can be produced annually.

Geiger Tree

Cordia sebestena

The attraction of this tree lies in its virtually continual succession of bright vermilion flowers, and its tolerance of dry conditions and salt-laden air. It is a popular ornamental tree in gardens and streets throughout its native range. It is sometimes also grown as a shrub. In addition, the tree has a number of medicinal uses, particularly in relation to breathing difficulties. The sweet, edible fruit is used in some areas as a remedy for coughs, while the bark, flowers or fruit may be used to make a sugary syrup.

Identification: The trunk is rarely straight and may be multistemmed. Interestingly, the stiff leaves are hairy and rough on the upper surface and smooth below. They are also dark green above and paler below, 6in (15cm) long and may have a slightly toothed margin. The veins are paler than the leaf and depressed on the upper surface. Each flower is funnel-shaped, 1½in (4cm) long and a similar width. The petals are crinkled like crepe, and there are central yellow stamens. The flowers are in terminal clusters and are particularly abundant in the summer. The white fruit is oval and ½in (1cm) long.

Distribution: West Indies and Venezuela.
Height: 26ft (8m)
Shape: Oblong to spreading (variable)
Evergreen
Pollinated: Insect
Leaf shape: Ovate

Left: The clusters of flowers include bisexual and male ones; the male flowers are smaller but occur in a greater numbers.

TEAK FAMILY

This large family contains well-known and useful plants. It is found mostly in the Southern Hemisphere and includes herbs, climbers, shrubs and trees, some of which are aromatic. Verbenaceae often have square-shaped twigs, and flowers with a long tube divided into five petals. The fruit is a hard capsule or fleshy with a hard stone, divided into four sections, each with one seed.

Teak

Tectona grandis

The wonderful hard timber of the teak tree was first taken to Europe in the early 1800s and has been introduced in the U.S.A. It has remained a constantly popular choice for quality furniture production ever since. As a result, the monsoon forests of which it is a native have been stripped of their specimens, and now few wild trees remain. Originally elephants would have been used to shift the timber before it was floated downriver out of the forest. Now, the fast-growing teak is planted in large plantations across its indigenous area.

Identification: The straight trunk carries many tiered branches and has pale gray, soft, fissured, peeling bark. The leaves are of colossal size, up to 32in (80cm) long and 16in (40cm) wide, with undulating margins and prominent veining. They are rough and leathery, mid-green above and covered in soft white hairs below. The tiny cream flowers are found in large panicles 18in (45cm) long in early summer. The fleshy fruit is round, ¾in (2cm) across and purplish-red or brown.

Distribution: Tropical India to Vietnam. Tropical America.
Height: 115ft (35m)
Shape: Oblong
Deciduous
Pollinated: Insect
Leaf shape: Widely elliptical

Right: The old bark peels off in small, thin, oblong pieces, revealing the yellow inner bark.

Left: The flowers appear after the tree has put on its new leaves in the wet season.

Florida Fiddlewood

Citharexylum fruticosum

This small, slender tree or shrub is often planted in gardens, hedgerows or alongside roads as an ornamental, and its fragrant flowers are attractive to honeybees. It is moderately salt-tolerant and is therefore often planted near the shore, where it grows well on sandy soils. Fiddlewood has heavy, close-grained timber, mainly used for rough building and fences, although, as may be guessed from its name, it has been used for musical instruments, including violins.

Right: The showy white flowers appear in the summer months, and provide a striking contrast with the leaves.

Identification: The young twigs have a characteristic four-angled shape. The leaves are opposite, and yellow-green with yellow or orange stalks. The flowers are borne in clusters (racemes), and the individual flowers are small, with a five-lobed white corolla. The fleshy fruit dangles down in tight clusters and is attractive to birds and other wildlife. Flowering and fruiting is throughout the year.

Distribution: Central Florida, south to West Indies; Venezuela to Surinam.
Height: 40ft (12m)
Shape: Variable, slender
Evergreen
Pollinated: Insect
Leaf shape: Elliptic

QUININE FAMILY

This is an important and virtually wholly tropical family of trees, shrubs, climbers and herbaceous plants. A number of the genus Rubiaceae have economic and/or ornamental value. The family is easy to recognize. Leaves always have smooth margins, and are most often arranged as opposites. Flowers are usually tubular with four or five flared petals, and the fruit is usually divided into two sections.

Quinine Tree

Cinchona officinalis

Distribution: Ecuador and Peru.
Height: 33ft (10m)
Shape: Oblong to rounded
Evergreen
Pollinated: Insect and hummingbird
Leaf shape: Ovate-lanceolate

One of the most important medicinal discoveries of all time was the quinine tree. The bark of *Cinchona* plants has provided the antimalarial drug "quinine" since at least 1638, when it cured the Countess of Cinchon in Peru. Commercial plantations were not developed though until the 1800s in India and Asia. After World War II synthetic antimalarial drugs were developed, but due to a build-up of resistance, quinine continues, to some extent, to be used. The trees naturally grow in humid lowland forests.

Identification: There is great variation within each *Cinchona* species, and hybrids are readily produced. The leaves of *C. officinalis* are generally smooth, shiny, mid-green and 3–6in (7.5–15cm) long. The tubular flowers vary from red to pale pink. They are covered in fine, silky hair, are often heavily fragrant, and found in terminal and axillary panicles. The ovoid fruit is ⅝in (1.5cm) long, and splits into two to release numerous winged seeds.

Right: The cinchona bark is usually harvested by either coppicing the trees every six years, or by carefully shaving the bark off two sides of the trunk at any one time, without damaging the cambium.

Genipap

Jagua *Genipa americana*

This widespread tree is frequently planted for shade and ornament, but also for the edible fruit and useful timber. It is also attractive to honeybees. The juice of the young fruit has been used as a dye, notably by Native Americans. The juice has been investigated for its antibiotic properties. The wood has a range of uses: tools, boxes, furniture, veneers, chests, barrels, and shipbuilding. The foliage is eaten by cattle, and the bark, rich in tannin, is used for curing leather.

Identification: A medium-size tree with an upright trunk, and large, dark green, opposite leaves. The flowers are large, five-lobed and pale yellow, in short, terminal clusters. The yellow-brown fruit has sour, edible flesh, sweetening slightly when over-ripe, and contains several flat seeds.

Distribution: Cuba, Hispaniola, Puerto Rico, Lesser Antilles, Trinidad and Tobago; Mexico south to Ecuador, Peru, Bolivia, Brazil, and Argentina.
Height: 60ft (18m)
Shape: Spreading
Deciduous
Pollinated: Insect
Leaf Shape: Elliptic

Far left: The ripe fruit makes tasty preserves, sour refreshing drinks, as well as various alcoholic drinks, when fermented.

JACARANDA FAMILY

Bignoniaceae is one of the more readily recognized families. Its members are native to the tropics and subtropics and include trees, shrubs, a few herbs and many climbing plants. Their funnel-shaped flowers are usually found in clusters and are some of the most flamboyant. Their compound leaves are opposite. The fruit is normally long, splitting into two to release numerous flat, winged seeds.

Candle Tree

Parmentiera cerifera

This tree is grown for the oddity of its fruit which hangs in great abundance from the trunk and branches of mature trees. The fruit has a distinctive apple-like scent and bears a strong resemblance to old-fashioned, hand-dipped candles, which is how the common name came about. In its native habitat the fruit is eaten and in many areas it is used as cattle fodder.

Identification: The tree often has many trunks and may grow as a large shrub. The leaves drop only briefly and consist of three ovate leaflets, each less than ¾ in (2cm) long, and have a winged leaf stem. The waxy flowers appear individually or in groups directly from the trunk and larger branches throughout the year. They are bell-shaped, pale greenish to creamy yellow, up to 2¾ in (7cm) long and open in the evening. The smooth, fleshy, cylindrical fruit is pale yellow, measures up to 24in (60cm) long and appears mostly in the drier months.

Distribution: Panama.
Height: 26ft (8m)
Shape: Rounded
Deciduous
Pollinated: Bat
Leaf shape: Trifoliate

Left: The candle-shape fruit has very waxy skin. Unusually for this family it does not split open.

Far left: The leaves turn yellow when they fall from the trees.

Left: These unusual-looking trees are said to have medicinal properties. They have spread from their cultivated areas and become naturalized in Australia.

Calabash Tree

Crescentia cujete

Distribution: Throughout Central America, northern South America, West Indies and southern Mexico.
Height: 43ft (13m)
Shape: Spreading
Evergreen
Pollinated: Bat
Leaf shape: Obovate

Calabashes are gourds, and were originally used as water carriers, but are now more likely to be seen as musical instruments, cups, ornaments or bags. Calabash maracas still feature in Afro-Caribbean music. The fruit is hollowed out, highly polished and often carved on the outside. To make an hourglass or other shapes, the fruit is tied with string while immature.

Identification: The short trunk has fissured, light gray bark and carries a dense to open crown of heavily foliaged, rarely branched, long, spreading, semi-pendulous branches. The leaves are in clusters of three to five, and they jut out along the length of the branches in an inelegant fashion. Each leaf is dark green, glossy and 4–6in (10–15cm) long. The unpleasantly scented flowers form directly from the trunk and larger branches; they are off-white with purple markings and 2in (5cm) long. The fruit is ovoid or round, brown when ripe and up to 12in (30cm) long.

Right: Calabashes are green while immature, ripening through yellow to brown.

Jacaranda

Jacaranda mimosifolia

Distribution: Paraguay, southern Brazil and northern Argentina.
Height: 50ft (15m)
Shape: Domed
Deciduous
Pollinated: Insect
Leaf shape: Bipinnate

While leafless the clear mauve flowers of the jacaranda cover the crown, creating a unique and unforgettable sight. The flowers fall to form a blue carpet below. In addition, this fast-growing tree has delicate ferny foliage justifying its use as a pot plant and in gardens of humid tropical areas, where it flowers less reliably. This is one of the rare trees commonly called by its botanical name.

Identification: The trunk has gray bark. The airy, well-shaped crown is as wide as the tree is tall. The leaves measure 8–18in (20–45cm) in length and consist of 8–20 pairs of pinnae, each carrying 10–28 pairs of leaflets. Each downy leaflet is bright green, ovate to elliptic and ½in (1cm) long. The dense terminal panicles of 2in- (5cm-) long trumpet-like flowers appear in spring and summer. The fruit is a 2½in- (5cm-) wide, flattened, round to oblong, rich brown, leathery pod containing winged seeds.

Above and right: The jacaranda is a beautiful tree. The fine, fern-like foliage casts delicate shade below.

OTHER SPECIES OF NOTE

Jicara *Crescentia alata*
From southern Mexico through to Costa Rica grows this 30ft (9m) evergreen tree. It has long, thin, stem-like branches and a short trunk. The trees were thought to have Christian significance, as the leaves form the shape of a cross. Each trifoliate leaf is composed of a winged leaf stem, and three leaflets arranged at right angles to one another. The entire leaf is 4½in (12cm) long and dark green. The flowers form in pairs on the trunk and larger branches; they are 2½in (6cm) long, greenish-yellow to brown with purple markings. The round gourd-like fruit reaches 5in (13cm) across.

Cow Okra *Parmentiera aculeata*
A small tree, to 33ft (10m), from secondary forest, in Central America and Mexico. It is grown for the edible fruit, medicinal properties of the roots, shade and ornament. In Australia it has become a weed, posing a threat to the native flora. It may grow with a shrubby, multistemmed habit, and has ascending branches and gray, fissured bark. The trifoliate leaves have thorns at the base and are dark green with paler veins. Leaflets vary in size up to 6in (15cm) long. The flowers emerge directly from the trunk(s) and older branches throughout the year. They are funnel-shaped, greenish-cream with purple markings and 2in (5cm) long.

Yellow Trumpet Flower

Tecoma stans

This fast-growing plant forms a large shrub or small tree. It can be grown as a hedge or screen and is popular in gardens, as it is reliable and flowers over a long period, specially in the spring and fall. If pruned after flowering, the tree is encouraged to produce more flowers. It grows well in arid and semiarid zones, but may cause problems for some people, as the flowers produce a large quantity of pollen.

Identification: This tree is often multistemmed, and the trunks have smooth, light gray to brown bark. The opposite leaves are 8–10in (20–25cm) long and consist of five to eleven leaflets. Each leaflet is 2½–3in (6–8cm) long, lanceolate, light green, smooth, thin and heavily toothed. The 1½in- (4cm-) long flowers are clustered in rounded terminal panicles. The fruit is an 8in- (20cm-) long, leathery, rich brown, thin bean-like pod. It contains the two-winged seeds.

Distribution: West Indies, Mexico, Central America and northern South America including Peru.
Height: 30ft (9m)
Shape: Spreading
Evergreen
Pollinated: Insect
Leaf shape: Pinnate

Above and left: The flowers are an attractive trumpet shape and a beautiful golden yellow.

Right: Leaves are somewhat variable.

Golden Trumpet-tree

Tabebuia chrysantha

Distribution: Mexico to Venezuela.
Height: 100ft (30m)
Shape: Rounded, spreading
Deciduous
Pollinated: Insect
Leaf shape: Compound palmate

Right: Breathtaking in flower, this tree produces a profusion of golden trumpets. In the wild, it grows in forested, riverine and coastal localities and is a feature of secondary forests.

This genus has earned a reputation as being one of the most worthwhile trees for planting in the Americas. There are numerous species to choose from, providing a vast choice of color, and the majority have outstanding displays of flowers over a long period, particularly in the winter months. Many are tolerant of coastal conditions, flooding or dry conditions, and are rarely attacked by pests and diseases. This species has deep yellow flowers in large clusters while it is leafless. Its timber yields a mulberry-color dye, and it is also valued for making furniture, flooring and bowls.

Identification: The tree often has an irregular trunk, and the narrow branches have a zigzagging habit, creating an open haphazard crown. The leaves fall in late winter or spring; they are up to 10in (25cm) across and divided into five hairy, ovate leaflets up to 7in (18cm) long. The trumpet-shape flowers have pink streaks inside, are lightly scented, 3in (8cm) long and appear toward the branch tips from late winter through to summer. The fruit pods are slightly hairy.

White Cedar

Tabebuia heterophylla

This is both a valuable timber tree, and also one of the most beautiful and ornamental of tropical trees. Widespread in forests, it is also popular in parks and gardens where it is notable for its abundant, large pink flowers, which sometimes cover the tree, even before the leaves are fully out, and which carpet the ground beneath when they fall. In areas with a pronounced dry season, leafless trees may burst into full blossom, standing out like beacons in the forest. The timber is fairly hard and strong, and takes a high polish, and is used for furniture and veneers. Several species are known by the name "Pau d'arco." Their inner bark has been used to treat a variety of diseases, from cancer to fungal infections, and a popular herbal remedy is said to stimulate the immune system.

Distribution: Caribbean islands, and naturalized in southern Florida.
Height: 60ft (18m)
Shape: Rather narrow-crowned
Mainly deciduous
Pollinated: Insect
Leaf Shape: Palmate

Identification: The bark is rough, furrowed, and gray-brown. The leaves are opposite, grow to about 12in (30cm) long, and usually have five leaflets. Each flower is tubular and five-lobed, and about 3½in (9cm) long. The fruit is a long, dangling pod containing many light brown seeds.

Right: The large, showy flowers make this one of the most beautiful of flowering ornamental trees.

Above: Tabebuia *species are coming under pressure from collection of their bark for use in herbal remedies.*

Pink Trumpet Tree

Tabebuia rosea

This tree is grown for its stunning floral display and handsome foliage, and as a shade tree for coffee and cocoa throughout the tropics. In areas without a pronounced dry season, flowering is reduced, and the tree may be virtually evergreen. It is also grown for lumber in forestry plantations, and the heavy, durable wood is used in construction and furnituremaking.

Identification: The massive straight trunk has rough, furrowed gray bark, is often buttressed and carries well-spaced branches. Dark green leaves are up to 12in (30cm) across and form from three to five elliptic leaflets of varying size, the largest measuring 6in (15cm) in length. Numerous terminal and axillary inflorescences carry clusters of trumpet-shaped, pale to dark pink to mauve flowers with crinkled petals in spring, and sporadically through the year. The fruit splits to reveal winged seeds attached to a central core.

Distribution: Mexico to Venezuela to Ecuador.
Height: 90ft (27m)
Shape: Oval to cylindrical
Deciduous
Pollinated: Insect
Leaf shape: Compound palmate

Left: Often grown for its timber, this multi-use tree is stunning when in full flower.

Far left: The fruit is a dark brown, straight, round pod.

African Tulip Tree

Spathodea campanulata

This outstanding tree is easy to spot and recognize. It is grown throughout the tropics, including the U.S.A., for its spectacular display of intense orange-red flowers radiating against the dark foliage. A pure yellow form is occasionally seen, too. In some places these fast-growing trees are used to mark land-ownership boundaries. Their soft wood is brittle, often resulting in damage in windy conditions.

Identification: The pale trunk carries only a few thick branches but a dense crown. The 24in (60cm), dark green leaves are composed of 9–21 ovate leaflets, each about 4in (10cm) long. The terminal flowers appear throughout the year, but are more pronounced in the wet season. Domes of tightly packed buds open in succession over many weeks. Each tulip-shaped flower is 4–6in (10–15cm) long, yellow inside, and red outside with a frilly golden edge to the petals and an unusual scent. The smooth, woody pods are 8in long (20cm), 2in (5cm) wide, and split open to release hundreds of winged seeds.

Distribution: Uganda.
Height: 82ft (25m)
Shape: Oblong
Evergreen
Pollinated: Bat
Leaf shape: Pinnate

Left and right: The finger-like flower buds are full of water and when squeezed will squirt water.

PALMS

The palms, Palmae, are monocotyledons. There are 200 genera and 2,650 species, the majority of which come from tropical and subtropical regions where they are a common feature in wild and cultivated areas. Most palms have hard, woody upright stem(s) giving a tree-like appearance. The stem does not branch, is pithy and topped with a crown of readily recognizable fronds.

Broom-palm

Brittle Thatch-palm *Thrinax morrisii*

This small palm grows naturally on limestone hills and cliffs, and also coastal sands, from sea level to about 1,000ft (300m). It is quite decorative and is sometimes planted for ornament. It is slow growing, with a single, slender, gray trunk, topped by a crown of about 20 large fan-like brittle leaves.

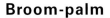

Left: As suggested by the common names, this tree's stiff leaves are sometimes used for thatching and making brooms.

Identification: The leaves are alternate and spreading, with blades to 4ft (1.2m) long. The uppermost leaves are erect, and are surrounded by outer drooping leaves. The leathery leaf segments are mostly forked at the tip. The cluster of flowers develops among the leaves and is 2–6ft (60–180cm) long. The flowers are slightly fragrant. The fruit has a whitish, rather bitter flesh, and a single shiny brown seed.

Distribution: Southern Florida, Bahamas, Cuba, Hispaniola, Puerto Rico, Virgin Islands; also Mexico (Yucatán) and Honduras.
Height: 15ft (4.5m)
Shape: Single-stemmed palm
Evergreen
Pollinated: Wind, insect
Leaf shape: Palmate, fan-shaped

Royal Palm

Roystonea regia

When one sees a dramatic, awe-inspiring avenue of palms in the tropics, it is likely to be *Roystonea*. Their fast, strong-growing nature, straight upright trunk and dense crown of feathery fronds makes them extremely useful for formal planting. Within the landscape gardening industry they are highly regarded and very widely planted, in both tropical and subtropical regions. The growing tip, which is called the palm heart or cabbage, is often eaten as a vegetable, but this involves killing the palm.

Identification: The thick, smooth, pale gray or white trunk has distinctive rings and becomes swollen in the center with age. The huge, arching fronds reaching up to 20ft (6m) in length are composed of numerous deep green, narrow pendulous leaflets, each up to 3ft (1m) long. The small, white flowers are found densely packed on 3ft (1m) branched plumes. The fruit is oval and ⅔in (1.5cm) long.

Below: The Royal palm requires a reliable supply of water to grow well. In the wild it can be found in swampy locations.

Distribution: Cuba.
Height: 98ft (30m)
Shape: Single-stemmed palm
Evergreen
Pollinated: Insect and/or wind
Leaf shape: Pinnate

Right: Ripe fruit is reddish purple.

Below: The elegant leaves arise from a deep green shaft.

Assai

Euterpe edulis

Large stands of this fast-growing graceful palm dominate damp areas of rainforest in the Amazon basin. The fruit is edible and can be used to make a nutritious drink, assai, by soaking in water. The palm hearts are also popular, although their harvest kills the palm. The heart is harvested from the young growing tip when the palm is three-and-a-half years old. The hearts are canned and exported from South America. Other species of *Euterpe* are multistemmed and need not be killed during the harvest of the heart.

Left: Assai is a fast-growing, tolerant palm.

Identification: The smooth trunk is slender, reaching about 6in (15cm) in diameter. It is gray with long, green, clasping leaf bases at the top. The deep green fronds are up to 10ft (3m) long and elegantly arching. Fronds consist of narrow, weeping leaflets up to 36in (90cm) long. The small white flowers on erect panicles produce large quantities of purple or black fruit, ¼in (5mm) across.

Distribution: Amazon basin, Brazil.
Height: 98ft (30m)
Shape: Single-stemmed palm
Evergreen
Pollinated: Insect
Leaf shape: Pinnate

Right: The fruit is popular with forest birds and mammals.

Left: Assai foliage is particularly elegant.

OTHER SPECIES OF NOTE

Ruffle Palm *Aiphanes caryotifolia*
From northern South America, this palm's widespread habitat includes deciduous and rain forests. It is common in disturbed areas, and is cultivated locally for the edible red fruit and seeds. It grows to 30ft (9m), with a single stem clothed in long black spines. The softly arching fronds have roughly tri-angular leaflets with jagged edges.

Carnauba Wax Palm
Copernicia prunifera
From low-lying areas of north-eastern Brazil comes this slow-growing, 40ft (12m), slender palm. The distinctive stem is clothed on the lower half only with old leaf bases. The tough carnauba wax found on the lower leaf surfaces is collected, and used in polish and foodstuffs.

Jelly Palm *Butia capitata*
This tough palm from the open drier areas of southern Brazil, Paraguay, Uruguay and northern Argentina grows in tropical to cool temperate environments. It grows to only 20ft (6m) with a thick trunk of up to 3ft (1m) diameter. The 1in (2.5cm) wide yellow fruit is found in huge clusters, and is harvested to make jellies and wine.

Coconut

Cocos nucifera

Tropical beaches would be incomplete without coconut palms, which are now thoroughly naturalized on tropical shores throughout the world. Coconut trees are also widely planted for their fruit, and as an ornamental. They can grow in sand and are incredibly tolerant of windy, salty conditions. Every part of this palm can be used: the leaves for thatch, the growing tip for palm cabbage, the trunk for construction, the flower for toddy, the fruit for food, drink and oil, and the fruit husk for matting and fuel. It is grown inland and in coastal areas.

Identification: Slender, often curved trunks are swollen at the base, where new roots emerge. The lightly arching fronds grow to 20ft (6m) with long, hanging, deep green leaflets. The 3ft- (1m-) long branched inflorescence carries small, cream flowers. The fruit is a hard, triangular sphere, 12in (30cm) long and green or yellow.

Left: The tough leaves can withstand strong coastal winds. Older leaves turn yellow before dropping off.

Distribution: Native to the tropical east, now widely naturalized and planted.
Height: 60ft (18m)
Shape: Single-stemmed palm
Evergreen
Pollinated: Insect and wind
Leaf shape: Pinnate

Below: A coconut fruit may float at sea for many months and still be able to germinate.

INDEX

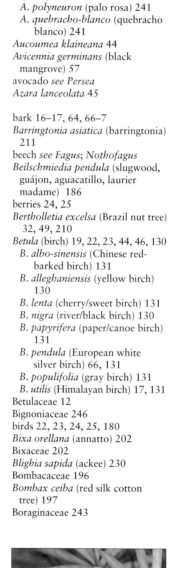

Note to reader
Many of the trees in this book have been given a zone range.

Plant hardiness zones
The Agricultural Research Service of the U.S. Department of Agriculture has developed a system of plant hardiness zones. Many trees in the encyclopedia have been give a zone range. The zones 1–10 are based on the average annual minimum temperature. In the zone range, the smaller number indicates the northernmost zone in which a plant can survive the winter and the higher number gives the most southerly area in which it will perform consistently. Factors such as altitude, wind exposure, proximity to water, soil type, snow, night temperature, shade and the level of water received by a plant may alter a plant's hardiness by as much as two zones.

Zone 1: Below -45°C   (-50°F)
Zone 2: -45 to -40°C   (-50 to -40°F)
Zone 3: -40 to -34°C   (-40 to -30°F)
Zone 4: -34 to -29°C   (-30 to -20°F)
Zone 5: -29 to -23°C   (-20 to -10°F)
Zone 6: -23 to -18°C   (-10 to 0°F)
Zone 7: -18 to -12°C   (0 to -10°F)
Zone 8: -12 to -7°C   (10 to -20°F)
Zone 9: -7 to -1°C   (20 to 30°F)
Zone 10: -1 to 4°C   (30 to 40°F)